Theory of African Music

VOLUME I

Chicago Studies in Ethnomusicology

A series edited by

Philip V. Bohlman, Bruno Nettl, and Ronald Radano

Editorial Board

Margaret J. Kartomi
Anthony Seeger
Kay Kaufman Shelemay
Martin H. Stokes
Bonnie C. Wade

Theory of African Music

VOLUME I

Gerhard Kubik

The University of Chicago Press

Chicago and London

Gerhard Kubik is a cultural anthropologist, ethnomusicologist, and psycho-analyst. A professor of ethnology and African studies at the Universities of Vienna and Klagenfurt, he also teaches at Sigmund Freud University, Vienna. Professor Kubik is affiliated with the Oral Literature Research Programme, Chileka, Malawi, and is a permanent member of the Center for Black Music Research in Chicago as well as an honorary fellow of the Royal Anthropological Institute of Great Britain and Ireland. His recent books include *Africa and the Blues* and *Tusona—Luchazi Ideographs*.

The University of Chicago Press, Chicago 60637
The University of Chicago Press, Ltd., London
© Copyright 1994 by Florian Noetzel Verlag, Wilhelmshaven
All rights reserved. University of Chicago Press edition 2010.
Printed in the United States of America

19 18 17 16 15 14 13 12 11 10   1 2 3 4 5

ISBN-13: 978-0-226-45690-4 (cloth)
ISBN-13: 978-0-226-45691-1 (paper)
ISBN-10: 0-226-45690-0 (cloth)
ISBN-10: 0-226-45691-9 (paper)

Library of Congress Cataloging-in-Publication Data
Kubik, Gerhard, 1934–
  Theory of African music / Gerhard Kubik.
    p. cm. — (Chicago studies in ethnomusicology)
  Vol. 1 previously published in 1994 by F. Noetzel.
  Includes bibliographical references and index.
  ISBN-13: 978-0-226-45690-4 (cloth : alk. paper)
  ISBN-13: 978-0-226-45691-1 (pbk. : alk. paper)
  ISBN-10: 0-226-45690-0 (cloth : alk. paper)
  ISBN-10: 0-226-45691-9 (pbk. : alk. paper)
  [etc.]
  1. Music—Africa—History and criticism. 2. Music theory—Africa.
I. Title. II. Series: Chicago studies in ethnomusicology.
ML350.K83 2010
780.96—dc22   2009042892

Contents

Preface to Volumes I and II

This book has been designed to serve as a reader in African musicology for students, scholars and people with a wide interdisciplinary range of interests. It contains ten chapters, originally written in English, and an introduction. The area it deals with is Africa south of the Sahara, with some sections devoted to specific musical cultures, others to regions and yet others to the musical concepts and practices of individuals. Among the culture areas relatively well represented in this book are those of southern Uganda (Ganda/Soga), central and south-western Tanzania (Gogo, Pangwa, Kisi, etc.), southern Malaŵi (urban musical cultures), eastern Angola (Ngangela/Cokwe), Central African Republic (Zande, Banda, Nzakara, etc.), Shaba Province of Zaïre (guitar music of the 1950s), Gabon, northern Congo and south-western Central African Republic (Fang', Mpyɛmɔ̃, etc.), Yoruba culture of Nigeria, Ewe/Fɔ̃ culture in Togo, and various musical cultures in southern Africa including the !Kung' (San speakers), Nsenga, Shona, Lozi, etc. This configuration reflects the regional emphasis of my particular fieldwork, which is the foundation of this book. Naturally, many other cultures and peoples also came into consideration with regard to selected aspects of their music/dance practice.

Some of the chapters have been written specifically for the present text: Chapter IX ("Genealogy of a Malaŵian Musician Family"), Chapter VI ("The Cognitive Study of African Musical 'Rhythm'") and the introduction. Some others are revised versions of papers that were first published between 1964 and 1969: Chapters I and II, Section 1 of Chapter III, and Chapter IV. My research in eastern Angola in 1965 is summarized in Chapter V, drawing on earlier articles. Finally, there are three papers, virtually without any revisions, but in one case considerably enlarged, which represent more recent emphases in my research and are therefore included here, although they had been published in other contexts: Section 2 of Chapter III on the San heritage in southern Africa, Chapter VIII on Yoruba chantefables and Chapter X on the *tusona* ideographs in Angola and north-western Zambia. Chapter notes give the source of each paper.

Although I have tried to keep revisions of some of the early writings, particularly those that became Chapters I, II, III (Section 1) and IV, to a minimum and preserve as much as possible their style and diction, the present book has its own dynamics; in the process of preparation I unavoidably had to read through the original texts again, eliminating inaccuracies, errors, a fair amount of misprints and occasional editorial interventions not sanctioned by me. Generally, it seemed necessary to bring the early texts a little more in line with my present-day approach and knowledge without, however, sacrificing their character and substance. Thus, in some places additions have been made, drawing on unpublished field data from the 1960s rather than data obtained on more recent field trips. Here I have tried to work selectively, exercising all the restraint needed to avoid damage.

Some chapters are compounded, i.e. two or more separate papers on related topics have been joined to form one chapter with sub-sections (e.g. Chapters III and V). In other instances the substance of a paper written earlier is preceded by a brief introduction written more recently (Chapters I, II, III, IV).

In organizing the ten chapters, I have tried to proceed from simple to more complex topics, re-enacting in some manner my own learning progression during the last three decades. This should be especially beneficial for students who are not yet very familiar with the subject. Thus, at least at the beginning, the chapters follow the order in which they were written, beginning with "Xylophone Playing in Southern Uganda" (completed in 1963), "Harp Music of the Azande . . ." (1964) and Section 1 of "A Structural Examination of Multi-Part Singing . . ." (completed in 1966). The chronological order, although broken in places, is visible as a guiding principle, and so it is not by coincidence that "African Space/Time Concepts . . ." (written between 1981 and 1984) concludes the book. For a number of reasons, mainly didactic, out of a need for some kind of grouping by region and subject matter, it was not possible to remain faithful to an absolutely chronological order. The final arrangement of the material, therefore, is a compromise in the interest of the student, who should now be able to study the texts without constantly turning pages.

While I introduce in this book a number of regional cultures, with their concepts of movement and sound, my overall approach in this work is comparative. Sometimes directly, sometimes indirectly, all the papers published here touch on theoretical issues ultimately concerning African music as a whole. For this reason the title *Theory of African Music* seems to be justified for this book. It should not be misunderstood, however, as programmatic. "Theory" here is a framework, interdisciplinary in its orientation, to bring our current database and its evaluation under some kind of umbrella. Neither is it to be understood in the narrow sense of "music theory" (for which reason the book is called *Theory of African Music* and not *African Music Theory*) or as being dogmatic in any manner. Actually, one of my objectives here is to make us a little more aware of what we may gain from a flexible methodology, and to teach methodology not merely by abstraction, but by application. I have tried to summarize for the benefit of readers from all nations and all cultures some of my field experiences in the course of attempting to understand African music and its conceptual background.

March 26, 1988

Introduction

For most researchers today the term "African music" refers to musical practices of the peoples of sub-Saharan Africa. Not normally included in the term are those in Arab-speaking North Africa, belonging to a Euro-Asian rather than African culture world. For similar reasons the music of European settler communities particularly in southern Africa, is not included.

"African music" in an extended sense also includes "dance;" both are intimately linked aspects of the same cultural complex. Further ramifications of African music/dance lead the researcher to include "oral literature," theatre arts and some aspects of visual anthropology in his area of study. But African music is also closely connected with language, to an extent that it is hardly possible today to study it without the necessary background in African languages. And finally, as Alan P. Merriam (1964) has stressed, there is the socio-cultural side of the phenomenon which requires the student to be well versed in the theoretical framework of current cultural anthropology.

African Languages and Music

Stylistic traits in African music have been found to be correlated with language in Africa, at least in its broad divisions, and in many cases also with regional ethnic/linguistic relationships. Christoper Ehret (1981:28) has observed:

> Polyrhythmic music and dance ... is often thought of as quintes-sentially African. In fact it appears to be a feature of culture particularly associated with Niger-Congo peoples. It has spread so widely because Niger-Congo societies, especially the Bantu, have covered so much of the continent and it has come to have an enormous impact on modern Western popular music and dance because so many of the African slaves transported by Europeans were of Niger-Congo background. Outside the Niger-Congo-speaking regions in Africa other musical styles, frequently based on stringed instruments, tend to prevail, along with quite different styles of dance.

It is important therefore to link African music studies to the language map of Africa. The broad divisions of the African language panorama form four super-families: I. Niger-Kordofanian II. Nilo-Saharan, III.

Afroasiatic and IV. Khoisan (Greenberg 1966). These are reflected in the musical panorama by the existence of broad style areas within Africa, inspite of intensive cultural exchange which has taken place across these boundaries since time immemorial.

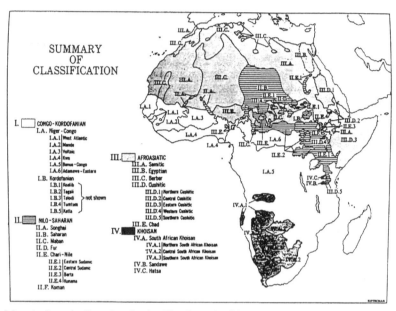

SUMMARY
OF
CLASSIFICATION

I. ☐ CONGO - KORDOFANIAN
   I.A. Niger - Congo
      I.A.1 West Atlantic
      I.A.2 Mande
      I.A.3 Voltaic
      I.A.4 Kwa
      I.A.5 Benue - Congo
      I.A.6 Adamawa - Eastern
   I.B. Kordofanian
      I.B.1 Koalib
      I.B.2 Tegali
      I.B.3 Talodi   } not shown
      I.B.4 Tumtum
      I.B.5 Katla
II. ▓ NILO - SAHARAN
   II.A. Songhai
   II.B. Saharan
   II.C. Maban
   II.D. Fur
   II.E. Chari - Nile
      II.E.1 Eastern Sudanic
      II.E.2 Central Sudanic
      II.E.3 Berta
      II.E.4 Kunama
   II.F. Koman

III. ☐ AFROASIATIC
   III.A. Semitic
   III.B. Egyptian
   III.C. Berber
   III.D. Cushitic
      III.D.1 Northern Cushitic
      III.D.2 Central Cushitic
      III.D.3 Eastern Cushitic
      III.D.4 Western Cushitic
      III.D.5 Southern Cushitic
   III.E. Chad
IV. ▓ KHOISAN
   IV.A. South African Khoisan
      IV.A.1 Northern South African Khoisan
      IV.A.2 Central South African Khoisan
      IV.A.3 Southern South African Khoisan
   IV.B. Sandawe
   IV.C. Hatsa

Map 1. Joseph Greenberg's classification of African Languages. Map and description reproduced from Greenberg 1966 [³1970]:177. "Congo-Kordofanian" = "Niger-Kordofanian" in a more recent version of the classification (Murray 1981).

In the micro-cultural dimension, however, it is not always possible to link stylistic traits in African music to invariable "ethnic groups." Remembering the iridescent character of many ethnic group designations, the confusion arising from the mixing up of self- and outsider-appellations, the frequent lack of clear delineation between "ethnic," "sub-ethnic," habitation area and clan names, as well as the influence of colonial administrations on ethnic terminology, it is often difficult to take existing "ethnic groups" as a reliable framework for reference. While in some areas, such as southern Uganda, ethnic names became markers of nationhood (cf. the Baganda = people of the Kingdom of Buganda), in many other areas terminology is not clear-cut. For example in eastern Angola there are people calling themselves VaLuchazi in the plural (literally: "the people who originated from the Luchazi river"), VaMbunda ("the red-earth people," i.e. people settled in areas of laterite soil), VaNkhangala ("the people building their villages in the dry forest") VaMbwela, VaLwimbi, VaNgondzelo, VaNyemba and so forth. But is there anything like a Luchazi culture, or Luchazi music in particular, to be distinguished from a Mbwela and Nkhangala music? – Certainly there are some differences from area to area. There are also differences linked to dialectal variants of the language, notably between Luchazi and Mbunda in the realm of phonology, but essentially it is the same culture. And VaMbwela as compared to VaNkhangala in the Kwandu-Kuvangu Province of Angola are virtually indistinguishable in their culture and language. What "distinguishes" them is merely their environmental preferences, with the VaMbwela settling close to the swampy river grasslands called *chana*, and the VaNkhangala a mere kilometer further "inland" on the edges of the forest zone (*musenge*).

All these languages belong to Malcolm Guthrie's Zone K, Group 10, in his tentative classification of the Bantu languages (Guthrie 1948) and this seems to be a more reliable reference, so that one can speak of a "Zone K-Group 10 musical culture," a clumsy term but scientifically much more tenable than "Nkhangala music" or "Luchazi music." In eastern Angola it is the appellation given these populations by outsiders that, in this case at least, seem to have hit the point more accurately. It was the Ovimbundu traders from central Angola who in the 18th and 19th century began to speak of all the eastern Angolan peoples as Vangangela (= "people of the aurora," "people of the east"), lumping together into one category populations with a widely identical cultural profile. Unfortunately this term is not acceptable to many of the people concerned (cf. also Chapter V).

From my own studies in African cultures I have gathered that musical styles and specific traits are rarely linked in a rigid manner to entities as small as "ethnic groups." More often they are linked to ethnically related population clusters, speaking languages belonging to the same zone. In addition there is also the phenomenon of sub-cultures (including musical styles) carried by even smaller units within the larger community, for example by professional associations in a stratified society, or, within a non-stratified society, by age-sets. And finally, there is the individual creative musical personality, long neglected by field workers in African music who have looked at it as "folk" or "tribal" (ethnic) music. As a leader, guide and innovator he plays a most important role in many African cultures.

Style Areas

In his Cantometrics scheme, aimed at a world-wide comparative sampling of vocal styles, "Africa" is divided by Alan Lomax into the following broad song style zones (1968:80): Western Sudan, Moslem Sudan, Guinea Coast, Eastern Sudan, Ethiopia, Upper Nile, Equatorial Bantu, Northeast Bantu, Central Bantu, African Hunters, South African Bantu and Madagascar. In Map 2 these broad delineations were drawn intentionally with a ruler in straight lines, demonstrating that it is impossible to make exact geographical borders between the style areas.

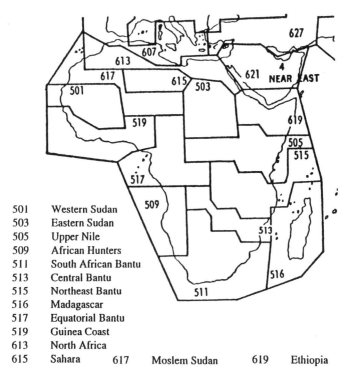

501	Western Sudan				
503	Eastern Sudan				
505	Upper Nile				
509	African Hunters				
511	South African Bantu				
513	Central Bantu				
515	Northeast Bantu				
516	Madagascar				
517	Equatorial Bantu				
519	Guinea Coast				
613	North Africa				
615	Sahara	617	Moslem Sudan	619	Ethiopia

Map 2. Alan Lomax's song-style areas in Africa. Reproduced from Lomax 1968:314, extract

Some reservations with regard to Lomax's methodology of sampling have been expressed by critics of the Cantometrics project, regarding external viewpoints in the rating system, the employment of exclusively Euro-American personnel during the investigation process etc. (cf. Pantaleoni 1970:131). However in spite of those criticisms Alan Lomax's African style areas seem to be much closer to reality than were earlier attempts to divide Africa into distinctive cultural or musical zones.

Alan Lomax observes a remarkable homogeneity in the song-styles within "Africa," interrupted only by the African Hunters (Pygmies and Bushmen), whose low representation in the quartile lists (15 percent) required that they be excluded ... Even this departure from the general homogeneity, however, is more apparent than real, for although the African Hunters appear low in the statistical ranks, their own quartile list is completely dominated by African areas (Lomax 1968:91–5).

Lomax's findings seem to confirm that the music of Khoisan speakers in southern Africa, as well as the music of the Pygmies in several pockets of central Africa, represent cultures apart from the mainstream of African music south of the Sahara, i.e. the music of speakers of Niger-Congo languages (I.A. in Joseph Greenberg's classification 1966). This picture, however, is blurred by two factors which have been given relatively little attention in the literature: 1. Bantu- and Khoisan interaction in southern Africa (including especially Lomax's areas 511 South African Bantu and 513 Central Bantu), 2. that Khoisan music and Pygmy music represent in fact, totally different musical culture areas, in contrast to impressions gathered previously[1] partly due to the lumping together of two unrelated peoples from the viewpoint of an evolutionistic interpretive framework. Thus, even the term African Hunters is too broad, quite apart from the fact that it can be even less geographically delimited than any of the other song style areas, due to the scattered distribution of hunter/gatherer populations in Africa.

As the "core," and even as an original historical point of dispersal of "black" African musical cultures, two zones appear foremost in Lomax's results: Guinea Coast and Equatorial Bantu. Lomax finds that an average similarity of 84% of the traits binds these two regions with those of the Central Bantu and the South African Bantu. Tracing these cross-relationships further, he finds that there are also remarkable similarities between the region Upper Nile and South African Bantu. Without doubt, the similarity profile reflects, in part, remote relationships in time, and the direction of past migrations.

Although the position of the African Hunters and their possible inclusion in or exclusion from the African culture world is a topic still to be discussed, the Afro-American style area on the other hand showed a sufficient similarity profile to be included.

The musical areas of North Africa and Sahara are excluded from "Africa" in Lomax's schema. They are considered to be fundamentally different from those of sub-Saharan Africa, particularly in vocal style. Most of the cultural zones described in George Peter Murdock's "Ethnographic Atlas" (1967) as "Circum-Mediterranean," were therefore excluded from the "Africa" style world (Lomax 1968:80). This does not

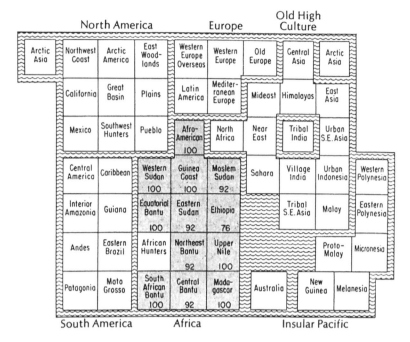

Ill. 1. African song style areas in global perspective. Reproduced from Lomax 1968:92

minimize in any way the enormous cultural exchanges which have gone on between north Africa and sub-Saharan Africa ever since an effective trans-Sahara trading network was established. There was considerable trade across the Sahara in Roman times between the Mediterranean and the western Sudan, as is testified in numerous rock paintings in the Tassili n'Ajjer (Algeria). It greatly intensified after the Islamic conquest of North Africa, the Islamic penetration of the early African states in the Western Sudan from ca. 700 A.D., and from trade and slavery. All this has resulted in the "Islamization" of African music in vast areas of west Africa, but also in a strong impact of African musical traditions in some areas of the Maghreb, notably in southern Morocco.

Lomax's Moslem Sudan is one of the Islamized musical regions. Another (not shown by Lomax as a separate zone) is the coastal strip of east Africa, as far south as Sofala in Moçambique. In east Africa, musical traditions displaying "Arab" or "Islamic" influences are found even far inland, for example in southern Uganda, and at Lake Malaŵi, not only along the Indian Ocean coast. Several musical instruments of Arab origin can be seen in both regions. The one-string bowed spike lute known in some parts of west Africa as *goje* or *goge* has been related to the Arabic *rebab*.

On the other hand some east African bowed lutes such as the one-string *endingidi* of southern Uganda, or the two-string *izeze,* popular among the Wagogo of central Tanzania, show much closer affinities to Chinese bowed lutes. This would not eliminate, of course, Arab traders as intermediaries between south-east Asia and the east African coast, especially in view of the substantial Omani control of the Indian Ocean trading network during the 10th to 18th centuries.

There are also vast areas in Africa which are virtually free from Arab or Islamic influences: Angola and northwestern Zambia is one of them. The traditional circumcision schools for boys found across Angola, with their dances and music, have a history not to be related to Muslim circumcision.

Apart from north Africa and the Mediterranean, "Africa" has had intensive contact with other parts of the world, particularly along the east coast. Cultural exchange across the Indian Ocean in historical times is a topic that has stimulated many writers including Hornbostel 1911, Kunst 1936, Jones 1959a, 1971b, Jeffreys 1961 and others. Here probably lies the explanation for a surprising finding by Alan Lomax, who remarks that the Guinea Coast and Madagascar, in his song-style sample, are linked by a score of 86%. Madagascar thus falls into the African culture-world on stylistic grounds. Looking at the pattern of similarities further east, Lomax found that

> only Western Polynesia (in the upper quartile of 60 percent of the African areas), Eastern Polynesia (30 percent) and Tribal India (30 percent) show any degree of affinity (Lomax 1968:94).

Within the vast expanse of the African continent, extremely distant areas often display similar, even identical traits, while adjacent areas may be set apart stylistically. The multi-part singing of the Baule of the Côte d'Ivoire, in triads within an equiheptatonic tonal system, is so close, even identical to the part singing style of Ngangela-, Chokwe- and Luvale-speaking peoples in eastern Angola, that this is immediately recognized by informants from both cultures. Why this is so is a riddle. The two areas are separated by several countries (Congo, Gabon, Cameroon, Nigeria, Benin, etc.) with different approaches to multi-part singing. Another historical riddle is the presence of practically identical xylophone playing styles and instruments in northern Moçambique (among Makonde- and Makua-speaking peoples) and certain peoples of the Côte d'Ivoire and Liberia, especially the Baule and the Kru. The *jomolo* of the Baule and log xylophones in northern Moçambique such as the *dimbila* of the -Makonde or the *mangwilo* of the -Shirima are virtually identical instruments.

1. They are both constructed over a base of two banana stems, some-times – especially among the -Makonde – over two stems of wood with isolating cushions placed on top, which are either grass bundles (Makonde) or bundles of dry banana leaves (Baule).
2. Slats, usually six, are placed over the support.
3. The slats are tuned to a hexatonic scale with narrow intervals of about 160–180 Cents and one large gap.
4. The instrument is played by two musicians sitting opposite each other, each holding two beaters and striking the slats on their ends.
5. It is played by young boys or adolescents, often in the fields outside the village to chase monkeys away from the crops. Though the music is mostly instrumental, song titles and implicit song texts refer to this subject.
6. The music is created by combining <u>interlocking</u> patterns. The first musician, who is often the disciple, begins with a basic pattern, while the second one, who is the expert and teacher, falls between with a more complex pattern and plays variations. Sometimes the same patterns are combined in canon-style (Herzog 1949).
7. Simultaneous sounds arise predominantly from striking two keys at a distance of "one empty key between." In the prevalent tuning of this instrument this gives "neutral" thirds.
8. Sometimes the experts player employs a cross-hand technique, i.e. striking the slats with hands crossed for example, if he wants to show the learner what to play.
9. It is common practice to exchange slats with each other to suit individual pieces. The order of the notes on a *jomolo* (Baule), *dimbila* (Makonde) or *mangwilo* (Shirima) is not always in the form of a "scale," but depends on the piece the musicians want to play. Occasionally, the same movement patterns are applied to a different layout of the slats, and this gives another tune.

Diffusionist theories of various kinds have been offered to resolve such riddles. A.M. Jones has assumed the presence of Indonesian settlers in certain areas of east, central and west Africa during the early centuries of our era who would have been responsible for the introduction of xylophones and certain tonal-harmonic systems (equipentatonic, equiheptatonic and "pelog"-scales) to Africa (Jones 1964a). Ethnohistorians on the other hand have tended to accentuate the importance of coastal navigation (implying the use of hired or forced African labour on European ships) as an agent of culture contact between southeastern Africa (Moçambique), west-central Africa (Angola, Zaïre) and the west African coast.

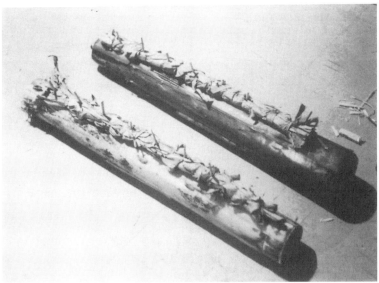

Ill. 2a – b. *Jomolo* – log xylophone of the Baule performed by Alexandre N'guessan (right) and Germain Kokoue. The second picture shows a characteristic in the construction technique of the basis: on top of the banana stems there is an isolation cushion made from banana stem leaves. Abidjan, Côte d'Ivoire, December 11, 1978

Ill. 3. A six-note *mangwilo* performed in the Mitukwe mountains, northern Moçambique. This picture shows the unusual case of a woman log xylophone player, Senhora Muhua, ca. 30 years old. Her partner, sitting opposite, is a small boy, aged ca. 10. At Settlement I in the Mitukwe mountains, north of "Cuamba" (Nova Freixo) Moçambique, October 14, 1962

Ill. 4. Interlocking-style performance in -Makonde xylophone music. An eight-note *dimbila* performed at Mitande, ca. 25 km east of Moçimboa do Rovuma, northern Moçambique, October 30, 1962

Another riddle is that the *timbrh* lamellophone music of the Vute of central Cameroon is based on the same duple-interlocking composition technique in pairs of octaves as is the *amadinda* and *embaire* log xylophone music of southern Uganda. Again, music recorded in areas lying in between is structured differently. No recent historical contacts can be adduced. Prehistorians could speculate here that the duple-interlocking style in octave pairs might have been an ancient technique of musical organization, already present in the music of proto-Bantu speakers

Ill. 5. An 18-note *timbrh* shown by the Vute master-musician Pain Sedu, ca. 60. Linté, seat of Chief Dimani Garba, central Cameroon, March 9, 1970. Archive No. G573

whose origin is supposed to be situated in present-day eastern Nigeria and central Cameroon. From there it would have spread to the Great Lakes before 300 A.D. with the first eastward migration of Bantu groups associated archaeologically with the so-called Urewe ware excavated in Uganda. The only problem is that the Vute are not speakers of a Bantu language (although settled in a zone of predominantly I.A.5 speakers) and that the kind of music displaying an interlocking style was qualified as "recent" by my informants in 1964 and 1969.

"Africa" is also linked to the New World, initially in a one-way relationship, i.e. from Africa to the New World; but it soon became a two-way relationship, a constant flux and reflux of cultural traits between African and African-American cultures reaching a new high point in the 20th century. Several African musical cultures have extensions in parts of the New World, for instance those of the Guinea Coast, the Congo/Angola area, and to a lesser extent some south-east African musical cultures from the Zambezi valley and northern Moçambique.

African-American music has inherited from Africa a specific approach to movement and the concept of "music" as an integrated aural, kinetic and visual event. In the course of three centuries African diaspora cultures have developed in the New World with a remarkable degree of autonomy from Africa, although it is still possible to trace single traits or clusters of traits in African-American music/dance back to specific African regions. In Brazil the music of the "Candomblé" religious cults is directly linked with 18th/19th-century form of *oriṣa* worship of the Yoruba of western Nigeria and Dahomé, including the bell patterns associated with individual *oriṣa* (deities). In a similar manner, "Umbanda" religious ceremonies are an extension of *umbanda* traditional healing sessions, still practiced in Angola today; and *vodu* religious music among the Fõ has extensions in Haiti and elsewhere in the Caribbean.

African musical instruments have been modified and sometimes developed in deviating directions in the New World, for example the central African friction drum, the idea of the lamellophone (in the Cuban *marimbula*) and numerous drum types. Two distinctive traditions of gourd-resonated xylophones known under the general term *marimba* in central and south America can be traced to specific African regions: a) a large variety on a stand, sometimes table-like, to the Sena/Nyungwe speaking areas of central Moçambique (Zambezi valley), b) a smaller variety with from only six keys (such as the *marimba* of São Paulo, Brazil) up to more than a dozen (such as those in Panama) to the Congo/Angola area. The latter type is characterized by a "rail" or arc, and may be carried in processions, as is still the case on the Ilha São Sebastião, near São Paulo, Brazil, during the festivities of the "Congada" (Pinto ed. 1986).

It has only recently become possible to relate various distinctive traits in African-American music/dance cultures with specific African regions and cultures. Gradually the "panorama" view of Africa from the other side of the Atlantic has been replaced by detailed field-work on both sides, and meticulous work in libraries, archives and collections, employing standard historical methods.[2]

African Music in History

The notion of African music as historically static has been abandoned in contemporary studies, and it is becoming possible today to reconstruct major portions of Africa's music history through a combined evaluation of archaeological artefacts, objects in collections, iconographical material, written and oral sources. In this context we prefer today to speak of "musical traditions" in Africa (as elsewhere in the world), rather than "traditional music" as a category (Kubik 1987b:2). Musical traditions in Africa have had individual life-spans, they started at some point in history and vanished at another. While some may have displayed extreme stability over time, others have not, and not only in the 20th century. Thus the shape of African music and dance as we know it today in the various regions of sub-Saharan Africa may be considered the (momentary and transient) result of a multitude of factors subject to historical change: ecological, cultural, social, religious, political etc.

Ecological change was a long-term factor affecting population patterns, driving people into other lands and thus provoking changes in the expressive culture, including music and dance. Since the drying out of the Sahara, populations have tended to shift south and southeastwards, as they are doing again today in some areas of the Sahel zone and even in east Africa. In Tanzania within the last twenty years, the pastoral Maasai, speakers of a II.E.1 (Eastern Sudanic) language, have been grazing their cattle increasingly further south and in 1977 they were a common view in Sangu country (that is as far south as the Tanzam railway, east of Mbeya). When settled populations accepted the intruders, they often adopted musical styles from them or new dance types. Thus, the choral singing style of the Maasai has had a fundamental influence on vocal music of the Wagogo of central Tanzania, as is audible in their *nindo* and *msunyunho* chants.

In ancient times the musical cultures of sub-Saharan Africa extended much further north. Between ca. 9000 and 3000 BC a markedly wet trend prevailed in the Sahara and promoted the extension of savanna flora and fauna into the southern Sahara and its central highlands (Tassili n'Ajjer, etc.). During this period human occupation of the Sahara greatly increased. Along rivers and small lakes a so-called "acquatic life-style" (cf. Sutton 1981) developed within Late Stone Age cultures, extending from the western Sahara into the Nile valley region. The acquatic cultures began to break up gradually between 5000 and 3000 BC, once the peak of the wet climate had passed, becoming more and more restricted to shrunken lakes and rivers. Eventually the population migrated towards places where a similar ecology was still intact. Today remnants of the acquatic civilization survive perhaps on the Lake Chad islands and in the Sudd region of the Upper Nile. Speakers of Nilo-Saharan languages are the most likely candidates to have developed the acquatic life-style. Today the distribution area of this super-family is dissected, a picture of complex migrations and intrusions by speakers of Afro-Asiatic languages (cf. Map 1).

The cultures of the "Green Sahara" left behind a vast gallery of iconographic records in the form of rock paintings, among which are some of our earliest internal sources on African music and dance. One, a vivid dance scene was discovered by Henri Lhote and his team in the Tassili n'Ajjer during his Sahara expedition of 1956. On stylistic grounds this painting has been attributed to the Saharan period of the "Neolithic hunters" (ca. 6000–4000 B.C.). It is probably one of the oldest testimonies of music/dance in Africa in existence. It is characterized by a rich dance decoration and clothing style, painted in white on the dark brown bodies. The flexible and athletic bodies of the men have a markedly flare-shaped leg dressing. Proceeding from Helmut Günther's theory of

Ill. 6. Reproduction of a Saharan rock painting found by Henri Lhote in the Tassili n'Ajjer, at Sefar. This picture shows what is most likely a scene of dancing involving men and women. In the Sahara chronology it is attributed to the "Période des têtes rondes évoluées" (before ca. 3500 B.C.) by Lhote. Reproduced from Lhote 1973, Fig. 53, next to page 137.

"dance signals," i.e. the fact that prominent motional centres in an African dance are often marked by decoration (Günther 1969), we can assume that the lower legs were important body areas in this dance, and possibly used in a heavy stamping action. The backs of the men are curved, the arms seem to swing backwards gaining energy. The dance decoration and movement style in the 6–8000 year-old picture are reminiscent of a dance style found in one present-day African area: the *indlamu* stamping dance of the Zulu documented by Hugh Tracey (1952).

In contrast to the men in the picture, the women, characterized by a rounded abdomen and what may be "stockings," if not painting on the legs, obviously show a less aggressive dance style. All the figures are linked by what may be a rope or some other object held in the hands. Some men seem to hold a stick or whisk.

While there are limits to the interpretation of such iconographic material, as there are to all "prehistoric art," an abundant amount of information can be obtained from many of the Sahara pictures.

Another somewhat controversial Saharan rock painting discovered by Henri Lhote during the same expedition relates to the history of the harp in Africa. It is a scene painted in brown, on a yellowish background, showing the silhouette of a harpist playing to another person. Although doubts have been cast on the authenticity of this picture since it apparently only exists as a redrawing preserved in the Museé de l'homme, Paris, internal evidence on the basis of organological features suggests that is it indeed a harp. The picture was described by Basil Davidson (1967:187) as "musical scene from the period of the horse," and dated ca. 800–700 B.C. However one may assess this dating, the value of this document of ca. 3000 years ago is enormous. The person on the left, sitting on a stool of a kind still found in areas of the central Sudan, performs on a six-string

Ill. 7. Performance on a six-string harp depicted in a rock painting found in the Tassili n'Ajjer (Algeria). This painting has been attributed to the Saharan "Period of the Horse" (ca. 1500–500 B.C.). Reproduced from Davidson 1967:50

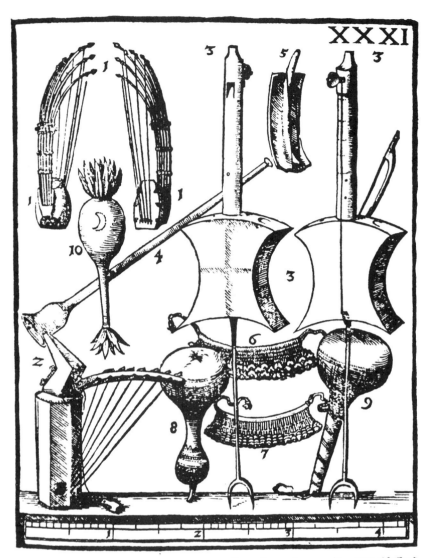

Ill. 8. Michael Praetorius' illustration, showing among other instruments a harp from Gabon probably in the collection of a German sovereign. Reproduced from Michael Praetorius: *Syntagma musicum*, Vol. II: De Organographia, Plate XXXI, 1620

harp with the neck towards the body, a playing attitude considered today as "old-style" further south, among the Azande of the Central African Republic (cf. Chapter II). From the organology of this harp, depicted clearly enough, it can be seen that this Saharan type belongs to Klaus Wachsmann's Type B of African harps ("tanged type") (Wachsmann 1964:85) whose distribution area today falls mainly into Chad and the Central African Republic, as well as some parts of northeastern Nigeria, northern Cameroon, southern Sudan and northeastern Zaïre.

Opposite the harp player there is a second seated person who is possibly listening to the musician. Both of them are drawn with stylized heads which in all probability show hair styles. The second person seems to have a beard and is seated on a somewhat larger chair or stool. The harp player's head is round, that of the second person oval.

West African students to whom I have shown this picture on various lecture tours almost unanimously interpreted it as a social situation. "The harpist is playing to the king, or chief." If correct, this would be a particularly fascinating testimony for the existence of social stratification and the role of musicians during the third period of Sahara rock paintings. The object in front of the "king" was interpreted with less confidence: (a) as a ceremonial staff, (b) as a bow, (c) a table, (d) a percussion beam.

Harps have a distinctive distribution area in present-day Africa, clustering characteristically just immediately south of the ancient aquatic cultures of the Sahara, and not extending into the sub-continent, the southernmost bridgeheads of the distribution area being Gabon and the western shore of Lake Victoria (Buganda, Karagwe), just slightly south of the equator. A seven-string harp from Gabon of the same type as used today among the -Kele was depicted by Michael Praetorius in 1620. On organological grounds Klaus Wachsmann (1964) has distinguished three basic types of African harps whose distribution areas are shown in Map 3:

> Type A: "Spoon in the cup"   o
> Type B: "Tanged type"   ●
> Type C: "Shelved type"   ⊙

Wachsmann defines the three types as follows:

> The first type derives its strength and rigidity almost entirely from the pull and tension of the strings. The neck rests like a spoon in a cup ... The second type has the simple and somewhat crude device of tanging the neck into a hole at the small end of the resonator, like a cork in a bottle. ... In the third type a shelf

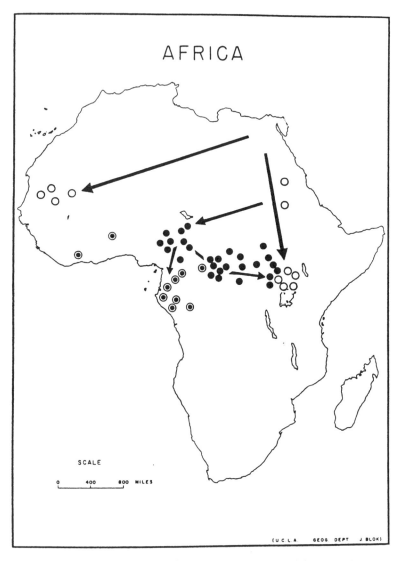

Map 3. Human migration and African harps. Reproduced from Wachsmann 1964:85

projects from the base of the resonator, to which the neck is laced with fibre or thong. ... At first sight these differences seem to have little meaning. However, if the distribution of these three types is marked in a map ... one notices at once that they occur in clusters, clearly separated from each other (Wachsmann 1964:84).

In his article "Human Migration and African Harps," Wachsmann (1964) correlated typology and present distribution areas with known migratory movements in Africa's history. In a letter to me a few years before his death he commented upon his earlier attempts as follows:

> ... the thick arrows are speculation or intelligent guesses whereas the thinner arrows are speculation closer to the ground or in tandem with regional traditions and legends as to migrations of populations. The whole business of musical instrument migration is very intriguing and I wish we knew more about the mechanism of inspiration to copy or to invent or to adapt.[3]

Some of our earliest sources on African music are archaeological. These are scanty, however, because in most climatic zones of sub-Saharan Africa, musical instruments made of vegetable materials or iron

Ill. 9. A terracotta ritual pot with relief figures, including an *igbin*-type drum (third motif from left), excavated by Frank Willet in Ife. Courtesy: Frank Willet, Glasgow

cannot survive in archaeological deposits. But Frank Willet (1977) opened up archaeological source material on Nigerian music by examining representations of musical instruments on stone or terracotta from Ife (Yorubaland). On the basis of this material he arrived at several worthwhile conclusions as to the history of Yoruba music:

> The representations of musical instruments on sculptures from Ife indicate, in general terms, a substantial accord with oral traditions. During Classical Ife times, approximately the tenth to the fourteenth centuries A.D., *igbìn* drums were used, probably for Ogbóni and Obàtálá, among others, though talking drums were not. The hourglass drum, *dùndún*, may have been introduced in the fifteenth or sixteenth century since it appears in Benin plaques of the Middle Period. The double iron clapperless bell (and by inference the single one also was known in Classical Ife, and thus seems to have preceded the talking drums. Pellet bells and small tubular bells with clapper appear to have been known by the fifteenth century, while pyramidal bells were probably introduced later (Willet 1977:386).

The drums of the *dùndún* set, now associated with Yoruba culture in an almost stereotypical manner, were introduced from northern Nigeria, where comparable instruments also occur, and are actually known in a broad belt across the Savanna region into neighbouring countries such as Burkina Faso. The Yoruba *dùndún* drums are used today as "talking" drums in relation with the poetry of the *oriki*.

Archaeological finds relating to African music have also included iron bells such as were excavated in Katanga and at several sites in Zimbabwe. Benin bronze plaques represent a further almost inexhaustible source for the interpretation of musical instruments depicted on them in ceremonial contexts, such as horns and bells, drums and even bow-lutes.

The existing historical sources on African music may be classified from various viewpoints; according to authorship as external and internal; according to the materials used and the medium of transmission we can distinguish the following categories:

(a) objects (archaeological, items in collections, museums etc.),
(b) pictorial sources (rock paintings, petroglyphs etc.; book illustrations, drawings, paintings etc.),
(c) oral historical sources,
(d) written sources (travellers' accounts, field-notes, inscriptions etc. in any language or script, African, Arab, European, musical notations),
(e) sound recordings (on wax cylinder, acetate disc, magnetic wire, magnetic tape etc.).

Ill. 10. Benin bronze plaque in the Museum für Völkerkunde, Berlin, depicting a performer on a double bell of the so-called "Guinea type." Inv.-No. III C 8401. Courtesy: Museum für Völkerkunde, Berlin.

Modern media such as movie and video-film would fall simultaneously under Categories (b) and (e).

Among the written sources (Category (d)) there are the writings of Arab travellers in the western Sudan (Ibn Baṭṭūta 1304–1377, Ibn Chaldun and others); there is Vasco da Gama's logbook (1497); there are the writings and illustrations by Jan Hughen van Linschoten (1596), Frei João dos Santos (1609, only writings), Giovanni António Cavazzi (1687), Girolamo Merolla (1692), François Froger (1698), Peter Kolb (1719) and others before the 19th century.

A specific category of writing is musical notation. Among the earliest attempts at writing down African music *in extenso* are the transcriptions of Asante and Fante songs by Thomas Edward Bowdich in Ghana (1819), Carl Mauch's notations of music for the *mbira dza vadzimu* in Zimbabwe (1869–72) and Capello and Ivens' sketches in inner Angola (1881). Clearly, this notation by travellers, commercial agents, missionaries and administrators with some training in the European music of their times does not match the complexities of African music. Rhythmic patterns were simplified and misunderstood, scalar and melodic patterns reinterpreted via the auditory habits of the transcriber's home culture. In addition there is the filter inherent in the Western notational system itself. However, some of the 19th century notations can be interpreted today and it is not impossible that one or another musical piece could be reconstructed.

Stability and Change: the 20th Century

Musical traditions in Africa have dramatically changed in the 20th century, and African-American music in particular has had a tremendous influence on the development of new urban styles of dance music from the 1920s up to now. Normally this is attributed to forces of "modernisation" or, in more scholarly language to "accelerating social change." However, these concepts are too broad and abstract to show what has really happened. They also do not explain why the specific changes we are familiar with have happened mainly during the second half of the 20th century, and not earlier. There were always periods of "modernisation" in human history and times of "accelerating social change." But in the 20th century a rather new situation emerged. The key factor is the rise of mass media technology. It is more important than other factors such as urbanisation, migrant labour, the rise of a mining industry for example in Shaba Province, Zaïre and on the Copperbelt in Zambia (cf. Kazadi wa Mukuna 1979/80), "detribalisation" etc. all of which played a visible role.

But only through the mass media, the spread of audition devices, from the hand-cranked gramophones of the 1920s to the 1960s, up to the transistor radios and present-day cassette industry and television, only thus did it become possible that musical traditions from one corner of the world could be heard almost immediately in any other corner, even the most isolated. Poverty was no barrier at all, because it is quite enough that one person in a village has a wireless set to make the youth of the entire village acquainted with the most recent musical fashions on the international record market.

Economic factors interacted in multiple ways with the new technology, but without the latter, African music in the 20th century would have taken a different turn. In Henry Morton Stanley's (1878) time the *sese* or *zeze* flat-bar zither and its music had to be introduced to Kisangani (ex-Stanleyville) in Zaïre by Swahili/Arab caravans from the east African coast. But around 1950 no Cubans were needed to introduce Cuban orchestral dance music to the Belgian Congo.

During a lecture visit to Kinshasa in December 1977, Lokwa Pascal and Magongo Sanga, two students from the Institut National des Arts, showed me the remains of their fathers' collections of 78 r.p.m. records, started in 1946. Among many records with the Ngoma label (produced by the Firme Jeronimidis in Leopoldville/Kinshasa during the 1950s) there were some old stuff, notably Woody Herman and, most momentous, there was Xavier Cugat and his Waldorf Astoria Orchestra's *"Ombo"* – Rumba Foxtrott, and *"Ca-Ta-Plun"* – Rumba (Hernandez).[4] To Zaïreans of the youngest generation the last title (*"Ca-Ta-Plun"*) could easily be passed off as an early Zaïrean record, so striking are the similarities with Zaïrean music of the "Cuban period" (late 1950s to mid-1960s). Cuban music was disseminated almost exclusively through the recording media and it has made a lasting impression, noticeable even today in the bel-canto singing style of current pop stars such as Sam Mangwana and others.

From the viewpoint of a general theory of stability and change it is evident that change in a specific tradition may occur through one or more processes which often take place simultaneously. The accessibilities created by the mass media constitute an external stimulus that may have a variety of totally different effects, depending on the reaction of the recipient culture. The nature of the acculturative processes thereby released is no different from that in earlier centuries. What is different, however, is that cultures around the globe are now universally affected by a highly monopolized and selective mixture of musical products, radiated at random into the environment.

While this is no doubt a new situation, the definable factors and processes which come into play when a tradition or culture changes are in principle timeless. Culture change may be generated by a combination of

(a) external (foreign) stimuli (*externally stimulated culture change*) and

(b) internal (intra-cultural) stimuli (*internally stimulated culture change*).

Among the external factors which promote, although not necessarily generate change in musical traditions we can mention:

(a) availability of new materials,
Examples:
- replacement of calabashes as resonators of string instruments by tin canisters, "bidons" etc;
- replacement of plant (fibre) materials for strings by nylon, usually taken from fishing lines;
- replacement of iron notes for lamellophones hammered out in the forge, by discarded umbrella ribs. The latter have been used in several cultures of Tanzania for the notes of box-resonated lamellophones such as the *ilimba* of the Wagogo and the *malimba* of the Wakisi;
- use of cigarette paper replacing the membranes of a spider's cocoon on gourd-resonated xylophones;
- use of factory-made textiles for dance costumes and decoration, replacing indigenous materials.

(b) availability of a new technology
Examples:
- employment of carpenter technology with the use of planks, nails, plane etc. in the making of African musical instruments. This has promoted, for example, the replacement of hollowed out wooden resonators made from a single block of wood by box resonators composed of several planks or boards nailed together, e.g. for lamellophones, xylophones, etc.
- employment of microphones during performances on stage. This has made it possible to exploit the human voice and certain musical instruments, e.g. mouth-bows such as the *nkangala* played by young women in Malaŵi, in a manner hitherto unknown.
- employment of electric amplification with certain "traditional" instruments such as the *agidigbo* of the Yoruba of Nigeria, especially when used in *apala* bands;
- music disseminated by the mass media responds even structurally to the new demands thus created.

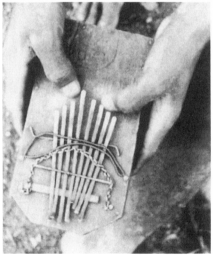

Ill. 11a–b. *Malimba* (lamellophone) with iron notes made from umbrella ribs, belonging to Laurenti, a Kikisi-speaking performer at Lupingu, Lake Nyasa. The musician happened to pose by chance with his spare umbrella, to be used one day for the next *malimba*. At Lupingu (then: Njombe District, Southern Highlands Province, Tanganyika), April 1960

(c) changes in a tradition provoked by interference of an ideological nature
Examples:
- rise of new music associated with separatist churches;
- rise of songs with a new political content, freedom songs, national songs, national service songs in Tanzania etc.

(d) changes in a tradition provoked by interference of a commercial nature
Examples:
- in the 1950s reduction of the duration of all recorded "traditional" music to a maximum of ca. 3 minutes for publication on 78 rpm singles;
- development of a fade-out performed by musicians heavily exposed to the record industry, for example by *kwela* flute bands in southern Africa, such as that of "Donald Kachamba's Kwela Band".

On the broadest level, the interaction of several of these factors may result, for example, in the ultimate total assimilation of a foreign tradition or foreign cultural traits into the local cultural mainstream. Alternatively, a local cultural tradition may totally change its content and nature by radical adjustment to a foreign tradition which becomes popular in the area.

Why and under what circumstances do external influences become effective in a culture? Clearly, there are psychological factors which play an important role in determining acceptance or rejection. In one case, external styles of expression, foreign objects, techniques, attitudes etc., which are associated with a foreign life-style, culture and/or language, are perceived by the members of the recipient culture as superior. Such feelings can be unleashed by: (a) the foreign culture's verbal claim to superiority, often accompanied by some form of indoctrination and/or (b) by its deliberate macho-type or show piece-like display of novel technologies. In the second case one subsection of the larger society in the recipient culture (for example an age-group) identifies with the foreign culture in revolt against an indigenous establishment, e.g. elders of their own society, authoritative parents, a preponderant aristocracy etc. The generation conflict is a natural phenomenon in many, also matrilineally organized societies, but it may receive dramatic fuel from a foreign culture within sight, which serves as an alternative.

Some traits in a culture may also be almost immune to factors, external or internal that would, under different circumstances, unleash culture change. For example, the so-called asymmetric time-line patterns (see below) so prominent in the music of the west African coast and in west-central Africa, as well as in extensions of African cultures in Brazil and the Caribbean, are virtually immune to forces of change. They may change their performance speed, their accentuation, the instruments or tools on which they are performed (for example from iron bell to glass bottle), and they may gradually change their distribution areas in Africa, thus disappearing from one tradition and reappearing in another, but they cannot change their numerical structures. There is no force in the world which can change the internal mathematics of the asymmetric time-line patterns, one of the most ingenious African inventions of the remote past.

What makes a culture reject a foreign element? Some researchers have claimed that a foreign element is easily assimilated if there is some accidental or historically-determined similarity with the recipient culture, allowing for a process Melville J. Herskovits (1941) has termed re-inter-pretation. It is true that one may explain the apparently easy assimilation of Cuban *rumba*, *chachacha*, *pachanga* and other Latin American dance patterns into the mainstream of the central African guitar-based music that was emerging after 1945, by the fact that Cuban dance music is heavily based on a central and west African heritage. When Latin American rhythmic, melodic, and other concepts returned to Africa via com-mercial records, these were immediately recognized as something "not far from home." These movement patterns not only affected guitar music but, for example, what were probably Calypso rhythms were assimilated into some lamellophone music of the Ogowe river area in Congo as far back as 1946. This is demonstrated by recordings made by André Didier and Gilbert Rouget during their 1946 expedition.[5] By comparison Jazz records had little impact on Zaïrean urban music during the 1950s, although the opportunities were there (cf. Jean Welle 1952). North Amer-ican Jazz has also made a "roundtrip" back to Africa (Mensah 1971/72), and – for reasons never fully explained – found a major foothold in only one cultural region of Africa, in South Africa, while elsewhere it was more or less rejected. Why in South Africa? Some authors have thought that a relatively simple beat, prevalent in much South African indigenous music, in contrast to the asymmetric time-line patterns of central Africa and the Guinea Coast may have facilitated the acceptance of Jazz. But it is clear that musical explanations alone do not suffice. Social scientists have explained the acceptance of Jazz in South Africa as being due to a social climate similar to that in the U.S.A. of the 1960s, a climate of racial tension combined with a high degree of urbanisation, etc. Even this is not a complete explanation. Jazz was also accepted with enthusiasm and imitated in postwar Germany for completely different reasons by young Germans who developed an attitude of identification with "black Amer-ican culture" across racial and language differences. Others eventually thought that the strong foothold Jazz gained in South Africa creating a Jazz-offspring such as *kwela* was merely due to a chance configuration of influences: the fact that, in the first instance, South African whites became interested in Jazz and imported records and films etc., while in Zaïre and west Africa there was no such background.

During the last 20 years, with the event of Rock and Soul music the situation has somewhat changed, however. While in Zaïre the influence of north American styles is still minimal, there are pockets in west Africa, where Rock, Soul and even certain traits of post-bebop Jazz styles have been assimilated; this is most clearly shown by some of Mose Yotamu's recordings (cf. 1979) of Dyula pop styles with electric guitars in the north of the Ivory Coast, and by some of our experiences in Dakar, Senegal in December 1981.

Understanding stability and change in African music in any century also requires the study of internal innovation. William Bascom wrote these remarkable observations:

> Every idea has its origin, ultimately, with some individual living at some time in some society, even though we may never know who, when, or where. In that creativity rather than conformity is expected, the forms of aesthetic expression differ basically from social, economic, political and even religious institutions. In this difference may lie the basis for their main contribution to the understanding of culture change (Bascom 1958:8).

Creating a musical composition in Africa – contrary to what has often been written by observers who project the concept of "folk music" onto African traditions – is usually not a collective undertaking. It is rather an individual one, even in musical forms that require the participation of many people.

The initial spark for a new song or composition always comes from one brain. The composer, sometimes referred to as the "owner" of a song, begins the process by conveying a basic musical idea or text which may have occurred to him in a dream to his potential helpers. Like a political leader, he then needs the response of others. So he invites friends or relatives and teaches them what they should do and how they should respond. These helpers may collaborate passively, or some of them may develop or modify the original idea. Thus, the ideas come from individuals, but the response is collective. Even the composer of a new ritual song is often remembered by name. As time passes the names of the composer may fade from the memory of the community, as is the case with very old songs whose "owners" are forgotten, songs of a ritual content, and songs which have migrated and have been adapted in areas far from where they were originally composed.

Since the instigators of creative change (innovation) are individuals, it follows that one must also look at the life histories and motivations of those creative individuals and at their relation to society at large. Human beings are naturally inclined towards cultural and psychological inertia. No one will change his patterns of thinking or his way of life without some external force exerted on him. Such a force may become effective in his close environment, e.g. family or professional milieu, but it may also originate at a great distance.

African Music/Dance as a Motional System

If there is any trait in African music/dance traditions of nearly pan-African validity, it is the presence of distinctively African concepts about and attitudes towards motion. Movement style is what sets Africa and Afro-America apart from the rest of the world, for example China, Japan, India, Melanesia, Europe, north America, Indonesia and so on. This is an area where research is even more challenging than is the study of the sounds produced. As far as Africa is concerned, dance research has been mostly descriptive, however, and from a Western angle. Only very recently, ethno-choreographic studies that include extensive notations of music and dance have become available from within specific African societies.[6]

One basic difference between African dance cultures and those mainly in the northern half of our globe, is that in the latter the body tends to be used as a single block, while in Africa it seems to be split into several seemingly independent body areas or "centres."[7] Helmut Günther has characterized African and African-American dances with the term "polycentric" and has also pointed to a prevailing body attitude, the "collapse" (Günther 1969). Olly Wilson in a lecture given at the Panel "African Roots of Music in the Americas" at the 12th Congress of the International Musicological Society, in Berkeley, 1977, pointed out that the most important trait which links "black" music in America with African music is motional behaviour. Indeed, motional style, at least in its basic principles, has been among the most persistent traits in African cultures. Motional styles are enculturated at an early age, when small children begin to move around among the community, dance, clap hands and beat out patterns. In Africa identical motional patterns and concepts embrace the two areas which are rigidly separated in Western cultures: music and dance. The late Daniel J. Kachamba (1947–1987), eminent guitarist from Malaŵi, once expressed it like this: "My fingers dance on the strings of the guitar."[8]

There are at least two motional centres in a given African dance. The same holds true of the playing of musical instruments. The musician not only produces sounds for their own sake, but he moves his hands, fingers, and in some cultures also head, shoulders, legs, etc. in certain coordinated patterns during the process of musical production. This is one of the reasons why African music is not written down by its exponents, in contrast to Western music. The non-use of notation systems in African music should not be regarded as a deficiency nor be mistaken for "musical illiteracy." On the contrary, the idea of writing down music and "playing it from paper" (Daniel Kachamba's expression) would be somewhat displaced in cultures where the auditory aspect in musical production is so much linked with the motional. Musical recitals from paper demand a totally different kind of mental alertness from that necessary for achieving the intimate relationship between body movement and sound which is so characteristic of African music/dance. For the same reasons, African-American musicians share with African musicians a reluctance to use comprehensive notation. This has often been misunderstood from the viewpoint of European-American cultures and qualified as a tendency towards "improvisation."

Analysis of films has been crucial in the study of dance movement in Africa, and many authors are now using this method.[9] On the basis of an analysis of a large number of music/dance films held in the Institute for Scientific Cinematography, Göttingen (W. Germany), A.M. Dauer (1967b) has proposed a geographical division of Africa into several dance style areas, for example Western Sudan, Sahara, West African Coast, Central African Bantu and Southern Bantu. These coincide to a great extent with Lomax's song-style regions. Acknowledging that African dances are "polycentric," Dauer's dance style areas are based on the observation that in different areas different parts of the human body tend to be emphasized in dance. Motional prominence of the pelvis, buttocks etc. especially in the form of pelvic thrusts or circular pelvis movements, is considered a diagnostic trait of the movement styles of the southern Zaïre/Angola region, while on the west African coast "multiplication" techniques in the leg-and-foot work are particularly important, often in acrobatic dances.[10] Sometimes the dance styles of ethnic groups are characterized by the prevailing use of certain "body centres." For instance, shoulder and shoulder blades in combination with an extreme "collapse" of the general body attitude play an important role in the dance style of the Fõ of Togo and Benin (formerly: Dahomé).

There is, however, considerable overlapping between the presumed dance style areas which can hardly be delimited geographically. In masked dancing of the large Ngangela group of peoples in eastern Angola, for example, many different movement patterns are used by the same community, and each is identified by a name. Which pattern is to be used depends on the character in action and the type of mask. Not all these patterns focus on the pelvic area, though Angola would fall within the central-African dance style zone. *Mutenya* is the term for a slow pelvis circle, while *kukoka* are pelvic movements characterized by tiny thrusts. On the other hand *chizukula*, so named after a mask, implies a movement pattern in which shoulders, arms and legs play a prominent role.

In solo dancing, especially masked dancing, there are also non-metrical types of movement, aimed at communicating with the audience or submitting certain coded messages. A masked dancer is an actor who has to play out the character his mask represents. This includes not only dancing, but pantomimic action, gestures, certain styles of walking etc., particularly non-verbal modes of communication of which Paul Ekman has distinguished: emblems, adaptors and illustrators (Ekman & Friesen

Ill. 12. The masked theatre as remembered history in eastern Angola: *Chikūza* – a mask representing the Chokwe king Mwene Kanyika (18th century). At Kambonge village, south of Longa, Kwandu-Kuvangu Province, south-eastern Angola, August 3, 1965

1969). As can be seen in some of our ciné films these play an important role in masked dancing from the Guinea Coast to central Africa. Masked performances have an interesting distribution area in Africa. They are widely found in west Africa and west central Africa, while they are rare in east Africa and absent in southern Africa (cf. Duerden 1974). The -Makonde, -Makua, -Ndonde, -Lomwe and -Cheŵa/-Mang'anja are the principal peoples in south-east Africa who make masks.

One of the richest African mask areas is the relatively culturally homogeneous territory comprising almost all of eastern Angola, north-western Zambia and some southern parts of Zaïre. Among these matrilineal peoples, the -Chokwe, -Luvale, -Luchazi, -Mbunda, -Nkhangala, -Lwimbi and others, there is an abundance of masked types, each specific in appearance, with a well-defined place in a hierarchic order, specific movement repertoires, gestures and pantomime.

Most of these masks represent ancestral members of an ancient court hierarchy. Kings and members of the royal families, their officials and retinue, including servants and slaves, are resurrected in the masked theatre. The mask *mpumpu* among the Mbwela/-Nkhangela in Kwandu-Kuvangu Province, south-eastern Angola, is said to represent Mwene Nyumbu, the founder of the traditional circumcision school. *Chikũza*, a mask of Chokwe origin, is said to represent the ancient ruler Mwene Kanyika. *Chileya*, a very popular mask throughout eastern Angola and north-western Zambia, represents a court fool, a slave who was very talkative and used to play around with the women. *Chileya* uses circular pelvis movements (*mutenya*) in its dance style, a parody of the dance style of young women undergoing initiation. In addition there are masks depicting animals, anthropomorphic or zoomorphic creatures from the forest and swamps, often grotesque, such as *ndzingi* (a giant with a big head and red "blood-thirsty" mouth) or *lifwako* (a creature imagined to live in rivers) (cf. Kubik 1969 b, 1971 b).

While the *akixi* (Chokwe), respectively *makishi* (Luvale) and *makisi* (Mbwela/Nkhangala) masked characters are inseparably connected with the institution called *mukanda* (boy's circumcision school) there is no such relationship, for example, in the *nyau* masks of the -Cheŵa and related peoples of Malaŵi, eastern Zambia and north-western Moçambique, which are part of men's secret societies.[11] The -Cheŵa do not practice circumcision.

Masked dancing occurs with a variety of social contexts and functions. This is evident from comparative studies of institutions such as *ɔmabe* (the "leopard" society) among the Igbo, Nigeria,[12] the *jenge* masked society among the Bangombe pygmies of the Upper Sangha (Djenda 1968 c) and the masked societies in the so-called matrilineal belt of south-central Africa (from Angola to the Ruvuma valley in Moçambique).

Ill. 13. *Chileya* masked dancer performing to the accompaniment of a *chinkuvu* slit-drum during the season of the *mukanda* circumcision school for boys. One of the predominant motional patterns used in the dance is a slow pelvis rotation (*mutenya*), expressing the lascivious character depicted by this masked dancer: a court fool who used to be very fond of women. At Sangombe village, Kwitu river area, south-eastern Angola, September 18, 1965

Movement organization in African music/dance cultures rigidly follows certain principles of timing, based on at least four to five fundamental concepts:

Concept 1

The overall presence of a mental background pulsation consisting of equal-spaced pulse units elapsing ad infinitum and often at enormous speed. These so-called elementary pulses (Kubik 1969a) function as a basic orientation screen. They are two or three times faster than the beat or gross pulse, which is the next level of reference.

Concept 2

Musical form is organized so that patterns and themes cover recurring entities of a regular number of these elementary pulses, usually 8, 12, 16, 24 or their multiples, more rarely 9, 18 or 27 units. These are the so-called cycles, and the numbers we call form or cycle numbers.[13]

Concept 3

Many of the form or cycle numbers can be divided or split in more than one way, thus allowing for the simultaneous combination of contradictory metrical units. For example, the number 12 which is the most important form number in African music, can be divided by 2, 3, 4 and 6.

Concept 4

Patterns inside the same form number can be shifted against each other in combinations so that their starting points and main accents cross. This is called "cross rhythm" (Jones 1934, 1959b). In certain instances they cross so completely that they fall between one another or interlock so no two notes sound together. There are two basic types of interlocking employed in various instrumental ensembles, from drums to xylophones, (a) duple-division and (b) triple-division interlocking. Performance in the interlocking manner implies that a performer refers his/her pattern to an "inner beat" that is different from that of his/her partner, and in addition may be different from that of the dancers. In some instrumental genres musicians combine strokes which represent for each participant the beat itself (such as in the two basic parts of *amadinda* and *embaire* music, Uganda). In other cultures a musician may strike what for him represents the beat with only one hand, interlocking it with the beat of his partner, while the other hand is free to play superimposed patterns. This is the case in the xylophone styles of northern Moçambique (cf. Kubik 1965c).

Ill. 14. *Ng'oma* dancers among the Wagogo, central Tanzania during a festival for Chief Mazengo. The *ng'oma* hourglass-shaped drums are exclusively used by females among the Wagogo. The technique of combining strokes in triple-division interlocking within a 12-pulse overall cycle is acquired at adolescent age. Mvumi, southeast of Dodoma, Tanganyika (Tanzania), January 1, 1962

This phenomenon of an "individual beat" in instrumental ensembles is frequently encountered in musical traditions of Bantu language speakers of east and east-central Africa (e.g. among the Baganda, Basoga, Wagogo, Anyanja, Wayao, Ashirima, Vamakonde, Babemba etc. to mention a few "ethnic groups") while in the musical cultures of west-central Africa and the Guinea Coast it seems to be less frequent.

The employment of interlocking techniques allows instrumentalists performing on the same instrument, or on instruments with identical timbre, to produce resultant patterns that are unbelievably rapid.

1st musician's beat:
2nd musician's beat:

etc.

Ill. 15. Duple-division interlocking

1st musician's beat:
2nd musician's beat:[14]

etc. or

etc.

r l r l r l r l   l r l r l r l r

Ill. 16. Triple-division interlocking performed by two musicians (or opposing groups)

1st musician's beat:
2nd musician's beat:
3rd musician's beat:

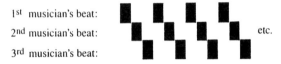

etc.

Ill. 17. Triple-division interlocking performed by three musicians

Concept 5

In certain areas there is yet a further principle of timing to be found: the so-called time-line patterns. These constitute a specific category of struck motional patterns, characterized by an asymmetric inner structure, such as 5 + 7 or 7 + 9. They are single-note patterns struck on a musical instrument of penetrating sound quality, such as a bell, a high-pitched drum, the rim of a drum, the wooden body of a drum, a bottle, calabash or percussion beam, concussion sticks (such as the Cuban claves) or a high-pitched key of a xylophone.

They are a regulative element in many kinds of African music, especially along the west African coast, in western central Africa and in a broad belt along the Zambezi valley into Moçambique. Broadly speaking they are found in those parts of Africa covered by the Kwa (I.A.4 in Greenberg's classification) and Benue-Congo (I.A.5) subgroups of the Niger-Congo family of languages but with the notable exception that they are not found in most areas of east and south Africa.

These are some of the most important time-line patterns:
a) the 12-pulse seven-stroke pattern
version a (mainly west African)

(12) [x . x . xx . x . x . x]

version b (mainly central African)

(12) [x . x . x . xx . x . x]

Distribution: especially along the west African coast, for example in the music of the Yoruba, Fõ, Ewe, but also in Zaïre, Angola, Zambia, etc.

b) The 12-pulse five-stroke pattern

⑫ [x.x.x..x.x..]

Distribution: central Africa, especially in Congo-Brazzaville, Zaïre, Zambia, Malaŵi; in West Africa, for instance, among the Baule of the Ivory Coast.

c) A 16-pulse time-line pattern

⑯ [x.x.x.x.xx.x.x.x]

Distribution: especially southern Zaïre (Katanga), eastern Angola and north-western Zambia. An isolated occurrence was observed in xylophone music on the Kenya coast.[15]

Time-line patterns of this kind are absent among most of the eastern branch of Bantu language speaking peoples, for example in the so-called interlacustrine zone (Baganda/Basoga) although there was one instance of the 12-pulse five-stroke pattern coming up as an inherent pattern in an *akadinda* xylophone piece (cf. Chapter II). Nor are they found among most peoples of Tanzania, unless recently imported with Zaïrean guitar music; but the 12-pulse five-stroke pattern has a long history in the Zambezi valley and at Lake Malaŵi (for example among the -Yao, -Kokhola, -Lomwe, -Mang'anja).

The longest time-line pattern used in African music was observed among the pygmies of the Upper Sangha river in the Central African Republic.[16] It is a 24-pulse pattern struck on a percussion beam, showing the following structure:

㉔ [x.x.x.x.x.xx.x.x.x.x.xx.]

It is used among the Bangombe pygmies in the accompaniment of a dance called *moyaya* in which pelvis motion predominates.

A time-line pattern represents the structural core of a musical piece, something like a condensed and extremely concentrated representation of the motional possibilities open to the participants (musicians and dancers). Singers, drummers and dancers in the group find their bearings by listening to the strokes of the time-line pattern, which is repeated at a steady tempo throughout the performance. Time-line patterns are transmitted from teacher to learner by means of mnemonic syllables or verbal patterns.

Ill. 18. One of Africa's longest recorded time-line pattern is the 24-pulse pattern struck on a percussion beam (*mbanda*) in the *moyaya* dance performed among the Bangombe, one of the two pygmy hunter-gatherer groups found in the Upper Sangha River area, where the borders of three countries meet: Central African Republic, Congo and Cameroon. The performer, Likito, headman of the pygmy camp Kanga-Tema uses two beaters, each in one hand, to strike it. At Kanga-Tema, south of Nola, Central African Republic, May 1966

Chapter I
Xylophone Playing in Southern Uganda

Buganda and the Interlacustrine Area

Archaeological excavations in the Lake Victoria area show a characteristic type of pottery classed as "dimple-based" or Urewe ware (Illustration 19) after a principal site on the northeastern shore of the Lake. It has been concluded from radio-carbon dates that an Early Iron Age culture established itself here in the so-called interlacustrine zone between ca. 400–300 B.C. (Phillipson 1977:228). The carriers of this culture are supposed to have been Bantu-speakers with an economy based on agriculture.

Bantu language speakers began to populate the sub-continent shortly before the start of the Christian era. It is generally accepted today that the "Bantu nucleus" where early Bantu speech developed falls into the northwesternmost edge of the present distribution area of I.A.5 languages (cf. Greenberg 1966) to which all the Bantu languages belong. Thus the original "home" of the Bantu or proto-Bantu is placed in a zone covering part of eastern Nigeria and the western Cameroonian highlands (cf. Murdock 1959). Between ca. 1000–400 B.C. some groups began to disperse eastwards along the northern fringes of the equatorial forest, while a parallel movement, dated by Phillipson (1977:227) as between ca. 1000–200 B.C. took place in southward direction to northern Angola.

It cannot be established whether any remnants of those early Iron Age Bantu were absorbed into the mainstream of Bantu speaking populations in southern Uganda of today, or whether they totally vanished. In any case many subsequent migrations took place but the Urewe ware represents the beginnings of both the Iron age and Bantu cultures in the interlacustrine area.

A decisive ethnic-linguistic boundary runs across Uganda today, roughly from Lake Albert along the Victoria Nile to Lake Kyoga and from there eastwards to Mount Elgon and into Kenya (Map 4). North of this line Eastern Sudanic languages are spoken (II.E. 1 in Greenberg 1966), i.e. Acooli, Alur, Lango, Teso etc., and in small pockets in West-Nile District also Central Sudanic languages (II.E.2) such as Madi. These populations, usually referred to as "Nilotes" in the ethnographic literature, came to northern Uganda and neighbouring Kenya in the course of the so-called Luo migration (cf. Ogot 1967), whose dating is uncertain,

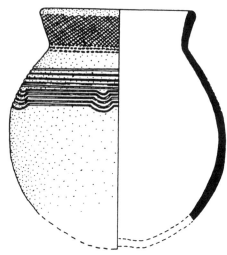

Ill. 19. Example of Urewe pottery, associated with the first migration of Bantu-speakers to southern and western Uganda (ca. 400–300 B.C.). Reproduced from D.W. Phillipson 1977:107

but which brought, in several successive waves, speakers of Eastern Sudanic languages from the Bahr-el-Ghazal in Sudan into their present settlement areas. South of this line, the languages spoken on Uganda territory belong to Zone E in Malcolm Guthrie's tentative classification of the Bantu languages (1948); the most important being: Luganda, Lusoga, Lunyoro and Runyankore.

During the later Iron Age in southern Uganda as well as in Rwanda and Burundi a series of centrally governed states began to form, from approximately the 14th century onwards, absorbing cultural traits from the environs. Archaeologically, the new development is typified by the appearance of a new type of ware, the so-called roulette-decorated pottery, excavated at Bigo in western Uganda.[1] Here extensive earthworks have been found. In oral traditions these sites have been called "ancient capitals" and their establishment has been attributed to the legendary Bachwezi, immigrants to Uganda, associated with long-horned cattle and a possibly pastoral life style such as continues today in some parts of Nkore (the country of the Banyankore in western Uganda). In many oral traditions of the interlacustrine zone the Bachwezi dynasty is referred to as the earliest, in some as the second, after the dynasty of the Batembuzi (cf. Mworoha 1977:67–71). The possible origin of the Bachwezi is still the subject of discussion. John Hanning Speke (1863) launched the hypothesis of a "hamitic" invasion of Uganda centuries ago which would have been responsible for the foundation of the interlacus-

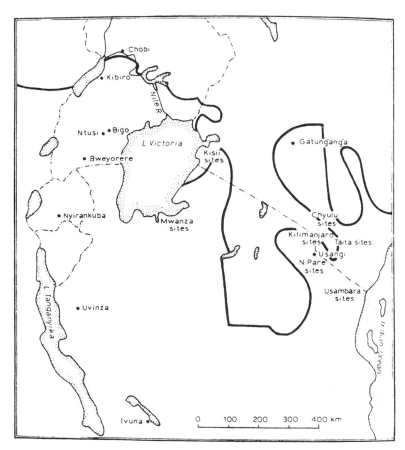

Map 4. Approximate boundary between present-day settlement areas of Bantu-
and non-Bantu-speaking populations in Uganda, Kenya and Tanzania; several
east African later Iron Age sites attributed to Bantu-speakers are marked. Reproduced from Phillipson 1977:162

trine kingdoms. As a possible area of origin of these pastoralists the Horn
of Africa was suggested. In Uganda the "invaders" would have lost their
language and mixed with the general settled population of Bantu-speakers.

With regard to archaeology, David W. Phillipson has stated that

> ... roulette-decorated pottery is demonstrably the work of
> Nilotic-speakers, ... and, indeed, its manufacture is widespread at
> the present time in the southern and central Sudan, where its
> development may be traced back to Meroitic times ... (Phillipson
> 1977:163).

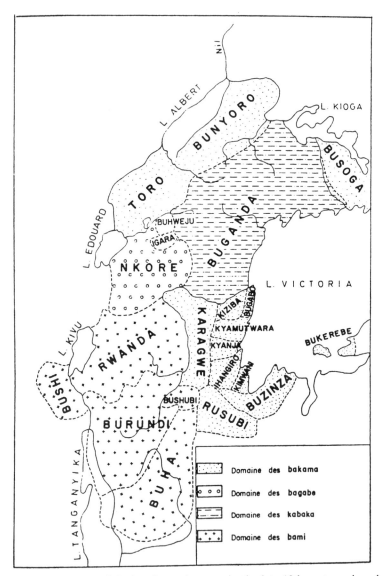

Map 5. The states of the interlacustrine area in the late 19th century classed according to the hereditary titles of their traditional rulers. Reproduced from Mworoha 1977:49

The "hamitic" hypothesis is considered simplistic and misleading today, apart from its racist overtones. Archaeological and linguistic evidence (cf. Ehret 1974) has suggested complex migratory patterns and interactions in East Africa during the last five thousand years.

The first state on the territory of present-day Uganda was Bunyoro-Kitara, under the dynasty of the Bachwezi. It reached the climax of its power and its greatest extension during the 15th century. In the following centuries, first Nkore and then Buganda seceded, and finally Tooro in the 19th century. By the middle of the 19th century, benefiting from coastal trade via Karagwe and Unyamwezi in Tanzania, Buganda became the greatest military power in the region.

Smaller territories such as Busoga (= the country of the Basoga), bordering on Buganda in the east, – the approximate boundary being the Nile between Lake Kyoga and Victoria – never reached the status of kingdom. During the 19th century, Busoga was a vassal of Buganda, and at the same time an important source for cultural innovation in the kingdom. Buganda's court music assimilated many creative impulses from Busoga. By the mid-19th century, as observed by Speke and Grant (1863), Basoga musicians were regularly recruited to the court of Kabaka Mutesa I.

The *endongo* or *entongoli* (lyre) figures among the instruments introduced to Buganda from Busoga.[2] The basic structural identity between *amadinda* and *embaire* log xylophone music testifies to the intimate relationship between the two musical cultures. By comparison, very little music in Buganda shows any traits linkable with the pastoralist musical cultures. This is a totally different picture from Nkore in western Uganda.

Court and ceremonial music in the area of the three traditional kingdoms of southern Uganda, Bunyoro, Buganda and Nkore, developed at an early stage. Besides the drums, insignia of royalty, various musical instruments were kept in the three courts. In Buganda, court music included the following ensembles which fulfilled their functions within the Kabaka's enclosure (*lubiri*) independently of each other: *abalere ba Kabaka* (the flute ensemble), *entamiivu za Kabaka* (the xylophone ensemble including a twelve-key log xylophone called *entaala*; outside the Kabaka's enclosure this instrument was called *amadinda*); *amakondere* (horn ensemble); *akadinda* (17-key xylophone) ensemble; *entenga* (drum chime consisting of twelve drums tuned like a xylophone) and other formations. In addition there were the soloists, particularly the performers on the *ennanga* (eight-string arched harp).

The first Europeans who visited Buganda searching for the "sources of the Nile," John Hanning Speke and James A. Grant, met Kabaka Mutesa I. in 1862, and repeatedly described musical scenes in the king's court. Mutesa I. who reigned from ca. 1854 to 1884, was himself a musician playing flute and xylophone.[3] Less than a kilometer from his palace there was the house of the queen-mother, who was often seen in the company of a blind harpist.

The continuity of Buganda's court music was interrupted in 1966 when Milton Obote, then Prime Minister of Uganda dissolved the kingdoms in the course of political problems. Only very recently, since the establishment of the Government of Yoweri Museweni on January 29th, 1986 have there been cautious signals that at least culturally, some of the splendour of the ancient kingdoms might be reconstructed one day. Peter Cooke, after a recent visit to Uganda, wrote to me in a letter dated March 16th, 1988:

> At Kidinda – the village where the *akadinda* musicians live they had built a new instrument for practice when they heard that the Ssabataka – the prince of heir – was visiting Uganda again for the first time – I found many younger and able players there ...

* * *

Musicology in Uganda began with the late Klaus Wachsmann, Curator of the Uganda Museum from 1948 to 1957. Ample space would be needed to fully assess Wachsmann's immense contribution, not only in his building up the collections of the Museum, the magnificent record collection (now preserved in the National Sound Archives, London), but also in his considerable influence on young musicians and composers in Uganda, notably Joseph Kyagambiddwa and Evaristo Muyinda. The latter was recruited by Klaus Wachsmann in 1949 as chief music demonstrator at the museum and became his research assistant.

I did not meet Klaus Wachsmann in Uganda, when I began my studies in 1959, but indirectly I benefited greatly from the facilities he created. My learning of the *amadinda* and *akadinda* xylophone traditions under Evaristo Muyinda's tutorship took place in a climate of friendliness and scholarship. To my teacher, Evaristo Muyinda, and to Merrick Posnansky, then Curator of the Uganda Museum, as well as to Charles Sekintu and Valerie Vowles I am greatly indebted.

The text which now follows is a transcript with amendments of a lecture I gave at the Royal Anthropological Institute, London, on March 28, 1963 – three years later. After publication of my experiences in Uganda between November 1959 and March 1960 (Kubik 1960), I had the opportunity to continue my studies during several visits to Uganda on our one and a half year research trip to east and south-east Africa: August 7, 1961 – January 10, 1963. This was my longest continuous trip to Africa and it was carried out jointly with a Viennese and a Tanzanian friend, Helmut Hillegeist and Basilius Saprapason from Lupanga, then Njombe District, Tanganyika.

In 1963 I was invited to London by the Transcription Centre (Director: Dennis Duerden) to make a few radio programmes and work in the sound archive of the Centre. That was an opportunity for me to meet Klaus Wachsmann and the Reverend A.M. Jones for the first time. Klaus Wachsmann was kind enough to introduce me to the distinguished audience at the Royal Anthropological Institute which, among other personalities, included William Fagg and Ernest K.K. Sempebwa. The following week I wrote up my talk, and the written version eventually appeared in the *Journal of the Royal Anthropological Institute,* Vol. 94, Part 2, 1964, under the same title as this Chapter.

The version printed here is revised and shortened in a few places, while supplemented in others. Tone and diction of my 1963 lecture, however, have been maintained.

March 29th, 1988
Gerhard Kubik

Xylophone Types

It is my intention to introduce today to you one of the most interesting kinds of east African music: xylophone playing in the area of the Kingdoms of southern Uganda. Since 1959 I have visited east Africa several times and my lecture is based on personal experience and research. For four months, in 1959–60, I was a student of Evaristo Muyinda, an eminent musician of the Kabaka of Buganda.[4] He taught me to play the *amadinda* and *akadinda* xylophones. I continued my studies for a few months more between November 1961 and June 1962, and in January 1963 I started to study the *embaire* xylophone music of Busoga in a small village called Bumanya, north of Kaliro in Busoga district.

Xylophones in southern Uganda belong to a category known as log xylophones. The base of the instrument consists of two fresh banana stems. A series of sticks is pushed into the soft stems. Then the keys are placed between. No resonator vessels are employed. In Buganda the keys are usually made of the wood of the *lusambya* tree.[5] In parts of Busoga, particularly near lake Kyoga, I found that *mukeremba*[6] was preferred (cf. also Trowell & Wachsmann 1953).

Performance Concepts

All Uganda xylophones are struck at their extremities. My Muganda teacher took great care that I beat the keys in a manner which gave the best sound, and that I kept my hands perfectly pliable, when moving in five-key spacing (parallel octaves) over the keyboard. The arms should be kept as still as possible. The sticks in the hands should derive their movement mainly from the wrist and not by moving the arms.

Among royal musicians in the Kingdom of Buganda "good" and "bad" ways of playing the log xylophones are distinguished by means of an impressive vocabulary, in which onomatopoeic syllables, or syllables which are constituents of words, as well as metaphorical comparisons are used for didactic purposes. My teacher used to describe different techniques of striking the notes of an *amadinda* (12-note xylophone) with a rich terminology in Luganda, the national language of the old Kingdom and in Uganda one of the important written languages.

Okubwatula is considered as a bad manner of xylophone playing. This term characterizes a manner of striking, whereby the performer does not hit the xylophone slats on their ends, but hits them hard with the tip of the beater on their surface. This can often be observed with beginners. The verb *okubwatula* contains the ideophone *bwa*, which may express, for example, the impact of a tree branch falling to the ground. Severe pain may also be described with the verb such as a severe headache; or the sound of a stroke causing a fracture or fissure.

Another mistake attributed to beginners is called *okugugumula*. It means: to strike a xylophone key at the end, but very hard and with stiff hands. Charles Sekintu[7] of the Uganda Museum, Kampala, who spent much of his valuable time with me discussing Luganda musical terminology, translated the word *okugugumula*, in its literal meaning as "to cause a crowd of birds to move at once." All these rather specialized terms in the musicians' language are metaphoric. Sekintu's translation may be understood in the sense of "to frighten away" birds through the noise of beating the keys badly.

Okuyiwa (Sekintu: "to pour down," "to let down," "to disappoint") denotes an irregular way of playing. Beginners often do that. They become slower and faster during the performance, because they have not yet acquired the necessary manual skill. *Okwokya* is a category denoting the opposite; it means: "playing hastily," "playing too fast." *Okukekemya* was defined by Sekintu as: "To cause something to make the sound ke-ke-ke, like a broody hen." It also describes a bad manner of striking the xylophone keys.

The most common and desired way of playing the *amadinda* is *okusengejja*. (Sekintu: "to sort things out, to clarify.") This possibly refers to the phenomenon of "subjective" or "inherent" rhythms (cf. Kubik 1960:12; 1962c), a term which I introduced to describe melodic-rhythmic patterns in Kiganda xylophone music which are clearly perceived by the audience, but not played as such by any of the performers. The musicians make them appear, "sort them out." *Okusengejja*, when Evaristo Muyinda demonstrated it, was a soft and even way of playing.

Sometimes a slightly different emphasis was given to each note, so that some of them would form into groups. Other ways of performance are to be regarded as special styles. *Okudaliza* is a strongly accentuated way of playing. Suddenly one note may be struck with great emphasis. Sekintu says: "To stitch a cloth together before you finally sew it". Some *amadinda* tunes are specially fit for being played *okudaliza;* for example "*Atalabanga mundu agende Buleega*" ("One who has never seen a gun should go to Buleega").[8] In the *okwawula* part of this composition the note transcribed as A occurs at regular intervals. Every third note in this part is an A. At the climax of the performance of this tune my teacher used to give strong accentuation to all the A's, if it so happened that he was playing the *okwawula* part himself. *Okudaliza* may have a disorienting effect upon listeners not yet familiar with this music, who then feel that the basic beat is completely shifted at the moment the players start to accentuate.

There is one manner of performance, where notes of the two basic parts of an *amadinda* composition can be dropped. Normally it does not happen in this entirely through-composed xylophone music. Such a style of playing is referred to as *okusita ebyondo oba ebisenge*. (Sekintu: "To erect corners [inlets] or to make walls.") It cannot be heard frequently. *Okusita ebyondo* essentially means that one of the basic parts is being played "broken up." The opposite musician meanwhile plays *okusengejja*. Some notes are left out, dropped, while others are maintained forming "corners," "walls."

During the performance of an *amadinda* tune the manner of playing can be changed ad libitum. Usually playing is started with *okusengejja*. Then other movement styles may be gradually applied. But changes should be sparingly used. *Okudaliza*, for example, leads at once to the climax. After *okudaliza* the performance should be stopped. (Steady movement at climax level means no climax.) The common way of performance is to play a tune strictly *okusengejja*.

Tunings

How are the xylophones of southern Uganda tuned? All instruments which I came across in Buganda, Busoga and Bunyoro were tuned to a pentatonic scale. This tuning seems to be identical in the three mentioned areas. It is used not only for the xylophone, but for other instruments as well, such as the *budongo* lamellophones of Busoga, the *ennanga* (Kiganda harp), the *entongooli* (Kiganda and Kisoga lyre), and other instruments. The exact nature of this pentatonic scale has not yet been found out. It has been suggested in previous musicological research that the scale is equidistant or at least subjectively is intended to be so by the traditional musicians. Measurements have been made with excellent equipment, which resulted in vibration numbers coming on average close to the ideal of an equidistant pentatonic scale (Wachsmann 1950; 1957).

Ill. 20. An *amadinda* in the Uganda Museum, one of the xylophones on which I was instructed in 1959/60 and on which I used to practise regularly. The two big keys at the near end of the instrument are referred to as *amatengezzi*. At the far end are the two *amakoonezi*. This specimen was constructed it seems in the 1930s. Subsequently it was used from 1949 onwards by the Uganda Museum's team of musical demonstrators, for visitors to the Museum. Kampala, February 1960

I have often been struck by the flexibility of Kiganda and Kisoga tuning. The different xylophones on which I used to play[9] had only approximately the same scale. Never, of course, did the scale lose its pentatonic identity. The flexibility could readily be explained by the suggestion that some xylophones might have been "out of tune," if the same phenomenon did not occur in the *budongo* music of Busoga as well. Between May 1962 and January 1963, during two visits to Uganda, I worked with two blind *budongo* players from Bulamoji County in northeast Busoga. One of them, Waiswa Lubogo, is a gifted singer and player of the *kadongo*. During a performance the two or sometimes three musicians used to retune (*okutuusa*) their instruments frequently. Here I felt that the tuning of the metal lamellae was not constant. Whenever they retuned their instruments, the tuning appeared slightly different from

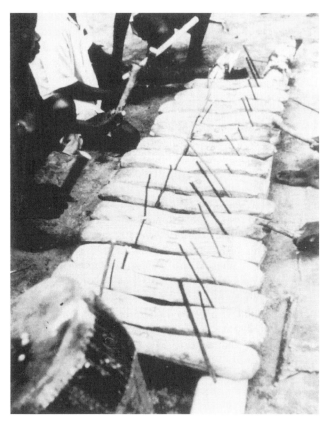

Ill. 21. Identification of the slats of an *embaire* xylophone with numbers painted in blue on the middle of the surface of each slat. The numbers, proceeding from the highest to the lowest note, are facing the *mulangalira* (on the right-hand side in the picture) who plays the opening part. This is the *embaire* ensemble of Venekenti Nakyebale at Bumanya, Busoga District. Archive No. B 374/1963

what it was before. Only the general layout or plan was strictly preserved by the musicians.[10]

I made similar observations in 1960 with another important troubadour of the *kadongo*, Mukama, a Mugwere from Kachuru near Palisa in Bukedi district. To him a deviation of almost a half tone was bearable on one occasion. Principally his tuning was the same as that of the Basoga players. The deviations, however, and this is probably the crux of the matter, were not systematic. For this reason, a pentatonic system with functionally different interval sizes can also be excluded from the range of possible theoretical explanations of the Kiganda tonal system.

It appears that the "true" octave is also disliked by the Baganda and Basoga musicians. This is remarkable, because in southern Uganda the only chord which intentionally occurs in instrumental music is the octave; and playing in parallel octaves (*myanjo* in Luganda) is very important in *amadinda, akadinda, embaire, budongo*, and *ennanga* music. On the *ennanga*, however, the total of eight strings restricts octave duplication to only three notes of the five-note melodies. All these instruments, as it seems to me, are tuned in approximate octaves only and in fact on purpose. The extent to which one may theorize at all on southern Uganda scales largely depends on the amount of deviation from perfect octaves that can be found in the different examples of tuning.

The word *myanjo* was first used to translate "octaves" by Joseph Kyagambiddwa. A Muganda church music composer, Kyagambiddwa was the first Western-educated student of Evaristo Muyinda on the *amadinda* xylophone. In his work (Kyagambiddwa 1955) he attempted to write down the songs he had learned in staff notation and formulate rules "governing" Kiganda music theory. With regard to the *myanjo*, however, it is necessary to consider some of the Luganda concepts behind this term. A class III noun, it is *mwanjo* (or *omwanjo* if one adds the initial vowel) in the singular; it is derived from the verb *kwanja*, meaning "to spread out," "to fold out." As a noun, *mwanjo* therefore, can be translated as "measurement", "dimension" etc., and accordingly, it is often used by traders of textiles who wish to describe the exact dimensions of a cloth.

Transferred to the musical realm, *myanjo* (plural term) can be translated as "different spans in space," "extensions," "distances." This alludes to xylophone practice. One of the obvious spacial "spans" in xylophone playing is when the performer strikes in octaves and preserves this striking distance of his two beaters wherever he plays on the keyboard (thus playing parallel octaves). The visual aspect of playing parallel octaves must have been what made Baganda project the term into music. *Myanjo* (in the plural) can therefore be used with justification to describe not merely the concept of an "octave" on the xylophone, but even more the concept of playing in parallel octaves.

Performance and Musical Structure

We need not solve the problem of tuning and scale to be able to discuss the structure of southern Ugandan xylophone music and to transcribe it. The reason is that we need not worry about harmonic patterns. I have already mentioned that no other "chords" or simultaneous sounds besides octaves are attempted. For Kiganda xylophone music there exists no transcription problem, provided that the transcriber does not believe that he can transcribe this music from tape without knowledge of how it is constructed. The comparative ease with which one may transcribe this music having learned to play it can also be explained through the fact that both *amadinda* and *akadinda* music are composed note by note.

The three illustrations (Illustration 23, 25, and 27) show three different xylophones from southern Uganda: the *amadinda,* the *akadinda* and the *embaire.* From these illustrations we note the positions of the players and the limited range for each of them and each of their hands. Under the drawing the scale is given. It should be regarded as a key to the transcriptions. Its purpose is to allow the student to find out on which key of the related xylophone every note in the transcriptions is struck.

It is important to note that this notation is all relative. The note which I have written as C therefore need not be the tonic in the mind of any musician and it is not necessarily at the same pitch on the different xylophones as well. Related to the European tone system it was near in two cases $F^\sharp$ (Kubik 1960). My friend and companion on the east African research trip August 1961 to January 1963, Helmut Hillegeist, photographer and musician, stated that to him there was more than one possibility for the feeling of a "tonic." And he showed me two or sometimes three notes on the xylophone, which could appear to him as the tonal basis on different occasions. He made the same statement about *budongo* music.

I have written the scales from top to bottom; this in accordance with the musicians' concept. There is evidence suggesting that the scale in southern Uganda is thought to start with the smallest and to end with the largest note. One is the tuning process, which apparently always starts by finding the exact interval of the two top notes (Wachsmann 1950; 1957). I have observed this many times myself. An interesting observation I made in Bumanya (Busoga) in 1963 was that the fifteen keys of an *embaire* xylophone in that village had numbers written on the surface, to make it easier for the musicians to assemble their xylophone quickly (to place the keys in the right sequence on the banana stems without trying their pitch first).

Key number 1 had the highest tone, and key number 15 the lowest. The same band was very sensitive concerning the sequence of pitches. During the recording session I suggested that the drums should be placed somewhere else, so that the lower xylophone keys could he heard more distinctly on the recording. The musicians refused. The drums, so I was instructed, were 'a part of the xylophone' and had to stand near the lowest keys of the *embaire.* They were regarded as a continuation of the xylophone keys into the deep register.

Illustrations 23 and 25 show two kinds of log xylophones used in Buganda, the twelve-key *amadinda* and the *akadinda* with seventeen keys.

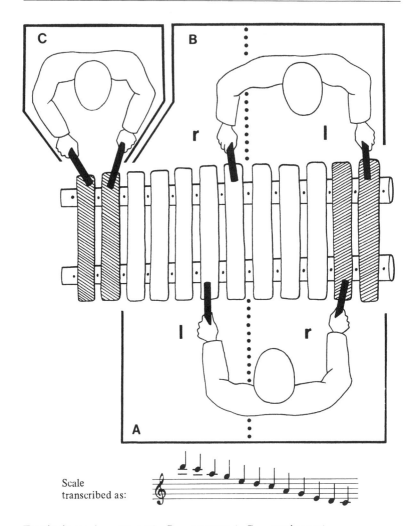

Scale
transcribed as:

Terminology: A = *omunazi*, B = *omwawuzi*, C = *omukoonezi*.

▨ = *amakoonezi* (sing. *enkoonezi*), the two top keys
▧ = *amatengezzi* (sing. *entengezzi*), the two bottom keys
r = right hand playing area; 1 = left hand playing area

Ill. 22. Performance on the *amadinda*. Demonstrator: Evaristo Muyinda, Kampala. The positions and playing areas of the three musicians are to be considered valid for all *amadinda* compositions. Their seats can, however, be exchanged with one another. It often happens that musician A sits in B's place (and vice versa); musician C can also sit next to A if he feels more comfortable playing his patterns left/right hand reversed (see also Illustration 23)

Ill. 23. The Uganda Museum's team of demonstrators showing the *amadinda* playing areas. Here the *omukoonezi* happened to sit next to the *omwawuzi*. Kampala, December 1962

Illustration 27 shows the *embaire*, the xylophone of Busoga with fifteen keys.

The method of combining the different performers' parts is identical in the three xylophone styles. We can say it is an interlocking way of playing. Those musicians who are sitting opposite each other (A and B) strike more or less the same keys of the instrument, each one at his own end. They strike, however, alternately, one being in the act of striking, and the other at the end of the stroke. Thus the patterns of each of the two opposite musicians fall in between another. In *amadinda* playing (Illustration 22) and in the kind of *embaire* music to which Illustration 26 refers[11] these basic patterns are always isorhythmic, each consisting of a series of equal-spaced notes. They combine like cog-wheels.

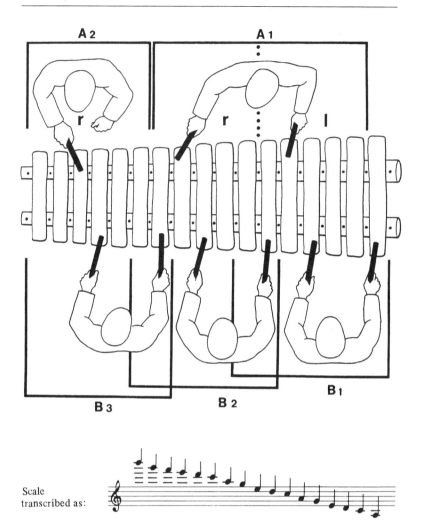

Scale
transcribed as:

Ill. 24. Performance on the *akadinda* (17-key xylophone). The positions and playing areas of the five musicians required to perform on the *akadinda*, as shown in
the diagram below, are correct for the composition *"Basubira malayika"* (see
Transcriptions, Example 10 at the end of this paper). They are slightly varied for
other compositions. The musicians whom Hugh Tracey recorded in the *lubiri*
(king's enclosure) in 1950, included two *abanazi* sitting with the lower keys on their
left, and three *abawuzi* sitting opposite them. Evaristo Muyinda reversed the order
when he taught the "Blind Musicians of Salama." There, for reasons not explicitly
discussed by him, the *abanazi* always sat so the lower keys were on their right. In
contrast to the royal musicians, there were also three on each side. Terminology:
A1 and A2 = *abanazi* (sing. *omunazi*); B1, B2 and B3 = *abawuzi* (sing. *omwawuzi*)

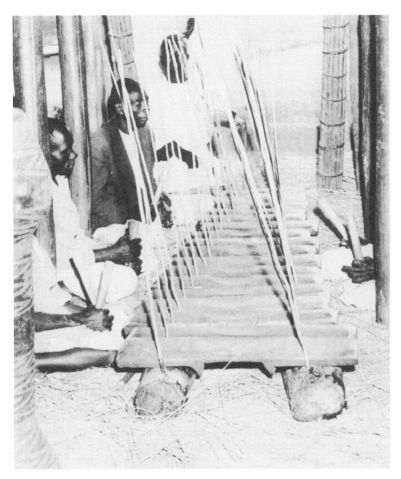

Ill. 25. The 17-key *akadinda* as it used to be, in a music house within the enclosure of the Kabaka's court. Notice the *amakundi* projections (lit. navel hernia) which prevent the slats from moving off the banana stem supports. In this picture, taken by Hugh Tracey during a rest between the recordings in 1952, one of the *abanazi* is (temporarily) absent. Photo: Hugh Tracey, June 26, 1952 (courtesy of the International Library of African Music)

In contrast to this style *akadinda* music requires triple interlocking. Here the *abawuzi* have to insert two notes between the strokes of their partners. Their part, performed with left and right hand beaters, is a rhythm pattern they keep in mind with the help of mnemonic syllables (see below). Only a few standard *okwawula* patterns exist for *akadinda*.

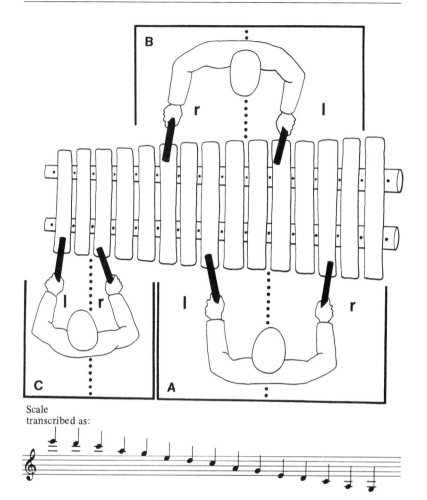

Ill. 26. Performance on the *embaire*. The positions and playing areas of the three musicians refer to the composition *"Njala eguire,"* as it was performed in Bumanya village, Busoga District, January 2, 1963. Terminology: A = *mulangalira*, B = *mugoiti*, C = *mudumi*

Looking at the *abawuzi* closely, one can interpret their task as combining the patterns of two musicians; it is justifiable to regard left and right hand parts of the *abawuzi* in *akadinda* as separate and autonomous lines.

From the following music examples 1, 2, and 3 we learn how the basic parts are combined in the three xylophone styles and what the total image, i.e. the combination of all the notes in the basic parts is like. This is performed at great speed, and the initial difficulty for the second performer (*omwawuzi*) or the second group of performers (*abanazi*) is to

Ill. 27. The *embaire* ensemble of Venekenti Nakyebale in Busoga performing on a 15-key log xylophone. The personnel includes the *mulangalira* with his sticks at octave spacing (right), the *mugoiti* sitting opposite him, and the *mudumi* playing on the five top keys. In addition there is a "helper" at the top end of the instrument, watching that the slats should not slide out of position, and there are the drummers near the lowest note of the instrument: two cylindro-conical drums characteristic of the interlacustrine region, *ngoma* (played with hands) and *kagoma katono* (almost covered by the former and played with sticks); the player of the long drum, *mugabe*, stands next to them. Bumanya, Saza Bulamoji, Busoga District, southern Uganda, January 2, 1963. Archive No. B 375/1963

insert their series or patterns at the correct moment, marked in the transcriptions by an arrow, and keep on at a steady speed, abandoning the beat of the opposite players. After my first experience with this in Kampala, December 1959, I wrote with reference to *amadinda* interlocking:

> When I started learning to play *okwawula* I made a mistake of great consequence. As the *okwawula* part falls exactly between the beats of the *okunaga*, the temptation is great to feel it syncopated. Indeed, from the point of view of the *Omunazi* the *okwawula is* syncopated. But an *Omwawuzi* who shares this view will never be able to fall in with his part. Whenever I started with the *okwawula* part of *"Olutalo Olw e Nsinsi"*, I still felt the beat of the *okunaga* part as being the basic one and "strong". My own notes which ought to be put between I therefore automatically felt to be

"light" and "syncopated". Playing a tune very slowly it was possible for me, with some concentration, to fill in my pattern and to keep on with my syncopation. But at a normal speed, which seemed to me as a beginner a terrific one, I always missed the short moment to add my "syncopated pattern". Until I found out that it was necessary to ignore the basic beat of the *Omunazi* and to create a second pulse for myself only. Until I found that the *Omwawuzi* has to "switch" in a split second and to abandon the pulse of the *Omunazi*. At the moment he pushes his first note into the counterpart he has to feel the notes as "heavy" ones and those of the *Omunazi* as "syncopated" (Kubik 1960:12).

And with regard to *akadinda* interlocking my experience was analogous.

1. Combination of the two basic parts in *amadinda* music

Title: *"Ganga alula"* ("Ganga had a narrow escape") (CD I/1). Historical song. "Ganga was a great friend of Nasolo (= first-born daughter of the Kabaka) with whom he fell in love. He was caught and had his fingers cut off, i.e. he was castrated." [12]
Total compass of combined melodies: five notes. [13]

Total image (36 notes):

Ex. 1a–b. *"Ganga alula."* a. Combination of the two basic parts in *amadinda* music   b. Total compass of combined melodies: five notes (cf. CD I/1)

2. Combination of the two basic parts in *embaire* music.

Title: *"Obukaire butusinye"* ("The older people . . .") (CD I/2). As performed by Yonasani Mutaki and his band at Bumanya. [14]
Total compass of combined melodies: six notes. [15]

Ex. 2a–b. a. *"Obukaire butusinye."* Combination of the basic parts in *embaire* music   b. Total compass of combined melodies: six notes (cf. CD I/2)

3. Combination of the two parts constituting *akadinda* music.

Title; *"Njagala okuddayo e Bukunja"* ("I Want to Go back to Bukunja"). – Modern song composed by Evaristo Muyinda and often performed at weddings.[16]
Total compass of combined melodies: seven notes.[17]

Ex. 3a–b. a. *"Njagala okuddayo e Bukunja."* Combination of the two parts constituting *akadinda* music   b. Total compass of combined melodies: seven notes. Part B

We see from Examples 1, 2, and 3 that, although the total compass of the combined melodies is different in all the three cases, each part in itself never exceeds the limited range of five notes. The *okwawula* part in *akadinda* songs such as *"Basubira malayika"* (cf. Example 10) could be an exception (the part performed by B_1 and B_2). But *okwawula* in *akadinda* music should not be interpreted as one melody. Musicians may appreciate the right and left hand movements as separate lines of equal status.

The music performed on all the xylophones in our illustrations is essentially composed. In *amadinda* and *akadinda* music no improvisation is allowed. Variation (*ebisoko*) is possible and practised in some songs, but it follows strict rules. The only variation normally used is dynamic in the widest sense and results from emphasis given to certain notes or note groups. I have described above some styles of performance which give rise to such variation.

In *embaire* music one performer may slightly vary his pattern. The kind of *embaire* music I describe here may appear at first similar to *amadinda* music, but it is built on different composing principles. These principles seem to be such that slight variation is not destructive to the music.

The following Example 4 will give an idea of the kind of melodic variation used in *embaire* music. In one composition recorded in January 1963, *"Njala egwire"* (CD I/3), it is player B (*mugoiti*) who varies his pattern. I have transcribed the basic form of his part and a series of five variations, after which he returns to the basic form. We soon observe that in none of his variations is the basic form completely lost, it always "shines through." Certain notes are substituted for others, but those which are unchanged remain at their exact time-place. And when the old notes appear again, it is always in their own place. The notes which constitute the basic pattern can be temporarily substituted but never shifted. And the formal length of the pattern, twelve notes, is strictly preserved in all variations.

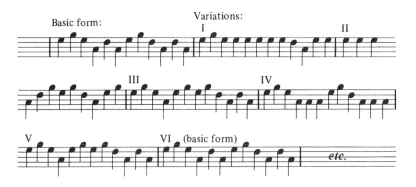

Ex. 4. Melodic variation in *embaire* music. Variation produced by the player B (*mugoiti*) in the composition *"Njala egwire"*[18]. The melody is played in parallel octaves. I have dropped the lower octave to make reading easier (cf. CD I/3).

The *embaire* xylophone of Busoga can be played accompanied or unaccompanied. At Bumanya village in Busoga both xylophones which I found there were accompanied by drums, which were considered an essential part of the music. The musical basis of the drum set was a "Uganda" drum, constructed exactly like the *baakisimba* drums of Buganda, referred to simply as *ngoma*. The second drum was a long instrument with a single skin, of the varanus lizard (*enswaswa*). It is called *mugabe* in the Lusoga of that area, /b/ to be pronounced as a bilabial fricative sound, phon. [ʋ]. This instrument is found in Buganda under the name *engalabi*. Both drums were played by the hands. The third drum was of the same type as the first, but smaller. It reminded me of the *nankasa* of the Buganda. The Bumanya musician just called it *kagoma katono* which means "small drum." This small "Uganda" drum was played with sticks. All these types of drums have been described by K.P. Wachsmann in Trowell & Wachsmann 1953.

Xylophone music in southern Uganda is played at an incredible speed. The lowest possible speed for *amadinda* and *embaire* music is 260 M.M. to the crotchet. For *akadinda* music it is 170 for the dotted crotchet. It is interesting to note that both speed indications are related to each other. *Akadinda* music is a music in triplets, *amadinda* music is in duplets. The speed of the smallest unit in both kinds of xylophone playing, written as a quaver, is intended to be the same. The speed of the quaver in all the transcriptions is more than 510 M.M.

From our illustrations we see that in *amadinda* music the spheres of musician A (*omunazi*) and musician B (*omwawuzi*) are like mirror images. These two players sit exactly opposite each other and the range of each of their hands covers the same five notes as the hands of their counterpart. In *embaire* and *akadinda* music this is not the case.

Subjective or Inherent Patterns

In *amadinda* music the melodic range of the two interlocking parts is restricted in total compass to five notes. From the illustrations of *akadinda* and *embaire* music we see, however, that the interlocking or opposite parts are obliquely shifted against each other, the exact shift varying from tune to tune. The illustrations refer to two particular compositions. When combined, the basic parts of *akadinda* or *embaire* compositions give a resultant melody of a larger total compass than *amadinda* tunes.

In *amadinda* and *embaire* music there is a musician C, whose task is quite different from that of the others and whose way of playing is not interlocking. This is the *omukoonezi* on the *amadinda* and the *mudumi* on the *embaire*. What is this third musician's task? Musician C (the *omukoonezi*) in *amadinda* music picks out all the notes heard on the two lowest keys of the instrument, called *amatengezzi*. And then he repeats these notes, the result of the combination of the interlocking parts of his partners, two octaves higher at the exact time-points when they occur. Evaristo Muyinda, my teacher, used to express it this way: "The *omukoonezi* listens to the *amatengezzi*, and plays what he hears on the *amakoonezi*." The musical task of the *omukoonezi* is called *okukoonera*. This is a verb which appears in the so-called "applied form" with the ending *-era*. The basic form of the verb is *okukoona* ("to knock," "to beat") with a strong by-meaning of tapping out rhythmically organized patterns, such as a visitor may do on a friend's door. *Okukoonera* therefore means "to knock," "tap," "beat" in relation to something, for some purpose or objective. *Omukoonezi* is the person doing so, *amakoonezi* are those high-pitched keys at the upper end of an *amadinda* intended for being "knocked on."

Listening into the deep register of the xylophone the *omukoonezi* discovers on the *amatengezzi* a melodic-rhythmic pattern which is almost ghost-like. In a sense it is a phantom, because nobody plays this elaborate pattern as such, it is inherent in the total structure arising from the combined basic parts. *Entengezzi* (singular of *amatengezzi*) is a term possibly rooted in the verb *kutengeeta* ("to tremble," "to shake," "vaccilate"). *Kutengeesa* is the causative form. *Amatengezzi* therefore are the xylophone keys that are vacillating, trembling, shaking. Associations with two nouns are also possible (1) *ntenga* (plural form) referring to swarms of noise-producing termites, and (2) *ntenga*, the drum-chime in the king's enclosure.

The pattern on the *amatengezzi* is constituted (in our notation) by all the C's and D's together, as they are struck by either of the two musicians sitting opposite each other. I have called such phantom-like patterns "subjective" or "inherent rhythms" (Kubik 1960:12) to be contrasted with A.M. Jones' (1934) "resultant rhythms." The latter are the summing up of all the constituent parts in a rhythmic-melodic combination (or as I call it the "total image"), while the former are the result of the breaking up of those resultant rhythms (or total image), into several autonomous lines in human perception. These subjective groups are not a random phenomenon in Kiganda music, but are clearly aimed at by the composers who use certain compositional devices to create structures which human perception must "break up" or "split up." Physically, they are not performed by any of the participating musicians.

When I discovered this during xylophone lessons in Kampala in December 1959, I gave the following account which may help the audience to understand what a culture shock it must have been.

    If we record the two parts *okunaga* and *okwawula* of "*Olutalo Olwe Nsinsi*" or any other *amadinda* or *akadinda* tune on a tape and listen to it afterwards, we are extremely surprised. We discov-

er that it sounds much more complicated on the tape and rather
different from what we played a few minutes earlier. We hear quite
a number of rhythm patterns which we are sure that nobody
played, and we also hear quite definitely variations. This confus-
ing phenomenon is very essential for Kiganda music and seems to
exist also in a number of other places in Africa. We very often hear
in our recordings of African music rhythms and melodies which
no musician has played. Certainly they exist and it is the *intention*
of the composer that we hear them. I should call them now
"subjective" or "inherent" rhythms. Returning to our *amadinda*
tune and analyzing the melodic and rhythmic structure of both
parts, it is not so difficult to find an explanation in part for this
phenomenon. The ear of a listener of course cannot find out
which note in one of the two parts was played by which musician,
because they both play on the same keys. It integrates the two
parts *okunaga* and *okwawula* and *constructs* out of them *new
rhythm patterns* which have never been played which run through
the mind of a listener but cannot be found in the movements of
the musicians' hands.

There is a psycho-acoustical fact which African composers,
particularly of instrumental music (xylophone, *likembe* etc.), are
delighted to take advantage of: that the human mind is inclined
to join together form objects of similar or equal qualities and
establish a "gestalt". In music the listener associates notes of
equal colour or loudness and of equal or similar magnitude. If,
further, notes of similar qualities are arranged in a definite rhythm
of occurrence, then association is enormously stimulated. This is
what many African composers are after by passion (Kubik
1960:12–3).

Evaristo Muyinda's way of describing the *omukoonezi*'s technique
("The *omukoonezi* listens to the *amatengezzi*, and plays what he hears on
the *amakoonezi*.")[19] is interesting in many respects. It is a direct reference
to the phenomenon of inherent rhythms. Muyinda's sentence also gives
us the key for playing the third part. Let us construct the third part of
the composition *"Ganga alula"* by writing together ("picking out") all
the C's and D's in the total image shown in Example 1. We see that the
result is a complex "additive" rhythm pattern (Example 5).

omukoonezi: (C)

r = right hand, *l* = left hand.

Ex. 5. The third part of the *amadinda* composition *"Ganga alula"* (cf. CD I/1)

It would be impossible to play this pattern at a speed of approximately ♩ = 300 M.M. by referring it metrically to either of the two basic parts. An expert *omukoonezi* listens to the *amatengezzi* and "absorbs" the pattern sounding out from these two keys. When the pattern has become firm in his mind and the rest of the composition sounds somewhat in the background he simply repeats two octaves higher what he hears. And while playing he continues to listen to the *amatengezzi* and (at least initially) avoids listening to any other patterns that might be heard in the total structure.

In *embaire* music the patterns performed by musician C (*mudumi*) are somewhat different from those of the *omukoonezi* on the *amadinda*. Like the latter, the *mudumi* picks out notes from the deep register resulting from the combination of the two basic parts. But in those *embaire* pieces I have analyzed so far, what the *mudumi* duplicated was not quite an inherent rhythm. In other words I did not perceive the *mudumi*'s part as something which had preexisted as an auditory image somewhere in the deep register before he actually played it. My impression was that his pattern, although in unison relationship with the notes played by his partners, was a new construction. But it will be necessary to record and learn a lot more *embaire* music of Busoga before I can give a final statement. My observations refer only to the area where I did research in January 1963, although I rather suppose that the *mudumi*'s technique is similar in the other parts of Busoga.

Another difference between the *mudumi*'s and the *omukoonezi*'s patterns is their melodic scope. In *amadinda* music the third part is always a two-note pattern. In *embaire* music it can be a five-note pattern.

In the *embaire* composition *"Sundya omulungi alya ku malagala"* ("Small insects eat only the leaves of the sweet potatoes") (CD I/4), which we recorded in January 1963, the *mudumi* played only a two-note phrase. However I could see clearly that this was not "*amakoonezi* technique." In most cases in *embaire* music a five-note pattern was played. The notes E and D were played by the left hand and the notes C, A and G by the right hand (cf. Example 4). The third part in *embaire* music, although not an inherent but a "built up" pattern, shows great regularity. As an example I would like to give the *mudumi*'s pattern of the composition *"Obukaire butusinye."*

Ex. 6. The third part of the *embaire* composition *"Obukaire butusinye."* The two basic parts are transcribed in Ex. 2 (cf. CD I/2).

Comparing with Example 2 it becomes clear that each note of the *mudumi*'s part corresponds with an equal note (in lower octaves) in one of the two basic patterns. If one keeps in mind that no other concords than octaves are desired in this music, the three parts can be fitted together quite easily.

"Obukaire butusinye" with its total image of only 18 notes is the shortest composition I came across in Busoga. Usually *embaire* compositions have a total image of 24, 36 or 48 notes. The same applies to *amadinda* music, although here a great number of irregular patterns can be found. The composition *"Agenda n'omulungi azaawa"* (cf. the score, Example 9) has 35 notes in each of its basic isorhythmic parts, which makes 70 notes in the total image. Another very long *amadinda* composition is *"Abakebezi abali e Kitende"* with 50 notes in the total image (not reproduced here). Generally it can be said the average length of xylophone compositions is longer in Buganda than in Busoga.

I have mentioned that in Kisoga xylophone music variation is sometimes employed. What consequences has variation of one of the basic parts on the *mudumi*'s part? I was very surprised to see that at least among those musicians with whom I worked, it had no consequences.

I did observe, however, that two musicians never varied at the same time. Normally all variation was left for one player to do. The others did not change their parts at all. I particularly concentrated on looking at the hands of the *mudumi*, but I never saw him "follow" any of the variations performed by one of his neighbours. This was surprising to me, because from the moment one musician started to vary, the principle of octave concord was broken. Immediately all kinds of simultaneous sounds appeared between the *mudumi*'s pattern and that of the varying performer. But it did not sound wrong.

That *embaire* variation breaks the principle of octave concord in places is evident, and unavoidable. However it is only transient and determined by concepts of melodic linearity. It is because of the inner logic of the melodic variations that the resultant "dissonances" do not disturb the ear. What comes out is a sort of transient "heterophony."

The *akadinda* Tradition

In the last part of my presentation I would like to explain in greater detail some essentials regarding the structure and performance practice of *akadinda* music, because I feel that it is this kind of Kiganda xylophone music that can make us better acquainted with the results of the interlocking composition technique so prevalent in southern Uganda.

At the king's court *akadinda* music is usually performed by five musicians without any further accompaniment. As much as the tasks of musicians A and B are identified in the terminology, so are the parts performed by them. The *abanazi* perform an action described by the verb *okunaga*. Charles Sekintu explained to me the meaning of this word as follows: "*Okunaga* is the beginning part, the part with which one starts to hit the xylophone keys." *Okunaga* also means (in daily language) "to shoot in the air," "to hit or catch something which is moving."

Musicians B, the *abawuzi*, perform the task of *okwawula*. Charles Sekintu believes that this word is related to the notion *okwawuza*, to be translated as "to divide:"

> The meaning of *okwawula* is to differentiate, to separate and to link at the same time. In religious practice the word *okwawula* is applied to the ordination of a priest, who by this is separated from all other people.[20]

The function of the *abawuzi* therefore is to "divide," to differentiate. *Okunaga* is the playing of the beginning part, *okwawula* that of the "dividing," "differentiating" or "constrasting" part. This terminology is valid for all xylophone types, for the harp (*ennanga*), and the *entenga* (twelve-drum instrument) kept in the Kabaka's enclosure.

So far I have come across four *okwawula* patterns for *akadinda* in Buganda. Two of these patterns occur frequently. The Baganda sometimes apply verbal phrases to them whose tonal patterns match those of the *okwawula* melodies. For example, the blind musicians of Salama used to call these two *okwawula* patterns shown in Example 7 *"kulya kulya kulya"* and *"katongole."*

Ku-lya ku-lya ku-lya   Ka-to - ngo-le
(to eat, to eat, to eat)   (Small chief)

Ex. 7. Two common *okwawula* patterns and their verbal associations

These word associations have become the names of the two patterns at Salama. Thus the blind musician Amisi Sebunya, who is one of the few remaining composers of *akadinda* music in Buganda could say to me one day, "Let me try whether *kulya-kulya-kulya* or *katongole* fits the *okunaga* melody which I have just composed." The origin of this sort of reference is connected with the fact that Luganda is a tonal language. When an instrumental melody is played to audiences, after a short time it may evoke verbal associations. I particularly observed this among Evaristo Muyinda's other pupils, who wondered that I could grasp a xylophone melody so easily without knowing the "meaning" of it. Thus the *okwawu-*

la patterns in Example 7 can evoke the word *kulya-kulya-kulya* respectively *katongole*. These of course are not the only possible verbal associations.

Many cases can be traced in Buganda where an abstract melody acquired a meaning through involuntary associations. The *baakisimba* drum pattern is associated by Amisi Sebunya and many other people with the sentence: *Kabaka ali nkuluze* ("The Kabaka is in the treasury"), a verbal patterns which both in accents and tonal structure represents the *baakisimba* pattern most accurately.

Charles Sekintu told me of an old woman he had met at the Kasubi shrine in Kampala, who had told him that whenever the *baakisimba* pattern was played it was as if she could hear the words *"Olunkutiza, olunkutiza"* sounding out of it. The exact meaning of this Luganda phrase was not clear to him, said Sekintu. Such associations occur in *amadinda* music as well. Normally the *okwawula* part is a many-note pattern rather like *okunaga*. But sometimes it can be a short ostinato pattern. The two *okwawula* patterns in Example 8 were associated with the words *tugende* and *gw'otunda* by the Salama musicians.

Tu - ge - nde

Gw'o-tu - nda

Ex. 8. Two *okwawula* patterns for *amadinda* and their verbal associations

All of these *okwawula* patterns cannot be applied arbitrarily to any xylophone composition. The *tugende* and *gw'otunda* patterns are applied to twelve-note *okunaga* parts in *amadinda* music. And the *akadinda* pattern *katongole* fits *okunaga* themes of eight and sixteen notes, while *kulya-kulya-kulya* is used for twelve-note *okunaga* themes.

Let us return to the discussion of the performance of *akadinda* music. How is the *okwawula* played by the *abawuzi*? In the Kabaka's musicians' style of *akadinda* playing, i.e. inside the royal enclosure (*lubiri*), the notes transcribed as quavers in our transcriptions (cf. Examples 3 and 9) are struck with the *abawuzi*'s right hand beaters, those notated as crotchets with the left hand beaters.

In the *akadinda* ensembles directed by Evaristo Muyinda outside the royal enclosure, such as that of the Blind Musicians' of Salama, the seating order has been changed. The *abawuzi* sit with the lower keys to their left, and consequently strike the quavers with the left and the crotchets with the right hand beaters. It is not clear why Muyinda changed the seat order in this "Kiganda orchestra," which includes many Kiganda instruments such as fiddles, flutes, and drums around an *akadinda* as its basis. One reason could be that in the "Kiganda orchestra," which is a "modern" phenomenon in Buganda, an instrument was included of which traditionally only one specimen existed, and was exclusively played in the king's enclosure: the *akadinda*. By changing the seat order possibly he wanted to stress that his *"akadinda"* (also different in construction) was different and his use of it therefore did not violate traditional custom. Whatever seat order is used, the essential thing here is that an *omwawuzi* must never feel his pattern "syncopated" in relation to the *okunaga* part. He must never feel his two notes as falling on "the two weak parts of a triple meter." We note the important fact that in *akadinda* music, as in all the other xylophone styles of southern Uganda, there are two "beats." If the musicians were to stomp their foot as some jazz musicians do (but they never do in Kiganda music) the *abanazi* and the *abawuzi* would stomp differently.

This psychologically interesting aspect of rhythmic combination in some African instrumental music was first discovered by A. M. Jones in the drumming of the Bemba and other ethnic groups in Northern Rhodesia. He transcribes and explains a kind of Bemba drumming called *ngwayi* (Jones 1949:44 ff.). Jones wrote the sentences which mark an epoch in our attempt to understand African music:

> Concentrate on your own drum. When drum No. 2 can hear his own rhythm well (i.e. when he is convinced that his beat is not the 3rd beat of number 1's bar, but is beat 1 of his own bar), then he can add his other tap (beat 3) (Jones 1949:44).

That is exactly as it is also in *akadinda* music. This kind of cross-rhythm is widely distributed in east and central Africa. Outside Buganda I have personally witnessed it in a Wagogo women's dance in central Tanganyika called *ng'oma*. The Wagogo women play it so exactly on their hour-glass drums that one could almost believe they learned it from A. M. Jones' book. The Wapangwa in the Southern Highlands Province of Tanganyika also use this combination. It is played in a very slow movement in one of their oldest dances, called *ngwaya* (Kubik 1961b).

In transcribing *akadinda* music I have always contracted the entrances of the two parts of the composition. One can hear from recordings, however, that the *abawuzi* do not fall in with their parts at once, but gradually. My transcriptions therefore start near the point in the recording where the full combination is achieved.

However, it is quite interesting to see how they fall in. In the recordings which Hugh Tracey made in the Kabaka's palace in 1950 [21], we note that the *abawuzi* fall in one by one with only one note, in the right hand (written as a quaver). And the moments of impact of their right hand strokes strangely enough do not exactly coincide with a triple division of the beat of the *abanazi*, i.e. they do not coincide with our reference points 2 in the transcriptions as we should expect, but come a little later, as if they wanted to divide the *abanazi*'s strokes in half. Only from the moment of full performance is the exact relationship established.

The fact that the *abawuzi* tend to enter with one hand only seems to confirm what I have suggested above, namely that left and right hand strokes of the *abawuzi* are conceptualized as two separate lines. When they feel safe enough with their right hand strokes in relation to their opposite partners, they then push in the left hand line. At the same instant the right hand beats seem to be delayed a little in tempo, so that they fall then exactly on reference number 2.[22]

We stated above that xylophone players in southern Uganda do not conceive of a common beat, as do musicians in a Jazz band, but refer their patterns to an individual beat relative to the performers opposite. If that is so, where then is the beat of the *abawuzi* when they play *akadinda* in the traditional style as in the king's enclosure (*lubiri*)? Do they sense it in the right or the left hand?

This seems to be an insoluble problem, because we cannot look into the musicians' mind. The impression gathered by an outsider observer, even if very familiar with the tradition, may be subjective, and in any case it is difficult to verify. Theoretically, the beat of the *abawuzi*, if they do not feel their phrases "syncopated" (which is impossible at that speed), must be felt either in the right or the left hand. There is no way for human beings to perform music without any recurring reference points, or by splitting one's "brain" and referring simultaneously to "two beats." And yet there is a simple and unambiguous answer. Hours together with Baganda and Basoga musicians soon made me realize that the beat of the *abawuzi* (in whatever position they sit, with the lowest keys to the left or the right) must be felt in the right hand, unless someone is left-handed. This connects with the general left-right symbolism in Kiganda thought. But the surest indication that the beat is in the right hand is precisely the fact that *abawuzi* on the *akadinda* often enter their part with one hand only. Since this is the right hand, the beat must be in that hand; it would be unconceivable and unnatural for them to feel their initial beats as "syncopes." And equally there is no reason to assume that they would "switch" from perceiving the beat first in the right hand then in the left, when the *okwawula* pattern is complete.

Beat perception, interlocking techniques and melodic combination are one side of our studies. The other is reception by the audience. If one listens to a recording, let us say, of "*Basubira malayika*"[23] which is transcribed in Example 10, one is struck by the conflict of several rhythmic-melodic lines which seem to be complex "additive" patterns. These <u>inherent rhythms</u> are not visible in the transcription of the players' patterns, but they can be made visible (cf. Example 10). In Example 10 two such inherent rhythms can be seen which were particularly obtrusive in Tracey's recording. I have transcribed them separately. They can easily be traced back to the total image of the composition. The one marked A is the most obtrusive and I think nobody can escape from hearing it clearly. (At this point the record was played.) Audiences are usually surprised, however, when I tell them that this pattern heard in the deep register of the *akadinda* was played by none of the musicians.

Almost all instrumental music in southern Uganda is constructed so that many inherent rhythms of this kind emerge. Compositions with inherent rhythms are multi-dimensional. One can "read" them from many starting points, listen to them from many different angles, and always discover regular patterns. It is somehow like a crossword puzzle, where every letter is at the same time an ingredient of two different words, only a little more complex.

What I call inherent rhythms are certainly not merely rhythm patterns. They are rhythms and melodies in one *Gestalt.* In many examples of Kiganda and Kisoga xylophone music they are predominantly two-note patterns. However, I could enumerate many compositions where inherent rhythms of a larger range appear in abundance.

If one can "read" these Kiganda instrumental compositions from many starting points, this process of reading will, of course, take time. One could not follow any inherent rhythms if the rather short cycles were repeated only once. To make all the inner dimensions of these musical picture puzzles gradually visible to oneself the total pattern must be repeated again and again. Only then is it possible to follow the conflicting inherent lines. If there were no repetitions, if the Baganda musicians had tried the kind of horizontal development of their art found in European classical music, there would be no chance for listeners and performers to appreciate this music in its highly developed vertical dimension. In Kiganda music every note is in a carefully devised multi-lateral relationship to every other note. Repetition is therefore indispensable in this kind of African music, because only thus can the inherent melodic-rhythmic patterns emerge to consciousness. Repetition and inherent rhythms seem to be functionally related to Kiganda music. Without such gestalt phenomena, the endless repetitions of a twenty-four note cycle would indeed become tiresome. By this I am not attempting to "explain" repetition in music. It would be a regrettable misunderstanding if someone were to say I had claimed that repetition in music is a result of inherent rhythms. I mention this because it did happen during a lecture and somebody came up with the argument that "repetition also exists in Bulgarian music."

Listening to African music demands different abilities from the listener than European music. It demands also a different direction of attention.

In European concerts one's attention is normally more directed to what will happen in the horizontal development of the composition. In African instrumental music this way of listening is certainly not absent, but it is less emphasized. A listener to African music has to direct his attention more to the inner dimensions of the compositions, which are so manifold that they cannot be perceived all at once in a split second. The listener has to change his own "position" gradually, just in the same way that one looks at an object from different sides.

If anyone finds African music "monotonous" or "repetitive," if it is tiresome to him to listen even for a few minutes, we simply see that he has not yet discovered how to listen to it.

Ex. 9. *"Agenda n'omulungi azaawa"* ("One who chases the beauties migrates away from his land"). Full score of an *amadinda*-composition. The song behind this *amadinda* piece is about the (secret) lover of one of the beautiful wives of the Kabaka

Ex. 10. *"Basubira malayika"* ("They are hoping for an angel"). Full score of an *akadinda*-composition. Note: Only one octave duplication has been transcribed here to avoid cluttering the score with too many notes and lines (cf. record AMA-TR 137 by Hugh Tracey, 1950).

Discussion

1. Mr. Sempebwa said: "I have been most interested in the work which is being carried out by Mr. Kubik in his research on the structure of the *madinda* and *kadinda* as played in the Buganda kingdom. I am, however, wondering as to how deeply Mr. Kubik has gone into the question of melody. He has spoken about an "inherent rhythm" and how the various combinations are produced and put together to give the desired but complicated movement. I am sure Mr. Kubik will agree with me that what is played on the *madinda* is what must have been at one time a sound produced by the voice. The primary instrument is the voice. The melody as produced by the voice is then played by the harpist on the bow harp with the four fingers. This can then be broken up into two parts and each part is allocated to one of the (two) players of the *amadinda*. The *madinda* players then produce the same song as played on the bow harp, and the idea is that that should be recognizable as the song which was produced

in the first instance by the voice. The question is this, can you recognize the melody when you listen to the bow harp or to the *madinda*? If not, where has the melody disappeared to? If you can recognize it, in what parts of the structure of the *madinda* can you locate the hidden notes which go to form the melody? Mr. Kubik may feel that this would require a quite different sort of research, in which he was not engaged recently. My point in making these remarks is that when studying the structure of the accompaniment, we should not lose sight of the main tune for which the accompaniment was intended. It is quite obvious that the *madinda* music, like the *ntenga* music, is in itself self-contained and self-sufficient. It would be wrong to expect this music to be used as an accompaniment because anybody trying to sing with the *madinda* or the *ntenga* would be completely drowned by the battery, but when the same music is played on the bow harp, it is intended to accompany the singer and it is then that the truth comes out of the existence of the melody in the complicated combinations produced by the harpist, or the *madinda* player or the *ntenga* player, and this should not be lost sight of."

Mr. Kubik replied that his teacher Evaristo Muyinda had often told him that *amadinda* music was originally composed for harp and voice, and that the harp music was later transferred to other instruments such as the *amadinda* and the *entenga* drums. The harpist's right hand part became the *omunazi*'s part on the *amadinda,* and the harpist's left hand part became the *omwawuzi's* melody. The vocal part (*okuyimba*) disappeared in the xylophone versions. But since the vocal part according to the principle of octave concord does not contain any other notes than those already existing in the two basic parts, it was not surprising that a Muganda can "pick out" or hear it out of the *amadinda* compositions. This vocal part, referred to by Mr. Sempebwa as "melody," however was not always an inherent rhythm. Further investigations are intended to find out for a large number of examples in what parts of the structure of an *amadinda, ennanga,* or *entenga* composition the "hidden melody" can be located. For this purpose, Mr. Kubik added, his plan was to make a series of analytical recordings of harp music with his teacher Evaristo Muyinda.

2. Dr. Jones commented on the similarity he detected between one of the resultant patterns produced by the xylophone playing and the clap-patterns used right across Africa from east to west. Such clap-patterns very often are built on a basic framework which may consist of these additive groups:

either $2 + 3 + 2 + 2 + 3$ units
or $2 + 2 + 3 + 2 + 3$ units.

Mr. Kubik said that the striking fact that some of the additive inherent patterns found in east African instrumental music were structurally identical with the forms of the "standard pattern" discovered by Dr. Jones, had brought him to a hypothesis on the evolution of these additive rhythms. He thought it was possible that the clap and gong patterns consisting of 2 + 2 + 3 + 2 + 3 units (without regard to the changing starting point) might have originated from inherent rhythms of the same structure. The process of evolution from inherent rhythms to separated gong patterns could have been the result of a kind of *amakoonezi* technique (technique of picking out the inherent rhythms and repeating them separately). In a later stage of the evolution, the basic isorhythmic patterns from which they were derived must have been lost, or must have been altered. After this the former "inherent rhythms" were remembered only as independent formulas and not according to their origin. This, of course is nothing more than speculation, Mr. Kubik added.

Appendix

Changes in Kiganda Musical Practice During the 1950s and 1960s

At the time when I first visited Uganda, there was a marked trend in Kiganda culture to loosen restrictions regarding the performance of court music. Some years before, an *akadinda* had been built outside the king's enclosure for the first time, for which Kabaka Mutesa II's permission was obtained (cf. Kyagambiddwa 1955). The immediate pre-independence period was an era of conflict between "traditional" values on the one side and values implanted from outside into a model British protectorate.

One of the ambivalent remarks frequently heard from European teachers and missionaries concerned the pentatonic system used in the music of southern Uganda. Some Baganda teachers reacted to this by trying to introduce a xylophone with a heptatonic tuning modelled on tonic sol-fa, such as the one I photographed in 1960 at Nkokonjeru Catholic Mission in southern Uganda.

Via mission and government schools local teachers began to introduce African music into colonial institutions. This was done in a manner that would be acceptable to the European superiors. Petero Kivumbi from Misansala, Masaka, constructed an "improved" version of the *amadinda* in the late 1940s. He replaced the banana stems, whose acoustical properties are partly responsible for its mellow sound, by a wooden frame, with strips of tyre rubber as cushions to isolate the keys, and iron nails to separate them from each other.[24] One of the reasons given for the

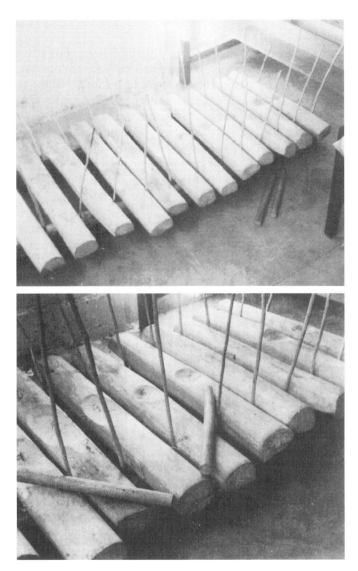

Ill. 28a–b. An *amadinda* with heptatonic tuning and slats numbered from 1 to 12, constructed by a Muganda teacher at Nkokonjeru Catholic Mission, May 1960. The slats of *lusambya* wood have the characteristic oval depressions, as the traditional *madinda*. The changes made include the replacement of the banana stems with ordinary tree trunks, without cushions, and the use of the diatonic heptatonic scale. Note that the numbering also proceeds from the smallest to the biggest slat. I did not hear the teacher play his instrument, and I believe it was not played much, but served more as a show-piece. (Nkokonjeru, southern Uganda, May 1960. Archive Nos. 33A/34, 36/36A)

change in construction was that it could be transported more easily on lorries.

Petero Kivumbi's model was readily adopted by another Muganda musical innovator of the closing colonial era: Evaristo Muyinda. He began to construct such types for his own band and for one of the groups he was training: The Blind Musicians of Salama (CD I/5). But Muyinda retained the pentatonic tuning. His innovative ideas did not concern "scale" and "melody", but orchestration. He wanted to create a popular "Kiganda orchestra" – as he called it in English – in which all the local instruments, more than one of each in some cases, would be combined for stage performances. Unfortunately, he did not have enough person-

Ill. 29. *Akadinda*, log xylophone with 22 keys, constructed in the manner of Petero Kivumbi's "improved" xylophone. The instrument was played by the ensemble "The Blind Musicians of Salama" (seen here during a performance at the Bugembe Stadium near Jinja, southern Uganda, in February 1960)

nel for carrying out his plan. But he recorded a prototype of his "Kiganda orchestra," involving musicians and dancers, at his home village Nabbale, in December 1961.[25]

Another group, the Blind Musicians of Salama, trained by Muyinda in the 1950s and 1960s, were relatively close to his ideal of a Kiganda orchestra, although he somehow always disdained their musicianship, perhaps due to ethnic reasons, because some of the members were Nilotic people from the north. It was during Klaus Wachsmann's days in Uganda, that Evaristo Muyinda began to develop his idea of a Kiganda grand orchestra that would unite all the instruments known in Buganda's traditions. Petero Kivumbi's idea of "improving" Kiganda instruments and Muyinda's ideas about orchestration converged on several occasions. No doubt as Wachsmann's research assistant since 1949 (cf. Chapter IV), he had opportunities to see classical European music performed on stage in Kampala. It is interesting, however, that Muyinda always considered himself to be a Muganda and a Kabaka's musician. Therefore it was out of the question for him to adopt guitars or the like, also because these were considered by him as "low-class" instruments, unworthy of the attention of a Kabaka's musician. So here was a natural barrier, rooted in a status-consciousness which had not eroded during the era of the British Protectorate. He wanted to transfer the court music into what he felt – confirmed by his mentors – to be a "modern" context of music performance: the festival stage, the theatre, the concert hall, institutions equally "high-class" and therefore acceptable to a musician of the King's court.

Chapter II
Harp Music of the Azande and Related Peoples in the Central African Republic

The area occupied by the large cluster of peoples referred to in the ethnographic literature as Azande covers part of north-eastern Zaïre (ca. 350,000 persons at present), and smaller portions of southern Sudan (ca. 250,000) and the eastern part of the Central African Republic (60–80,000).[1] Colonial borders have divided Azande territory into three parts, with the consequence that since the establishment of colonial rule Zande speakers in the three territories have developed in somewhat divergent directions. While the schooling system is based on French in Zaïre and the C.A.R., it is based on Zande in southern Sudan, where the first linguistic studies were undertaken by American missionaries.[2] These studies have had a remarkable impact on the language itself. The Viennese ethno-medical researcher Armin Prinz tells me[3] that the use in the Sudan of a Zande orthography with the letter r has resulted in making Sudanese Azande pronounce what would elsewhere be a flapped [ɾ] (cf. Westerman & Ward [5]1966:74–7) as a rolled r. In Zaïre, on the other hand, this is not the case. Missionary influence has also been enormous on the didactic and syntactic aspects of Zande in the Sudan. In his preface to E. C. Gore's "Zande Grammar" (Gore 1926), the then British district Commissioner at Yambio (Sudan) stated some of the objectives concerning the language:

> The slow but sure emergence of a new type of Zande, mentally and morally on a plane far higher than the old, is due to their [the C. M. S. missionaries] efforts, and is the reward of their self-sacrificing labours.

On reading the translations of some of the songs I recorded in 1964, such as "*Nzanginza mu dukporani yo*" (Ex. 31) by Maurice Gambassi or "*Ana ka wio kumba kua de o*" (Ex. 34) by Jérôme Sournac, or the same theme in variation in a song sung by the twelve-year-old Ouzana "*Ana ka binga dar'akumba o*" (Ex. 42), one can probably understand how horrified missionaries in the 1920s must have been.

Italian Catholic missionaries, among them Father Filiberto Giorgetti, author of a book on Zande music, have had a notable influence on Zande culture and music in the Sudan. Their promotion of an indigenous church music among the Azande also had certain repercussions across the border in the Central African Republic, where, during my visit in 1964, the Dutch priest Piet van Horne was experimenting along different lines from those of Father Giorgetti, but with similar objectives.

The Zande language is classed as an I.A.6 language (Adamawa-Eastern) by Joseph Greenberg (1966). It must be noted here that the I.A.6 languages include those of the neighboring Nzakara, Banda, Ngbandi and Sango. Sango is an important trade language in the Central African Republic. And this is also the direction in which one may look for the more important cross-cultural exchanges, as far as the Azande are concerned. My observations in 1964 confirm that intensive exchanges in the field of music were taking place at that time, particularly with regard to harp performance, where a "Banda style" was identified as such by Azande musicians at Rafaï and Zemio. Many new harp compositions by young people were performed in the Sango language.

In the ethnographic literature the Azande have often been lumped together with the Mangbetu in north-eastern Zaïre, and it is obvious that cultural exchanges have also taken place in that direction, particularly in music, where the Azande share with the Mangbetu almost identical musical instruments. Both are known in the literature as nations of eminent performers on the harp. Mangbetu harps fill ethnographic collections by the thousands and they feature among the earliest products of the tourist and souvenir industry in central Africa. Soon after Stanley's visit, Mangbetu carvers began to produce harps for the European market which were elaborately carved from ivory, the body covered with reptile skin.[4] Linguistically, however, the Azande and Mangbetu should be strictly separated, as the latter speak a II.E.2 language (Central Sudanic) which is classed with other languages in north-eastern Zaïre such as Madi, Logo and Lugbara.

With regard to their pre-colonial history, one theory is that the Azande as a whole migrated to their present habitats from the north and northwest, subjugating and assimilating local peoples, thanks to their rather tight political organization. The original "tribe" was said to be the Ambomu who were dominated by an aristocratic class called Avongara.

These aristocrats seem to have founded numerous small chiefships among the subjugated peoples. The multi-ethnic original composition of what is now the Azande people is perhaps reflected in the complex terminology relating to ethnic sub-groups. In 1964 I frequently heard my companions qualify the people of one or other of the villages we visited as for example Zande-Gbaya or "pure Azande."

The ethnologist Pierre Vidal stated that in the Central African Republic there is only a minority of Zande speakers (Vidal n.d.). He says that their origin from the "Salamat Tchadien" is clearly established from the evidence of their civilisation which was documented in the 19th century. He points to "la bèche montée à soie, trait caractéristique de la civilisation néo-soudanaise."

Azande society shows a "dual stratification into a hereditary aristocracy and a lower class of ordinary commoners or freemen" (Murdock 1967:58). Class stratification was still prevalent during my visit in 1964, when I had the opportunity to work at least with one representative of the hereditary aristocracy, Chief Zekpio and his retinue. At his residence in Dembia harp music and performance on the *manza* xylophone played an important role. Here it is worthwhile to note that succession of chiefship in Azande society is hereditary "by a patrilineal heir who takes precedence over a son" (Murdock 1967:59). The same applies to inheritance of real and movable property, where the principle of primogeniture is also applied.

Considerable ethnographic work has been carried out among the Azande; foremost that of E. E. Evans-Pritchard[5] and of the linguist A. N. Tucker of the School of Oriental and African Studies, London (Tucker 1933a, b) who was the only European I knew who could play the *ɽekembe* (lamellophone) and sing Zande songs to its accompaniment.[6] With regard to music and oral literature Eric de Dampierre's work among the neighboring Nzakara and his documentation of song texts as performed by various old harp players (Dampierre 1963) is of immediate relevance in comparison with my own findings. More recently, Manfred Kremser and Sabine Haller[7] have carried out extensive documentation of Zande music and dance in north-eastern Zaïre. The ethno-medical studies of Armin Prinz, particularly some of his cinematographic documents, also have considerable implications for the study of music and dance (Prinz 1978; Prinz & Heke 1986).

With the exception of a brief encounter with a Zande *likembe* (lamellophone) player in Bondo, Zaïre, on July 8, 1960[8] I have had contact with the Azande only once, during 1964, when I worked in several Azande villages in the Central African Republic. Besides my work with the harpists, however, I was also able to document many other aspects of the musical culture and general ethnography. My lessons in Zande harp playing were part of my third "expedition" across Africa (June 1963 to August 1964), carried out alone. It turned out to be the most difficult trip I have ever undertaken, in terms of physical hardship, lack of finance and problems resulting from the confused post-independence administration in some of the countries visited.[9]

The present chapter is essentially a reprint of my article "Harp Music of the Azande ..." (Kubik 1964a), however with some corrections and

extensive additions, particularly song texts, photographs and some discussion of *kponingbo* (xylophone) music.

March 28, 1988
G.K.

Since the travels of Georg Schweinfurth from 1868 to 1871 and others
during the second half of the 19th century into the "heart of Africa," the
Azande have been known for their beautifully shaped harps and their
fine playing of this instrument. In particular, the carved heads on some
splendid museum pieces continue to arouse the admiration of art collec-
tors.

Ill. 30. Schweinfurth's 19th-century illustration of harps in the Azande or
Mangbetu area. Reproduced from Dampierre 1994:21.

When I first visited the Central African Republic in 1964[10] I did not know much more than that about the Azande, because one of the essentials of my field methods – when beginning to work in a new area – was not to read the ethnographic literature prior to my personal experience. Obviously this contrasted sharply with what was normally required from university students preparing for their field work. But my argument was that acquaintance with the impressions of previous visitors to the area could bias the newcomer's data collection and observations. For this reason, I would only begin to read through the available literature after I had studied there for myself first and written down my own observations.

The study presented here has the character of a proto-testimony dealing with one specific aspect of the music of the Azande in a limited area of the Central African Republic and in the context of the mid-1960s. It was carried out only four years after the foundation of the Central African Republic (ex-Oubangi-Chari), formerly a part of French Equatorial Africa.

I had come all the way from Oshogbo in Nigeria on a small Solex autocycle. This tour took me about four months until I arrived at Gamboula (a border post between Cameroon and the Central African Republic) on the 17th March, 1964.

From there I went first to study among the Mpyɛmɔ̃ in the southwestern corner of the C. A. R., but by the beginning of April I was back on my way to the east, via Berberati and Carnot. Only two days driving on the lonely road and some bad news – the tyres were finished ...

This happened somewhere near Carnot. How I got to Bangui on the sandy tyre-eating track was a miracle, thanks to unknown friends on the road. Wherever I broke down, the village youngsters patched up the torn tyres; later they sewed them with iron or copper wire, exchanged broken Solex spokes for bicycle spokes, tied together the broken carrier with lianas, and inventive men repaired my recurrent motor troubles. In this manner I was passed on from village to village until somewhere near Boda, where military units took me to Bangui in a jeep. Here I was able to get my cycle repaired and prepare for the second part of the tour to the east.

It was during the long evenings in the villages that I became conscious of a characteristic of this country: the great popularity of harp playing. It is no exaggeration to say that the Central African Republic is a land of the harp.

I met the harp for the first time in the African quarter of the Plantation Molois near Carnot, where I stayed for the night. The player was a Karre, who had come from the area of Bozoum to work here for a white "patron." His five-string harp which he called *kundeŋ* was tuned penta-

Ill. 31. Finger technique in the playing of *kundeŋ* by a Karre musician from the area of Bozoum, who came to the Plantation Molois near Carnot as a migrant worker, April 5, 1964 (Archive No. III/2A)

tonically, and he played it in the "vertical" position, with the neck of the harp held towards the body. His harp playing was the backing for a female chorus, singing mainly in unison with occasional fourths. The music had that typical Centrafricain "flavour" that is difficult to describe, but so easily recognized from recordings.[11]

At the same place I also recorded the music of a young Gbaya-Kara from Bouar, who played a two-string guitar he had made. He called it *baizo*, a word obviously derived from "banjo" (in the French pronunciation). He could produce four notes by two alternating fingerings. His music was almost indistinguishable from traditional harp music. Listening to the recordings alone one would hardly believe that it is <u>not</u> a harp.[12]

A similar observation has been reported from an area I did not visit. The Radio Diffusion Centrafricaine has a recording of a Banda guitarist named André Savat who plays a "real" guitar, but entirely in the harp style. In Rafai I later met two Azande guitarists (the only ones I saw), one of whom played compositions of his own that were close to Azande harp music. With the exception of band guitar music in Bangui, which is tuned to the hits of Brazzaville, guitar playing among the Banda, Azande and other peoples of the Central African Republic is mainly an extension of harp playing. But in spite of this the harp is by far the more popular instrument today. Harp music as I heard it everywhere on my way from west to east all had a great similarity both instrumentally and in singing. The various harp styles of peoples such as the Karre, Buru, Banda, Nzakara, Azande and others seem to be related. There is a current exchange of themes, tunes, patterns, etc. Tunes are invented somewhere and spread in various directions.

At Galafondo, north of Bangui on the road to Fort Sibut, I recorded a harp player of the Buru people: Jean Nquimale.[13] He, like his relative, Dimanche Malekete, a talented thirteen-year-old harp player, held the five-string harp in an oblique "horizontal" position in the lap. He used a pattern of fingering that I saw again later in harp playing of the Banda and Azande (compare the "Banda beat").

Some pieces were sung solo. For other pieces the harpist just provided an instrumental backing to the voices of the women. They were singing in parallel pentatonic harmony. For comparison with Azande and Banda patterns one of the harp patterns recorded at Galafondo is reproduced at the end of the scores.

It took me five days on my Solex to get from Bangui to Rafai. Once again the tyres were finished. I arrived at the Vovodo river late in the night of April 23. The ferry was closed. On the other side of the river was Rafai, the first town of the Azande country. Through the evaporating humidity of the river I distinguished the shimmer of kerosene lamps on the other side. I tried to shout, but in vain. Nobody would come to the river by this time. So I looked for a place to pitch my tent and escape the greedy buzzing of the gathering mosquitoes. Tomorrow I would go and see the Catholic priest, Father Piet van Horne, to whom I had been recommended. I had heard a lot about his Zande church compositions, so I was anxious to meet him...

Rafai was a surprise. I have never seen so many harp players amusing themselves in the streets of a town. They were mostly young people playing the harp, walking up and down near the market, where honey wine was being sold by the women. I arrived at the mission, a house of raw bricks with a grass roof on top, and found Father van Horne sitting in front of the house surrounded by a swarm of children. He was very surprised when I explained what I had come to Rafai for. I must mention that my intention was still to study *kponingbo* xylophone music in order to see if there was any similarity to East African xylophone playing, which I had known before. Fortunately, I was told there would be a *kponingbo* dance in the town that evening.

Attracted by my arrival, a number of harp players came to the Mission and after some talk said they would be glad to teach me the harp. This overthrew my original plan and in the following weeks of my stay in the Azande country it was harp music that I would mainly study. There were many difficulties to overcome at the beginning, because I had never really played the harp before. But my various teachers proved patient and they had a remarkable pedagogic gift, being able to explain slowly, and play the right and left hand parts at reduced speed.

I spent a week at Rafai learning to play the harp and recording all kinds of Azande music. Here, like in Zemio and some other places, I learned the contemporary style of Azande harp playing and it is this music that will be analysed on the following pages. My tutors were all young people. In Rafai I was taught by Maurice Gambassi, aged 16, from Agoumar village, 5 kms northwest of Rafai; Jérôme Assas, aged approximately 23, catechist of the Catholic Mission, Rafai; Jérôme Sournac, pupil of the Jeunesse Agricole Bangassou, aged 17, from Rafai. In Dembia I was taught by Mockys Dieudonné Yves, aged 15, and in Zemio by Samuel Ouzana, aged 12. Various other harp players gave me occasional instruction. I should like to mention Antoine Gbalagoume, aged approximately 30, from Djema, and Bernard Guinahui, aged approximately 30–35, from Makanza near Rafai.

When Father van Horne went to Zemio, the larger Mission station, I went along with him and made Zemio my base for long foot-slogs as far as Djema in the north and Dembia (the seat of the great Chief Zekpio) in the west.

These walks through Azande country lasted several weeks and they were all in the company of two twelve-year-old schoolboys from the Mission School at Zemio: David Kamoundé and Samuel Ouzana. During our walks through the wide savannahs, Ouzana used to play a small, high-tuned *kundi* (harp) as he walked, carrying the bag containing my small tape recorder on his head at the same time. Kamoundé carried our food (on his head as well), and I carried a big rucksack with our camping equipment, camera, tapes, paper and other stuff. In this manner we toured large parts of the Azande country and touched on the best of *kponingbo*, harp and other music.

Kamoundé and Ouzana were often quarreling jealously and accusing each other so as to make me prefer one of them. Only in areas where we were frightened of a buffalo appearing at any moment from the vast and lonesome bush was it quiet: no laughing, no quarrels, no sound from Ouzana's harp.

My two companions had remarkably different characters. Ouzana was an artist, a charming dancer and composer of his own harp songs.[14] On our journey he steadily increased his repertoire by learning with phenom-

Ill. 32. Field recording of Azande music at Djema. My tape recorder Stuzzi Magnette Typ 671 B, is progressively falling apart . . . . Here I am using an external loudspeaker taken from an old radio, since the Stuzzi's own loudspeaker had packed up. Ouzana's head is visible at the table, with his small *kundi* in front of him. In the foreground is Kamoundé wearing a beret. Djema, May 1964 (Archive No. V/7)

enal speed from harpists we had been recording on the way and whose music we used to play on the tape recorder in the evenings. I learned very much from Ouzana, not only his current songs, but what he himself had picked up on the way. For example he could quickly find out the finger-ing of a harpist just by listening to the tape, and teach me later. Kamoundé was different. He neither played the harp well nor could he dance very well. He was an intellectual. It is to him that I owe the transcription of seven hours recordings of harp and vocal music, word by word in Zande. In addition he transcribed with grim persistence 21 *sangbatule* stories from the tapes. In spite of a "special" orthography of his own, his Zande text transcriptions are of great value. We spent four to five hours every day transcribing. Ouzana transcribed at the same time, at the same table, for the sake of comparison, but his writing was unsatisfactory. He had no concentration. He was "distrait" as I once criticized him in Kamoundé's presence and so unfortunately grieved his artist's heart and gave Kamoundé new arguments.

The following map shows all the places where we recorded harp and other music. I have not been able to visit the area of Obo on the Sudan border, where a number of refugees of the Azande people have recently come from. This paper only deals with harp playing as I studied it in the area shown in Map 6.

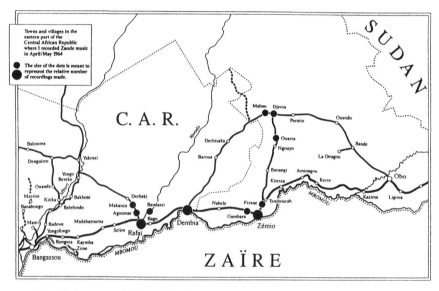

Map 6. Towns and villages in the eastern part of the Central African Republic where I recorded Zande music in April/May 1964

Azande harps can frequently be seen in the showcases of museums in Europe. These samples mainly come from that large portion of the ancient Azande empire which is now under Zaïrean administration. Usually they are tall instruments with a carved head at the end of the neck.

In the region visited I very rarely came across harps with a carved head. Even the old players, such as Lazaro Tourgba from Zemio, who possesses a harp constructed in the days of Chief Ikpiro, or Chief Zekpio from Dembia, did not play such instruments. One small harp with a small, not very elaborate, head (approximately 3.5 cms high), I bought at Djema. It was very old and broke on the way to Europe. I cannot assess all the factors responsible for this unexpected absence of carving. Personally I do not think that the absence of carved instruments is a recent phenomenon. It seems that the northern Azande (and I know only these well) are different in some of their cultural patterns from those living in Zaïre, who have had cultural contact with the Mangbetu and with Bantu language speakers.[15]

Construction and Playing Attitudes of Zande Harps

I shall confine myself to a general description of harps as I have seen them in the region shown on Map 6. The construction of harps was identical in the places visited. The resonator consists of a piece of hollowed-out wood having at one end a tube-shaped hole. Along this resonator "boat" a hard wooden rib with five holes is laid (Illustration 33a).

The resonator body appears in various forms. In the region visited I have seen the following shapes, which are simply variants of <u>one</u> basic idea for the shape of the harp (Illustration 33b–c).

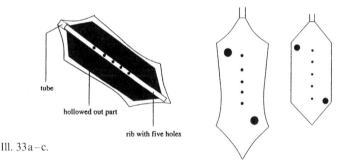

tube

hollowed out part

rib with five holes

Ill. 33a–c.

Now the resonator body (with the wooden rib across) is covered with antelope skin which is sewn together on the under side with a cord (Illustration 34). On the top surface five small holes are cut into the skin directly above the holes in the rib below. Two big holes are cut into the top surface of the skin, lying obliquely opposite each other (Illustration 33b–c). These are not only "sound holes" but essential for threading the strings.

Ill. 34.

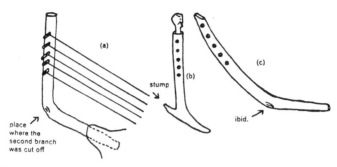

Ill. 35a–c.

The neck of the harp is cut from the <u>fork</u> of a very hard bough. Its definite shape depends on the natural angle of the fork. Usually one branch of the fork is cut off completely, but it is always evident where it was. Only a fork has enough strength to prevent the neck from bending when the strings are tightened. In one case the stump of the second branch was left on by the maker giving the shape in Illustration 35. The following neck shapes are frequent:

The neck of the harp is pushed into the tube but not attached; it can easily be pulled out again. It is held mainly by the tension of the strings. Five holes are pierced for the pegs through the upper part of the neck.

Now the strings are put on. Everywhere nowadays in Azande-land of the C.A.R. nylon strings are used which are cut from fishing lines sold in the shops. Each of the five strings is passed from outside into one of the holes in the rib and pulled out through the nearer of the two big holes in the skin (Illustration 36a). The string is now tied round a little piece of wood and pulled back so that the "anchor" is held against the inside of the wooden rib. The procedure is the same with all five strings of the harp. Then each string is simply attached to its peg as in Illustration 36b. The pegs are slightly split at one end.

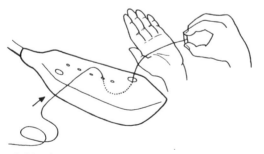
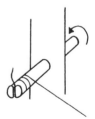

Ill. 36a–b.

Harps of mainly two sizes were used by the various musicians I met: the first a very small instrument, about 40–45 cms long, measured from the top end of the neck to the front end of the "boat." The body itself is about 25 cms long. This kind of harp is very often played while walking. The second type is a large harp with a body almost twice as big as the small harp (ca. 40 cms), and a total size of 60 to 75 cms from end to end.

The term almost universally used in the Central African Republic to denote a harp is *kundi,* in any of its variations, such as *kunde* or *kundeŋ* (among the Karre, see above). *Kundi,* pronounced with a clear [i] at the end, is said to derive from the old word *kundhi* according to Father Filiberto Giorgetti (1965) who worked on Zande music in neighbouring Sudan. He believes that this term is composed of the morphemes *ku* (translated by him as "pure," "simple") and *ndhi* ("to play", "to be joyful") (cf. Giorgetti 1965:74). A legendary harp performer, about whom many harpists at Rafai and other places used to sing in 1964 and possibly even today[16] was Kpyoza, also known as Kpyázá in southern Sudan according to Giorgetti. He used to play harps in the old style, i.e. with the string-bearer towards the performer's body, as in the photographs showing the harpists Tourgba and Zekpio. For this reason, says Giorgetti the harp was also called *sagiru,* which means "turn (*sa*) its back (*ru*) to the player (*gi*)" (Giorgetti 1965:74).

Another designation of the harp which I constantly came across during my stay in Zande country was *nzanginza.*[17]

Among the Azande in the C.A.R. two traditions of holding the harp are common, existing side by side: the "vertical" attitude and the „horizontal" attitude in Hugh Tracey's terminology (H. Tracey 1948b). Parallel to the different ways of holding the harps there was in 1964 a local differentiation between the historical and the contemporary style of harp playing. The older generation in the region played "vertical" harp: the musician holds his instrument with the neck towards the body. For plucking the strings, the old harpists used three fingers of the right and two fingers of the left hand.

Almost all the younger people I have seen played "horizontal" harp with the neck away from the body, or, as Ouzana explained it: "one holds the harp like the *sanzu*" (lamellophone). The "walking harp" is also played in this way.

Horizontal harp playing and dancing to *kponingbo* music were in 1964 the most popular kinds of entertainment among the Azande of the C.A.R. The *sanzu* was very rare. I only recorded it in Djema. But I had heard of a *sanzu* player at Rafai and there was probably one in Zemio too. Guitars were also very rare. There was, however, plenty of thought association between these instruments and the horizontal harp. Ouzana's

Ill. 37. Lazaro Turugba, one of the oldest harpists at Zemio in May 1964 (Archive No. IV/3A)

remark was probably not a random idea. The idea of playing a small harp walking might have come from imitating the attitude of the *sanzu*. Likewise there was an association with guitar playing. In French conversation young harpists always refered to their instrument as "guitar" and when singing, quite often one could hear the triumphant exclamation *"Gita!"* (guitar) or *"Guitariste!"* at climax points, particularly when they wanted to give a "push" to an instrumental interlude after the last sung verse.[18] Many young horizontal harpists played their instrument in the fond belief that they were famous guitarists. Once in a village on the road from Rafai to Bangassou – I do not know whether I was in Azande or already into Nzakara territory – I saw a harp with a body exactly the same shape as a small guitar, being covered with a "skin" made of sheet iron and painted red.

The horizontal and vertical attitudes of playing have a deeply different effect on the player. One only comes to realize this after having tried both for oneself. When playing vertical harp, the neck of the instrument leans against the chest, while the end of the body is propped in the lap. When plucking the strings, one feels the vibration going through one's chest and resonating strangely in it, as if the harp were part of one's body. I can imagine that this must create a music of different content than the horizontal harp does. It is an inward music, while one is tempted to call modern Azande harp playing, especially the walking music, a forward music.

In the following illustrations the two playing positions of the harp and the fingerings are compared.

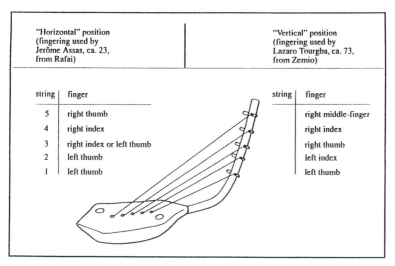

"Horizontal" position (fingering used by Jerôme Assas, ca. 23, from Rafai)		"Vertical" position (fingering used by Lazaro Tourgba, ca. 73, from Zemio)	
string	finger	string	finger
5	right thumb		right middle-finger
4	right index		right index
3	right index or left thumb		right thumb
2	left thumb		left index
1	left thumb		left thumb

Ill. 38. Playing positions and fingering techniques of Azande harp players compared

How are the Zande Harps Tuned?

In the Central African Republic and neighboring areas the harp is usually a solo instrument, although at Makanza near Rafai I once recorded a harp duo, Bernard Guinahui and François Razia playing the same melody together on the two harps tuned in unison (CD I/6). I was

Ill. 39 a–b. The eminent Azande chief Zekpio playing a small *kundi*, surrounded by his grandchildren (a). He normally performed together with his relative Martin Abirasse, expert player of a five-note *manza* log xylophone (b). Village: Dembia, May 1964 (Archive No. V/12 and V/15)

even more surprised when I found the eminent Zande Chief Zekpio at Dembia playing the harp together with a small log xylophone (CD I/7). The two instruments were tuned to each other. The xylophone, called *manza*, was played by the second in line of the village elders, Martin Abirasse. In contrast to the *kponingbo* it only had five wooden slats arranged over the two banana stems and was played by one musician alone – and unusual for log xylophones – the slats were struck in the middle and not at their ends[19] (Illustration 39a/b). The xylophone slats were placed in irregular pitch order: seen from the performer's side the tuning was as follows: (1) 567, (2) 524, (3) 420, (4) 389.5, (5) 607 c.p.s. (Hertz), from left to right.

The tuning of the two instruments together constituted a strange pentatonic scale, characterized by two narrow, two wide and one middle-size interval. The narrow intervals were close to a European semitone, the wide intervals close to a major third. The following table makes this clear.[20]

MANZA			KUNDI		
xylophone slat no.	C.p.s.	Cents intervals	harp string no.	C.p.s.	Cents intervals
			1	835	98
			2	790	439
5	607	118 - - - - -	3	613	93
1	567	137 - - - - -	4	581	156
2	524	383 - - - - -	5	531	
3	420	128			
4	389.5				

Table 1. Pentatonic tunings of *manza* xylophone and *kundi* harp in comparison

Obviously this is a kind of tuning which had almost disappeared from the music of the Azande in Central African Republic by 1964. The young generation tuned its harps (and also the *kponingbo* log xylophone) according to the speech melody of a spoken formula: *wili pai sa sunge*.[21] The approximate translation of this phrase into English is: "Something a little, that is of work." The harp players explained the meaning of the phrase to me thus: "This is an encouraging advice to the harpist: 'Something of value needs work. Only a little effort and there will be a good result.'"

Musically, this spoken pattern yields a descending pentatonic scale which one can safely notate with the (relative) pitches of the European tone system: E, D, C, A, G (from top to bottom) although the intervall E – D was usually somewhat narrower than the corresponding step in Western music.[22] The Azande scale is always thought of as descending. There is further evidence for this besides the descending tonal structure of the tuning formula. At Zemio and at Fizane I noticed a funny habit with players of the twelve-key *kponingbo* log xylophone. Normally the xylophone keys are kept apart from their banana stems in a hut. In order to rearrange the keys quickly at actual performances – without testing the pitch of each key first – the musicians had painted numbers on them! And these numbers always went from the smallest to the biggest note (key).

When tuning the harp, it is the phrase *wili pai sa sunge* which is engraved in the harpist's mind and not a sequence of wholetone plus wholetone plus minor third plus wholetone. On the other hand, because a harmonic sound is expected between certain left and right hand notes plucked simultaneously, there is some tendency towards "pure" intervals. The actual tuning seems to be a sort of compromise. Tuning circles around a nucleus that is determined by the intervals of the speech pattern, the desire for harmony and the margin of tolerance. An individual musician's tuning is not usually consistent over a long time but alters slightly. When two harp players performed together, as I recorded once at Makanza, there was also some difference between the notes of their two harps, which were thought to be in unison. By measuring the notes of the two harps we can perhaps assess the margin of tolerance to be expected in Zande tunings.[23]

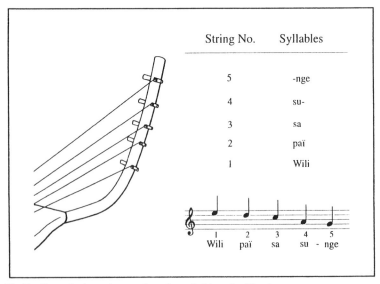

Ill. 40. How the harp is tuned to the syllables of *wili pai sa sunge*

Ill. 41. The harpist Raymon Zoungakpio, ca. 40, with the children who accompanied his performance. He was a most popular performer of the *nzanginza* in 1964, playing it in the "vertical" position. At Fizane near Zemio, May 1964 (Archive No. IV/37A)

Flattening of the E by up to a quarter tone is usual with Azande harp players, also in singing. A few musicians, for example the middle-aged harpist, Raymon Zoungakpio, from Fizane (CDI/8), inclined to an idiosyncratic interpretation of the speech formula which used narrower intervals down to a semitone and a neutral third. I heard similar tunings in Rafai.

The history of this tuning among the Azande cannot easily be reconstructed. Its identity with that of the *kponingbo* log-xylophone, however, is striking and possibly significant. Present-day *kponingbo* music came to the Azande with a wave of cultural influences from the south (Zaïre); this is not only suggested by a careful analysis of historical resources and references to the region (such as kept in the Musée Royal de l'Afrique Centrale), but also by the analysis of the stylistic and organisational traits of *kponingbo* music, as we know it today, some of which point to connections as far south as Katanga (Shaba province of Zaïre). One significant trait is the appearance of a 16-pulse, 9-stroke time-line pattern, characteristic of south-central Africa (the Luba/Lunda cultures). It occurs in several *kponingbo* themes, for example in the following song about the late President Boganda, which I recorded in Fizane and of which I learned to play the main xylophone part (CD I/9).

Ex. 11. *Kponingbo* theme: "Song about Boganda," learnt and transcribed from a live demonstration by a musician at Fizande, 15 km east of Zemio, April 1964 [24] (cf. CD I/9). Relative notation
    r = right-hand beater
    l = left hand beater
The note a" is the highest pitch on the instrument. The theme was duplicated in octaves by a second player, sitting next to the first and playing one octave lower

Kponingbo is a log xylophone with 12 or 13 slats, laid out over two parallel banana stems. The slates are carved from *mbuka* wood. They are approximately 13 to 14 cm broad and almost half a meter long. The xylophone is usually played by two musicians sitting next to each other, one striking within an area of deep tones identified as *ba-kponingbo* (father-xylophone), the other within an area identified as *na-kponingbo* (mother-xylophone). Sometimes a third musician – sitting opposite the two – may join in. He usually performs on the notes marked as No. 8 and 9 in Illustration 42. During the performance of a *kponingbo* village dance more instruments are involved: *guru* (large slit drum) and *gaza* (double-membrane cone-shaped drum). Some 50 to 60 persons may take part in a *kponingbo* dance. Several dancers hold metal bells (*nzoro*) in their hands. The instruments are placed in the centre of the dancing ground. The dancers form two circles around the instruments, an inner and an outer circle.

The dancers in the outer circle move facing the centre with sideways steps and pantomime gestures. The inner circle is usually formed of young girls and boys leaning slightly forward and dancing with vigorous movements concentrated on breast and pelvis. As in African round dances elsewhere, both circles of dancers move in an anti-clockwise direction.

I reproduce below some of my field-drawings from Fizane, May 1964, about the *kponingbo*, the terminology used for specific playing areas of the slats and the other instruments used in the dance.

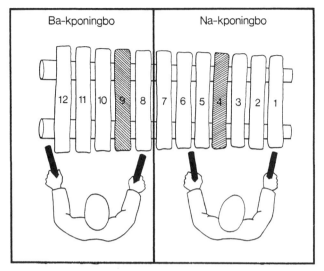

Ill. 42. Playing areas of the *kponingbo* xylophone

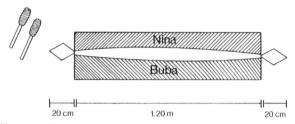

Ill. 43. The *guru* slit drum

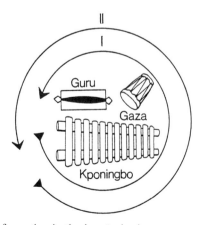

Ill. 44. The dance formation in the *kponingbo* dance

Terminology for pitch-differences on the slit drum is analogous to that of the *kponingbo:* the higher sound is called *nina* ("mother"), the lower *buba* ("father"). Identical concepts exist in harp music. The slit-drum is struck with rubber-headed beaters. It is placed with the higher note towards the xylophone. The "mother" corresponds in tuning with note No. 4 on the *kponingbo,* the father with note No. 9 (which is the fourth note from the bottom). I have marked these special notes in the drawing.

This may suffice as an introduction to some of the concepts concerning pitch and tuning of various instruments. It is evident that harp tunings cannot be studied in isolation, but must be compared with the tunings of other instruments, particularly the *kponingbo.*

Ill. 45. The instruments used in the *kponingbo* dance at Fizane (Orig.-Tape No. 46/A) and photopraphed the day after: *kponingbo* with the low notes to the left, the *guru* slit-drum and the *gaza* membrane drum. Fizane, 15 km east of Zemio. April 1964 (Archive No. V/1)

There is no absolute pitch for tuning commonly agreed on by all Azande harpists today. *Wili pai sa sunge* can be spoken by a boy with a small voice and by adults. Similarly it can appear at tone levels according to the size of the harp. Each player seems to tune his instrument to fit best the range of his voice and that of the chorus, if there is any to respond to him. The various players I recorded at Rafai, Zemio, Djema, Dembia, Fizane and Makanza, had tuned their harps to different pitches.

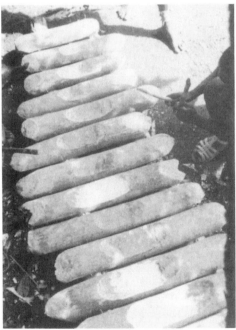

Ill. 46a–b. Performance on a 13-key *kponingbo* xylophone in Zemio by two musicians sitting opposite each other. (Ouzana standing, hands in pockets, next to the far musician.) Zemio, May 1964. Archive No. IV/1A and IV/2

On the other hand, I could observe that one tuning pitch was particularly frequent, one where the biggest note (to the syllable *-nge*) was around an A or an A-flat. Further, harp players from the same village often had the same pitch. When a *kponingbo* xylophone was near, the harp was often at the same pitch as the xylophone. (Although *kponingbo* and harp are not played together, harp tunes are played on the *kponingbo* and vice versa).

I received the following measurements of some of my recorded Azande harp tunings <u>after</u> I wrote the sentences above. It may be interesting therefore to compare these independent results with my previous statements which emerged entirely from aural observation.[25]

Harp of B. Guinahui				Harp of François Razia			
C.p.s.	Cents	Cents interval	Cumulative Cents	C.p.s.	Cents	Cents-interval	Cumulative Cents
(1)734.5	1334		380	(1)711	1276		322
		145				113	
(2)676	1189		235	(2)666	1163		209
		221				227	
(3)595	968		(12)14	(3)584	936		1182
		314				282	
(4)495.5	654		900	(4)495.5	654		900
		165				169	
(5)451	489		735	(5)450	485		731

Table 2. Two harps playing in unison. Musicians: Bernard Guinahui and François Razia, age: ca. 30–35, recorded at Makanza, near Rafai. "Horizontal" position.

C.p.s.	Cents	Cents-interval	Cumulative Cents
(1) 697	1242		373
		148	
(2) 639.5	1094		225
		225	
(3) 562	869		0
		335	
(4) 463	534		865
		169	
(5) 420	365		696

Table 3. Tuning of the old harp player Lazaro Turugba, age: 60–65, recorded at Zemio. "Vertical" position. Relative pitches[26]

For comparison now the tunings of two *kponingbo*-xylophones, since these instruments are also tuned to *wili pai sa sunge*:

Absolute pitches:		
(1)	791	SA
(2)	682	SU
(3)	606	-NGE
(4)	498	WILI
(5)	457	PAI
(6)	389	SA
(7)	333	SU
(8)	293.3	-NGE
(9)	250	WILI
(10)	229	PAI
(11)	201.5	SA
(12)	?	SU[27]

Table 4. *Kponingbo* xylophone at Rafai. The instrument was regularly played and rather carelessly treated. Some notes are probably slightly out of tune. But this was still acceptable to the players who worked it daily with vigour. I suppose that the instrument once had 13 keys, because the tuning starts with *sa*, and that the biggest key was lost. It would be logical with the tuning phrase to be complete with a *-nge* at the bottom.

Absolute pitches:			
(1)	971	SU	
(2)	844.5	-NGE	
(3)	698	WILI	
(4)	636	PAI	
(5)	562	SA	tuning area of Turugba's harp
(6)	485	SU	
(7)	426	-NGE	
(8)	357	WILI	
(9)	325	PAI	
(10)	280.6	SA	
(11)	236	SU	
(12)	212	-NGE	

Table 5. *Kponingbo* xylophone at Fizane. Played by virtuoso musicians

All these tunings demonstrate the character of *wili pai sa sunge*. The two big gaps from *sa* to *su* and from *-nge* to *wili* are at once recognizable. From the skill of the performers I have presumed that the Fizane *kponingbo* is a very well-tuned instrument. The two harps at Makanza show to what extent deviations from unison are acceptable to the players. After I had taken the tuning they immediately continued to perform.

Comparing the tunings of Turugba's harp with that of the *kponingbo* at Fizane, we see that they are practically at the same tone level. Of course I have only relative pitches for Turugba's harp, and for the *kponingbo* at Fizane Father Jones had to add 10 cents to each vibration number to arrive at the absolute pitches. But even if we are suspicious of the speed of the tape recorder and allow a certain amount of cents to be added or subtracted from Turugba's harp, still the two instruments have the same audible tone level.

I do not want to make a theory out of this coincidence, since I have not found a similar case so far. But the fact that the harp of a personality like Turugba is nearly in perfect tune with an excellently tuned *kponingbo* in a village 15 kms away from his town is at any rate remarkable.

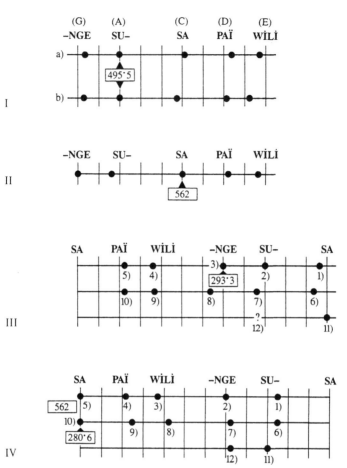

Ill. 47. I–IV. Comparison of Zande tunings (graphic layout based on Stroboconn measurements)

The graphs demonstrate that the interval *wili-pai* is regularly smaller than a second, at least in these four examples. The two notes are pitched towards each other. In comparison with the European notes both Zande notes are a little "off". *Pai* appears to be augmented and *wili* lowered. *Pai-sa* is regularly wider than a second, and the interval *wili-sa* is a little smaller than a major third, but never quite reaching a neutral third, in these four examples. Secondly, when notes appear diverging it is always a chain or sequence of notes diverging in the same direction. Look at the notes *wili-pai-sa* in the tunings of the two harps playing in unison (I), at notes No. 6, 7 and 8 in relation to 1, 2 and 3 of scale III, and at 7, 8, and 9 in relation to 2, 3, and 4 of scale IV. There is hardly any isolated divergency of a note. Perhaps this is so because Azande musicians conceptualize the scale in intervals of neighbouring notes when tuning.

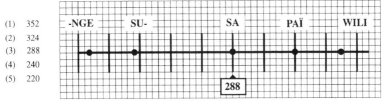

(1)	352
(2)	324
(3)	288
(4)	240
(5)	220

Ill. 48. A Zande harp tuning taken by Hugh Tracey in the northern Congo (Reference No. 74W-8)

Further, the divergencies look "organized" and are possibly meant to be a deliberate distortion of the octave and the unison sound, to obtain the desired dissonant "friction" effect. More, since there are always some "reference notes" in pure octaves or unison.

Hugh Tracey has been kind enough to send me a number of harp and xylophone tunings of the Azande that he measured in 1952 in the Congo (Zaïre). One among the two harp tunings is identical with that of Chief Zekpio at Dembia, and the other is clearly the "wili pai sa sunge" tuning.

In the following analysis of harp music, we shall be confined to horizontal harp playing as practised mainly, but not exclusively by the younger generation.[28]

Learning to Play the Harp

All harp players with *wili pai sa sunge*-tuning are expected to play an introductory phrase before starting with the tune:

> *Wili pai sa sunge.* (2 ×)
> *Mu ta kundi ki bi bialeu kindi.*
> *Kuluo pai sa sunge.*

Approximate translation:[29]

> Something a little, that is of work.
> One must play the harp and sing its song too.
> The old things are the work.

The tone pattern of these words is played on the harp. Example 12 gives the phrase as played in the horizontal technique. I have written the text below, so that it may be clear which note represents which syllable. But the text is not sung. Further, the durational value of the notes and the tempo are not exact, it is a free (speech) rhythm:

By means of the phrase *wili pai sa sunge* the harpist tests the tuning, playing it twice. With *mu ta kundi ki bi bialeu kindi* he tries the pentatonic harmony in "arpeggio:" E/C, D/A, C/G. And by playing the third phrase he confirms the scale. Then he starts with the tune:

♩ = approx. M.M. 130-144

Wili païsa su-nge. Mu ta ku-ndi ki bi bia-le-u ki-ndi. Ku-luo païsa su-nge

Ex. 12. Words and tone patterns of the introductory phrase *"Wili pai sa sunge"*

The structure of this introductory pattern reveals the main principles by which the harpist tunes his instrument: spoken pattern and harmonic sound. One can often see harpists playing the introductory phrase for some time, and suddenly stopping at one point because they are not satisfied with the sound. Some notes are then altered. And the harpist starts again until the phrase sounds right.

The fingering of the pattern is easy (cf. Illustration 49 below right). In more formal performances the introductory phrase is always played. But otherwise harpists often just start without it, particularly when walking alone on the road.

All horizontal harp playing found in the region I visited consists of two parts: a left and a right hand part, which are functionally different.

The musician starts the tune with the right hand (unless he is a left-hander like the above-mentioned blind harpist).

In the first type of harp music that we shall study, his right hand plays a short basic pattern of two or three notes. Then he adds the left hand part, which is often an interlocking pattern, sometimes a pattern in another meter, or simply a pattern phrased "off beat" at times.

We first learn a composition called *"Nzanginza mu du kporani yo"* ("The harp is in our village") (CD I/10). Two performances of it are reproduced in detail in Ex. 31 and 32. Maurice Gambassi will be our tutor.

We hold a small high tuned harp horizontally in the lap and place the fingers in a way that they are near to their prescribed areas. As in all horizontal harp playing of this country we use just three fingers: thumb and index of the right hand, and thumb of the left hand.

For the composition *"Nzanginza..."* as well as for many others the range of the fingers is this:

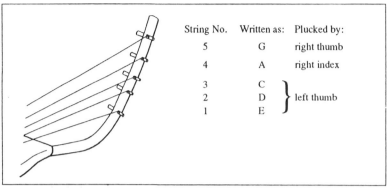

String No.	Written as:	Plucked by:
5	G	right thumb
4	A	right index
3	C	
2	D	} left thumb
1	E	

Ill. 49. Fingering pattern I

Now we learn to play the right hand part, at a comfortable speed at first. It is a simple two-note pattern repeated over and over:

Ex. 13. The two-note pattern of the right hand

We now try to play the left hand part separately, using only the thumb. It is this:

Ex. 14. The left hand part

The combination of the two parts is <u>bimetric</u>:

Ex. 15. Left and right hand together

This is what the harpist plays throughout the song at the speed of 144 MM to the dotted quaver. There is no variation of the instrumental part for this tune.

The vocal line develops along this basis. But before learning to sing to the harp, I believe we have to clarify one important point: How does the harpist think about the above bimetric pattern? Where does he feel his beat? (if he feels one at all). Does he feel it with the right or the left hand?

This is, indeed, a difficult question to answer scientifically, although personally it is clear to me where the beat is. How can I prove it to the sceptical reader? I became absolutely certain of it from the moment I learned to sing the first vocal phrase to the harp pattern. It is simply impossible to "get" it to a wrong beat.

Theoretically there are three metrical conceptions possible for this pattern:

Ex. 16. Three possible metrical conceptions for the harp pattern

How can we look into the harpist's mind? We cannot ask him, because as he thinks it, that is unquestionable to him. He cannot even understand our question which typically arises from a comparative look at musical traditions. The harpist normally does not stomp his foot either and, even if he did, this would signal the opposite for the Azande because they "lift" the beat and incline to an emphasis of the "after-beat" at least in those harp songs related to *kponingbo* tunes.

I can only offer one significant observation: at Dembia, while one harpist was playing this theme, I noticed a small boy beating on the table with his right hand in a regular pulse. It was exactly the beat which I had also felt. On another day I tried to get my harp tutor to tap the beat when I played the tune. But he was entirely perplexed, and I could not, of course, show him what I wanted without running the risk of influencing him in some way.

I had better let on now where the beat is felt. It is as indicated in the first line above at *a*. This beat, however, is no more than a kind of "background" orientation. The right hand part is not conceived as "off-beat" but as a pattern in its own right.

As for the rest I am afraid I can offer nothing more than the advice to the reader to play the harp yourself and try to sing the vocal part of *"Nzanginza..."* to the wrong beat. See whether you can manage it and feel comfortable.

Relation Between Voice and Instrumental Part in Azande Harp Music

Generally, one sings at one's natural voice level. Occasionally Azande harpists prefer head voice or falsetto. Quite often the tone level of the harp is higher than the voice, e.g. when playing a small instrument.

At first it is necessary to acquire a certain repertoire of "text phrases". In performance these are just intelligently "strung together" in the horizontal development of the music, and quite often interrupted by instrumental interludes. The singer has much freedom in arranging the text phrases. He does this spontaneously during the performance. But he is always bound by two rules: *(a)* to return sometimes to the main phrase or "theme" and *(b)* to observe the meaning of the text. You can alter the sequence of phrases *ad lib.;* you can start at various points or cut it into half – for example, you may start with the second half of the phrase as in bars 1, 2, 10, 19 and 20 of *"Nzanginza..."*, if it gives verbal sense, if it gives the desired meaning in Zande.

This is practically all the "free improvisation" an Azande harpist can do. Azande harp music sounds very much "improvised" to an outsider. But in reality it is essentially composed, by which I mean that the performer knows in detail beforehand what he is possibly going to sing and play. He knows the "material" of the tune. And if there are instrumental variations, as we shall get to know later, he has played them many times before. They are likely to be standard variations. It is comparatively rare for a really new phrase to be invented during performance.

Example 31, which follows further on in this chapter, shows one performance of the tune *"Nzanginza..."*. There are a hundred others and all a little different. For example, the singer could well start with the basic form of the theme as it appears in bar 6. Or, where there is a repeat made three times, next day he will repeat it only two times or leave out the phrase entirely and sing it in another context. He may also take sections of the text ahead, or he may sing melodic variations.[30] The latter however has to follow certain rules as we shall soon see.

If we look at Example 31 (and the other ones) analytically, we can observe one fact concerning the relationship of the voice part to the instrumental part: Virtually every note in the voice part is represented by the same note in the instrumental part. Very rarely, and we estimate only for some particular reason, is this rule broken, to create a sort of transient heterophony.

We can see from Example 17 how the voice part strictly follows the constituent notes of the instrumental part. The words *"Nzanginza mu"* duplicate notes of the right hand part. But then the melody jumps into the left hand part with the syllables *du-kpo* duplicating the E of the harp pattern. In the next moment the voice goes to G of the right hand part with the syllable *ra* and back to the left hand D in a counter movement. Contrary motion from unison into octave and the reverse is a frequent practice in Azande harp music.

Nza - ngi - nza mu du-kpo ra n'yo,a-na-ta - ta.

Voice:

Harp:

Ex. 17. A performance of the tune *"Nzanginza ..."*

We can also see from Example 17 that, as a result of this technique, the voice part shows some rhythmic features that have come to be described in such terms as "off-beat" phrasing of melodic accents (from the vertical point of view) and "additive" (from the horizontal point of view). Perhaps equally important is, however, that the notes of the voice part are thought of as congruent with notes in the instrumental backing.

We can see that the voice part is nothing "new," but that it is somehow hiding in the total structure of the instrumental part. One can hear the voice part looming up out of the notes of the harp, even if it is not sung. And the slightest accentuation of certain notes of the instrumental part can bring it out clearly at once. This seems to be true for all those African musical traditions where the voice proceeds in unison with constituent notes of the instrumental part. The term unison, of course, I take here in a wider sense, including octaves, since the octave is generally regarded in these traditions as the same note only of different pitch level.

In Azande harp music the voice part can "pull out" any notes of the total pattern of the right and left hand parts and duplicate them either in unison or at the octave. In Ex. 17 there is one exception to the unison principle: the note A to the initial letter of the phrase "Anatata" coincides with a G in the harp pattern. This note, I believe, is thought of by the harpist as a G. There may be various reasons why it did not become one. I suggest that G was too low (too big) and out of the range of the singer's voice, so he sang the nearest note, an A! The unison principle is occasionally broken in variation too, in parallel harmonic singing, and through passing notes.

A frequent form of variation is the substitution of different notes by a sequence of equal notes at a certain tone level. This seems psychologically to have a relieving effect and thus the emerging heterophonic dissonance is motivated and justified to the singer. I should mention here that, of course, every variation sung has a psychological meaning to the singer. It is a never ending game with the "level" of excitement. That is why it is sufficient to play the harp when walking alone. The end effect is psychocathartic. In the variation of bars 20 and 21 we can see that the notes A, E, E, G for the syllables *mu du-kpo-ra* are substituted twice by four G's, which are no longer in unison relation to the harp part. This is a "strong" variation and can only occur at a climax of the "level". It has a relieving effect and could not be found for example at the beginning of a performance.[31]

If we try to invent the melody of a text phrase, we understand that there are always two possibilities for setting it out. Quite contrary to other traditions of African music further east (as for example in Southern Uganda), Azande harp playing has a harmonic aspect. The left hand's notes for example are really thought to have duration as written. Thus there is simultaneous sound at any point of the harp pattern. The word "Nzanginza" sung to G, A, G could in principle be sung to three D's since the D is present all through the first (small) bar and half of the second one.

The possibility of melodic variation and consonance arises from the fact that there are always two notes of the harp backing at the singer's disposal for composing the voice part. The second restricting and modifying factor in variation comes, of course, from the tonal character of the language. Although all kinds of movement are possible in Azande chorus singing, a tone language minimizes contrary movement and favours parallel movement.

The Zande language, however, is not as tonal by far as some other African languages, Yoruba for example. Hence we frequently find contrary movement both in melodic variation and in chorus singing. Text invention in Azande harp music is largely subject to two musical factors: the unison principle and tonal laws.

There are essentially two ways of starting to compose a song. The musician may first have an idea for a text phrase, usually topical, referring to a recent event, and try to fit a suitable harp pattern to it. The latter usually contains fill-out notes, and so will have more notes than the text phrase. Or he may have an instrumental idea and try to fit words to it.

Whatever the start may be, the second and more difficult part of the creative process is to invent additional text phrases, which now have to fit into the repeated instrumental backing.[32] From this stage on at any rate he has to follow the second technique: fitting words to a given instrumental structure. Here the training of the musician from early childhood, to think of melodies as representative of words and vice versa, comes to his help.

However, this simple and natural way is easily veiled by too much analysis. An Azande harpist will not compose a new song in the anatomical way we necessarily had to go through to describe the results. He does not "pull out" notes. Nor does he compose his text phrases placing notes on an assembly line. He rather listens to the structure of the harp bakking, and hears the looming inherent melodies, whose tonal pattern represents possible text phrases, and soon ideas come to the mind. It is interesting in this context to observe how the singer gets different text themes by following different parts of the total structure.[33]

Although the harp is very much a soloist's instrument, we often find harp players gathering a chorus of girls in the evening and singing with them in antiphony. The chorus basically sings in unison with frequent harmonic variation. When one singer of the chorus follows the left hand notes on the harp and another one the right hand notes, the result is a harmonic sound.

A kind of polyphony emerges from simultaneous singing of different text phrases, especially in duets. But here as for all singing the same rule is valid: the singers usually sing a harmonic sound that is already present in the harp part.

Example 37 (further on in this Chapter) with extracts from a performance of *"Limbiayo"* gives an idea of the possibilities. In Ex. 37/I one vocalist sings a sort of "riff" while the other one sings independent text phrases.[34]

A similar kind of polyphony emerges between voice part and whistling part (Ex. 37/II). In group performances of Azande harp music there is often a "whistle" (*nvilili*): The performer blows the edge of the tightened skin between thumb and index of his right hand. The *nvilili* is talking. In Ex. 37/II it says: *Araba tissaro Kpyoza*, a remark about the historical Azande harpist Kpyoza, who is said to have "invented" harp playing.

In addition to these two examples a case of parallel harmony can be found in Ex. 38 (*"Wen'ade gbua"*) (CD I/11). Here the unison principle is broken at one point for the sake of consecutive parallelism. Azande multi-part singing shows of course the characteristics of pentatonic parallelism (cf. Chapter III).

From the presence of a harmonic style we should also expect a progression of different tonal steps. I have very rarely heard any African music where there was no tonality shift – be it music containing no chordal harmony, like the Kiganda-Kisoga tradition in Uganda, or music containing bichords as with the Azande.

In Azande harp music one can always distinguish two or three tonal steps, one of which we can confidently call the tonic. The other ones I would call "contrasting steps." Looking into the scores we can see that many of the Zande songs contain similar progressions of chords in one or the other variant, which we shall give in Ex. 18 below. By "chord" I mean here a sound of two notes. No triads are played on the harp or sung. When two strings are plucked simultaneously, they will always represent (with very few exceptions arising from purely melodic or motor reasons) one of the four chords shown in the standard progression of Ex. 18.[35]

It is striking that most of the horizontal Zande harp themes end on the tonic. Exceptions are: *"Wen'ade gbua"*, Ex. 38 and *"Ngbadule o"*, Ex. 39.

T.   = tonic
CS I   = contrasting step I
CS II   = contrasting step II
Int. Ch. = intermediate chord

|Int. Ch.|CS II|CS I|Int. Ch.|CS II| T. |

Ex. 18. A standard harmonic progression in horizontal Azande harp music

Harmonic contrast is mainly created by the left hand notes, the contrasting bichords, CS I and T, having the same lower note.

Now let us learn the harp pattern of a tune called *"Limbyayo."* It is representative of another series of tunes for the Azande harp with slightly overlapping ranges for the fingers. Jérôme Assas will be teaching us the fingering pattern II (indicated are the ranges for *"Limbyayo"* and other pieces:

5 – Right thumb
4 ⎫
3 ⎬ Right index
  ⎭
3 ⎫
2 ⎬ Left thumb
1 ⎭

Here, unlike *"Nzanginza ...,"* the basic pattern consists of three tones:

Ex. 19. The basic three note patterns of *"Limbyayo"*

The right hand part has to be repeated twice to fit the length of the left hand part as follows (left hand notated with uptails):

Ex. 20. Patterns of the right and left hand combined

This pattern seems to stimulate instrumental variation. When varying, however, only the left hand part is usually altered. The "bass" of the right hand is fundamental and invariable.[36] The variants are often achieved by the subtle means of shifting just one or two notes, but it immediately gives a new image to the pattern.

In addition to the score of Jérôme Assas' performance of "Limbyayo", I should like to give here a standard variation to the same tune as played by Jérôme Sournac and by Bernard Guinahui.

Ex. 21. Standard variation of "Limbyayo"-harp pattern

The second type of harp music performed in the "horizontal" position does not emphasize rhythmic independence of the left and right hand parts so much as parallel movement. It is represented in Exs. 38, 39, 40, and 41. The rhythm in these examples is dominated by asymmetric or irregular phrases, particularly groups of 5 + 5 within the regular cycle length of 24 units. This is the impression an "additive" interpretation would give. While this may be justified in analysing the internal structure of the cycle, it is not possible to conclude from this how such patterns are conceptualized by the Azande harpists themselves.

Equally one must have reservations about interpreting them as composed in "hemiola style," as Rose Brandel (1959) applies this term to African music. All my experience contradicts any assumption that Azande harpists "think of" their patterns as metric particles strung together horizontally. No one could sing to his own harp accompaniment. There must be constant and recurring reference points, if one wants to sing to the harp. Further, if the music is played on the *kponingbo* xylophone, people dance to it.

For this reason, the "inner beat" is propably as important in Azande music as it is in other forms of African music, although an outsider may have difficulty in finding it, particularly in asymmetric pieces. In addition, there is a vague and general awareness of an orientation "screen," which, however, runs much quicker than any "beat". It could be described as a series of quavers – the smallest units. Metaphorically, this propensity for rhythmic orientation is just the same orientation that enables people to balance a heavy load on their head for hours and not let it fall. In Zande music one does not normally beat one's foot. And when one plays "walking harp" or the *sanzu* one does not think of one's notes as being "on" or "off" one's walking feet, but fingers and feet move quite independently, yet relatedly.

How are such asymmetric harp patterns as in *"Wen'ade gbua"* (Ex. 38), *"Ngbadule o"* (Ex. 39, CD I/12) and *"Ouzana"* (Ex. 41) really conceptualized? – It may help if we realize that there are probably several simultaneous levels of reference:

(1) the elementary pulsation which always seems to be 24 pulses in the asymmetrically organized pieces. This is the most basic level, on the border between conscious and unconscious, by which I mean that this level is ever-present, but one would not "count" or in any way objectify these elementary pulses. They function as an inaudible orientation screen guiding the spacing of one's action units on the harp.

(2) the reference level of the beat or dance step, that is an awareness of a series of recurring reference points, usually spaced three elementary pulses apart in the "asymmetric" pieces, and coinciding with the steps of the dancers. On this level certain notes are "on" and others "off" beat.

(3) the level of internal groups of numbers, possibly unconscious, which correpond with our analysis of the "additive" make-up of the phrases.

(4) the level of length and structure of text phrases, text lines etc., sometimes not sung but implied in the instrumental phrases.

All four levels depend on each other. With regard to level 2, however, where is the beat in these pieces (if there is one)? This is the question anyone who wants to play this music may legitimately ask.

One can find it relatively easily by looking at the dancers. But failing that it is also possible to discover it by analysing the music. Here it is useful to proceed by analogy from the known to the unknown. Azande harp music is probably one system, not two or three. Thus it is to be expected that an individual Zande harpist's behavioural patterns and modes of thought will not alter from piece to piece in his repertoire, and that he will conceptualize both the asymmetrical and symmetrical harp patterns in an analogous way. In the (symmetrically organized) song *"Nzanginza..."* (Ex. 31) the beat coincides with the fourth syllable of the word *anatata*, thus it is marked audibly. In *"Limbyayo"* (Ex. 37) it falls between the impact points of the two syllables of the word *Kpyoza*. Here then, the beat is not marked acoustically. Since Azande music, particular-

ly *kponingbo* music, is characterized by a delight in after-beat accentuation, i.e. the second of each pair of reference beats in 4/4 time (1 **2** 3 **4**)
to express it in the Western manner, this is not surprising. In *"Limbyayo"*
the accent falls on the acoustically marked after-beat, namely on the first

note a' of ♪ played by the harpist's right index.

Once we know this, we have almost discovered the whole schema.

The overall rhythmic structure of *"Limbyayo"* is generated by the
repeating pattern of the harpist's right hand part which, in theory, could
even be struck on a bottle like a time-line to accompany the harpist. In
relation to the inner beat, the pattern is this:

⑫   x.xx.x.x.x.x
     1 2 3 4

Ex. 22. Inner beat and right hand pattern of the harp player

Or, conceptualized the other way round, i.e. starting on 3:

⑫   .x.x.xx.xx.x
     1 2 3 4

Ex. 23. The right hand pattern started on 3

It has to be repeated to fill out the 24-pulse cycle. The harpist accentuates the notes falling on the after-beat (numbers 2 and 4 above) i.e. a' and
c' in our transcription (Ex. 33).The after-beat is invariably hooked to the
right index-finger as it were, while the other steps of the beat are hooked
"into the mind," so to speak, and may be objectified by any finger stroke
or simply left out.

A glance at the asymmetric themes in our collection then reveals that
the *"Limbyayo"* rhythmic structure is contained in them, but only in the
second half of these 24-pulse themes (Ex. 24). If we write the harp theme
of *"Limbyayo"* vertically aligned with the other themes, so that the
rhythmic structure of their second halves is congruent, by projection
from *"Limbyayo"* we can then find out where the beat must be in all of
them. The result can be tested practically on the harp. That the inner beat
should fall here, for example in *"Ngbadule o"*, is at first surprising – and
the revision of my earlier notation of this song (cf. Kubik 1964a:69) is
perhaps painful – but there is a compelling logic behind it if one regards
this harp music as one system. One can now sing Ouzana's words quite
easily to the harp accompaniment.

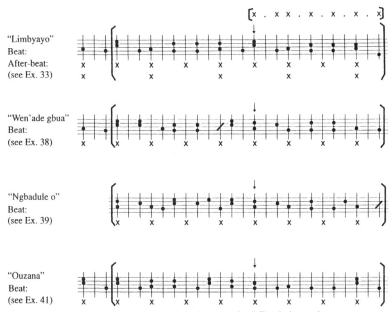

Ex. 24. Beat identification in asymmetrically organized Zande harp pieces.

Our comparison reveals that the structure of Ouzana's masterpiece *"Ngbadule o"* (Ex. 39) follows *"Wen'ade gbua"* (Ex. 38) quite faithfully. Only the sequence of bichords and the resulting tonal progressions are different. The main asymmetric accents fall mostly in the same places. The transcription also reveals that the harp part of *"Wen'ade gbua"* consists structurally of a five-pulse entity repeated four times, concluded by one four-pulse entity, adding up to the 24-pulse cycle.

$$\textcircled{24} \quad \text{x.x} \left[\begin{matrix} 5 \;+\; 5 \;+\; 5 \;+\; 5 \;+4 \\ \text{x.x.xx.x..x.x.xx.x.x.x.x} \end{matrix} \right]$$

Ex. 25. The 24-pulse cycle of the harp part of *"Wen'ade gbua"*

The third type of Azande harp compositions I documented in 1964 is not a Zande style at all, but comes from their close environment. This large body of harp songs is said to be of Banda origin, and it is largely played by young boys. The ethnic group called Banda lives to the west of the Azande. Like them, the Banda speak a I.A.6 Adamawa-Eastern language (Greenberg 1966). The Banda element appeared to be recent in the contemporary Zande styles I recorded in 1964. Banda tunes were all sung in the Sango language, the vehicular language in the Central African Republic.

One can easily distinguish them from the majority of the Zande tunes by the movement of the "bass" (right hand), which is always a quick two-note pulse. The music is essentially monometric and very rarely contains asymmetric passages as we have seen in the second type of Zande tunes. The notes of the left hand divide this unvarying two-note pulse usually into halves, sometimes constantly interlocking as in *"Mbi kote kote ngo"* (Ex. 44), sometimes temporarily as in *"Tade so zo koue M.E.S.A.N."* (Ex. 45) and sometimes just in the form of a rhythmic click as in *"Kolongo"* (Ex. 43). There are many other elements to distinguish this music from the tunes of Zande origin, but it would take us too far to discuss them all here.

The most frequent right hand part of the Banda tunes is the one we already know from *"Nzanginza..."* In the Banda tunes, however, it is not a component of a bimeter. Incidentally, the right hand part of *"Nzanginza..."* might be a recent adoption of the Banda beat. Moreover, it is the only case of a Banda beat in harp songs sung in the Zande language. Ouzana once made a strange remark, claiming that the old people played the right hand part of *"Nzanginza..."* differently. And he showed it to me, holding the harp, however, in the horizontal position. The pattern is interesting and also sounds nice. One can sing the tune to it in the same way:

Ex. 26. Right hand pattern

The most interesting composition in the Banda style in the scores is the political song about the M.E.S.A.N. as performed by Jérôme Sournac (Ex. 45). The harpist starts very fast with a four-note pattern having the A – G Banda beat and interlocking E notes.

(Fingering pattern III)
Right hand:
Played on strings:
Fingering:

4　1　5　1
Th　I　Th　I

Ex. 27. Fast four-note pattern

Now the left hand is played in between this pattern, between both rhythmically and melodically. It is transcribed in this way in the score. Here I should like to give the resultant rhythm that is heard from it:

Ex. 28. The resulting rhythm

By subtracting the notes given in Ex. 27 from the resulting pattern, one can easily find out how the pattern is played, even without looking into the scores. At one place there is a clash between E and D, arising, however, purely from melodic necessity.

One day Ouzana introduced me to something very new and exciting: he said the harp tuning we had used was not the only one. A second one existed for certain tunes. "One can also play en anglais!" he said I began to listen. What did he mean by this? And I asked him to explain it to me. Now Ouzana lowered the third string of the harp a semitone and said that the notes *wili pai sa su-nge* were now to be sung like this:

String No.:
Syllables:

Ex. 29. Harp tuning *"en anglais"*

I began to understand. The scale can be transposed! When the harp is tuned "en anglais" by lowering the third string the tuning formula begins at a different place and with it the position of the fingers is also exchanged accordingly.

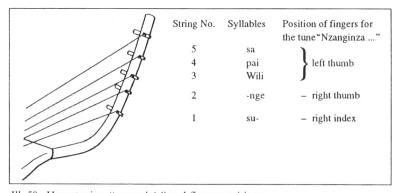

String No.	Syllables	Position of fingers for the tune "Nzanginza ..."
5	sa	} left thumb
4	pai	
3	Wili	
2	-nge	– right thumb
1	su-	– right index

Ill. 50. Harp tuning *"en anglais"* and finger positions

Now Ouzana explained how the tune *"Nzanginza..."* can be played *"en anglais"*. The starting points of *wili pai sa su-nge* having been shifted, the two parts of the harp pattern are turned upside down, the right hand part ("bass") now appearing in the treble, and the left hand part in the bass.

Ex. 30

This was a novel experience to me. The singing, of course, and all the harmonic intervals are entirely the same, only transposed.[37] Ouzana said that all the Banda tunes can be played *"en anglais,"* but not tunes like *"Limbyayo"* with a three-note bass. And there are also special compositions for performance *"en anglais"* such as *"Ana kabinga dar'akumba"* (Ex. 42). I often heard this brisk little song played by boys when walking.

The theoretical implications of Ouzana's transposition process are far-reaching. For example, it may be totally excluded that the Zande tone system is based on any kind of equitonal ideas. Here, in contrast to southern Uganda for example, differing intervals are conceptualized within a pentatonic system, and harmonic sounds which include fourths, fifths and a somewhat neutralized third. The reversal of the harp parts in Ouzana's *"en anglais"* tuning also seems to reveal that in the old days there must have been a lot of theoretical experimentation in harp music. What the teenage boys showed me, although of value in itself, is probably only the last few drops of a drying spring.

I have racked my brains over the question of how Ouzana and other boys came to this remarkable terminology. None of them could give me a Zande term. Ouzana normally distinguished in this way: the tuning in question is *"en anglais"* and the other (normal) one is *"la vraie guitare"* ("the true guitar"). After some time on the journey with me he started to say *"la vraie harpe,"* after he had heard me calling the instrument harp. I have thought of the possibility that the tuning comes from the "English" side of the Azande country, from the Sudan, and hence the term. This has not been verified up to now.

Ouzana's term also made me think of another strange expression. At Rafai I heard about the *mami wata* or *mama ime,* a female water spirit that is thought to have a body with a human upper part and a belly like a fish. This woman is said to live in rivers such as the Vovodo river at Rafai. The *mami wata* legend was common knowledge in all the places I visited. Any really good harp player (or guitar player) is supposed to have some obscure relation to this woman. He opens his engagement by correspondence. A letter is taken to the river and left under a certain stone. Once a man has entered into a relationship with the *mami wata* many things change strangely. For example he loses his shadow. He cannot see his shadow in the sun any more. Others of course can see it.

It need not be emphasized that the *mami wata* myth has implications for studies in depth psychology. To pursue this topic – although much has surfaced more recently in this connection – would exceed the scope of this chapter. It must be noted however, that the term *mami wata,* so pronounced, is known in wide areas of the Guinea Coast and in Cameroon. Without doubt it is Pidgin English: "Mammy water" (mother of the water). There is even a popular Highlife record in Nigeria about the *mami wata.*[38]

This would suggest that Azande knowledge of the term in Central African Republic could be a result of diffusion from the west (via Cameroon or Zaïre), rather than from the east (Sudan). How long the *mami wata* myth has been known among the Azande could only be clarified after laborious examination of oral traditions and the existing literature. It is possible that it converged with older indigenous Azande ideas about a female water spirit. In a note on my Zande harp paper (1964a) dated February 9, 1978, Klaus Wachsmann[39] seems to have thought of this possibility when he remarks:

> The reference to the *mami wata* or *mama ime* myth is fascinating. There are harps from this region that have a neck (or arch) that is carved in the form of a woman being devoured by a crocodile. In many Mangbetu harps only the head is carved, but K. states explicitly that in his locality heads hardly occurred.

The Transcriptions

In the transcriptions I have followed tape recordings, but <u>after</u> I had learned to play and sing the songs myself. I have preferred to transcribe the recorded versions in order to give a demonstration of "live" performance, so that we can study some of the variation techniques of the harp players both in singing and playing. I hope to show by these transcriptions how the preconceived text material is actually spread out and arranged in each performance. It is to be understood, however, that every performance is different; the "material" of the tune is always the same.

For the harp part the right hand notes are written with downtails and the left hand notes with uptails, except in the tunes of the second (parallel) type of harp playing, where all the notes are written with downtails.

At the beginning of each score there is an indication as to the special fingering used for the piece. The tuning of the harp in the particular performance is indicated as well. It always refers to the actual pitch of the key note – the note sounding the syllable *sa* and written as C, respectively as G in the *"en-anglais"* transposition.

All tunes have been notated with "reduced" bar lines. The double bar lines indicate the expiry of one formal unit or summary meter of the harp pattern.

With regard to the text transcriptions of the harp songs I had considerable problems, in contrast to other research areas. In Azande country I depended on interpreters, and in view of my ruinous financial position on the 1964 tour, I could not recruit a "professional" translater. In writing the Zande texts I therefore had to follow the rather "intuitive" orthography of Ouzana and Kamoundé.

This may even have one advantage, that it reflects more closely the actual pronunciation of the words in the particular Zande dialects spoken in Zemio and elsewhere in the area than any of the standard orthographies (which have their own inherent problems). Sometimes I have deliberately altered their orthography for musical reasons. Thus I have written *du kporan'yo* (Ex. 31) and *du kpuran'yo* (Ex. 32) instead of *du kporani yo; –* or *Nadwakit'yo* instead of *Naduakiti o!* (Ex. 40). In the Sango texts I have followed the official orthography of this language, which reads like French (ou = u etc.). Here Maurice Djenda, my co-worker on my second trip to the Central African Republic in 1966 was of great help and he produced the transcriptions and translations published here. He could not do anything about the Zande texts, however, since he is not a Zande speaker.

For many years, many pages of song transcriptions made by Ouzana and Kamoundé (not only of harp song texts, but also *kponingbo* and other music) remained untranslated and uninterpreted. We did not know anything about their content. In January 1985 my colleague Armin Prinz, researcher in ethno-medicine at the University of Vienna, offered to have some of the harp songs I had recorded in 1964 retranscribed and translated from tape by his Zaïrean co-worker Laku Heke. Subsequently I sent a cassette copy of some of the songs to Zaïre.

The result was a very readable and carefully written manuscript for which I am most grateful to Laku Heke and Armin Prinz. But as I had anticipated, several texts transcribed from the same tapes as transcribed by Ouzana and Kamoundé on the spot in 1964 are somewhat different not only in orthography but in the words.

I am of course conscious of the dangers of working with an informant from another area in Zande country, on material which must be distant to him both in space and time, 1964 to 1985. The divergencies are probably the result of three factors:

(1) Kamoundé and Ouzana made many mistakes in their transcriptions.[40]

(2) Although Armin Prinz assures me that the Zande language is not split into widely varying dialects, there is a possibility that some words may not have been properly understood by the new transcriber.

(3) The new transcriber may have approximated the texts in pronunciation and orthography to the Zande as spoken in his area in Zaïre.

Although I am thankful that we now have transcriptions and translations into French of some of the songs, which I did not have in 1964, the problems have not diminished. They are probably not seriously relevant to the subject of our chapter, harp <u>music,</u> but on the other hand I would not wish to claim absolute accuracy in the text transcriptions and translations which follow.

etc. *) spoken words. The musician is saying his name. (On the repeat of bar 13 onlys). – There is a small mistake in harp playing at this place, which I have not transcribed.

etc. +) The player repeats the first half of the harp pattern. – Probably a mistake.

Ex. 31. *"Nzanginza mu du kporani yo."* Performed by Maurice Gambassi, aged 16, from Agoumar village, near Rafai (cf. CD I/10), Language: Zande. April 1964. Orig. Tape No. R 44/B. Tuning: *sa* = approx. f″ Fingering: pattern I.

Translation of some text lines provided by Father van Horne:

Nzanginza mu du kporani yo, anatata.
Ba kpere gundo o, mo ye ka nyangareni.
Nyekere nyekere mbai ti mbosoro, ako anatata.
Tataha liye koyo, ko ye ka nyangareni.
Wili Gbaya tia ko, Agumara gaya.

La harpe est dans notre village, on va se promener, anatata.
Grand fumeur du tabac, tu viens pour m'embêter!
La mauvaise odeur qui sort de tes fesses, ako anatata!
Il s'est promené, il a mangé, il vient pour m'embêter!
C'est un fils de la race Gbaya, Agoumar est leur village.

("The harp is in our village, we are going to walk, anatata.
Big tobacco-smoker, you are coming to trouble me!
The bad smell which comes from your buttocks, ako anatata!
He has walked, he has eaten, he comes to trouble me!
This is a son of the Gbaya ethnic group, Agoumar is their village.")

2. *Alternative text versions by other players:*
3. (a)   Mo da li e ko yo o, ka i ka yo da ni (from Rafai).
   (b)   Ba mbi li gund o, kumba ku natata (from Dembia).

Ex. 32. *"Nzanginza ni ku kpurani yo"* (condensed version). Performed by Samuel Ouzana, from Zemia. Language: Zande. Tuning: *"en anglais." sa* = e″. Fingering: transposed pattern I.

Ex. 33. *"Limbyayo."* Performed by Jérôme Assas, aged approximately 23, from Rafai. Language: Zande. April 1964. Orig. Tape No. R 42/B. Tuning: *sa* = approximately b'♭. Fingering: pattern II

Ill. 51. *Kundi* harp performer Jérôme Assas. Background centre is the harpist Maurice Gambassi. At Rafai, eastern part of the Central African Republic, April 1964. Archive No. III/15.

Translation of some text lines (Jérôme Assas):

Aropka gumere nga kundi Kpyoza!
Araba tissara Kpyoza!
Araba tissara komesa Kpyoza!
Syaduwa na kpoli le mi 'ya ti wa!

Bale ku Dergadi, 'wen'ade ni pai ku ngbale.
Bale ku Zamburo, 'wen'ade ni pai ku ngbale.
Bale ku Zekpio, mya ni li gi kondo ni kpai mbiro.
Araba tissaro o Kpyoza!

("Arokpa, my friend is the harp, Kpyoza!
Eight! Nine! Kpyoza!
Eight! Nine! Ten! Kpyoza!
My friend who cries about me and the mother!
One should take me to Dergadi, so that the beautiful girls embrace me.
One should take me to Zamburo, so that the beautiful girls embrace me.
One should take me to Zekpio, where I will eat my chicken with palmoil.
Eight! Nine! Kpyoza!")

Notes: This song treats of the legendary harp player Kpyoza and it is
said that he once sang it or perhaps even composed it. Dergadi, Zamburo
and Zekpio are chiefships in the surrounding area. Dergadi is about
100 km north of Rafai. "Arokpa", also pronounced "araba", "tissaro"
and "komesa" are not Zande words according to local opinion. They are
apparently local pronunciations of the Arabic numerals eight, nine and
ten. The singer obviously adopted these lines with the song when he
learned it.

Ex. 34. *"Ana ka wio kumba kua de o"* (short extract). Performed by Jérôme
Sournac, aged 17, from Rafai. Language: Zande. April 1964. Orig. Tape No. R
44/A. Tuning: *sa* = b♭. Fingering: pattern II. The note C is plucked as indicated
by the letters r and l below

Text (as written by Jérôme Sournac):

Ana ka wio koumba kua de o (3 ×)
Kamo ya hi! mi taloata ho!
Mya folo nzapa lago guilio he die
Mo sengui ni na, mo sengui ni na.
Moyanga fi, moyanga ngoto koumba koua de he
Bolingo te he sene gano nga koussa koumba
Mya folo nzapa lago guilio dit prendre koumba
Ana ka wio lo aviliakolo toni wele

French translation (by Sournac):

Nous allons les bosser, les femmes mariées.
Si tu dis comment, je vais te bosser
Je te dis chérie, la femme mariée il faut jouer.
Tu as injurié maman pour la cause de ta femme?
Si tu dis encore deux fois le nom de ma maman tu verras!
Chérie tu ecoutes ce que dit ton marie?
Mais c'est rien. Et que peut-il faire de moi?
Je te dis, Dieu, il fait jour. Ton mari est au seuil de la porte.
Nous allons les bosser les femmes mariées.

("We are going to fuck them, the married women!
If you say how, I will fuck you!
I am telling you, darling, with a married woman one must play!
You have insulted Mother because of your woman?
If you say the name of my Mother another two times, you will see!
Darling, do you hear what your husband says?
But that means nothing. And what can he do to me?
I tell you, by God, it's already morning! Your husband is at the door step.
We are going to fuck the married women!")

Notes: The text of this song is not completely in Zande. There are some words in Sango, French and even in Lingala, *bolingo,* a famous term meaning "love" in the guitar music from Kinshasa and Brazzaville which is heard in the Central African Republic.

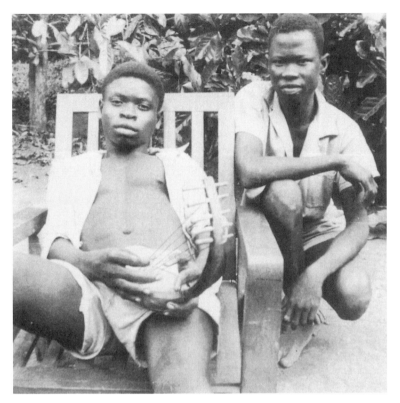

Ill. 52. Jérôme Sournac with *kundi*. (I have reinforced the harp strings to make them more visible). Next to him is Maurice Gambassi who performed the song "*Nzanginza...*" (Ex. 31)

Ex. 35. *"Agbe ni nduandu ngboro."* Performed by Samuel Ouzana, aged 12, from Zemio. Language: Zande. May 1964. Orig. Tape No. R 45/B. Tuning: *sa* = approximately a'. Fingering: pattern II

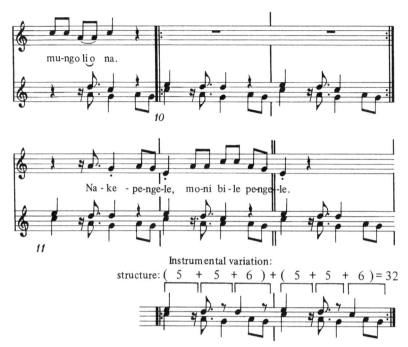

mu-ngo li o na.

10

Na - ke - pe-nge-le,   mo-ni bi - le penge -le.

11

Instrumental variation:
structure: (5 + 5 + 6) + (5 + 5 + 6) = 32

Ex. 36. *"Nakepengele."* Performed by Jérôme Assas, aged approximately 23, from Rafai. Language: Zande. April 1964. Orig. Tape No. R 42/B. Tuning: *sa* = b'$_\flat$. Fingering: pattern II

Text transcription (by Jérôme Assas):

Nakepengele, nakepengele
moni bile pengele nakepengele
A mawa ti kpai te
Mu binga Natata
Mi abi na sambia di?
Mi abiri ti mungoli o na.
Nakepengele moni bile pengele

French translation by Jérôme Assas:

Ou aurais-je celle qui ecrase le mais?
Ou aurais je une femme?
Le malheur n'est rien
Tu vois Natata
Je la verrai par les rires
les femmes de Bakambia sont deux
L'autre est courte, *l'autre est* geante

("Where shall I find the one who pounds the maize?
Where shall I get a wife?
Misery, it does not matter!
You see Natata (= a name)
I will see her by her smiles,
the wives of Bakambia are two,
one is short, one is tall.")

Notes: The song contains some Sango words, for example *"mawa"*
(= misery, bad luck).

Example I

Example II

Ex. 37. Extracts from *"Limbyayo."* Performed with two harps by Bernard Guinahui and François Razia, aged 30–35, from Makanza near Rafai. Language: Zande. April 1964. Orig. Tape No. R 44/B. Tuning of the harps: *sa* = near d″. Fingering: pattern II.
I: Duet of the two harp players.
II: Passage with *nvilili* (whistling) and vocal part.
Both extracts are taken from the same performance (cf. CD I/6)

Ex. 38. *"Wen'ade gbua"* (condensed version). Performed by Antoine Gbála-goume, aged approximately 30, from Djema (cf. CD I/11), Language: Zande. May 1964. Orig. Tape No. R 46/B. Tuning: *sa* = approximately e♭". Fingering: pattern II. (The note C is plucked by the left thumb, when alone or in a C/G chord)

Transcription and translation of song text into French by Laku Heke, Zaïre, February 1985:

Text:

Mi a dia gi gbegbere de kabangita wene ade gbua;
Mi a dia kina gbegbere de kabangita wene ade gbua.

Translation:

Je me marierai à une laide femme afin d'engendrer. Les belles femmes ne valent rien;
Je ne me marierai qu'à une laide femme. Les belles femmes ne valent rien.

("I will marry an ugly woman, to beget children with her.
The pretty women are worth nothing.
I will only marry an ugly woman. The pretty women are worth nothing.")

Ex. 39. *"Ngbadule o."* Performed by Samuel Ouzana, aged 12, from Zemio (cf. CD I/12), Language: Zande. May 1964. Orig. Tape No. R 45/B. Tuning: *sa* = approximately a″. Fingering: pattern II. (The note C is plucked as indicated by the letters l and r in the score)

Ill. 53. Samuel Ouzana posing for the camera. At Chief Raphael Zekpio's village, Dembia, May 1964 (V/17)

Transcription and translation of song text into French by Laku Heke, Zaïre, February 1985:

Text:

Nagbele o mi a nya wai da gbadi buda na gime;
Ako o mi a nya wai aboro gbata na u re;
Ako o mi a nya wai Nagbadibute na u re;
Ngbadule o mi a nya wai da gbadi buda na ime;
Gitare – Ozana – Samuel.
Ngbadule, Robert da mangi buda na ime;
Tamere o mi a nya wai da wari buda na pere
Ako o mi a nya wai Nagbali buda na ga re.

Translation:

Nagbele, que dois-je dire? Tu as préparé la boisson avec beaucoup de fumée;
Ah, que dois-je dire? Les citadins s'enrichissent;
Ah, que dois-je dire? Nagbadibute s'enrichit;
Ngbadule, que dois-je dire? Tu as préparé la boisson avec beaucoup d'eau;
Guitare – Ozana – Samuel;
Ngbadule et Robert vous avez préparé la boisson avec beaucoup d'eau;
Mon (ma) cadet (te), que dois-je dire? Tu as préparé assez de boisson dans le pot;
Mon (ma) cadet (te), que dois-je dire? Tu as mis trop d'eau dans la boisson;
Ah, que dois-je dire? La soularde rentre.

("Nagbele, what shall I say? You have prepared the drink with a lot of smoke;
Ah, what shall I say? The townsmen enrich themselves
Ah, what shall I say? Nagbadibute enriches herself
Ngbadule, what shall I say? You have prepared the drink with much water;
Guitar! Ozana Samuel!
Ngbadule and Robert, you have prepared the drink with much water!
My younger brother/my younger sister, what shall I say? You have prepared enough drink in the jar!
My younger brother/younger sister, what shall I say? You have put too much water into the drink!
Ah, what shall I say? The drunken woman is coming in again").

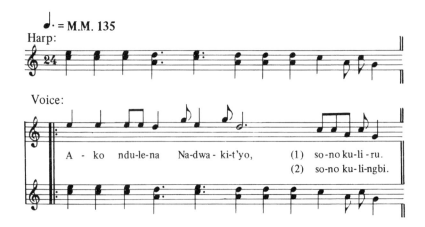

Ex. 40. *"Ako ndulena"* (condensed version). Performed by David Kamoundé, aged 12, from Zemio. Language: Zande. May 1964. Orig. Tape No. R 45/A. Tuning: *sa* = g″. Fingering: the note C is plucked *always* by the right index, the note A <u>always</u> by the right thumb

Ex. 41. *"Ouzana"* (extract). Composed and performed by Samuel Ouzana, aged 12, from Zemio. Language: Zande. May 1964. Orig. Tape No. R 45/B. Tuning: *sa* = a″. Fingering: pattern II. (The note C is plucked as indicated by the letters r and l in the score)

Transcription and translation of song text into French by Laku Heke, Zaïre, February 1985:

Text:

Samuele e Samuele Ozana
Nzanginza du re wiri pai sa Ozana;
Nzanginza ni kuru yo wiri pai sa Ozana;
Nzanginza ni kuru yo wiri pai sa Samuel;
Ozana, Ozana, Ozana pai were;
Nzanginza ni kuru yo wiri apai uwe Ozana;
Guitariste – guitariste, Ozana.

Pour une moindre chose, ce *nzanginza* accuse toujours Ozana;
Pour une moindre chose, *nzanginza* accuse toujours Ozana;
Pour une moindre chose, *nzanginza* accuse toujours Samuel;
Ozana, Ozana, Ozana. Il y a ceci ou cela;
Pour deux moindres choses, Nzanginza accuse toujours Ozana;
Guitariste, guitariste, Ozana.

("For a little thing, this harp always accuses Ouzana!
For a little thing, the harp always accuses Ouzana!
For a little thing, the harp always accuses Samuel!
Ouzana, Ouzana, Ouzana, there is this or that!
For two little things, this harp always accuses Ouzana!
Guitarist! Guitarist! Ouzana!")

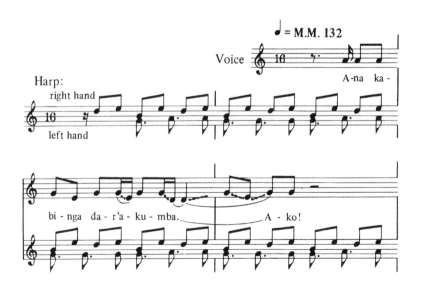

Instrumental variations:

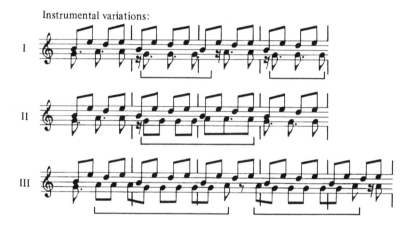

Ex. 42. *"Ana kabinga dar'akumba."* Performed by Samuel Ouzana, aged 12, from Zemio. Language: Zande. May 1964. Orig. Tape No. R 45/B. Tuning: *"en anglais."* sa = approximately e″

Transcription and translation of song text into French by Laku Heke, Zaïre, February 1985:

Text:

Mi na kabinga dere akumba, ako;
Mo nya dokpo mo ye kani;
Mi na kabinga dera akumba;
Mi na kawinga dere akumba, ako
Ai nda ai;
Mi na kapinga na dere akumba;
Dere akumba a... dere akumba;
Guitare – *Ozana – Samuel.*

Translation:

Ah, je vais regarder les femmes d'autrui;
Si tu ripostes; viens; je te frapperai à te faire déféquer;
Je vais faire l'amour avec les femmes d'autrui [langage impoli];
Je vais coucher avec les femmes d'autrui;
Les femmes d'autrui... oui; les femmes d'autrui.
Guitare – Ozana – Samuel.

("Ah, I will look at other people's wives!
If you want to answer back, just come! I will beat you till you shit!
I will make love with other men's wives!
I will sleep with other men's wives!
The other men's wives... Yes! Other men's wives!
Guitar! Ouzana Samuel!")

Notes: In the recording the main line of the text clearly sounds
"...dar'akumba" rendered by Laku Heke in written Zande as *dere
akumba*. I have not changed this in the scores, but it should not pose any
problem. As in many other Zande songs, the exclamation "Ako!" is also
used. Laku Heke does not translate it, and there is indeed no real translation possible.

Evans-Pritchard (1962–65) in a lucid analysis of a Zande text taken
down in 1928 from Kuagbiaru in the old Zande kingdom of Gbudwe
(Sudan) explains some of the occasions on which *ako* may be uttered in
Zande.

> *"Ako"* is the most often heard of all Zande interjections of ejacu-
> lations, but it is not always easy to find quite the right word in
> English by which to translate it, though "alas!" and "oh!" will
> usually convey the meaning fairly well, though the tone of the
> exclamation cannot always be adequately conveyed. In its verbal
> form it has usually, if not invariably, the sense of "to bemoan" or
> "to sigh" with sadness or resignation.

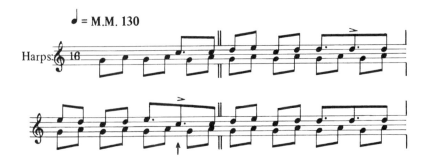

A -nnée soi - xan - te!

↑ = starting point of the second harp.
The second harp never varies.

Ex. 43. *"Kolongo."* Performed by Mockys Dieudonné Yves and his friend, with two harps. Approximate age 15, from Dembia. May 1964. Orig. Tape No. R 49/A. Tuning: *sa* = approximately g″. Fingering: pattern I

Text in Sango:

Kolongo ga ti goué goué ngo,
Kolongo jia mbi na passi.
Kolongo ga ti goué goué ngo,
Kolongo jia mbi na Bangui.
O! o! é! Mawa! Année soixante.

Translation into French (by Maurice Djenda, C.A.R.):

Kolongo vient de partir,
Kolongo m'a laissé avec une grande douleur
Kolongo vient de partir,
Kolongo m'a laissé à Bangui.
O! o! é! Misère! Année soixante.

("Kolongo has just departed
Kolongo has left me behind with a terrible pain
Kolongo has just departed,
Kolongo has left me in Bangui.
O! o! é! Misery! The year 1960.")

Notes: "Kolongo était un agent de police bien connu parce qu'il était très méchant et frappait toujours le gens. Image d'un agent de police pendant le temps du gouvernement Dacko. *Passi:* On emploie le mot "passi" pour exprimer une douleur, une peine, une souffrance et des émotions de douleur; avoir une douleur à cause de l'absence de quelqu'un." (Maurice Djenda, 1966)

("Kolongo was a policeman who was ill-famed because he was extremely unfriendly and used to beat the people. This is the image of a policeman in the times of the Dacko government. *Passi:* This word is used for expressing grief, pain, suffering and all emotions of pain; it means feeling pain because of somebody's absence.")

Ex. 44. *"Mbi kote kote ngo."* Performed by David Kamoundé, aged 12, from Zemio. Language: Sango/Zande. May 1964. Orig. Tape No. R 45/A. Tuning: *sa* = g″. Fingering: pattern I

Text in Sango:

Mbi koto koto ngo, kuya.
Mo jia mbi na Bangui mbi sala nié ita ti mbi?
Kolongo jia mbi na Bangui mbi sala nié wali ti mbi?
Ceinture mbi vovongo.
Culotte mbi vovongo.
Pantalon mbi vovongo.
Chemise mbi vovongo na koli ti mbi.
Na ndu kué ki na poli kanzu kanfua mo ngiwa.

Translation into French (by Maurice Djenda, C.A.R.):

Je pince, kuya!
Tu m'a laissé à Bangui, qu'est-ce que j'ai fait mon frère?
Kolongo m'a laissé à Bangui, qu'est-ce que j'ai fait, ma femme?
La ceinture je l'ai achetée.
La culotte je l'ai achetée.
Le pantalon je l'ai acheté.
La chemise je l'ai achetée, mon mari!
[Phrase zande non-traduite.]

("I pinch [you], kuya!
You have left me behind in Bangui,
what have I done, my brother?
Kolongo has left me in Bangui,
what have I done, my woman?
A belt, I have bought.
Shorts, I have bought.
Trousers, I have bought.
A shirt, I have bought it, my man!
[Zande phrase not translated.]")

Notes: Koto koto ngo: On emploie ce mot quand on pince la peau de quelqu'un avec un petit bois ou les ongles des doigts pour faire mal ou bien le blesser. (Maurice Djenda, 1966)
("*Koto koto ngo:* This phrase is used if you pinch someone's skin with a little piece of wood or the finger-nails in order to cause him pain, or even hurt him.")

(Instrumental interlude):

Ex. 45. *"Tade so zo koue M.E.S.A.N."* Performed by Jérôme Sournac, aged 17, from Rafai. April 1964. Orig. Tape No. R 44/A. Tuning: *sa* = approximately b♭″. Fingering: pattern III

Text in Sango:

Boganda koui aoué,
a zo koué Mesane.
Boganda a tene,
e koué gui na tole,
Kolongo fa na mbi Sango!
Boganda a tene,
fa dé so zo koué Mesane.
I sara da koué gui na mole,
Boganda!
Wali mbanda fa na mbi mbanda
wali mbanda!
Kolongo fa na mbi mbanda,
fa na mbi Sango!
fadé so zo koué Mesane,
wali mbanda!
Sanga na li ga bassima,
sanga na li ga tessani.
Zingui na lidou bassima,
zingui na lidou tessani.
Kolongo fa na mbi Sango!
wali ti mbi,
wali ti jia mbi na passi.

Translation into French (by Maurice Djenda, C.A.R.):

Boganda est mort déjà
et tout le monde est M.E.S.A.N.
Boganda a dit
que tout le monde ait la tôle,
Kolongo enseigne-moi le Sango!
Boganda a dit,
maintenant tout le monde est M.E.S.A.N.
Faisons toutes les maisons en moule,
Boganda!
Femme de *mbanda,* montre moi le *mbanda,*
femme de *mbanda!*
Kolongo enseigne-moi le Sango,
enseigne-moi le Sango!
tout le monde est M.E.S.A.N.
femme Mbanda!
[Phrase zande non-traduite.]
Kolongo enseigne-moi le Sango!

ma femme,
femme qui me laisse en souffrance.

("Boganda is already dead,
and everyone is M.E.S.A.N.
Boganda said
that everyone should have a corrugated iron roof,
Kolongo, teach me Sango!
Boganda said
now everyone is M.E.S.A.N.
Let's build all the houses with dried bricks, Boganda!
Watchful wife, show me your watchfulness,
watchful wife!
Kolongo, teach me Sango,
teach me Sango!
Everyone is M.E.S.A.N.
Watchful wife!
[Zande phrase not translated.]
Kolongo, teach me Sango!
my woman,
woman who leaves me suffering!")

Notes: "*Mole:* signifie en français 'moule' ou 'brique'! Une maison en moule est une maison faite de motte de terre en forme de ciment rectangulaire ou carré. *Mbanda:* exprime une qualité de jalousie, d'accusation que font les femmes en defendant leurs maris de rester avec d'autres femmes en cachette. L'action que fait une femme en défendant l'amusement de son mari avec d'autres femmes est appellée mbanda." (Maurice Djenda, 1966)

("*Mole* derives from French "moule" which means mould. A mould house is one made of clay shaped like rectangular or square cement bricks. *Mbanda* expresses a quality of jealousness, the kind of accusations women make to prevent their husbands from staying secretly with other women. The action a house-wife takes to prevent her husband from enjoying himself with other women is called *mbanda.*")

♩ = M.M. 138

Ex. 46. Harp pattern of Jean Nquimale, a *Buru* musician, aged approximately 30, from Galafondo, near Fort Sibut. April 1964. Orig. Tape No. R 42/A. Tuning: the note written as C is near e″. Fingering: right hand part with downtails, left hand part with uptails. The G/A Banda–beat is played on the *third* and *second* string of the harp with the usual fingering

Chapter III
A Structural Examination of Multi-Part Singing in East, Central and Southern Africa

This chapter combines and compares some of the results of my work on patterns of multi-part singing in several societies of sub-Saharan Africa. In contrast to Chapters I and II it is not devoted to a single population cluster, but to a number of cultures across East, Central and southern Africa. My theoretical outlook here largely stems from my observation in the 1960s in Tanzania and elsewhere that there is a certain reciprocal structural relationship between specific multi-part singing styles (with the simultaneous sounds created) and the tonal systems of the music of a community. This relationship seems to be so tightly knit that the researcher can reconstruct theoretically the nature of a tonal system from a representative sample of the multi-part singing of an area.

Instrumental tunings can be measured with devices such as the Stroboconn, the Korg Tuner Model WT-12 and more recent electronic pitch-measuring equipment, or the standard I.L.A.M. set of 54 tuning forks (212–424 c.p.s.) used in the field, but the figures obtained are not conclusive by themselves. Stroboconn measurements in particular, with their extreme accuracy, may falsely suggest more restricted pitch values than the actual margin of tolerance in a given musical culture. It may also be difficult to interpret the considerable deviations visible in the measurements from the theoretical "scale" ascribed to a culture by the researcher. The measured tunings may require totally different explanations in different circumstances. One also has to assess the intra-cultural meaning of the acceptable tuning fluctuations that may occur regularly in an individual musician's day to day tuning.[1] Without the help of informants to introduce the researcher to local musical theory[2] one can easily go astray. Thus, Zande xylophone tunings from Zaïre have been held to be "gapped" equiheptatonic (cf. Jones 1971 b : 41–44) or "pélog-type" (pp. 59–61), and, more recently Robert Gottlieb (1986 : 56–76) has claimed that the "musical scales" of the Gumuz, Berta and Ingessana peoples in the Republic of Sudan are equipentatonic. Neither claim is substantiated by my own research among the Azande in 1964 or among the Ingessana people of Sudan in 1977.[3]

While, in Africa, there are many incidences of equipentatonic tunings[4] and equiheptatonic tunings[5] they have never been confirmed from the II.E.1 Eastern Sudanic, II.E.3 (Berta) and neighboring languages areas (Greenberg 1966).

For historical reasons too this is an unlikely zone for the development of equidistantly conceptualised tunings, as my investigations of a broad comparative sample of sub-Saharan musical styles have shown over many years (cf. Kubik 1968c, 1985). Looking at this large sample certain likelihoods emerge, and one of them is that equidistantly conceptualized tunings are intimately linked with the historical presence in an area of instruments that have a sound spectrum with a preponderance of non-harmonic overtones, such as xylophones and lamellophones. Where string instruments devoid of spectrum-modifying buzzers have played a dominant role, such as in parts of the so-called Sudanic belt and among Khoisan speakers of southern Africa, we are unlikely to observe the development of a tuning temperament.

One can obtain a fairly accurate picture of the nature of instrumental tunings in Africa with an integrative analysis such as I have attempted in the papers combined in this chapter. While the study of instrumental tunings in isolation is mostly inconclusive, it can become revealing if one relates the figures to regularities observed in the choice of simultaneous sounds and the order of their appearance in the music itself. Any regularities thus discovered will by no means be coincidental, but will reflect structural characteristics of the underlying tonal system. It may then be easy to assess whether the tonal system in question operates with the notion of partials or is based on other concepts such as equidistance.

Section 1 summarizes my early findings in East and Central Africa about the interrelationship between sung harmonic patterns and underlying tonal systems. The examples come from the -Pangwa, -Kisi, -Gogo etc. in Tanzania, -Mbwela, -Cokwe etc. in Angola, and various peoples in Congo, Gabon and the Central African Republic. This section is an English translation, with amendments, of part of my booklet "Mehrstimmigkeit und Tonsysteme in Ost- und Zentralafrika," (1968c). In this section various inter-regional theoretical concepts such as the "span" or "skipping" process are introduced. These will also be needed for understanding parts of Chapters IV and VI.

Section 2 deals with structural interrelationships between multi-part singing and tonal systems in south-central Africa (Zambia, Zimbabwe, Angola), a zone of historical contact between Bantu and San speakers. It gives us a glimpse of a musical culture outside the Niger-Congo family of languages, and at San and Bantu interaction in music. Besides reconstructing what might be the San tonal universe, I am also attempting to reconstruct a portion of the music history of southern Africa, linking it with data from the cultural and population history of the region. This is a recent paper, only completed in 1987 and first published 1988 in *Ethnomusicology* 32 (2). Although its inclusion in this compounded chapter breaks the chronological order of the papers faithfully observed up to this point, there was no other more suitable place in this book. The considerable time-span between my writing sections 1 and 2 is noticeable in style and method, but they are linked by an overall theme.

June 5, 1990

G. K.

Section 1
Homophonic Multi-Part Singing in Bantu Musical Cultures of East and Central Africa

A Common Procedure for Obtaining Simultaneous Sounds

During my first visit to Tanzania in 1960 (then: Tanganyika) I stayed for some time in the southwestern highlands of Upangwa and Ubena (in present-day Rudewa and Njombe Districts, Iringa Region) and walked down from Madunda Catholic Mission to Lake Nyasa. When I learned songs in Kipangwa, Kindendeule, Kimanda and other local languages spoken in that area, I noticed that most of the songs followed quite strictly a characteristic procedure for obtaining simultaneous sounds. A kind of counter-note principle seemed to be at work as a harmonic rule. Each note in one singer's voice required a distinctive harmonic counter-note in the other singer's voice. In Kubik 1961 a I published a transcription of a song in Kindendeule as an example of this counter-note pattern. It is reproduced in the transcriptions at the end of this section.[6]

The two voices combine in quite a rigid way, and they are strictly interdependent. Given the first voice, if one knows the basic idea behind this kind of part singing, one can reconstruct the second one in most of the songs performed by the people of this area.

Among the Wapangwa, Wandendeule, Wangoni, and in some music of the Wakisi and Wamanda at Lake Nyasa (CD I/13) the basic organization of harmonic part singing follows the structure as shown below. All these groups sing predominantly in a pentatonic system with whole tones and minor thirds as the constituent intervals:[7]

(1) *E* in the upper voice requires *C* in the lower one. Resultant consonance: a major third.

(2) *D* in the upper voice requires *A* in the lower one. Resultant consonance: a perfect fourth.

(3) *C* in the upper voice requires *G* in the lower one. Resultant consonance: a perfect fourth.

(4) *A* in the upper voice requires *E* in the lower one. Resultant consonance: a perfect fourth.

If we write this down in staff notation, we can see that in the two-part harmonic singing style of these peoples some consonances must recur with regularity.

3   4   4   4

Ex. 47. Counter-note pattern prevalent in the music of the Wapangwa, Wandendeule and other ethnic groups in the Lake Nyasa area (Tanzania)

Such harmonic patterns are common in pentatonic traditions of vocal music in south-western Tanzania and many parts of Malaŵi, where we have recorded several representative examples, particularly in story songs[8] (CD I/14).

The logic behind this type of parallelism in several perfect fourths, interrupted in one place by an isolated major third becomes clear, if we link the harmonic pattern of Ex. 47 to the pentatonic system used in the music of these ethnic groups.

Scale:

Simultaneous sounds:

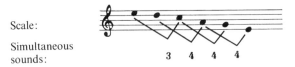

3   4   4   4

Ex. 48. Counter-note pattern in a two-part harmonic style within a pentatonic system

Comparing Exs. 47 and 48 we can observe that all the simultaneous sounds are obtained by singing a given note together with the next note but one in the scale, skipping one step. E goes with C, D with A, C with G and A with E.

In principle a second singer finds his note by duplicating the pitch-line of the first singer at a different level. However, his level is not arbitrary, but exactly two degrees higher or lower than the first one. The second singer finds his note by skipping one note of the scale. This process is comparable to a xylophone player moving his two sticks in parallel over the keyboard, always leaving one note between the two keys which he strikes simultaneously. If the xylophone is tuned to this kind of pentatonic scale similar sounds to those described will result.

It seems that we are here on the track of a typical procedure in the organization of homophonic forms of multi-part singing in Africa. My investigations since 1960 have shown that this process is widespread and widely, though not universally, valid in African music. I have found it operative in the music of Malaŵi, northern Moçambique, Angola, Central African Republic and other countries.

In his ecclesiastical work *"Misa Baba Yetu"*, the Tanzanian composer Father Stephan Mbunga from Peramiho follows very closely the traditional harmonic patterns of the Lake Nyasa area. *"Misa Baba Yetu"*, published in 1959, is perhaps one of the most beautiful African masses ever composed. The *Gloria ("Utukufu kwa Baba mbinguni...")* is an especially lucid illustration of the harmonic pattern we have discussed (cf. Example 63).

Among the Wandendeule and others this system also embraces the possibility of transposition. In most songs of these peoples the tonal basis is the kind of pentatonic scale shown in Example 48. This can be used, however, in combination with a transposed form of itself, beginning a fifth lower. A five-note descending pattern $G - E - D - C - A$ is then combined with its transposed form $C - A - G - F - D$ to form an extended scale:

a) scalar patterns combined

b) resulting harmonic sounds

Ex. 49. "Hexatonic" extension of the "Lake Nyasa" pentatonic system

An important difference between this hexatonic extension and genuinely hexatonic systems as they are found in many other parts of Africa, is that there are still not more than five notes within one octave in either of the combining pitch-lines (see Ex. 49 b). The E and F notes are mutually exclusive; E occurs in the upper part of one voice and F in the lower part of the other. Often the F only appears in the closing phrase of a song. The song then ends on the lower G which is introduced by the F below it, resolving upwards, or by the simultaneous third F plus A.[9]

Various forms of "tonally bound" parallelism[10] in East African multi-part singing which have remained a riddle to observers can thus be explained by the fact, that harmony is obtained by the simultaneous singing of notes separated by one degree in the scale. I would like to call this procedure the <u>single skipping process</u>. Now it also becomes clear, why in so many types of multi-part singing in Africa there cannot be absolute parallelism in the intervals. If the skipping process is applied to the type of anhemitonic pentatonic scale found in the area of Lake Nyasa (Example 48 above), the inevitable result is a parallelism in perfect fourths interrupted in one place by a major third. This isolated third is structurally determined by the nature of this scale and it always occurs in the same place.

The application of the skipping process to the following mode of the anhemitonic pentatonic scale results in an absolute parallelism of fourths:

Ex. 50. Counter-note pattern in a pentatonic mode resulting in parallel fourths

Several communities in northern Zaïre and in the Central African Republic use a two-part harmonic singing style based on parallel fourths, for instance, the Karre, Buru and Manja, but also the Azande in some of their songs.[11]

If the single skipping process is applied to a heptatonic system the logical result is the appearance of chains of thirds; in a hexatonic system either thirds or alternating thirds and fourths, depending on the mode. In a diatonic heptatonic system of the kind which A. M. Jones has called "nature's own scale" (Jones 1959a) the result within a two-part harmonic singing style is alternating major and minor thirds. In an equiheptatonic system the simultaneous sounds would be neutral thirds. Abundant examples of two-part singing in parallel thirds occur in wide areas of Central Africa, especially in Zaïre, Cameroon, Angola, and Zambia. Two-part harmony with thirds chains can also be found in some music of the -Bemba (Zambia) studied by A. M. Jones (1959b).

Ex. 51. Application of the single skipping process to a diatonic seven-note scale

It is no accident that the same chains of thirds also occur split up melodically on instruments such as lamellophones and xylophones in those musical cultures which use a heptatonic system in combination with two-part harmony. In these cases the thirds melodies are mostly played in descending sequence. Gradually it becomes clear why in heptatonic systems the resulting harmony is so often in the form of parallel thirds, while in the pentatonic areas of Africa parallelism in fourths is common.

There is a fundamental correlation between tone systems and multi-part forms in the Central and East African culture areas. The explanation of this interdependence can be found in the common method of obtaining simultaneous sounds, which I have described above and which is valid across many different cultures in this part of Africa. I have proposed to call it the skipping process. Thus the different forms of homophonic multi-part singing we encounter in different regions within this broad East/Central Africa culture area simply result from the application of the same skipping process to different tone systems. The first hint leading to the discovery of this principle was the rigidity of the harmonic patterns I noted in south-western Tanzania and the Lake Nyasa area.

The knowledge of this organizing principle now makes it possible for us to understand the relationship between tone systems and multi-part forms in a new way. Since the two realms are related structurally and functionally, we can even reconstruct one from the other.

For instance, it is possible to deduce the exact layout of the scalar pattern, underlying the music of a given people from the kind of harmonic sounds which occur in the voice combinations of the singers or instrumentalists. It is even possible to discover the layout of a tone system by observing which substitute notes are used for melodic variation, because these notes too are often obtained by the same process.

Some More Multi-Part Patterns in Pentatonic Traditions

The following observations are based on my field-work in Central Tanzania among the Wagogo. Between January and May 1962 I visited the Wagogo several times in the company of the two members of my field-trip to East Africa, Helmut Hillegeist, Vienna, and Basilius Saprapason from Lupanga (Njombe District).[12] On these trips we were able to document Gogo music comprehensively on tape in both Dodoma and Manyoni Districts, where we visited many, often remote villages.[13]

Gogo music represents an elucidating case of multi-part organization. Some writers have described the harmonic part-singing style of the Wagogo as an "organum in fourths." A closer study of Gogo music reveals, however, that a completely different principle operates at the root of this music. Some harmonic sounds are so typical that Gogo music can be easily identified by ear. In songs and also in instrumental playing such as, for example, in the performances on the *ilimba* (lamellophone) the following harmonic cycle appears again and again; a descending two-part harmony, beginning with a fourth, followed by a diminished fifth and ending with a perfect fifth. With it the harmonic cycle reaches its conclusion:

I   II   III

Ex. 52. Harmonic style in Gogo music

Wherever we went in Gogo country, I was struck by the omnipresence of this harmonic cycle. It is found in *nindo, msunyunho,* in *ilimba* music and many other types. From Mvumi, south-east of Dodoma, where we were the guests of the late Chief Mazengo, up to the remote village of Iseke in Manyoni District this was as good as a hall-mark of Gogo music (CD I/15). What is the explanation of this ear-catching sequence of harmonious sounds in the music of the Wagogo? Is it just a "broken parallelism" or is there some coercive logic behind it?

From the evaluation of our recordings and measurements of the instrumental tunings it is evident that the use of natural harmonics is the formative element in the tone system of the Wagogo. Actually it is an extract of the harmonic series, basically the section from the 4th to the 8th partial, resulting in a tetratonic system. This "scale" is, however, often extended upwards to include the 9th partial (which we represent as D in staff notation) and occasionally even the 10th (E).

The nature of the Gogo tone-system can be seen in the following illustration. From the structure and the layout of the notes it is easy to explain how the famous Gogo chords come about:

Gogo tones:

Corresponding to partial No.:

Harmonic sounds obtained by application of the skipping process:

Ex. 53. The tone-system of the Wagogo

As in the music of the Wandendeule, Wapangwa, Wangoni and others in south-western Tanzania, the harmonic sounds are obtained by application of the skipping process. In the Gogo case, however, it is applied to a totally different "scale." The result is the harmonies shown in Exs. 52

and 53, above. The characteristic "diminished fifth" bi-chord results from one voice singing a note representing the 5th partial (E), while the other sings with the 7th partial, i.e. the flat B♭ of the harmonic series.

But why is the section from the 4th to the 8th, respectively to the 9th partial so attractive to the Gogo ear? Why do the Wagogo not make use in their music of the lower partials? The answer is that the melodically useful part of the natural harmonic series really begins with the 4th partial and continues upwards where the intervals become narrower. Partials 1 and 2 of the harmonic series form an octave, 2 and 3 a fifth, 3 and 4 a fourth on top of each other. Such large intervals, stretched out over the range of two octaves could not be used melodically to make songs.

Ill. 54. The *ilimba* (lamellophone) player Mirindi. Nondwa, central Tanzania, May 1962

The Gogo system is based on harmonics over a single fundamental. As we shall see later there are other musical cultures in Africa, especially where the musical bow comes into the picture, in which harmonics over two fundamentals became the formative element to constitute the tone system. Our notation of the Gogo notes with Western symbols is only an approximation. The Gogo tones do not exactly correspond with the respective notes on a Western tempered instrument, because the Western tones often deviate rather radically from natural harmonics. The "natural" major third formed by the 4th and 5th partials, for instance, is 386 cents wide, in contrast to the major third of 400 cents on a piano. Even greater is the difference between the B_b of the harmonic series (the 7th partial) and the minor seventh in the Western tempered system: it is no less than 31 cents, a very audible magnitude. By comparison with the tempered B_b of 1000 cents the Gogo B_b is only 969 cents wide.

The Gogo chords result logically from the application of the skipping process to the Gogo tone system, as shown in Ex. 53. A major characteristic is that the notes which fórm the scalar pattern underlying Gogo music are laid out in their original order as in the harmonic series. The 9th partial, represented by a D, maintains its position in the series and is not transposed an octave down to form a pentatonic tone-row in the lower octave. If it were transposed the resultant harmonic sounds would be entirely different from what we have shown in Exs. 52 and 53. The Gogo system thus represents the interesting case where the formative tone material is spread out over a range wider than an octave. The basic note C (4th partial) and the D (9th partial) of this "scale" form a ninth.

Accordingly, the D is only used in certain combinations. Normally it appears only melodically in the songs, but in the rare cases that it is used in multi-part singing, it is sung together with the B_b (the 7th partial). This results in the rare thirds heard in the Gogo harmonic system. If, at the same time the lower voices combine at the level of the 5th and 7th partials (E and B_b) a strange chord between the three voices results: $E - B_b - D$ (from bottom to top).

We have a recording of a *msunyunho* vocal performance from Iseke village, May 1962, where this voice combination can be heard. On that occasion, literally hundreds of men, holding herdsmen's sticks in their hands assembled to perform in the late evening. *Msunyunho* is danced when the millet and maize are ripe for harvest, usually in May. But it is also danced in January, if the rains have stopped, then it becomes a "cry for rain." There are two movements: the first consists of a chorus with long-held chordal harmony; the second is in a faster tempo and the men vocalize syllabic patterns, including the guttural *hrr hra*. This is called *kilumi*.[14]

Occasionally the Gogo system is extended to the 10th partial (an E). In vocal music this note is normally used melodically, as far as I could assess, and it appears in the leader's part. On the *izeze* (bowed lute) however, especially in the music of the two-string variety, I have also heard it used harmonically. Here the extended Gogo scale leads to the presence of one more simultaneous third of 368 cents. It arises not between the *izeze* notes themselves, but between the *izeze* part and the human voice (with a timbre quality very similar to that of the bowed lute).[15]

The voice sings below, the *izeze* line is on top. The chordal pattern regularly heard is shown in Example 54. The high-pitched C − E bi-chord between voice and *izeze* usually appears at the start of the theme. Characteristically, it is immediately followed by the other third we have already mentioned, the B♭ plus D combination (standing for partials 7 and 9). Gradually, the harmonic pattern continues, passing through the G plus C bichord, then through the "diminished fifth" (E plus B♭), finally reaching the point of rest (C plus G).

The extended tone system of the Wagogo and the resulting harmonic sounds in *izeze* music can be shown as follows:

Extended scale   Resulting harmonic sounds

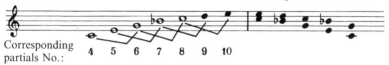

Corresponding partials No.: 4 5 6 7 8 9 10

Ex. 54. Extended tone system of the Wagogo

On further analysis it becomes evident that the inner structural order of the Gogo tone system and the resulting harmonic sounds are only two inseparable aspects of a structural whole. The Gogo harmonies, as we have described them, are actually only possible if what is shown in Exs. 53 and 54 is indeed the inner order and layout of the Gogo "scale." But there are also other traits in the musical practice of the Wagogo which support our thesis:

(1) the blowing of natural harmonics on horns;
(2) the use of yodelling in boys' *msunyunho* and other kinds of vocal music;
(3) the use of "over-tone" singing as a special vocal technique, as demonstrated by Hukwe Zawose;[16]
(4) the intonation in vocal music which clearly corresponds with the positions of partials 4 to 9;
(5) the tuning of musical instruments, especially the *ilimba* and the characteristic tuning layout of the notes revealing structural relationships.

We can analyse Gogo instrumental tunings. Here I should like to have a closer look at the tuning of a 23-note *ilimba* which I recorded in Ugogo in 1962. The measurements were kindly made by the Rev. Dr. A. M. Jones with a Stroboconn at the School of Oriental and African Studies, London. The frequencies were sent to me, as we agreed, without comment. The interpretation of these data is entirely my own.

The *ilimba* (Kigogo term), which is also known as *malimba* or *marimba* in Tanzania, is a lamellophone with a rather large rectangular wooden box resonator. In some organological features it seems to be related to Zaïrean box-resonated types but in others it differs from them. The Gogo instrument has many more lamellae than the Zaïrean box-resonated models that were popular along the trade routes from Ujiji (at Lake Tanganyika) into Zaïre towards the end of the 19th century. In 1962 I saw instruments with 18, 22, 23, 33 and 36 metal notes. Varying numbers of lamellae are used for the Gogo *ilimba* (CD I/16).

Gogo lamellophones have a sound hole in the centre of the front side of the resonating box and a second one on the top side (pointing away from the musician). These are covered with the membrane of a spider's cocoon, i.e. a spider's nest covering as found in local houses, which is glued on. When one strikes the lamellae, especially the long ones, their vibration is sympathetically resonated by these mirlitones and the result is a louder buzzing sound. There is a third sound-hole on the back of the resonator box within reach of the left middle finger. This is the vibrato and sound modification hole. By alternately opening and closing it the player can modify the sound spectrum of whatever note he is striking. This device is found on most lamellophones in Tanzania, from those on the coast to the small *malimba* types of the Wapangwa, Wabena, Wakisi, Wanyakyusa and other peoples in the south-western highlands and at Lake Nyasa.

Wagogo musicians play with the thumbs. The notes are divided into three areas, one each for the left and right hand thumbs, and in the centre a section consisting of a series of shortish lamellae with high-pitched tuning. These are never used for playing. They function as reference notes in the tuning process and also vibrate sympathetically when the other lamellae are struck. Actually their number varies in individual instruments, but our player here had five. The player was Mirindi, then ca. 25 years old, an expert on the *ilimba,* whose acquaintance we made at Nondwa village in Manyoni District.

According to Mirindi the central tone and point of departure for the tuning process of his *ilimba* was lamella No. 10. This is the lowest (longest) of the five reference lamellae in the centre of the instrument. I have written it as C in the following illustration showing the layout of Mirindi's tuning and related all the other notes to this keynote in accordance with the structure of the Gogo tone system.

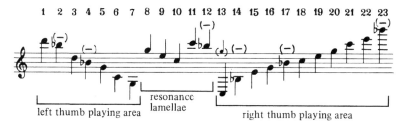

Ex. 55. The tuning of the 23 lamellae of Mirindi's *ilimba* with playing areas

The measurement of the 23 *ilimba* notes is shown in the following Table 6. Column 1 identifies the lamellae with their number as in Example 55 above. They are written in order from the highest (smallest) to the lowest (biggest) note. Column 2 shows the frequencies in Hertz (c.p.s.), Column 3 the cents intervals. A last column shows the cents values building up within one octave (cumulative cents), a method which makes the actual position of each note within the octave visible (cf. also Jones 1971 b).

In a note the Reverend A. M. Jones sent me on May 10, 1963, together with the c.p.s. of various of my tunings he pointed to the possibility that the fundamental tones of some lamellophone notes may be so weak, that "the Stroboconn registers quite plainly what must be their 3rd or 4th harmonic. From this one can easily calculate the v.p.s. of the fundamental..." Though Jones did not refer to Mirindi's instrument particularly, I think that the Stroboconn must have registered the 6th harmonic with lamella No. 13, for which Jones gave me the value of 613.3 c.p.s. This was, however, the longest and quite obviously the deepest note of Mirindi's instrument. It was tuned to a (relative) C, two octaves below the central tone of No. 10. With earphones on one can hear it in the recording of the tuning, but the high note (G) registered by the Stroboconn is absolutely dominant.[17]

According to my calculation the fundamental of lamella No. 13 is 102.2 c.p.s., forming a fifth of 691 cents with the next note, lamella No. 7. In the Table 6, following, I have used the calculated value for this note.

Number of lamellae	Hertz	Cents	Cumulative Cents
23.	1478.6		1040
22.	976.4	721	319
1.	925.6	91	228
21.	813.6	223	5
11.	806	17	1188
12.	719	198	990
2.	712.8	15	975
20.	618.5	244	731
8.	589.6	83	648
19.	508	259	389
9.	507	4	385
3.	457.2	179	206
10.	406.4	206	0
18.	405.2	4	1196
17.	355.8	223	973
4.	354.5	5	968
5.	305	263	705
16.	303.3	11	694
15.	251.5	319	375
6.	203.3	375	0
14.	175.3	256	944
7.	152.2	244	700
13.	102.2	691	9

Table 6

In the following Table 7 the tuning of this *ilimba,* covering more than three octaves, is expressed in cumulative cents related to the pitch of 0 (lamella No. 10), and compared with the cents values of the "scale" given by harmonics Nos. 4 to 9.

Notes of the harmonic series expressed in Cents (Nos. 4–9)	Ilimba notes (Unisons are shown on the same line)	
	Lamella No.	Cents
969	23	1040
702	–	–
386	22	319
204	1	228
0	21,11	5 1188
969	12,2	990 975
702	20,8	731 648
386	19,9	389 385
204	3	206
0	10,18	0 1196
969	17,4	973 968
702	5,16	705 694
386	15	375
204	–	–
0	6	0
969	14	944
702	7	700
0	13	9

Table 7

A comparison of the *ilimba* notes with the respective partials of the harmonic series (cf. Tables 6 and 7) reveals a convincing correspondence. Quite obviously Mirindi was a musician who tuned his instrument carefully. The central tone (lamella No. 10) is tuned to 406.4 v.p.s. on this particular *ilimba*. Since it is the starting point in the tuning process I have given it the number 0 in the column of cumulative cents. Going from this keynote and calculating the intervals to the other notes in cents, we see that lamellae Nos. 5 (705 cents), 7 (700 cents) and 16 (694 cents) are tuned in perfect fifths. The thirds, i.e. lamellae Nos. 9 (385 cents), 15 (375 cents) and 19 (389 cents) correspond almost ideally to the cents values of 386 for the 5th partial of the harmonic series. The crucial low B_b of the harmonic series (969 cents) is well represented in the tunings of lamellae Nos. 2 (975 cents), 4 (968 cents) and 17 (973 cents) and less accurately in No. 12 (990 cents) and No. 14 (944 cents). None of these lamellae is tuned to 1000 cents as in the Western scale.

Of the 23 notes on Mirindi's lamellophone only three are considerably out of tune. Characteristically, these are the two highest ones (lamellae Nos. 22 and 23) which is not surprising in view of the remote position of these lamellae on the instrument; they may easily have slipped out of their extreme positions during playing. The third one is No. 8 which is 54 cents out of tune. It is one of the "reference notes" in the centre of the instrument never used by the musician in musical performances. The likely explanation is that Mirindi did not retune the reference notes before his recording with us, since they are not used for playing.

A conceptualized identity of the *ilimba* pitches with partials 4–9 of the harmonic series (duplicated in the various octaves) is obvious. This is suggested both by the choice of specific intervals in the tuning procedure, as well as the logic behind the layout of the notes on the instrument (cf. Ex. 55). The absence of the D (representing the 9th partial) in the deep register further confirms it. Actually this marginal note is only found in two places on Mirindi's instrument. All the other notes appear duplicated from 4 to 6 times within a range of more than three octaves. This confirms my impression gathered earlier from the analysis of Gogo vocal music that the Gogo tone system is basically tetratonic. The note D widens this system into a pentatonic scale, but it is something like the tip of a pyramid, only hesitantly accepted and, because of its upper position in the harmonic series, not represented in the deep register of the instrument.

From Example 55 showing Mirindi's tuning in staff notation we can also see that the five reference notes in the centre actually represent the Gogo tone system in its nuclear structure. Significantly they are divided into two groups (rising from right to left): C, E, G and B_b, C. If we write them on top of each other we obtain the famous Gogo chords G C and

E B♭, I have shown in Example 52 above. The reference lamellae reveal the inner plan of the Gogo tone system, of which the actual tunings are only a replica. It is also significant that the note D is absent in the reference notes.

The Wagogo are not the only people in Tanzania who make use of the natural harmonic series. There are indications that the Wakisi, a people of potters and fishermen settled on the northeast bank of Lake Nyasa do so as well, at least in one musical type, though much of their music is influenced by the pentatonic harmonies prevailing round Lake Nyasa. In some songs of the Wakisi and in tunings of the *malimba* lamellophone, such as we recorded at Lupingu, the notes plainly correspond in their layout and cents figures to the partials 5–11 of the harmonic series (notes: E – G – B♭ – C – D – E – F₊). It seems that the 11th partial (a note between F and F sharp) is also present in the tuning of a *mangwilo* log xylophone we recorded from expert players among the Ashirima of northern Moçambique (Kubik 1965c:39).

In 1964 I became acquainted with another region where comparable pentatonic systems are used: in the area of Fort Rousset, in the northern part of the Republic of Congo. In the village of Ihuda, on the road from Liweso ("Liouesso") to Makua ("Makoua"), not far from the river ferry of Yengo, I recorded Victor Opombo, ca. 25, a player of the notched-bridge stick-zither *ŋgɔmbi*. This musician belonged to an ethnic group known as the Makua.[18] His instrument was tuned pentatonically. The melodic line of his solo voice was in unison relationship with the instrumental basis. However, in the instrumental playing itself he sometimes used harmonic bi-chords. Here a diminished fifth occurred again and again.[19]

Example 64 gives a condensed transcription of the instrumental part, played at high speed. It shows the short theme and one melodic variation. The "counter-note principle" in this music is not very difficult to detect. The kind of variation used by the musician and the presence of a diminished fifth bi-chord also give us a clue.

Actually, the pentatonic system of this Makua musician is also inspired by the natural harmonic series, and it makes use of partials 4–9. However, the resultant bi-chords and melodic exchange notes in the variations are different here from those in Gogo music, because of the different layout of the notes which constitute this system. As in the preceding examples, counter-notes are obtained by the skipping process:

Ex. 56. Counter-note pattern in a pentatonic system from Congo based on harmonics

Although the Makua musician Victor Opombo from Congo and Wagogo musicians of Tanzania obviously use the same tonal material, based
on the recognition and selection of partials 4–9 of the natural harmonic
series to constitute their tone systems, we have two structurally different
pentatonic systems before us. In the Makua case the 9th partial, written
as D in Ex. 56, is integrated into the scale by octave transposition. It is
transposed an octave down from its position in the harmonic series. The
result, and most likely the motivation behind it, is to form a real scale in
which all the constituent notes should be contained within the limit of
one octave. This kind of layout with all its structural consequences marks
the fundamental difference between the system of our Makua musician
and the Gogo system. The Gogo "scale" is only pentatonic in the sum-
mation of its constituent notes, but it is not a pentatonic "scale" in the
strict sense of the word, because the series exceeds the range of one
octave. In its fundamental structure it is tetratonic with a rather cautious-
ly annexed fifth note. In the tuning of the Makua stick-zither, on the
other hand, the note representing the 9th partial has become a firmly
integrated part of the system, sharing equal right with the other notes.
The result is a scalar-type note series which no longer corresponds to the
order of the harmonic series. From the Makua layout of the same tones
there arises a multi-part structure which must be different from that of
the Wagogo.

In my 1964 field notes to Example 64 there is a sketch of the instrument which I have reproduced here (see transcriptions) with the tuning
of the strings given in staff notation. The musician's right hand controls
the notes C, E, G, B♭ (relative notation) in rising order as they move away
from the musician's body. These notes correspond in their intervals and
layout with the order of partials 4, 5, 6, and 7 in the natural harmonic
series. The continuation of the row is found in the left hand playing area
in which the strings are tuned to B♭, D, E and G. These notes are,
however, transposed down one octave to form an integrated scale between left and right hand notes. The highest note in the right hand area
(B♭) reappears in the left hand, an octave lower, followed by the tone D,
the transposed 9th partial, and by E and G which duplicate the right
hand notes of the same pitches.

Melodic variation also follows the counter-note principle resulting
from the skipping process. It is not possible, in the music of Central and
East Africa, to use any arbitrary note from the tone material for melodic
variation. Variation follows an exchange procedure, and in certain traditions that are oriented towards harmonic sound,[20] the exchange notes
are often identical with the harmonic counter-notes. This holds true for
both vocal and instrumental performance. Only occasionally, in these
traditions, is this principle broken by melodic anticipations, passing

notes or held notes, mainly in vocal music and in the melodic variations of a leading instrument within an ensemble.

Thus from the skipping process result both the harmonic counter-notes and the exchange notes in melodic variation. In the transcription (Ex. 64) we can see how Victor Opombo, in varying the short theme he plays on his stick-zither, exchanges one D for a G and the lower B♭ for a D. These are the only possible exchange notes he can find in his left-hand playing area. As is obvious from a quick glance at the scale shown in Ex. 56 above, these variant notes are motivated by the counter-note scheme.

From merely observing the layout of the notes on African instruments, such as zithers, stick-zithers and lamellophones, it is possible to predict the likely counter-note scheme ruling the music concerned and reach tentative conclusions about the structure of the tone system because the counter-notes must be within reach of the fingers. An important distinction arises, however, between unison style, in which only melodic exchange notes are used, and harmonic style, with extensive use of simultaneous sounds.

In order to retain the motor image unchanged in the player's variations (which is an important principle in African music) melodic exchange notes are found in the same playing area of the layout, while harmonic counter-notes are found in the opposite playing area. The latter include octaves. Exceptions are found in playing styles where one finger strikes two notes at once, or where four fingers are used for playing, thumb and index fingers of both hands, as in the lamellophone music of the Tikar of central Cameroon.

Since the same notes in multi-part music may be used harmonically in one context and as melodic exchange notes in another, one can often find them duplicated in the different playing areas of an instrument. This is the case, for example, in the tuning of the stick-zither of Victor Opombo (cf. Example 64), where identical notes (E and G) occur in the left and right hand playing areas.

From the above discussion alone it is evident how different structurally the various pentatonic "scales" in Central and East Africa must be. African pentatonic systems – this is only an omnibus notion. Cross-regional comparisons based on the number of notes in an octave are, therefore, not always conclusive, and sometimes even misleading. As to pentatonic systems I have been able, so far, to trace the following important types:

(1) Near-equidistant or "slendro-type" pentatonic scales.

These seem to be concentrated in Uganda among the Baganda and Basoga, for instance, and in some parts of northern and north-western

Central Africa, for instance among the Gbaya, Manja and in some music of the Central African Republic. It is significant, that people usually sing in unison and octaves with instruments tuned in such a manner.

(2) Pentatonic systems resulting from the use of a section of the natural harmonic series over one fundamental.

Whatever actual forms may occur the hall-mark of these systems is the occurrence of a diminished fifth interval $(E-B_b)$ and bi-chord in a certain place of the tonal/harmonic pattern. It represents the jump from the 5th to the 7th harmonic (leaving out the 6th by the skipping process). In these systems the spectrum of natural harmonics is exploited as far as the 9th partial, sometimes as far as the 10th (which is the octave of the 5th). We have enlisted the Wagogo of Tanzania and the Makua of the Peoples' Republic of Congo as examples of ethnic communities where this may be found.

(3) The so-called anhemitonic pentatonic scale.

It is based on the recognition of perfect fourths. Alternating intervals in seconds and minor thirds characterize this system. The notes are not audibly different from those in Western music sounding from the black keys of a piano. Consequently, songs in this system can be represented with acceptable results in staff notation. The ethnic groups using such a pentatonic system often have a two-part harmonic organization of their vocal music. The prevalent feature of the pattern of simultaneous sound arising from this scale is consecutive fourths with an isolated major third recurring in a well-defined place. This kind of tonal/harmonic system is found among peoples all around Lake Nyasa (Lake Malaŵi), but also among the Nguni peoples of South Africa, from where it may have been brought to the Lake Nyasa area with the Ngoni migration in the second half of the 19th century. The Lake Nyasa group includes among others the Wapangwa, Wandendeule, Wakisi on the Tanzanian side, and in Malaŵi all communities who were affected by the Ngoni invasions, i.e. the -Tumbuka especially, but also various -Nyanja groups. Ultimately the "anhemitonic" pentatonic scale in these parts of southern Africa could have been inspired by musical bow harmonics such as produced on the *mqangala* mouth-bow (South Africa) and its derived versions known as *nkangala* in southern Malaŵi and *mtyangala* on the Tanzanian lake shore. Mouth-bow players, who are always women in this culture area, use two fundamentals about a whole-tone apart. Amplifying partials 3, 4 and 5 over fundamental I and (only) 3 and 4 over fundamental II results in tonal material identical with the "anhemitonic" pentatonic scale.

Mouth-Bow Harmony and Multi-Part Organization

There are regions in Africa where a closed system of melody, harmony and counterpoint emerges from characteristic traits in the playing of the mouth-bow. Percival R. Kirby, as is well-known, has pointed out on several occasions the interdependence of tone systems and the recognition of bow harmonics in the music of Khoisan speakers and South Africans who speak Bantu languages (Kirby 1934, 1961). It seems that something similar may also have happened in some areas of West-Central Africa. An essential difference, however, between mouth-bow generated tone systems and others based on the recognition of harmonics per se, like that of the Wagogo in Tanzania, is that the former are built on harmonics over two fundamentals, as against one in the latter.

In West-Central Africa (Gabon, Congo etc.) the harmonic spectrum is mostly used up to the 6th partial of both fundamentals, giving tonal material which forms a hexatonic system. The mouth-bow used by the Fang' in Gabon called *beŋ,* is an example (CD I/17).

The bow is quickly made. The string-bearer is cut from a tree branch and bent in the form of a parabola. At its ends a tape-shaped string is attached; it is cut from the little stem of the liana palm known as *oncocalamus* (bot.). The musician holds his musical bow diagonally when playing. His mouth is positioned near the right end of the string. The string passes very close in front of the mouth cavity. With his left hand the bow player holds the string-bearer and a short stick with which he stops the string from time to time. The stopping point divides the string to give two fundamentals approximately a whole-tone apart.

Fang' musicians make extensive use of the technique of forming melodies from the partials appearing on a musical bow. By increasing or decreasing the mouth cavity the musician reinforces those harmonics he wants to come out prominently. The result is that one can clearly hear melodic phrases above the two basic notes. Fang' players go relatively high up in their use of partials, actually as far as the 6th harmonic. The result gives hexatonic tone material in the bow music. It consists of the two fundamentals and their harmonics up to the 6th partial.

Ex. 57. Tone material of the mouth bow among the Fang' (Gabon) arising from harmonics over a two-note bass tuned a whole-tone apart (cf. CD I/17)

A short analysis of a cult song accompanied with the *beŋ,* recorded at a syncretist church in a Fang' community in Gabon (cf. Example 65) shows: The singers follow the notes of the bow and sing in the same hexatonic system. From this tone material the musical bow player forms the song. The actual "melody" of the song is drawn from partials 4-6 of the higher fundamental, and partials 5-6 of the lower one.[21]

On the musical bow the pitch lines made up by harmonics and fundamentals (the latter reinforced by the strong 2nd partial) behave like a harmonic counterpoint in which all types of motion are possible: parallel, oblique and contrary. This counterpoint can be heard clearly during the solo bow interludes between the sung sections.[22]

The harmonic counterpoint of the singers is identical with that of the musical bow. The "counter-note principle" results in this case from the two "chordal blocks" produced by the musical bow (cf. Example 57

Ill. 55. Mouth-bow *(beŋ)* playing among the Fang'. The performer seen in this picture is André Mvome, the priest of a syncretist religious community known as Angome-Ebogha (friendship of the *ibɔyɔ* hallucinogene). Oyem (Gabon), July 1964

Ill. 56. While the mouth-bow represents the male principle in the cosmogony of the Angome-Ebogha religious community, the *ŋgɔmbi* eight-string harp represents the female; the harp held in this illustration by the priest André Mvome in front of the cult-house is considered the "home" of the female spirit called Nyiŋgɔn-möböɣə (*"Esprit Consolateur"*). The tuning of the harp is hexatonic and is probably related to the mouth-bow harmonics. The Fang' harps fall in Klaus Wachsmann's category III (shelved-type) in his classification of African harps. (cf. Introduction). Oyem (Gabon), July 1964

above). Only notes within each of the two blocks can occur simultaneously to form harmonic sounds or be interchanged in melodic variation. The singers follow this principle strictly. Thus the notes we have transcribed as C, E and G can combine or substitute for each other. The same applies to B_b, D and F. Since there are two possible counter-notes for each tone in this harmonic system, the voice movement in the sung parts is not rigidly determined, but is variable. Each singer always has a choice between two notes, both being correct. This approach to variation can be noticed both in the playing of the bow and in the vocal parts.

The song *"Nan' engongol!"* transcribed here begins with a short instrumental introduction in which the theme is presented. Then the female soloist and the responding chorus enter. The members of the chorus follow the bow melody at any octave level suitable to their voices. In several places the vocal parts branch into bi-chords (thirds). The formation of melodic variants is an important trait. There is no three-part harmony in this style. Even outside the context of bow music, I have found little tendency towards three-part singing among the Fang'. The same song as played on the musical bow is also performed on the sacred harp called *ŋgɔmbi.* [23]

Multi-Part Organization in Heptatonic Traditions

We have seen in several earlier examples how widespread the skipping process is as a structural principle in the formation of simultaneous sounds, and how it enabled us to explain chordal patterns and melodic variations which would otherwise have remained unexplained. Tonal systems derived from mouth-bow harmonics also form part of this picture. A diagram of the tonal material used on the *beŋ* (mouth bow) which also coincides with the tuning of the eight-string *ŋgɔmbi* (harp), reveals that all the sounds that can go together are spaced one apart.

The skipping process could generally be explained as the result of a scalar layout of the harmonic columns over two fundamentals except that this process also determines the simultaneous sounds in some traditions where harmonics are derived from one fundamental, as among the Wagogo.

But what happens in heptatonic traditions with that kind of lush chordal harmony in three parts, characteristic of so many areas of West Central Africa? In African music three-part harmony does not usually occur within pentatonic systems, but was found in almost half of the hexa- and heptatonic musical cultures in my earliest recorded sample (1959–1966) from eleven East and Central African countries (cf. Kubik 1968 c : 11–26). It is possible to explain why this is so.

Two-part harmony requires only one skipped note, i.e. via a single application of the skipping process in one direction. In three-part singing styles two notes must be skipped, applying the skipping process twice (in two directions). Such is the case in many heptatonic traditions in Central Africa. In pentatonic traditions it would not give acceptable results in most cases, because it would lead to two superimposed fourths, e.g. a chord consisting of D + G + C. This seems to have little musical appeal to the peoples in the areas concerned. The -Henga people (a -Tumbuka subgroup) in Malaŵi are the only community in my earliest recorded sample in which I have found a pentatonic system with occasional three-part harmony. In several songs performed by the prophet and healer Chikanga Chunda and the crowds of people he attracted to Thete village near Rumphi in June 1962, there were three-part harmonic progressions from an A – D – G chord to G – C – E, occasionally even to A – C – E.[24]

In a heptatonic system the application of the skipping process in two directions inevitably leads to a chain of triads. This is shown in the following schema:

Double skipping process   Resultant tri-chords

Ex. 58. The bi-directional skipping process and the resulting triads

Among heptatonic groups the double skipping process opens up a new dimension for harmonic-melodic organization. Now each singer has two counter-notes at his disposal. To the A of one singer a second vocalist can sing either F or the high C (compare Ex. 58). If the first singer arrives at G, the second one can sing either E or B and so on. Thus the individual singer has a choice. The consequence is less rigid shaping of the individual voice lines than we found in the pentatonic traditions of East Africa, and the possibility of improvisational variation in the voice parts.

One of the most impressive areas of heptatonic multi-part singing may be encountered in the north of the Republic of Congo, among ethnic groups such as the Bakota and Bongili (cf. recordings Orig. Tape No. 57/II at Mekome, a few kilometers south of Liweso, Congo; cf. short extract on CD I/18). These peoples sing in three to four parts in clusters of triads in a system that is apparently diatonic. This heptatonic system is probably derived from a hexatonic background rooted in mouth-bow harmonies, but extended to include a seventh note.

Of course, "African heptatonic tone systems" is as much an omnibus notion as is "pentatonic systems" and there are several structurally different types which have little to do with each other, as for example, the heptatonic "scales" of the Wanyamwezi in Tanzania,[25] the -Chopi in Moçambique[26] and the Luo in Kenya.[27] But there is reason to assume that one large group of heptatonic systems, particularly in West-Central Africa (Gabon, Congo, western Zaïre and Angola) has remote hexatonic origins.

Depending on various factors operating in the wider conceptual realm of a musical culture, the introduction of a seventh note into an originally hexatonic system can give rise to conflicts. It may put singers and instrumentalists into a dilemma, and is therefore not rarely referred to as an "outlaw" in local musical theories.[28] While a mouth-bow generated harmonic system based on two fundamentals, F and G, with their harmonic columns $F - A - C / G - B - D$, allows singers to enjoy the euphony of these sound clusters, the introduction of yet another third on top of the $F - A - C$ chord,[29] namely $F - A - C - E$, leads to the concept of a diatonic scale and thereby, of diatonic modality.

While such a development probably came about in areas like northern Congo (Bongili, Bakota etc.) without any stimulus from Western music, there is evidence that in many other areas of West-Central Africa, diatonic modality had not become an accepted regulator of chordal progression.

In these areas harmonic sensitivity is basically conditioned towards accepting only major triads as the standard euphony-generating simultaneous sounds, perpetuating the cultural memory of the musical bow harmonies. In multi-part singing the vocalists' basic concept is then to maintain those lush sounds throughout the scalar system. This is, however, impossible to do from the moment it has been cracked by a seventh note. The behavioural consequences which resulted from this conflict and provided the second option for a harmonic style in a heptatonic system (besides the Bongili/Bakota solution) can be described as follows:

(1) Vocal themes began to proceed increasingly by steps until they rarely exceeded the range of a fifth or sixth in total compass;

(2) To avoid the "minor chords" that would inevitably arise by shifting the triads, for instance to the step created by the intruding seventh note (E), singers gradually learned to make constant adjustments of intonation.

The result was nothing less than a "temperament" with the crucial third neutralised in many places. Foreign observers have reacted to the kinds of tonal/harmonic systems found in West-Central Africa and in several areas along the Guinea Coast (West Africa) in a characteristic manner. A historical description of the impression made upon a visitor with a background in European classical music can be found in Pechuël-Loesche 1907:115. The author also gives transcriptions which may be reinterpreted on the basis of our present-day knowledge. They refer to the music of the Loango Coast, in particular to the Bafioti. Obviously the Bafioti used a non-modal heptatonic system in three-part harmony. However, this was a bewildering experience for Pechuël-Loesche and, like many others before and after him,[30] Pechuël-Loesche reacted with perceptual disorientation.

> But closer attention teaches us that the voices, entering at different pitches, move parallel on the average, and that chords formed of tones proper to the scale play the major role. ... Since most of the pieces lack any strict organisation, the performers don't keep them firmly in their memory. ... They enter wrong, feel

for the sounds, slide here and there, take up tempo rubato, drop to intermediate tones which we can't even write in staff... This results in a mixture between oscillations, pleasant chord sequences, horrible discords, such as one may hear at home in village inns and spinning-rooms. Precisely because of this undecidedness of the singers, it often remains doubtful whether a piece is to be taken in major or minor. These people seem to be indifferent to modality. Therefore one cannot rightly say whether minor is a misconceived major or the reverse. For hours the same phrase sounds now like this, now like that and also, as already mentioned, divergent in tone sequence and melodic accent to such an extent, that one really doesn't know what one should write down.[31]

Eastern Angola is a good demonstration area for heptatonic multipart singing in a style that is perhaps comparable to what Pechuël-Loesche heard on the Loango Coast at the turn of the century: the musical cultures of the -Chokwe, -Luvale and various peoples belonging to the so-called Ngangela group (-Luchazi, -Mbwela, -Nkhangala etc.).

Ex. 59. Extract from the chorus part of the song *"Chiyongoyongo neza"* (Chiyongoyongo has come). Orig. Tape No. 63/I/3 a, at Sakateke village, north of Kwitu-Kwanavale, Kwando-Kuvangu Province, south-eastern Angola, August 1965 (cf. CD I/19)

Our example, the song *"Chiyongoyongo neza"* (CD I/19) in a three-part harmonic style, comes from a concentrated area of hexa/heptatonic systems: Kwandu-Kuvangu Province in south-eastern Angola. It is only performed in the secluded lodge of a *mukanda* boys' circumcision school. Men and youths from the village form a circle together with the *tundanda* (initiates) round the fire inside the lodge and sing this kind of song in impressive multi-part heptatonic harmony, often all night long.

In their hands are secret instruments: concussion sticks called *mingongi*. Some of the men also play vertical wooden slats *(tutanga)*. Two groups form, combining their stick patterns in a 2 against 3 relationship. Chiyongoyongo is a person who thinks very much. This kind of song is an ancient heritage in the area and often the text is not fully understood by the present generation.

As seen in staff notation (Ex. 59) the chorus part of the song starts off with what is clearly parallel perfect fifths between the two voices forming the framework, i.e. the highest (Voice I) and the lowest (Voice III). The lowest voice then moves up stepwise in contrary motion, resulting in a major third (F − A) over the text syllable *-z'e* in bar 4. If this were a Western song in the diatonic system the two lines would logically end on a minor third (D − F) over *-lo* in bar 6, but in Mbwela music this is not acceptable. All the lines end on a neutral third with the upper voices fluctuating – in Western notation – somewhere between F and F sharp.

This is a description by comparison. Intraculturally, there is of course no notion of sharps let alone of "neutral thirds" as against "major thirds." This is the crux of the matter. Mbwela auditory perception aims at standard intervals that Western-educated observers would describe as thirds and fifths, but Vambwela informants as three voice levels coming together in "agreement" *(kwivwasyana)*. In practice, however, the thirds fluctuate anywhere between ca. 320 and 390 cents and they are unconsciously adjusted according to context. This is measurable and therefore also a kind of reality. Obviously the basic aim in this multi-part singing style is to achieve a euphonic overall effect while maintaining a heptatonic division of the octave. In other words, the voices must come together in a harmonious manner and in their combination there must not be more than seven notes in the octave. Actually, in many songs the individual voices moving by step do not even exceed a fifth.

The basic concepts within this system of multi-part singing can be summarized as follows:

(1) The tone material within the octave (1200 cents) is hexa- to heptatonic without any fixed modality.

(2) One voice on its own does not fully exploit the range of an octave, but usually moves within the range of a fourth or fifth, in some cases a little more.

(3) All voice movement is predominantly by step and downward.

(4) The objective of the multi-part combination of voices is euphony: a full-sounding, harmonious, mostly three-part combination of voices in intervals which are perceived as consonant.

(5) Intervals called fifths, fourths, octaves and thirds in Western music are perceived as consonant by the singers. While the fourths and fifths seem to be intoned close to their "natural" sizes of 498 and 702

cents, the thirds fluctuate between "neutral" thirds of about 340 cents and "natural" major thirds of theoretically 386 cents, which are 14 cents narrower than the tempered thirds used in present-day Western music. These values are measurable.

(6) Singers aim at consonant sounds of this kind on all steps (or degrees) of the melodic lines.

(7) However, since this is not structurally possible in any heptatonic system, be it "equiheptatonic" (with a standard interval of ca. 171 cents) or diatonic (with major and minor thirds) the singers have to correct their intonation, expecially at points where sounds are held on. Thus the impression of euphony and equivalence of harmonic sounds can be maintained throughout as much as possible.

(8) For a Western observer the thirds, which are the crux of the system, appear to be "unstable" in many places. From the singers' viewpoint on the other hand, this comment is irrelevant.

(9) Another implicit concept of this multi-part musical system is linearity, i.e. each voice exists in its own right, though at the same time there remains the perspective of simultaneous vertical sound (see above). All participants sing the same text, but their melodic lines are not parallel throughout, as might be expected from the tonal inflections of the language. On the contrary, oblique and counter-movement is consciously employed in order to emphasize the individuality of each participating voice. Contrary motion is not always perceptible in recordings because the voices merge with one another. In practice an individual singer in the group can change the direction of his melodic line whenever he likes. The desired chords are guaranteed, because nearly all movement from one harmonic combination to the next goes by steps. From the viewpoint of the Vambwela vocalists it is of little importance, therefore, whether a singer proceeds up or down to the next chord. He will inevitably land on one of the correct notes. An individual singer can also string together several variants of his voice part successively along the time-line. In *"Chiyongoyongo..."*[32] for instance, there are dozens of simultaneous variants possible and each is perceived as correct. This leads to a very lively style of variation, in which each individual voice is conceived to be linear and independent while contributing to the euphonic whole.

Where the precepts of tonal languages permit it – and this is the case in eastern Angola – we can thus find a kind of multi-part singing which transcends the "parallel harmony," so often described by authors as typical of one or the other African style. The multi-part singing style of the peoples of eastern Angola, including the -Mbwela, -Luchazi, -Chokwe, -Luvale and others is only parallel in theory. The creation of harmonic sounds is accomplished within a relatively loose combination of individual voices, fluctuating between triads, bichords and more or less dense accumulations of notes. The exact shape of the chords, the duplication and omissions of individual notes in the total pattern may change with every repetition.

The Mbwela/Luvale/Chokwe solution to the challenge of a multi-part harmonic style in combination with a heptatonic tone system is the second of several possible solutions. A third is the use of harmonic clusters built over roots that are a semitone apart. This creates a kind of pseudo-chromatism probably inspired by mouth-bow tunings with fundamentals a semi-tone apart and harmonics reinforced up to the 6th partial. My example is Mpyɛmɔ music, to be accurate one specific genre of it, namely *sya* story songs.

Mpyɛmɔ (in the literature also "Mbimou," "Mbimo" etc.) is the self-appellation of a small, Bantu language speaking people of forest agriculturalists in the south-western corner of the Central African Republic. Maurice Djenda (cf. 1966/67, 1968 b and c) and I carried out an extensive research programme in that area in 1964 and 1966, particularly on oral literature and its connection with music.[33]

Mpyɛmɔ musical culture is a synthesis of several styles and converging influences from neighbouring peoples such as the Bangombe pygmies on one side and the Gbaya on the other, speakers of a I.A.6 (Adamawa-Eastern) language. More than one tone system is used. Some musical instruments, for example the *kembe* box-resonated lamellophone – a 20th-century import from Congo – are tuned equi-pentatonically with no simultaneous sounds besides octaves in the music. On the other hand various types of vocal music sung in the Gbaya language show strict parallel fourths, while yet other types of songs are polyphonic with yodel, demonstrating the assimilation of a pygmy musical style.

During my first visit to the area in 1964 I recorded songs with a specific harmonic style exclusively found in *sya* chantefables. Later in 1966 Djenda and I recorded 51 such stories systematically, some of them lasting over an hour. The extraordinary length of *sya* stories is due to the constant interruption of the narrative by songs that do not actually belong to the particular story, but merely serve, in the informants' words, "to prolong the session." These songs come from the bulk of the *sya* chantefables of which several hundred exist.

Mpyɛmɔ vocal music is characterized by parallelism in strict intervals and the *sya* songs are no exception. However, some of them are remarkably different from other Mpyɛmɔ vocal traditions in that their harmony moves in major thirds over a semi-tone root progression. Chord clusters going higher up than major thirds can even be built, as some of our recordings demonstrate (CD I/20).

(a) two voices in
parallel major thirds

(b) three voices in
major triads a semitone apart

II   I   I   II

Ex. 60. *Mpyɛmɔ* harmonic core based on semitone roots (as in some *ṣya* story songs (cf. CD I/20)

The use of narrow intervals (tones and semi-tones) in combination with strict parallelism in major thirds creates a dilemma of course, even if the semi-tone appears at the bottom of the voice lines. From the moment parallel major thirds are rigidly transposed by steps, going only one degree beyond roots I and II, already introduces a note alien to the system.[34]

Another important characteristic of this type of *ṣya* songs is that melodies move within a relatively narrow compass, rarely more than a fifth. But within the interval of the fifth (cf. Example 66) there are definitely only five different notes, not more. Each individual voice sticks to that. Parallel major thirds on three degrees of the scale then result in a "chromatic" alternative to one note: E♭ versus E in the resultant image of the two voices in the chorus. This does not disturb the individual members of the chorus of course, because each individual singer still has no more than five notes within the fifth. But for the lead singer it does pose a problem. While the chorus conceptualise their voices as duplications of the same melody (in octaves and major thirds) at absolutely identical intervals and are happy with it, the lead singer, whose melodic line has its own identity, must sing in tune with their resultant harmonic pattern.

Many *ṣya* story songs demonstrate how a lead singer gets around the dilemma in practice. His solution is acutally a sham: pitch adjustment of the "alien" note such that its identity as a major third for the chorus does not get spoilt while for the lead singer his fifth continues to be divided into five (and not more) different notes. In the story song *"Syelinga nɛ Nkuminjɛli…"*[35] (CD I/21) the chorus response is sung by male and female voices together. The total melodic compass is a fifth (from G to C in my notation). Characteristically for this type of *ṣya* songs the semi-tone step falls between the two bottom notes of the scale, written as C and D♭. The primary line is the one sung in parallel octaves. Some participants then duplicate the words *dadami n'aja yɛ* in major thirds below this line. This harmonic duplication is strictly "interval-parallel" in major thirds, i.e. the lower melody maintains absolute identity with the higher line, as far as intervals are concerned. This introduces, however, the harmonic progression:

$$\frac{G}{E_\flat} > \frac{F}{D_\flat} > \frac{E}{C}$$

and an alien note in the resultant image: $E_\flat$. While this is acceptable to the chorus, the lead singer has to seek a compromise, otherwise he would introduce a "chromatic" distinction between an E and an $E_\flat$. Theoretically he could sing an E over the syllables *'njɛ-lye* followed by $E_\flat$ a bar later over the syllables *-da-mi n'a-* (from the lower voice line). But this is precisely what is impossible. It would mean that the singer conceptualizes six notes dividing his compass of a fifth, thus distinguishing $E_\flat$ and E as two different tonemes. The singer's behaviour indicates that he does not do so. On the contrary, he reacts with minor adjustments of his intonation, singing a somewhat flattened E (or sharpened $E_\flat$) in those places, and giving the impression that in his mind the pitches for *-njɛ-lye* and *da-mi n'a-*, are the same note. So he maintains his division of the fifth into five degrees, while not contradicting the parallel major thirds principle to which the chorus adheres. Thus two conflicting concepts find some sort of accommodation.

In the story song *"Nconcoli syalɔmɛ…"* (Example 67) the situation is similar. Here the basic chorus line in parallel octaves has a range of only a minor third. G − F − E in my transcription.[36] Other singers then duplicate the words *syalɔmɛ ye* in parallel major thirds, above the primary line in this case. By sticking to absolute parallelism this second voice line introduces, as usually, an "alien" note, transcribed here as $G_\sharp$. Once again, the conflict thus created is solved by intonation adjustments. The lead singer and story-teller, Calixte Tumba, while introducing a $G_\sharp$ quite clearly at the solo beginning of the song, avoids it as soon as the chorus enters, by following the lower chorus line.

Even in the chorus itself some singers adding the second voice in major thirds tend to adjust the $G_\sharp$ towards G in several places, as far as I can judge by ear. The song is accompanied by *makɛkɛ,* clapping of a time-line pattern whose pivot point coincides with the last (and lowest) note of the chorus phrase.

As we have seen Mpyɛmɔ vocal music does not use oblique or contrary motion. This is in contrast to the music of Eastern Angola. It is steered by the concept of parallelism at a fixed interval created by a tonality in major thirds shifting over three neighboring steps of the scale, the lowest two a semitone apart. This preference for absolute parallelism, as well as the common division of the melodic ambitus of a fifth into five degrees could be linked with certain tonal characteristics of the language. The Mpyɛmɔ language is situated in the so-called northern Bantu borderland on the map of Bantu languages (Richardson 1957), a transition zone between Central and West Africa. It seems to be much more tonal than for instance the Bantu languages of Malcolm Guthrie's Zone K (eastern Angola). Besides semantic tone, grammatical tone is also important. Maurice Djenda has given me several examples of words which may give the opposite meaning merely with a change of intonation, e.g. *aṣiyã* (_ ¯ ¯) = he does not know, as opposed to: *aṣiyã* (¯ – –) = he knows.

It is obvious that in Mpyɛmɔ̃ music any departure from parallelism could easily give rise to verbal misunderstandings.

Transcriptions

♩. = M.M. 120

Singing: Ki-ta - ndo-li ma-ta - la,   Ki- ta - ndo-li ma-ta - la,   ku
Hand-claps: x· x· x· x·   x· x· x· x·

nyu - mba ya - ngu e - na!   Ki - ta - ndo-li ma-ta - la,   ku
x·   x·   x·   x·   x· x· x· x·

nyu - mba ya - ngu e - na!   *etc.*
x·   x·   x·   x·

Ex. 61. *"Kitandoli matala"* (Song about the advantage of bigamy). Sung by Elzear Nyoni, aged approximately 17 and his group of youth, from Madunda, Rudewa District, Iringa Region, southwestern Tanzania. Language: Kindendeule. April 1960. Orig. Tape No. 21. Relative pitches. Transcription first published in Kubik 1961 a

Text:	*Approximate translation (Elzear Nyoni):*
Kitandoli matala,	I should like to have two women,
Kitandoli matala,	I should like to have two women,
kunyumba yangu ena!	in my house, indeed!

Ex. 62. "*Mphezi-mphezi iwe*" ("You thunder/lightning!"). *Nthano* story song performed by Anasibeko, aged approximately 40 and his group of children and adults in a traditional story telling session, at Singano village, near Chileka, Malawi. Language: Ciyanja/Chichewa. March 1967. Orig. Tape No. 2/1967.

This is a story about a man who kept *mphezi* i.e. thunder and lightning, in his house in a pot. When the children uncovered the pot, the thunder/lightning escaped. The ruthless man ordered his wife to go and call "his" lightning back. The lightning responded to her call and killed all her seven children, one by one. Eventually she drowned herself in the lake.[37]

Text:	Translation:
L.: Mphezi-mphezi iwe!	Thunder/lightning, you!
Ch.: Mwanjenje	Mwanjenje.
L.: Mphezi-mphezi iwe!	Thunder/lightning, you!
Ch.: Mwanjenje	Mwanjenje.
L.: Ana wanga!	My children!
L.: Andituma	I have been sent
L.: Kagwire mphezi.	to catch the thunder/lightning.
L.: Mphezi talira iwe!	Thunder you cry out!
Ch.: Mwanjenje, ili patali mphezi.	Mwanjenje, it is very far, the thunder/lightning.

Kiongozi anasoma 'Mwanzo' (introitus) wa siku ile katika misale
au anaanzisha «Sala ya Daraja».

2. Gloria

«Jina lako litukuzwe»

Kwa furaha (M. M. ♩ = 208)

V. 1. U - tu - ku-fu kwa Ba - ba mbi-ngu-ni
    2. Twa- ku - si -fu na twa -. ku - a - bu-du,
    3. U - tu - ku-fu kwa Mwa- na wa pe-kee
    4. U - li-ye-mtu-ma ku - tu-ta-fu - ta si - si,
    5. U - tu - ku - fu kwa Roho Mta-ka - ti - fu
    6. A-tu -ja -li - a - ye u - zi-ma wa -ko, Ba - ba,

W.1-6. Na a - ma-ni kwa wa-tu du-ni-a-ni!

Mwisho: V. A - mi - na, W. A - mi - na, A - mi - na.

Kiongozi anasoma Sala, Epistola na Enjili katika misale, au anaanzisha 'Sala' katika Chuo cha Sala na baadaye unai-
mbwa wimbo unaofuata, kadiri ya nafasi mpaka mwisho
wa enjili.

Ex. 63. Gloria – *"Jina lako litukuzwe."* Extract from Stefan Mbunga's *"Misa Baba Yetu,"* published by the Benedictine Mission Peramiho, Tanganyika. Language: Kiswahili. 1959[38]

Construction of the ŋgɔmbi: The string-bearer is a raphia stem leaf of about 1 m length, from whose surface four idiochord strings are pealed off. These run over the notches of a stick-shaped bridge pierced through the string-bearer in the middle. Movable rings from plant fibre are slung round the two ends of each string and the string-bearer. These are the tuning rings. By moving them it is possible to shorten or lengthen each section of a string, until the note desired is obtained. In some places of the string-bearer there are small metal buzzers attached. The resonator is a gourd fixed under the notched bridge. The division of the four strings by the notched bridge gives eight notes to the stick-zither. In the following Example 64a I have transcribed them in their relative pitches.

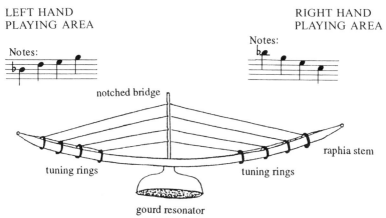

LEFT HAND
PLAYING AREA

RIGHT HAND
PLAYING AREA

Ex. 64a. Tuning and construction of the *ŋgɔmbi.*

In the musical example I am first giving the instrumental part in its basic form which is constantly repeated, and then one variation that can be heard in the recording. The instrumental part is structured such as to create a strong inherent-pattern-effect. All the deep notes, E, D, C and B♭ form an independent *Gestalt* in the listener's auditory perception.

Played pattern:

An auditory image
(inherent pattern):

Ex. 64b. Instrumental part of a song accompanied by a four-string notched-bridge stick-zither (local name: *ŋgɔmbi*). Performed by Victor Opombo, aged approximately 25, at Ihuda village, on the road from Liouesso to Makoúa near the river ferry of Yengo, in the north of the Republic of Congo. Ethnic group and language: Makua. July 1964. Phonogrammarchiv Vienna, No. 8755 a and b.

Ex. 65 begins with an introduction by the musical bow. The melody formed by the harmonics already suggests the theme of the song. Then the two voices enter. Their movement follows a loose counter-note principle with the result that the man's and the woman's vocal lines sometimes sound in octaves and sometimes in parallel thirds (removed one octave). In some places there are short episodes in contrary motion.

With the exception of a short phrase with the words *nan'ezag bö bya* which is sung by the woman alone, while the mouth-bow player characteristically leaves out his harmonics (!), the voice lines follow the counter-note principle exactly, as shown in Example 59. This lone exception occurs for formal reasons.

During the sung parts the melody of the bow harmonies is not heard on the tape, therefore I have not transcribed it. But I know that the player continued in the same way as where it can be heard.

The notation is relative. The original recording sounds about a semi-tone lower than notated. As a matter of convenience I have transposed the upper harmonics of the bow one octave down. At the end of the transcription I have indicated two variations in the bow melody, as they occur regularly in the instrumental interludes.

Variations in the bow interludes:

Ex. 65. *"Nan'engongol!"*("Mother! Forgive!"). Beginning of a song from the syncretist cult of *Angome-Ebogha* in a Fang' community, Gabon. Performed on the mouth bow (*beŋ*) by the priest André Mvome, together with two vocalists. Language: Fang'. Recorded in Oyem, northern Gabon. July 1964. Phonogrammarchiv Vienna No. B 8756[39] (CD I/17).

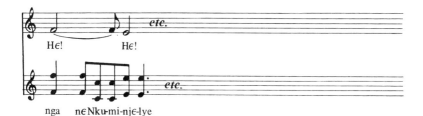

He! He!

nga nɛNku-mi-njɛ-lye

Ex. 66. *"Syelinga nɛ Nkuminjɛli"* ("Syelinga and Nkuminjɛli"). *ṣya* chantefable. Song performed by Ignace Bawando, aged approximately 45, and a group of women and children, at Bigene village, Nola District, Department Haute-Sangha, Central African Republic. Ethnic group and language: Mpyɛmɔ̃. April 1966. Phonogrammarchiv Vienna No. B 10748. Relative notation (cf. CD I/21)

Harmonic core of the chorus phrase: $\begin{matrix} \text{G} & \text{F} & \text{E} \\ \text{E}_\flat & \text{D}_\flat & \text{C} \end{matrix}$

Text in Mpyɛmɔ̃:

L.: Jɛo! ɗadami n'aja yɛ
Ch.: Syelinga ne Nkuminjɛlye ɗadamin'aja yɛ
L.: Syelinga ne Nkuminjɛlye ɗadamin'aja yɛ, Syelinga ne Nkuminjɛlye
L.: Hɛ! hɛ! n'aja yɛ, hɛ -nga ne Nkuminjɛlyo, ɗadamin'aja yɛ (rep).

Translation:

L.: Jɛo! My village is very far
Ch.: Syelinga and Nkuminjɛli! My village is very far.
L.: Syelinga and Nkuminjɛli! My village is very far, Syelinga and Nku-minjɛli!
L.: Hɛ! hɛ! it is very far, hɛ! -nga and Nkuminjɛli! It is very far!

♩. = M.M. 120

Leader:

Ncɔ - ncɔ-li sya - lɔ 'mɛ ye, Ncɔ - ncɔ-li sya-lɔ

mɛ nɛ mɛna 6a wɔ! Sya - lɔ |mɛ ye, Ncɔ - ncɔ-li sya -lɔ

Chorus:

Sya - lɔ mɛ ye, Ncɔ - ncɔ-li sya-lɔ

Ex. 67. *"Nconcoli syalɔme ye"* ("Nconcoli take me to the other side of the water-course"). *ṣya* – story song. Sung by Calixte Tumba, aged 25, with a group of women and children, at Bigene village, Nola District. Ethnic group and language: Mpyɛmɔ̃. June 1964. Phonogrammarchiv Vienna B 8834. Relative notation. During the song the participants in the chorus clap a common five-stroke time-line pattern with their hands. This is called *makɛkɛ*.

Harmonic core of the chorus phrase: $\begin{smallmatrix} B & A & G_\# \\ G & F & E \end{smallmatrix}$

Text in Mpyɛmɔ̃:

L.: Nconcoli syalɔ mɛ ye, Nconcoli syalɔ mɛ, nɛ mɛna ɓa wɔ!
Ch.: Syalɔ mɛ ye, Nconcoli syalɔ mɛ.
L.: E mɛna ɓa wɔ! E mɛ na ɓa wɔ!
L.: Nɛ mɛ na ɓa wɔ.
L.: Nɛ ɗambi ronce.
L.: E baγo, e mɛ na ɓa wɔ!

Translation:

L.: Nconcoli take me to the other side of the watercourse, I shall be married to you.
Ch.: Take me to the other side, Nconcoli, take me to the other side
L.: I shall be married to you! I shall be married to you!
L.: And I shall be married to you!
L.: War is coming!
L.: The truth is I shall be married to you!

Nconcoli is a bird always seen at rivers and watercourses. It feeds on fish. In the story the hero asks this bird to safe his life and take him to the other side of the river.

Section 2
Nsenga/Shona Harmonic Patterns and the San Heritage in
Southern Africa[40]

San-speaking communities were once widely distributed in Southern
Africa. In the course of the last two thousand years they have been
gradually forced away into climatically unfavorable regions, decimated
and brought into economic dependence by Bantu-speaking populations
who eventually occupied the area after immigrating in several waves and
with complex migration patterns[41] (cf. Phillipson 1977). In some areas
San people have been physically absorbed, as for example in South
Africa especially among the Xhosa, where segments of the present-day
population display anthropologically Khoisanid[42] elements that can
hardly be overlooked.

In many parts of southern Africa the San preinhabitants, even where
they have been extinct for several centuries, still play a role in the oral
literature of Bantu speakers as well as having influenced certain Bantu
cultural traits. For example, specific patterns in the San hunter-gatherer
life-style are often reenacted by young boys belonging to the large Ngangela group of peoples in eastern Angola and northwestern Zambia during
the *mukanda* seclusion (Kubik 1982a). The phenomenon of macronym-
phia, often discussed in the ethnographic literature of southern Angola
(Almeida 1956), which is the result of physical manipulation during girls'
puberty ceremonies, is a San heritage, adopted by Bantu speakers in
southern Angola.[43]

Occasionally, the memory about San people survives in short didactic
texts and verbal formulas transmitted over several generations. In Northwestern Province, Zambia, -Luchazi children learn the riddle *kasekele
wamana hacana* ("A Bushman is standing still in the river grasslands").
Answer: *mwila* ("Tall grass"). The word *kasekele*, pl. *vasekele* ("people
of the porcupine") is the term with which Ngangela speakers used to call
the !Kung'. In riddles learned by children far away from any present-day
contact with San speakers it is still transmitted, although no longer
understood.[44]

An ancient contact zone between Bantu peoples and the San was a
broad belt of savannah land south of the Benguela railway, stretching
through central Angola to the eastern Muxiku Province, into Northwestern Province, Zambia, and then across the subcontinent up to Malaŵi.
In this area no San speakers are found today. But legends abound
concerning the San preinhabitants. Among the -Luchazi of Kabompo
District, Zambia, old people talk to young children about the *tumonapi*
or *wanjimwena kuli*. They tell young children that should they ever see
one of these short beings somewhere in the bush and be asked by him:

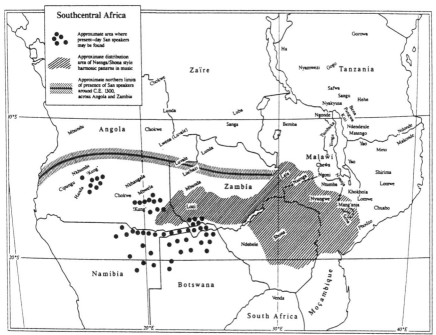

Map 7

Wanjimwena kuli? ("Where have you seen me?") they should quickly reply: *Kuze!* ("Over there"). Only then the man would not do any harm to the child.[45]

This same magic formula for neutralizing the power of the autochthonous people who have vanished can be found 1500 km further east. In Chicheŵa/Cinyanja, in fact in all the languages of the Maravi-cluster, elderly people tell young children: "If the small man asks you, *Mwandionera kuti?* 'Where have you seen me?' you must reply, *Uko ku phiri!* 'Over there on the mountain!'"[46]

The preinhabitants of Malaŵi, who were met by the Maravi immigrants in the distant past, are referred to in legends as *akafula* (sing. *mkafula*).[47] The linguist, physician, and anthropologist George T. Nurse has written two important papers on the *akafula* and their likely San identity in the prehistory of Malaŵi (Nurse 1967, 1968a).

In southernmost Africa there is evidence that extinct San populations have had a tremendous impact on local cultures and also on music, especially among the Xhosa, in whose language they left click consonants in no fewer than 2,395 words (de Wolf 1983: 270). Although Xhosa music and dance have not been examined systematically for traces of a San heritage, many of the data from Deirdre Doris Hansen's field research

seem to suggest it (Hansen 1981). Preliminary comparison of recordings of San and Bantu music in the southcentral African belt, from southern Angola into Botswana, Zambia, and Zimbabwe has led me to the conclusion that a San heritage is particularly pronounced among those speakers of Bantu languages in this zone and perhaps among some others further south who show the following background:
(a) a strong pastoral component in their economy (including a taste for milk);
(b) long-term presence in the area, going back to the so-called Early Iron Age Industrial Complex (Phillipson 1977); and
(c) a remote East African migration background of some of their population components.

The influence is particularly demonstrated in Angola, where the cattle-keeping and milk-producing -Nkhumbi, -Handa, -Cipungu, and related peoples of the Province of Wila (Huila) in the southwest, have assimilated and adapted essential traits of San music. In the midst of this population there are still small communities of !Kung' (San speakers of southern Angola and adjacent areas) to be found. From them was adopted the idea of using a hunting bow as a mouth-bow in two different techniques: (a) by inserting one end of the bow stick into the mouth and (b) passing the middle of the bow stick by the lips.[48] The name for this instrument – used as a hunting bow or as a mouth-bow – is *onkhonji* in Luhanda, one of the languages of this group of peoples. There are also shiver dances performed by the southwestern Angolan peoples which were obviously adopted from the !Kung', although their current name, *musakalunga,* is Bantu. Both -Nkhumbi/Handa and !Kung' men and women participate in this dance.[49] Perhaps because the San were always a small minority in southwestern Angola, the Angolan pastoralists/agriculturalists, by comparison, have not attained the degree of interpenetration and ultimate fusion with San cultures that has occurred in the case of the pastoralist Khoi ("Hottentots") further south. They have reached, nevertheless, a stage of symbiosis unparalleled elsewhere, a symbiosis that is not merely founded on economic cooperation between the two groups, but includes intensive cultural exchange as well.

By comparison, the Ngangela-speaking peoples in eastern and southeastern Angola, who have settled in Kwandu-Kuvangu Province only from the 17th and 18th centuries onwards, have not adopted any San elements in their music. Until the present turmoil in southeastern Angola, i.e. definitely up to the mid-1960s when I conducted research in that area, the Ngangela peoples and the few bands of !Kung' hunter-gatherers used to live in strict separation but practiced economic cooperation, something less, perhaps, than a full symbiosis. The Bantu-speaking peoples mentioned are classified as Zone K/Group 10 by Malcolm Guthrie

(1948) and belong culturally and historically to the Lunda cluster (Murdock 1967). It is from the larger Lunda empire that they have emerged. In contrast to the semi-pastoral peoples of southwestern Angola (within Guthrie's Zone R), the Ngangela peoples have a Central African cultural background and a kind of music characterized by an approximately equiheptatonic tonal system, multi-part singing in clusters of thirds or thirds plus fourths, an emphasis on percussion instruments, and many other traits that are totally disparate with regard to the San musical world.

The Southcentral African Belt

A question which could be crucial for unlocking the remote cultural history of southern Africa is the following: What happened culturally in that broad strip of land in southcentral Africa, approximately south of the 14°–15° latitude, where there are no San groups left today but where they are remembered and where contact came about between San speakers and early Bantu migrants? According to our present knowledge such contact must have been taking place between San groups and Bantu speakers of the "Eastern Stream" of the Early Iron Age cultures (cf. Phillipson 1977:223–5, 229). The inception of such contact may be tentatively dated between 300 and 400 A.D. This encounter took place hundreds of years before the so-called third Bantu dispersal from the Katanga area came into effect, dated by Phillipson (1977:230) to approximately 1000–1100 A.D., which brought the ancestors of the present-day -Bemba and others to the northern and northeastern parts of Zambia.

If contact between the San and early Bantu speakers within the southcentral African belt was accompanied by some cultural exchanges, for example in music, is it possible to find an echo of such an encounter even today? How can we identify such echoes? Methodologically, this is an extremely difficult undertaking. Given the lack of any contemporary written sources and the impossibility that sound could have been preserved, even indirectly, in archaeological finds, we have no choice but to look at present-day traditions. Looking more closely at the Bantu musical cultures within the "belt", we may make at least two observations that encourage us to persist on this path:

(1) San music, as it survives in southeastern Angola and among San-speaking minorities in Zambia's Western Province and elsewhere (in the Caprivi strip, for example), is based on principles that are likely to be traditions of some antiquity and relative stability – especially with regard to tonal-harmonic preferences – such as the tonal possi-

bilities inherent in the use of a hunting bow as a musical instrument and the specific nature of San vocal polyphony; [50]

(2) Bantu music south of the 14° – 15° border line dividing Zambia from west to east is remarkably different in its tonal-harmonic configurations not only from musical cultures north of that line but also from any multi-part music elsewhere in Africa, Central and West Africa in particular. In fact, the tonal-harmonic system in this zone is unique by any measure and has often startled observers (cf. Jones 1949; Kubik 1968 c). In that broad belt north and south of the Zambezi we find peoples using a hexa- to heptatonic system in combination with harmonic part singing in fourths and fifths.[51] This combination is very unusual in Africa. Normally people with heptatonic traditions and multi-part singing use parallel thirds or thirds-plus-fourth trichords in parallel, oblique, and/or contrary motion, but they would not combine a heptatonic system with the exclusive use of bichords in fourths and fifths. On the other hand fourths and fifths, sometimes intersected by an isolated third, are the predominant simultaneous sounds in many pentatonic traditions (Kubik 1968 c: 28).

Elsewhere I have shown that tonal systems and multi-part patterns in African music are always interdependent and that the type of harmonic progressions prevalent in one or another culture follow strict rules which depend on the structural nature of the tonal system (Kubik 1968 c: 18 – 20; 1984 b). One cannot break out of a tonal-harmonic system in African music without destroying it. The combination of a hexa-/heptatonic system in the southcentral African belt with a regular progression order of bichords in fourths and fifths, therefore, requires a structural examination. Perhaps related to this peculiar harmonic style is the fact that in the same culture area is also found a unique polyphonic vocal style that has been described by A. M. Jones for the -Manyika (Jones 1949) and by Andrew Tracey for the -Shona (Tracey 1974).

The existence of a sharp border line across Zambia with regard to tonal-harmonic styles was first observed by A. M. Jones, and it is reflected in his "harmony map" (1959 b). In Jones's account most of the peoples south of approximately latitude 15° south figure among the ethnic groups using a harmonic system based on fourths, fifths, and octaves – in particular, the -Nsenga, -Lala, -Lenje, -Soli, -Ila, -Tonga, -Lozi, and others – while north of that line there are many peoples who sing in thirds – especially the -Bemba, -Usi, and -Biisa – a harmonic style area that extends into Katanga with the -Luba, -Hemba, and -Lunda peoples. This situation was also noted by the Zambian musicologist Mwesa I. Mapoma, who like me has racked his brains over why this should be so:

As stated earlier, the Lala are part of the Bemba. They share many common cultural practices and speak the same language ciBemba. However, musically they belong to a non-Bemba group... The Bemba as well as the Luvale people harmonize in parallel thirds with occasional fifths while the rest of Zambia harmonizes in fourths. The Lala, Lamba, Swaka, and presumably a few more ethnic groups within the Bemba harmonize their songs in fourths.

No convincing explanation is available for this musical difference among a people who share several cultural traits including language. I have only attributed some of this to the influence of the dialect (Mapoma 1980). The Lala, Lima, Lamba, and Swaka to mention only these for the time being, seem to belong to the same dialectal group while the Bemba of Luapula and those of Northern Province belong to two separate dialectal groups which also correspond to the two other categories of Bemba music. While the dialectal explanation is offered within the same groups, none can yet be found for it when the problem is considered across the linguistic groups. The musical difference among a people who share most cultural practices raises a number of questions. The first is why should there be such a difference? The second is, did the Lala, Swaka, Lamba who share the same dialect and musical idiom ever organize their music in the same way as the other people in the Bemba language group? If they ever did what caused the changes and when did the change occur (Mapoma 1982 : 7, 9).

Considering that any present-day situation is but the most recent manifestation in a chain of events generated by complex historical forces and countless interactions in the past, we can safely assume that the present picture is not a chance product. Obviously, there is somewhere an unknown "gravitational" force in the historical background of the area that has contributed to the present configuration and that nobody seems to have thought about before.

The -Lala, -Lamba, -Swaka, and others were more or less assimilated by the later arriving -Bemba, with their distinctive culture, but for some reason this process of assimilation exempted musical traits. These peoples share today a tonal-harmonic system with peoples further south and southeast such as the -Nsenga, -Shona, -Manyika, and others too distant to have been affected by the -Bemba influx. Obviously, the -Lala, -Lamba, and -Swaka have retained, in common with the peoples further south, a music of pre-Bemba cultural heritage in spite of -Bemba assimilation.

It is precisely this pre-Bemba cluster of tonal-harmonic traditions that gives rise to questions regarding the remote music history of Zambia, Zimbabwe, and southern Angola. What was paramount in Zambia and

Angola before the influx of "thirds peoples" such as the -Bemba in the central part and the Luvale/Cokwe/Ngangela group in the west?

My thesis is that the tonal-harmonic system shared today by the Nsenga, -Shona, -Lala, -Lamba, -Swaka, -Lozi, and others – in short what we may term "the southcentral African tonal-harmonic belt" – was once

(1) more coherent in its distribution area than it is today, that is, at a time before it was geographically "cracked" by the influx of the "thirds people" on its northern fringes; and

(2) is in itself the long-term result of an early, transculturative encounter in this region between heterogenous musical cultures, namely, those of the early Bantu migrants associated with the Early Iron Age Industrial Complex and of the San hunter-gatherers once occupying this area. Broadly speaking, this encounter took place during the first millenium A.D.

Thus the "unknown gravitational force" behind the present picture in the southcentral African belt seems to be San music in some of its historical forms which would have been assimilated and developed in various directions by people with a mixed economy based on agriculture and animal husbandry and belonging to early migrations of Bantu-speaking peoples. The resulting synthesis was probably complete long before new waves of migration brought the ancestors of the present-day -Bemba to Zambia and the Ngangela peoples to eastern and southeastern Angola. By that time San inhabitants had long disappeared from much of the southcentral African belt. The new immigrants, therefore, remained unaffected by San music. The earlier synthesis between Bantu and San tonal-harmonic ideas (and it is especially in this realm where the San heritage can be recognized) could not be repeated. But it has been passed on and survives today among modern ethnic groups in the south-central African belt, such as the -Nsenga, -Shona, -Lala, etc., in areas where the influx of the "thirds peoples" from Central Africa either did not become effective (the -Shona case) or where it was rejected musically (the -Lala, -Lamba, and -Swaka cases).

The encounter as a "pre-Bemba" event should therefore at least partly explain the sharp borderline in Zambia separating the harmonic styles south of approximately 15° from those in the north and northeast. This borderline which is in no manner straight (cf. Map 7) indicates on the one hand the maximum penetration of musical influences from Later Iron Age migrations of "thirds peoples", and on the other – perhaps also more or less – the approximate northern borderline of San occupation of the area by 300–400 A.D.

We can never know for certain, what the music of the San preinhabitants of this area was like. But considering the possibility that the San life-style, where it survives today in the more southerly areas, may have changed little since prehistoric times, one may make tentative inferences about the remote past based on present-day data obtained in areas of San retreat (e.g., southeastern Angola). We next begin, therefore, with a discussion of some San musical traits which, for internal structural reasons, must have been relatively stable. The data for this discussion comes from my research done in 1965 among several camps of the !Kung' in southeastern Angola (cf. Kubik 1970 b; 1987 a).

The !Kung' Tonal-Harmonic System

!Kung' music, both vocal and instrumental, is based on the selective use of natural harmonics. This has been known for a long time,[52] but only recent studies have brought to light what makes the !Kung' use of harmonics so particular.

Not all African music is based on tonal systems. And several tonal systems are based on nonsonic principles, for example distance, as seems to be the case in some of the equidistant tonal systems found in certain areas. But many African tonal systems are based on the recognition and selective arrangement of harmonics, sometimes only lower harmonics, sometimes surprisingly high ones, e.g. the 11th harmonic.[53] In studying these harmonics-based systems, however, we have to distinguish two fundamentally different procedures by which the constituent notes are obtained. Is the tonal material derived from the harmonics of one or two fundamentals? A case for the first is the tonal system of the -Gogo of Tanzania (Kubik 1967 b, 1968 c) and some other East African peoples classed as "pentatonic". A case for the second is the tetratonic system of the !Kung' in southeastern Angola. Two fundamentals also form the basis of the hexatonic system of the -Nkhumbi and -Handa of southwestern Angola (Kubik 1975/76), the -Xhosa of South Africa (Hansen 1981), the Fang' of Gabon (Kubik 1968 c), and others.

The evolution of tonal systems based on one fundamental may not necessarily have been in connection with the knowledge of musical bows, but the evolution of those based on two fundamentals apparently has been. Practice of other musical instruments and even certain vocal techniques alone may also have led in the past to the discovery and selective use of natural harmonics over a single fundamental. The latter is probably the case with the Wagogo of Central Tanzania (or, possibly, with their predecessors in the area) who do not use musical bows. Philip Donner[54] possesses a crucial recording of a Gogo mouth-resonated vocal technique, performed by Hukwe Zawose, by which the harmonics-based Gogo system, using harmonics 4 to 9 (even up to the 10th), is instantly generated.

Tonal systems based on the use of harmonics over two fundamentals are, on the other hand, frequently encountered in areas where the musical bow is known, particularly the mouth-bow in its varieties. These fundamentals are yielded either by the two segments of the string when it is divided by means of a brace or noose or on an unbraced bow when the string may be stopped with a finger or a stick and thus shortened to obtain the higher note.

The next distinguishing feature to be observed in our studies is the height of the harmonics used i.e. what section of the natural harmonic series is selected to form the tonal system. Depending on these two variables (namely the number of fundamentals and the height of the harmonics used) completely different tonal-harmonic systems may be encountered among those African peoples whose music is based on the natural harmonic series. The tonal system of the !Kung' of southeastern Angola is tetratonic with frequent pentatonic extensions. My surprise finding, however, while doing research in the area of Kwitu-Kwanavale in 1965, was that the !Kung' tetratonic system manifests itself in three different phenotypes with different intervals, depending on the width of the basic interval to which the musical bow is tuned (Kubik 1970b:69, 1985:44). Unaccompanied vocal music is totally in line with the bow harmonics, and a song stands in any of the three phenotypes, unless of course, it is pentatonic.

Another important point regarding the !Kung' tonal-harmonic system is that the natural harmonic series of each fundamental is not used beyond the fourth harmonic. This is why the system is tetratonic with two fundamentals and why fourths, fifths, and octaves are the characteristic simultaneous sounds, besides unisons in !Kung' polyphony.[55]

Melodic and harmonic results

Ex. 68. Musical bow tuning at an interval of ca. 400 cents (tuning *a*). Melodic and harmonic results (cf. CD I/23a)

Melodic and harmonic results

Ex. 69. Musical bow tuning at an interval of ca. 300 cents (tuning *b*). Melodic and harmonic results (cf. CD I/23b)

Ex. 70. Musical bow tuning at an interval of ca. 200 cents (tuning *c*). Melodic and harmonic results (cf. CD I/23 c)

Among the tonal-harmonic patterns generated by the three !Kung' musical bow tunings, the most peculiar one, in the sense of being so different from the others, is that resulting from tuning the musical bow at an interval of ca. 400 cents (Example 68). The harmonic patterns yielded by an alternation of the two roots (F = root I; A = root II) contain a semitone progression, (F − E) downwards (from I to II) or upwards (from II to I). The melodic and harmonic results of this tuning are so characteristic of San concepts that they may be considered as diagnostic of a San heritage in any music of southern Africa where they occur. According to which harmonics of the bow tuning are reinforced or which notes of the system are picked out by singers, the following progressions may then come up frequently in !Kung' polyphony based on this tuning:

Ex. 71. Harmonic progressions in !Kung' polyphony based on tuning *a*

In all these progressions only system-inherent pitches are used, and yet a variety of parallel, oblique, and contrary motion is possible. The chordal progression $\frac{E}{A} \rightarrow \frac{C}{F}$ with its reverse is something like a hallmark of a substantial part of !Kung' music (Example 86).

Next, from the comparison of my sample of !Kung' bow music recordings in Angola[56] and the measurements of the fundamentals,[57] it seems that these tunings and their harmonic columns are interrelated in their absolute pitches, forming a "chain" with tuning *a* (that of Ex. 68) the lowest, tuning *b* (Ex. 69) in the middle, and tuning *c* (Ex. 70) the highest.

For example, Lithundu Musumali, a !Kung' performer on a gourd-resonated braced bow, used two different bow tunings during the same recording session (see below). While using tuning *b* (at a "minor third" interval) he tuned the lower fundamental (I) at $A_3 + 15$ cents, and the higher one (II) at $C_3 - 10$. The resulting "minor third" interval was 275 cents wide. When he changed to tuning *a* (at a "major third" interval), he also changed the overall level by tuning his lower fundamental (I) a "major third" down from fundamental I of his first tuning and his higher fundamental (II) in unison with the remembered note of fundamental I of the first tuning. The "major third" interval was 420 cents wide. Lithundu Musumali's bow tunings were measured with a Korg WT-12 tuner:

Higher tuning (orig. tape 76/II/13):	$A_3 + 15$	$C_3 - 10$
Fundamentals:	I	II
Lower tuning (orig. tape 76/II/14−15):	$F_3 + 10$	$A_3 + 30$
Fundamentals:	I	II

From this it follows that different bow tunings used by this musician were "anchored" in his memory in their absolute pitches. $A_3 + 30$ and $A_3 + 15$ were without doubt, conceptualized as the same pitches.

Looking further into bow traditions of the !Kung', I then discovered that another performer, Chief Vimphulu, who used a mouth-bow and tuning *c* (i. e. an interval of ca. 200 cents), had his overall pitch still higher, apparently linking it with the $C_3 - 10$ of fundamental II of Lithundu Musumali's "minor third" tuning. Although recorded in the same camp, the two bow players had no immediate contact with each other.

I would not contend on the basis of these data alone that !Kung' bow tunings throughout southeastern Angola are invariably related in their absolute pitches. But the evidence of one player linking his two different tunings in the manner described and of a second one apparently joining the cycle is a warning to the effect that at one time in !Kung' musical culture there could have been the notion of a generalized "anchoring" of the three bow tunings, in the following manner. A hypothetical cycle of !Kung' bow tunings (relative notation):

Tuning

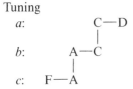

Thus, the three common bow tunings observed among the !Kung' and their resulting tonal-harmonic patterns could be understood as three phenotypes within a single system.

With justification, the attentive reader might ask here: Why should there be just three bow tunings among the !Kung', and if there are, what is their primary inspiration? Why three, and why should they have ca. 400, 300, and 200 cents separating their fundamentals? What generated these three bow tunings in the first place – and more specifically – in what kind of concept does the "major third" (ca. 400 cents) as an interval of tuning *a* originate? What kind of experience might have preceded both rudimentary scales and these bow tunings in !Kung' music? Could the "major third" be based in the experience of higher harmonics of a stretched string?

Although it is difficult to answer questions aimed at the reconstruction of possible evolutionary sequences, some can perhaps be answered. Kirby (1961:6) claimed to have observed San people producing higher harmonics than the fourth from a stretched string, but with regard to the !Kung' I have never found any evidence for that, nor has David Rycroft, examining Westphal's material (Rycroft 1978:18). This is not to throw doubt at the accuracy of Kirby's observation, but if there was ever an experience among the !Kung' and other San (not influenced by Bantu or Hottentot musical concepts) of higher harmonics (i.e. beyond partial 4) in connection with braced bow, it would seem incomprehensible why they should have reverted to using only lower harmonics today. My main argument, however, is that components of a closed system cannot be explained by, or derived from, concepts outside the system. Thus, the "major third" cannot have an origin in higher harmonics (i.e. something outside the system), while being an integral part of a system that excludes the notion of higher harmonics.

So where then does the "major third" come from? And indeed the three tunings? I have already offered an explanation with illustrations in Kubik 1987a. The basic argument is: the !Kung' ear, by recognizing and making use of harmonics up to partial 4, became conditioned to consonance ideas embracing the octave (interval between harmonics 1 and 2), the fifth (between 2 and 3), and the fourth (between 3 and 4). Once conditioned in that manner, human beings will always be guided by such a primary experience in further developments that come about. Therefore, somewhere on the evolutionary line, far back in the past, when it was discovered that a second fundamental – with analogous harmonics – could be obtained by stopping or dividing the string, the ancestors of the present-day San would have been naturally inclined towards attempting to repeat their primary consonance experience in the extended system. They would have attempted to divide the string at such points that

(a) two analogous columns of harmonics are obtained, with the same number of notes each, and that

(b) the emerging intervals between these constituent notes of the analogous columns either repeat any of the primary consonant intervals (as is the case in the chains $I^2 - I^3 - II^4$ and $II^2 - I^3 - I^4$ of tuning c) or represent subdivisions of the former which do not disturb the primary consonantal order.

In tuning c, therefore, the second and the minor third appear as derivative intervals. Knowledge of this fact, then, could have been projected to create tuning b (containing the concept of a "minor third" in its basic interval). In this tuning then we find the first appearance of a major third in cross-column relationships, $II^2 - I^3$. The latter experience in turn would have been projected to create tuning a, leading to yet another novel experience: the interval of a semitone. With tuning a the scope of the system is concluded, the limit reached. Whether this might have been the evolutionary sequence cannot be decided so quickly, but in any case the relationships outlined above should explain, at least in part, why there cannot be more than three bow tunings and what the origin of the thirds interval could be, in any case a "melodic", not a harmonic, experience.

It may be noted that the margin of variance between the three spacings of the tuning noose on the bow that generate the fundamentals of the three bow tunings is extremely narrow: expressed in sound, not much more than 200 cents (the approximate difference between the intervals of tunings a and c, i.e. the difference between a "major third" and a "second"). The three bow tunings represent the maximum exploitation of consonance possibilities within the overal !Kung' tetratonic idea. If the bow were tuned at an interval of a fourth, this would be unacceptable, because in this case only a tritonic system would emerge, with I^4 duplicated by II^3. Similarly, tuning the bow at a semitone interval (such as occurs among some Bantu ethnic groups in West-Central Africa) would not appeal to San consonance experience.

What surprised me, however, when continuing this analysis and what heightened my suspicion that the three bow tunings and their columns of harmonics were perhaps conceptualized as "anchored" in the !Kung' mind, was the discovery that a merger of the note sets of two adjacent bow tunings creates scalar and harmonic patterns actually used in some San vocal music that is pentatonic. Here, it has to be noted that not all !Kung' music is tetratonic. In my 1965 sample of !Kung' music of southeastern Angola 10 out of a sample of 34 songs were pentatonic (cf. Kubik 1970b: 57–62). For a long time, it was unclear whether the pentatonic songs represented some foreign influence, or whether they represented a step in an evolutionary sequence within San music, leading from tetra- to pentatonic music. For example, a merger of the tonal material obtained from tunings b and c, i.e. the two fundamentals plus their harmonics up to the 4th harmonic, yields an anhemitonic pentatonic scale exactly of the type used in my 1965 recordings of pentatonic vocal music of the !Kung' in Angola. Clearly, no pentatonic material can arise from !Kung' solo bow playing, if no use is made of harmonics beyond harmonic 4. To produce pentatonic music would require two bows with "neighboring" and thus overlapping tunings to play together. Although I have never seen this, and the tonal material of all my !Kung' bow recordings, except that of the Bantu-introduced friction bow *(kawayawaya)* is tetratonic, it must be conceded that what is not performed can exist as an abstract idea, and perhaps it materializes in some totally unexpected quarter. Thus, a !Kung' combining the experience of two imaginary bow players with tunings *b* (ca. 300 cents) and *c* (ca. 200 cents), would arrive at a tonal-harmonic merger that constitutes precisely the pentatonic scale mentioned above.

Ex. 72. Merger of !Kung' bow tunings *b* and *c* (including their harmonic) and its tonal-harmonic result

Further above I have suggested that the three common !Kung' bow tunings might be conceptualized by the !Kung' as "anchored", each having one fundamental in common with its neighbor. There is some evidence that such a relationship, if it exists, must be a circular one, with the top D column (in relative notation) also linked to the bottom F column (see Exs. 70/II and 68/I). The best method to visualize such a structure is to use David Rycroft's circular transcription method introduced in Rycroft 1954, here however, not applied to the transcription of a song, but of a system of tonal relationships:

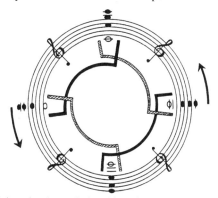

Ex. 73. The infinite circular relationship of !Kung' musical bow harmonic columns

From this abstract representation of what appears to constitute the !Kung' and perhaps the San tonal universe, it follows that any neighboring two columns within this system can be combined to form a tetratonic, and any neighboring three to form a pentatonic configuration. Our model should be able to explain the abundance of apparently unrelated scalar and harmonic patterns documented by various authors among San groups in Namibia, Botswana, and elsewhere, in particular those transcribed by Nicholas M. England in his article "Bushman counterpoint" (England 1967).

For example, if the harmonic columns over A, F, and D (in relative notation) are linked, the resultant pentatonic scalar pattern and its associated simultaneous sounds correspond with that in England's transcription of the song *"!Kāī ‡əm ‡əm"* ("Tree Stump"), accompanied by a pluriarc *(!Gauka)* (England 1967:60). The pluriarc is not a San instrument, but was adopted by the San from the southwestern Angolan Bantu cultures of Guthrie's Zone R, mentioned earlier in this paper. It was immediately integrated into the San musical universe and tuned precisely as if two musical bows had been "anchored", thus objectifying what has been detected as an "abstract idea" further above. This is plainly visible in the *!Gauka* tuning given by England (1967:60), whose pentatonic material, characteristically containing a "major third" and the "semitone" is derived from the linkage of our A, F, and D bow-associated harmonic columns:

Bow-derived harmonic columns:

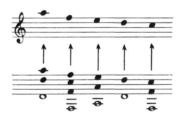

Ex. 74. Structural origin of a *!gauka* (pluriarc) pentatonic tuning among the ʒũ'l' wasi of Namibia. *!Gauka* tuning (after England 1967:60)

Among the !Kung' of southeastern Angola who do not use the pluriarc because their Bantu contacts were different, I did not find this particular pentatonic scalar pattern and the simultaneous sounds that follow from it.[58] But E. O. J. Westphal recorded !Kung' music in Namibia that uses precisely the same scalar-harmonic pattern.[59]

The Nsenga "Harmonic Cliché"

On the basis of our probe into the deep structure of San music we can now set out to look at the tonal-harmonic patterns used in the musical cultures of that broad belt of Bantu languages speaking peoples, stretching across Zambia and northern Zimbabwe between approximately 15° and 20° latitude south, where music is strangely different from anything we know elsewhere in Africa. Long ago, in precisely this area, A. M. Jones stumbled over a surprising "harmonic cliché" in Nsenga music "consisting of one fourth, one fifth and one octave"[60]. I am reproducing below Jones's transcription from his handwriting in his letter; but it can also be found in Jones 1959b:218, although written in another key.

Ex. 75. A.M. Jones's Nsenga "harmonic cliché." Copied from Jones's letter, October 6, 1964

It should no longer be a problem to solve the riddle of this pattern. To anyone who has been strongly exposed to !Kung' or other San bow music, as I was in southeastern Angola in 1965, and even to someone who has merely scrutinized the previous pages, this pattern inevitably produces an effect of *déjà-vu* (or rather a *déjà-ouçu*). A. M. Jones's Nsenga "harmonic cliché" and the harmonic progressions that arise from !Kung' bow tuning *a* (with the fundamentals ca. 400 cents apart) are congruent. Suddenly, the Nsenga pattern is no longer strange, but makes sense by its internal logic:

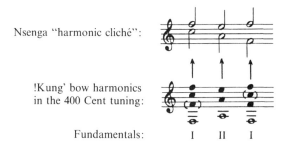

Ex. 76. A.M. Jones's Nsenga "harmonic cliché" and its roots in musical bow harmonics Note: Since I have used F as a basis in our notation of !Kung' bow harmonic columns further above, I have had to transpose Jones's notation in Ex. 75 from C to F in order to make it comparable.

We can instantly recreate Jones's Nsenga "harmonic cliché", if we take a !Kung' hunting bow, tune its two fundamentals by means of a tuning noose roughly ca. 400 cents apart, and then, using it as a mouth-bow (with one end inserted in the mouth) reinforce only harmonics 2 to 4 over each fundamental played alternately. Vocalists who would pick up those sounds would naturally arrive at the Nsenga "harmonic cliché", as shown in the example above.

I do not mean to suggest that the Nsenga "harmonic cliché" derives from any present-day bow tradition, whether San or not. We are dealing here with evolutionary processes that are at least several centuries old and cannot be related to any specific present-day ethnic group (whose ethnogenesis remains undetermined) only because the latter has become the surviving carrier of the tradition. How -Nsenga musicians might react to a musical bow demonstration as outlined above, is a worthwhile experiment to be undertaken by whoever will have the opportunity to do so. But at this stage all we can do is to elicit obvious structural analogies. With regard to the example above, the "secret" of the Nsenga "harmonic cliché" dissolves immediately when we project the !Kung' bow harmonies of tuning pattern *a* onto it. They cover each other perfectly, with the !Kung' fundamentals explaining not only the nature of the bichords, but also why a specific inversion occurs in a specific place and no other. Thus, the first bichord of the Nsenga pattern turns out to duplicate harmonics 3 and 4 of fundamental I, the second, harmonics 2 and 3 of fundamental II, and the third, into which the progression resolves, harmonics 2 and 4 of fundamental I. The "cadence" itself is a shift between two roots: $I - II - I$.

The Nsenga "harmonic cliché" is something like the core, the nucleus of a whole system, and it is surprising how widely distributed it is in one or the other inversion in the southcentral African belt. The westernmost area where this kind of harmonic pattern has been observed, so far, is the country of the -Lozi (Barotse) in Zambia's Western Province, and its largest distribution area is to the south of the Zambezi among the -Shona. There, it is part of one of the most ingenious harmonic systems of Africa: the famous Shona chord sequences.

A "Common and Striking Harmonic Particle"

Like A. M. Jones among the -Nsenga, Andrew Tracey when studying Shona music and *mbira* (lamellophone) playing in particular was startled by a "common and striking harmonic particle", characteristic of harmonic movement in the majority of Shona music (A. Tracey 1970b:40). As can be seen in the following illustration, Jones's "harmonic cliché" and Andrew Tracey's "harmonic particle" are one and the same structurally. The "particle" is part of the "cliché" and represents a one-step progression, while the "cliché" represents a two-step progression. Furthermore, the identity is merely veiled by inversion of intervals and also because each author writes it in a different key.

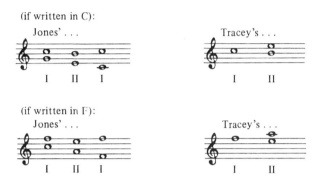

Ex. 77. Comparison of Jones's "harmonic cliché" and A. Tracey's "harmonic particle"

We can now repeat our experiment and take up again the !Kung' bow tuned at 400 cents. The following example illustrates how A. Tracey's Shona "harmonic particle" is contained in !Kung' bow harmonics. On the basis of this illustration, we can define the Shona "harmonic particle" structurally as a progression from a note in one harmonic column (I) to two notes in another (column II), with both columns based on hidden fundamentals that are a major third apart. The first note of the Shona "harmonic particle" represents the 4th harmonic of column I; the bichord into which it progresses represents harmonics 3 and 4 of column II.

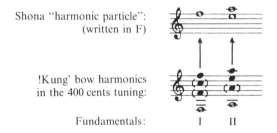

Ex. 78. Comparison of Shona "harmonic particle" with !Kung' bow harmonics

A Merger of Musical Bow Harmonic Columns

Once upon a time there were three San men or *tumonapi* setting out on a long journey. As usual they had their hunting bows with them, and as is the custom even today, they frequently converted their hunting bows into musical bows playing along their path or in a shady place for rest. This used to be most entertaining when travelling in solitude. But on that day they were three, and all of them had their bows for hunting and playing music. If each of them played his own music in his own tuning, there would be no consensus and the journey would not go well. What to do then? The three men decided to find a method so that they could play together.

First they had to find links between their different bow tunings. They had to tune their instruments in a manner that the sounds would form a chain like three people holding one another's hands. The first bow player tuned his instrument to the fundamentals F and A (400 cents apart), the second to A and C (300 cents), and the third to C and D (200 cents). By doing so they wanted to share the music so that each of them would have one harmonic column in common with his neighbor. Consequently, together they now had at their disposal a total of four harmonic columns or "chords": $\frac{C}{F} \frac{E}{A} \frac{G}{C} \frac{A}{D}$. In order to play their bows together they formed a circle and played alternately, each player just performing a short set of strokes on one chord, bow player 1, 2, and 3, round the clock. The fun of it was that each player, when his turn came, had a choice between either of his two columns (chords). After some practice they saw that their music had arrived at a chord sequence, consisting of different arrays of the four bichords which are derived from the four fundamentals.[61]

Myth or reality? – A dream? Pure speculation or intuitive reconstruction of the past? I have tried to use the style of a narrative to explain to the reader how people in southern Africa might have arrived at a total integration of the components forming the tonal-harmonic universe depicted in an earlier, circular illustration (Ex. 73), thus creating a hexatonic harmonic system based on progressions among four chords. In Example 79 this bow-derived chordal sequence is given in two different relative notations, the reason for which will become obvious later in this paper.

a) if written based on F:

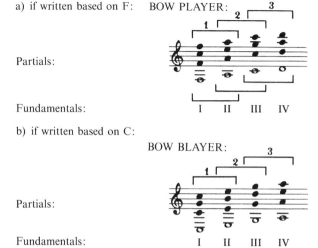

Ex. 79. Bow-derived chord sequences obtained from !Kung' (San) tonal universe (cf. Example 73)

From our thought experiment we have gained a new insight, namely that !Kung' (San) bow tunings and their associated harmonic columns (up to harmonic 4) are capable of forming a total merger. Whether this actually occurred in musical bow performance practice in the history of any San music or not is irrelevant for our subject of discussion. It is possible that the model existed only as an abstract concept. What is relevant, however, is that the hexatonic system with an array of four bichords thus obtained actually occurs in southcentral Africa. Apparently it does not occur in any present-day San music but in Bantu music within the southcentral African belt. In the following part of this paper we shall detect it in various tunings and harmonic patterns of this area. The first culture to be looked at is that of the -Lozi (Barotse) of Western Province, Zambia.

Here we are obviously on track, because many Lozi *silimba* (xylophone) tunings open up in the low register with a wide interval, often a major third, before ascending in scale-like manner to form a hexatonic pattern. We are now very familiar with this major third.

Silimba (Xylophone) Tunings

Atta Annan Mensah studied Lozi xylophone construction and tuning in 1970 and described in detail the tuning process and its results:

A few clear objectives had been revealed in the process of *silimba* tuning observed on the two occasions. The *silimba* maker had not only been setting a definite pitch pattern on his instrument, but had also been aiming at increasing its power range and trying to achieve a particular form of beauty in the appearance of the instrument.... The musical objectives may be studied at three levels, the ultimate level being the achievement of a seven-note scale with a triadic pattern in the three lowest keys. This objective was verified on other *lilimba* (plural of *silimba*) that Kanjele and Sililo had completed, as well as on samples by other makers previously and afterwards studied.... There was also a consistency in the appearance of a triad in the lowest keys; but again different members of the Lozi *silimba* scale have been found in this triadic formation on various specimens of the instrument, and the intervallic order varied accordingly, featuring both near major and near minor triads on different speciments. Few exceptions to this tuning pattern were found during the course of this study. The specimens examined varied in their number of keys. The numbers ranged from ten to fourteen. On the larger specimens the pattern of keys fell into three segments, consisting of two scalic rows, one an octave below the other, separated by a wider interval; then followed the triadic spacing among the lowest three keys. On two large specimens made in the Mongu District in the Western Province of Zambia, for instance, the keys were arranged thus in ascending order (the cipher notation here should be read only as an approximation of the major scale):

Thirteen-Keyed Specimen: 54321-6-54321-6-4
                         (a)   (b) (c)

Fourteen-Keyed Specimen: 321765-321765-3-1
                         (a)   (b)   (c)
(Mensah 1970b: 21)

Mensah then gives the tuning layout in cipher notation of two more, smaller xylophones which are heptatonic and apparently represent a tradition different from the other two (above), so that we do not have to discuss them in this paper.

With regard to the cipher notations, it is clear that the two specimens have an identical tuning layout. Although Mensah uses different series of ciphers, the only difference is that the 14-key instrument has one note more at the top. It is also clear that Mensah must have related by ear the 13-key instrument to the Western key of F, so we can confidently write his cipher 4, at the lower end of the scale as an F in staff notation (Ex. 80); and the cipher 1 in the second tuning as a C (Ex. 81).

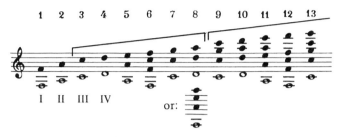

Ex. 80. !Kung' merger model projected on *silimba* tuning (basic note written as F)

Note: The top line is the actual *silimba* scale; the bottom line is that of the (hidden) fundamentals guiding the tuner of this xylophone.

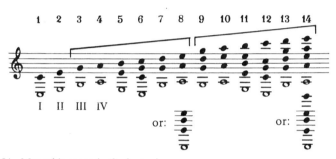

Ex. 81. Mensah's second *silimba* tuning

For our present analytical purposes cipher notation is no asset, because it would simply replace staff notation, if not tonic sol-fa, without adding any further information. We can therefore rewrite Mensah's tunings in staff notation, retaining the relative pitches, and then repeat the experiment we made with Jones's Nsenga "harmonic cliché" by projecting San harmonic columns onto the *silimba* notes, here however using the complete merger model as shown in Example 79 above.

The pattern fits absolutely and thus defines the *silimba* tuning layout as derived from a chain of four fundamentals with the intervals (ascending) F – A – C – D, if written with F as a basis, and C – E – G – A, if written with C as a basis.

One note (No. 8) in the first tuning (Ex. 80) and two (Nos. 8 and 14) in the second tuning (Ex. 81) allow alternative interpretations: they can be derived either from fundamental I or IV. Which is acceptable can be found out by watching a performer to ascertain with which other notes he strikes them. There is, however, some indication from chordal structures used in *kang'ombyo* (lamellophone) music of the -Lozi (CD I/24) and in the related *kankobele* and *ndimba* of the -Lala of central Zambia

– all sharing identical tuning structures – that this particular note is always conceptualized as ambiguous.[62] Note No. 8 on the *silimba* can therefore be struck together with either No. 4 or 5 and 10 or 11 respectively. Mensah's second *silimba* tuning gives the same picture. It is intriguing to see how, by the projection of our !Kung' merger model onto the *silimba* tuning, we obtain instant information about musical performance, i.e. which notes may be struck simultaneously with the xylophone player's rubber-headed beater and which not. The unwritten law is that only notes representing harmonics of the same fundamentals may be sounded together. Thus, on a *silimba* with hexatonic tuning and 13 to 14 keys, such as illustrated above, the following (system-inherent) simultaneous sounds may occur:

1 + 6,6 + 12 (octaves only).
2 + 5 (fifth), 5 + 11 (octave).
Alternately: 2 + 8 (octave), 5 + 8 (fourth), 8 + 11 (fifth),
    11 + 14 (octave).
3 + 7 (fifth), 7 + 9 (fourth), 9 + 13 (fifth).
4 + 8 (fifth), 8 + 10 (fourth), 10 + 14 (fifth).

Any other simultaneous sounds, besides these bichords, would fall outside the system.[63] Occasionally, it may happen that individual performers strike other chords, but these can easily be traced to influences from alien cultures, for example, other ethnic groups or Western influences. Marjory Davidson (1970) reported something like that in patterns for the Lala *kankobele* (lamellophone) but was then able to interpret the occasional alien thirds and sixths.

Summing up, the bichords listed above are those a performer with two beaters can strike while remaining within the boundaries of this tonal-harmonic system. Accordingly, the resultant sounds produced by *silimba* players have been described correctly, although indiscriminately, as "octaves", "fifths", and "fourths" by observers. As we have learned, however, for internal structural reasons these bichords cannot appear just anywhere on a *silimba,* but are confined to specific places (CD I/25).

Thus, the four lowest notes on a *silimba* of the type documented by Atta Annan Mensah (1970) can be defined as representing four fundamentals of a harmonics-based tone system. These four fundamentals, at the intervals F − A − C − D (respectively, C − E − G − A), generate all the notes of the *silimba* that represent harmonics of any of these fundamentals in a certain order.

The Basic *Kalimba* Core

A. M. Jones's Nsenga "harmonic cliché" was the starting point of our investigation linking Bantu musical traditions in the southcentral African belt with the musical heritage of a vanished San population. With the discovery that the Nsenga "harmonic cliché" and related patterns probably derive historically from musical bow harmonics of type *a* (surviving in the music of San speakers elsewhere up to the present) we came to appreciate this "harmonic cliché" as a nuclear structure and a point of departure for tonal-harmonic patterns prevalent in musical traditions of the southcentral African belt.

We do not have to go very far in order to find yet another testimony for this relationship. Andrew Tracey, in a remarkable paper entitled "The Original African Mbira?" (Tracey 1972), argues that all the various *mbira*-type lamellophones in the Zimbabwe/Lower Zambezi culture area and in Zambia have tunings that are historically interrelated. In spite of variations and divergencies, somewhere hidden in a *mbira* tuning of this culture area there is a "tuning core" of certain interval relationships. He calls it the "basic *kalimba* core."

Andrew Tracey's "basic *kalimba*" is not merely a theoretical model, it does exist in the form of the eight-note *kankobele* of the -Lala people in Zambia (cf. Jones 1949; Davidson 1970). This is a lamellophone of the fan-shaped variety. Both the *kankobele* and the larger *ndandi* share the same tuning system, although the layout is different, but it is especially the layout or array of the notes in the eight-note *kankobele* which unlocks the concept behind this tuning:

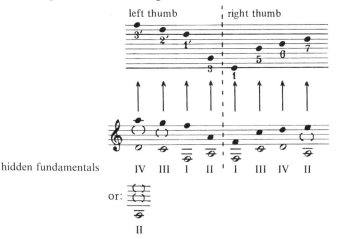

Ex. 82. The hidden roots of the *kankobele* or "basic *kalimba*" core (reproduced from A. Tracey 1972:88)

The basic *kalimba* core corresponds with the lower eight notes of a Lozi 13–14 note *silimba,* as documented by Atta Annan Mensah. In addition, the *kalimba* array reveals the harmonic structure of the music even more unequivocally, because the thumbs are restricted to right and left hand playing areas that cannot be trespassed.

On the *kankobele* as on the *silimba* the unwritten harmonic rule is that only lamellae representing harmonics of the same fundamental may be sounded together. Of all the eight notes, each has its eternal partner, except one, or as Marjory Davidson has quoted a villager: "One row of keys represents boys, the other represents girls and we choose a boy and girl who go nicely together" (Davidson 1970:104). The one exception is the "smallest girl" in the array (note No. 3' in our example). She is undecided and likes two boys equally, Note No. 3' can be sounded together with No. 6 or 7. As a partner of No. 6 it represents the 3rd harmonic of Column IV, while as a partner of No. 7 it assumes the role of the 4th harmonic of harmonic Column II. This is exactly as on the *silimba.*

The system-inherent simultaneous sounds that can be created on the "basic *kalimba*" or *kankobele* are therefore the following:
3' + 6 (fifth), alternatively (if the girl goes with the other boy): 3' + 7
2' + 5 (fifth)
1' + 1 (octave)
3 + 7 (fifth)

In staff notation this shows us the four bichords used on the "basic *kalimba.*" Order and sequence are variable:

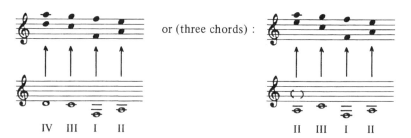

or (three chords) :

IV	III	I	II			II	III	I	II

Ex. 83. Bichords on the "basic *kalimba*" and their roots

Neither Andrew Tracey nor the late Marjory Davidson has ever suggested that the "basic *kalimba*" tuning of the -Lala and others in its chordal patterns represents a harmonics-based system, deriving from the lower harmonics of four fundamentals, but such an interpretation is advantageous because it explains the reason for the bottom third combined with the Nsenga style semitone progression, the structure of the four bichords, and, in fact, the logic behind the whole layout.

In search of the "original African *mbira*" Andrew Tracey has spoken of a "secret link between all of them" (1972:85), tracing the various forms of lamellophone in the southcentral African belt back to a sort of "ancestral" form which he called the "basic *kalimba*". What he really discovered, however, was perhaps not so much a kind of *Ur-kalimba*, as a perfect structural layout of the tonal harmonic system permeating much of the music of the southcentral African belt. This is what the "basic *kalimba* core" really is.

An analysis of the above illustration reveals how rigorously this system is structured. From the layout it is plainly visible why some notes must be in the right thumb playing area and some in that of the left thumb. Each harmonic column, i.e. the four fundamentals of the system and their selected harmonics, is represented "double", once in the left thumb, once in the right thumb playing area. That in turn explains why the basic *kalimba* must have eight notes. A further reason for having eight notes is that the harmonic system, as we have seen, is in bichords, i.e. two simultaneous sounds. Therefore each thumb must have access to four notes in order to make the system complete.

The internal order of the four notes in each thumb's playing area and the overall layout of the eight notes are determined by the following two factors:

(1) Harmonic notes must be positioned in the opposite playing area;
(2) The overall layout is intended to form a scale: 3' 2' 1' 7 6 5 3 1, with the basic notes (1 and 3, an octave above the hidden fundamental) placed in the middle.

The actual layout is then a compromise between these two principles plus the overall principle of having the four hidden fundamentals present in both playing areas.

The Shona Chords and Their Evolutionary Background

The final topic to be discussed in this paper is the Shona chords and their internal logic. While some earlier writers have suggested that the Shona tonal system might be equiheptatonic (cf. Jones 1971 b), people who perform Shona music have tended to go along only reluctantly with this idea. It has often been observed that the Shona system is rooted in distinctively harmonic ideas[64] based on fourths, fifths, and octaves, and that there are relationships with the music of peoples to the north of the -Shona, particularly in Zambia (Blacking 1961; Davidson 1970) (CD I/26).

In 1961, after being instructed by the *mbira* musician Jege A Tapera, Andrew Tracey first stated that Shona music is generally based on progressions between four bichords, which he gave in the key of G. It requires no further analysis here to show that these bichords are structurally identical with those heard on the *kankobele* (lamellophone) of the -Lala and in various traditions across the border in Zambia. Regional traditions may prefer one or the other inversion of the bichords and reshuffle the chord sequence in accordance with local fashion and the exigencies of the particular songs. But their relationships remain constant, proving that this is a closed system, a universe in itself.

If we project the !Kung' merger model on the Shona chords the result is immediately revealing:

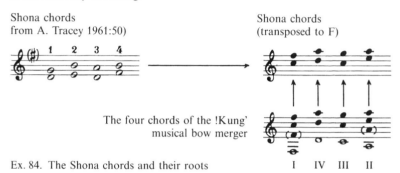

Shona chords
from A. Tracey 1961:50)

Shona chords
(transposed to F)

The four chords of the !Kung'
musical bow merger

Ex. 84. The Shona chords and their roots   I   IV   III   II

This illustration makes clear why, in the Shona chords, fourths and fifths must follow each other in precisely the inversions they do, why there must be four chords, and why there can be no thirds. The inherent logic of the Shona chords and their harmonic relationships (in whatever sequence they may occur in a musical piece) becomes transparent from the moment one recognizes them as representing 3rd and 4th harmonics over four nonsounding roots: F, A, C, and D in my notation. Certainly, the Shona chords are not necessarily played in the order given in Andrew Tracey's early (1961) publication. This does not alter however, their vertical layout which is the diagnostic marker linking them to the harmonics of our !Kung' merger model of harmonic columns. The evolutionary secret of the Shona chords, if I may express myself symbolically, is that our three San musical bow players in the hypothetical myth above, have learned to act like a single brain; they have learned to sound their bow harmonic columns alternately in a certain order built on consensus, like the members of a *nyanga* panpipe ensemble. Example 84 suggests that the two fourths in the Shona chords written as C−F and E−A (the first and the last chord in Andrew Tracey's earliest description) arise from the 3rd and 4th harmonic of the F/C−A/E harmonic columns. The two fifths, D−A and C−G, are identical with the 2nd and 3rd harmonics of the C/G and D/A bow tuning. In addition, the third and fourth of the Shona chords, in the order written by Andrew Tracey (1961 : 50), are also contained in harmonics of the A/E−C/G bow tuning, which is anchored between the other two in the merger model. Further, it can be seen that Andrew Tracey's "common and striking harmonic particle" is hidden in notes of harmonic columns I and II.

Summing up, we can characterize the Shona chords in the following manner:

(a) There are four different bichords.

(b) The simultaneous sounds in the harmonic progression, in whatever order these chords may be used in individual compositions, are always fourths or fifths; it is a typical 4–5 harmony in the sense of A. M. Jones's harmony map (Jones 1959 b).

(c) These simultaneous sounds may appear in inversions which are strictly determined by what harmonics of one of the four roots they represent; fifths are the objectified harmonics 2 and 3; fourths represent harmonics 3 and 4; octaves represent harmonics 2 and 4 of any of the hidden fundamentals.

(d) A hallmark of this system is the occurrence of a melodic semitone progression which is treated harmonically in a distinctive manner; it is part of Andrew Tracey's "most common and striking harmonic particle", also of A. M. Jones's Nsenga "harmonic cliché".

(e) Two of the four fundamentals in the basis of this system are a major third appart; the semitone progression in the system is generated by the major third interval between these fundamentals. It comes about through progression from harmonic 4 of the lower fundamental (I) to harmonic 3 of the higher (II) or the reverse.

(f) This system is effectively visualized in the tuning layouts of *mbira* instruments.

The Shona harmonic system is independent of the type of instrument used and operates in the same manner in vocal music. Some of the Shona threshing songs collected by Hugh Tracey in the 1930s and transcribed by Andrew Tracey (Example 88 in this Section) can be explained note by note by projecting our four fundamentals under the chords. Each note in these threshing songs stands exactly in places where the 3rd or 4th harmonics of those fundamentals would stand.

Heptatonic Shona Music

Much of the present-day Shona music, especially instrumental playing such as *mbira,* is heptatonic. How did the Shona get their heptatonic system? Is it the result of an equiheptatonic influence from the Lower

Zambezi valley? In his article on the *matepe* lamellophone of Zimbabwe, Andrew Tracey has described a prevalent heptatonic chord sequence in Shona music:

> Some of these chord sequences can be discerned in the mbira songs of a very large area, from the northern Transvaal through the eastern half of Rhodesia (excluding the largely hexatonic Ndau) to the Zambezi in the Mozambiquan pedicle. One sequence in particular is so predominant that I am tempted to call it the "standard" Shona chord sequence. ... This can be written with tonic C, as in 'Msengu': C E G, C E A, C F A, D F A, ... Now we are faced with the question – what is the logic, the sense of this chord sequence *C E G C E A C F A D F A?* ... Why do these chords follow one another in this particular way? It seems to me that each harmonic movement from chord to chord must embody something that is right to the Rhodesian ear ... the repeating sequence C E G, C E A is basic to much Shona music. Threshing songs, among other types of music, use it extensively.... The "standard" sequence can be considered as a statement of this shorter sequence followed by a contrasting statement of the same sequence a *fourth higher* ... (Tracey 1970 b : 38 – 41).

This is indeed the clue. We can understand the "standard" Shona chord sequence if we realize that its cycle is bipartite, and – although the total chord sequence appears to be heptatonic – that each of its two sections, A and B (cf. example below), taken by itself, is still hexatonic. Once this is clear it also becomes obvious that the bichords of sections B and A are merely transpositions of one another. Since this is a reciprocal relationship it would be pointless to ask which of the two sections is structurally the basis and which is the transposition.

"Standard" Shona chord sequence: (repr. from A. Tracey 1970: 40)

The harmonic columns of the ! Kung' musical bow merger model:

Ⓐ   Ⓑ

Ex. 85. The "standard" Shona chord sequence and its logic

The logic behind the "standard" Shona chord sequence, however, only becomes clear if we project our !Kung' merger model onto it: onto section B in the notation based on F and onto Section A in a transposition to C (cf. Ex. 79). The result is absolute congruence in sonic content and spatial layout (inversions) between the bichords in the "standard" Shona chord sequence and the harmonics of the four harmonic columns of the !Kung' merger model (Ex. 85).

Summary

Some of the observations in this paper may have appeared to be a trip into fanciful speculation. After all, no three San bow players have been observed to date combining their harmonics-derived harmonic columns in the manner described to create a unified system, although the harmonious playing together of three to four musical bows by Cape Hottentots was once reported (Kolb 1719:527), and, ironically, the "pluriarc" (*!Gauka*) seems to have provided a modern realm for at least a partial fusion of this kind. On the other hand, it is not illegitimate for the scientist to construct models, such as I have done in this paper, and test them out. If these are put into the right slot at the right moment, unexpected discoveries may come about.

My analysis of !Kung' music in southeastern Angola has shown that three common bow tunings with their harmonic columns (up to harmonic 4) constitute a generating basis for tonal-harmonic patterns in !Kung' vocal music, and that the tunings seem to be related in their absolute pitches by some performers I observed.

A merger of the tonal material obtained from the three bow tunings then provided us with a theoretical model of a unified !Kung' (or even San) tonal system. This merger model, to be understood as an abstract idea of relationships, something like the Rutherford/Bohr atomic model, was then projected on various tonal-harmonic patterns not only in San-speaking areas, but in the music of Bantu speakers of a broad southcentral African belt, characterized musically by hexa-/heptatonic tunings with multi-part patterns in fourths, fifths, and octaves.

Our surprise finding was then that all these tonal-harmonic patterns fit neatly into our !Kung' tonal-harmonic merger model in the sense of absolute congruence in sonic content and configuration of interval relationships (inversions of chords, etc.). Since the harmonic system in the southcentral African Bantu musical cultures is distinctively different from tonal-harmonic systems in other parts of Africa, and since its present distribution area can be related to certain convergent facts about the population history of this zone, I came to the conclusion that the present tonal-harmonic system of the -Nsenga, -Lala, -Shona, and others in this zone displays traits of a San heritage. The question has been left open, however, whether the hexatonic merger system with its four bichords represented a Bantu development of San harmonic ideas adopted in the remote past, or whether the total merger (cf. our model) already existed as an abstract idea in past musical cultures of the San. In any case, the theory of a San heritage in the tonal-harmonic concepts of the -Nsenga, -Shona, and others in Zimbabwe, Zambia, and adjacent areas, advanced in this paper would appear to make pointless earlier ideas by certain authors comparing the -Shona, -Manyika, and -Nsenga polyphony in "fourths and fifths" with European 12th-century polyphony. One of the insights we have gained from projecting our !Kung' tonal-harmonic merger model onto tunings, harmonic patterns, and polyphonic vocal music of the people mentioned, was that their music does not merely contain "fourths" and "fifths" of any sort, but constitutes a system of bichords in fourths or fifths that appear in a certain sequential order, with each distinctive inversion allocated to a specific place within the system.

Determining to what extent an assimilation of San concepts by the Bantu took place in the remote past in this area may still be open to discussion, but the fact that there is a San heritage in the music of the -Lala, -Nsenga, -Lozi, -Swaka, -Shona, etc. will be difficult to deny. The idea that one of the most extraordinary harmonic systems of southern Africa could have a remote San background also surprised me greatly when I first made note of my observations in my diary on May 29, 1975. I hesitated for several years before publishing them, owing to various reservations I had and a few points that had to be clarified. But now the issue displays itself in a different light. The question now is how otherwise could the congruence between Bantu tonal-harmonic patterns and the San tonal-harmonic merger model be explained? I may have constructed the merger model, but I did not construct the congruence.

The illustrations have hinted at an evolutionary secret of the tonal-harmonic system found in the Bantu southcentral African belt. The result of the investigation has been that in all likelihood even the famous Shona chord sequence and the structure of Shona polyphonic singing is to be understood as a Bantu development of an ancient San musical heritage in southern Africa. The connection with the San heritage is very remote and is probably a strange idea to -Shona contemporaries, but south of the 14° latitude there is a harmonic world so totally different from that of any other part of Africa, West, Central, and East, that some explanation of a historical nature is due. This was an early contact zone between Bantu and San peoples, beginning 300–400 A.D. Thus, anyone looking deeper into the history of southern Africa might discover that the ancestral spirits of the autochthonous inhabitants survive in the most unexpected quarters.

Acknowledgements

A first draft of this paper was informally circulated at the ESEM Meeting at the School of Oriental and African Studies, London, 20–23 May, 1986. I am extremely grateful to Dr. David Rycroft for having invested valuable time and energy to read and reread my paper before publication and for having come to my help with constructive criticism and invaluable suggestions for its improvement, based on his thorough experience of southern African musical cultures. I feel that without his help I would have never completed it. Naturally, many imperfections remain, but these are entirely my own responsibility and not that of my benevolent reviewer.

Transcriptions

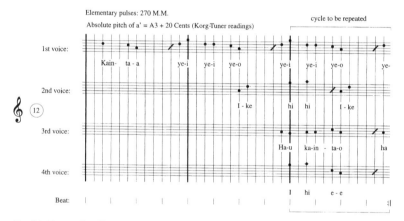

Ex. 86. Example of !Kung' polyphonic singing in southeastern Angola (CD I/27)

The performers recorded at the !Kung' camp Vimphulu near Kwitu-Kwanavale in December 1965[65] were four women, whose leader, Nthumba, ca. 45 years old, accompanied herself with a stamping tube (called *bavugu*) manufactured from three gourd shells of the Strychnos spinoza fruit. The instrument (not transcribed below) is struck with the right hand on the upper orifice and the sound is dampened in intervals against the left thigh.

Songs accompanied by the *bavugu* are an exclusive affair of women, and it was held that long ago, the instrument and the songs were connected with women's rites among the !Kung'. In the performance transcribed

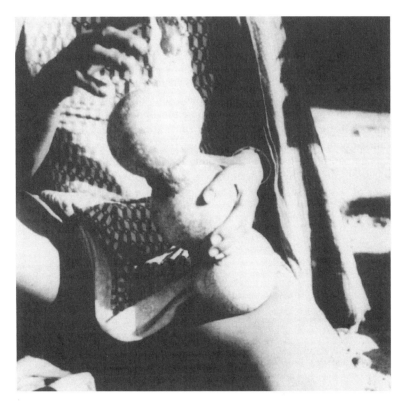

Ill. 57a–c. !Kung' vocal polyphony performed by Mrs. Nthumba (with *bavugu* stamping tube) and female group. Camp Vimphulu, near Kwitu-Kwanavale, southeastern Angola, December 1965. (Archive No. VIII/20, 23 and 21)

there are four singers combining their different voices in "hocket" fashion, each line with its own "text." This "text" however consists mostly of syllables, sometimes executed in yodel fashion (particularly voice No. 2), as is characteristic of many forms of vocal music among the !Kung'. A few words, probably from neighbouring Bantu languages which I cannot unfortunately identify, have been interwoven with the syllables.

The combination of simultaneous sounds is absolutely strict: although no musical bow accompanies the women, the harmonic patterns follow the CG/DA sub-system of !Kung' bow-tunings which results in a tetratonic melodic repertoire. In the vocal combination the four voices enter in a staggered manner with the *bavugu* beats providing a clear rhythmic reference line. After the last voice (No. 4) has entered, the 12-pulse cycle of voice combinations is repeated on and on, with some accentual and melodic variation.

My transcription below follows a notation system I developed departing from ciné-transcriptions (cf. Kubik 1965c, 1972c). In this system – to be explained in greater detail in Chapter VII – the durational principle of Western notation has been abandoned. The vertical lines represent the elementary pulsation, i.e. the smallest action units conceptualized in African music. For notation only black dots are employed. They are written on the vertical lines, marking the impact points. Each note marked in this manner is to be held out until it is cancelled either by another note or by the symbol for "stop" (/). The reinforced vertical lines are comparable to bar-lines identifying the 1 (one) in the reference beat, as conceptualized by the performers. The horizontal lines in our notations of !Kung' music have the same meaning as in Western staff notation.

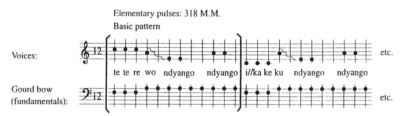

Ex. 87. Example of !Kung' musical bow performance in the F – A tuning (southeastern Angola) (CD I/23c)

The performer on the gourd-resonated bow (an ordinary hunting bow with a gourd of the *strychnos spinoza* tree held against the stave) is Lithundu Musumali, approx. 45 years old. I recorded him in December 1965 in the camp of !Kung'-leader Vimphulu near Kwitu-Kwanavale, Province Kwandu-Kuvangu, Angola.[66]

The instrument called *n//kau* was braced near the centre of the string and held diagonally by the player. The measurements of the bow's fundamentals gave the following result: Fundamental I = F_3 + 10; Fundamental II = A_3 + 30, the interval thus was 420 cents. I am transcribing these notes below as F and A respectively.

Accompanying himself with repetitions of a 12-pulse cycle on the muscial bow, Musumali sang a song with mixed !Kung' and Bantu words, while another man joined in too, in unison.

My transcription is a condensed version of the performance. It demonstrates how voices and musical bow in their polyphony operate note-by-note within the bow harmonies characterized by the presence of two fundamentals tuned a major third apart and the use of harmonics (by changing the distance of the resonator's orifice (from the breast) not higher than the 4th harmonics. The harmonics of a gourd-resonated bow

are very difficult to transcribe, and I have omitted them, but the sung part moves strictly at the level of those harmonics, as can be easily calculated from the transcription.

This polyphonic song is set in typical Shona chords. To demonstrate my point that the Shona/Karanga type of harmonic system has roots in bow harmonies, I have added under b) the four roots and their lower harmonics discussed in the main part of this paper. Since Andrew

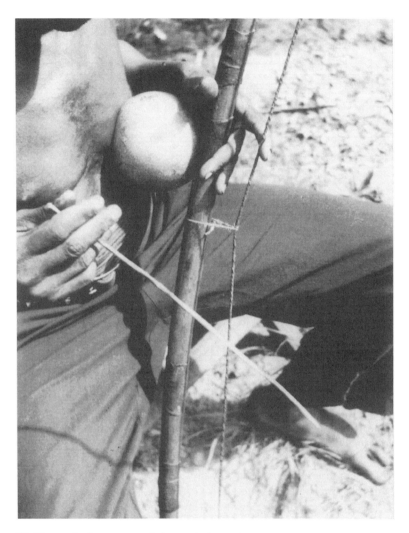

Ill. 58a–c. Performance technique of the *n//kau* (calabash-resonated musical bow) by Lithundu Musumali. An ordinary hunting bow is transformed into a musical instrument by dividing the string with a tuning noose and holding a resonator against the stave, the opening towards the musician's chest. By slightly changing its distance from the skin, the musician creates timbre melodies on top of the two fundamentals provided by the two segments of the divided strings. Notice the diagonal position of the stave at the end resting on the ground and the characteristic way in which !Kung' performers hold the leather stick used for striking the string. In addition, the left segment of the string may be lightly touched with the index finger of the left hand (c). The lower segment of the string has the deeper note ($F_3 + 10$), the upper segment the higher one ($A_3 + 30$). !Kung' camp at Vimphulu, December 1965 (Archive Nos. IX/27A, 28 and 28A)

a) Andrew Tracey's original transcription (courtesy A. Tracey)

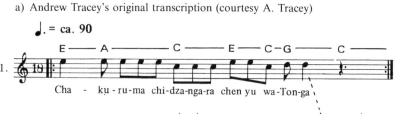

b) Hypothetical bow roots of a)

Ex. 88. Andrew Tracey's notation of a Shona threshing song, recorded at Gutu, Zimbabwe, in 1932 by Hugh Tracey. Archive of the International Library of African Music. Language: Shona/Karanga. With musical bow roots and harmonics added by G. Kubik to interpret the harmonic system

Tracey's transcription is in the key of C, the four bow roots F, A, C, D had to be transposed here to C, E, G, A.

The harmonic clusters constituted by the bow roots and their lower harmonics form something like a "resultant image" of this threshing song. I think that the illustration well demonstrates that all the notes constituting the elaborate polyphony of this threshing song (cf. Andrew Tracey's transcription under a) have counterparts among harmonics in my added bow harmonies under b).

If you are five people and you sing this threshing song to the accompaniment of an electric bass guitar (lacking musical bows) which would follow the roots I have added, but break them up rhythmically, you will experience something similar to what modern Zimbabwean musicians such as Thomas Mapfumo have discovered in the 1970s by using the traditional Shona harmonic system in their contemporary dance music.

Chapter IV
Composition Techniques in Kiganda Xylophone Music. With an Introduction into Some Kiganda Musical Concepts

When this paper was first published (Kubik 1969a), the kingdom of Buganda already no longer existed as a political entity within the larger Uganda. The Kabaka's residence and all the musical instruments in the *lubiri* (king's enclosure) had been destroyed. The court music had ceased to function.

After Uganda's independence in 1962 domestic political tensions between the central government of Milton Obote and the kingdom of Buganda became more and more obvious. By mid-May 1966 a crisis situation had arisen. Kabaka Edward F. Mutesa II had put an ultimatum before the Prime Minister of Uganda, Milton Obote: by the end of the month the central government should quit the territory of Buganda, including Kampala the capital. After this the Uganda Army was ordered to assault the Kabaka's residence on the night of the 24th of May 1966. Parts of the palace were destroyed, including the sacred drums of the Kabaka, the "house of music" with the xylophones, *entenga* drum chime and other instruments belonging to the court music ensembles. Equally the Kabaka's regalia and many other objects of inestimable historical value were destroyed.

Kabaka Mutesa II managed to flee from the burning palace. After weeks of marching on foot through Western Uganda he reached Burundi. Subsequently he lived in England, where he died years later under mysterious circumstances. In his book "Desecration of my Kingdom," London 1967, he recalled what had happened in Buganda:

... Among the sad news of who is dead, who is in prison and what is destroyed comes the confirmation that the Royal Drums are burnt. I saw this work begun and feared that it must have been completed. These drums of which there are more than fifty are the heart of Buganda, some of them hundreds of years old, as old as the Kabakaship. To touch them was a terrible offence, to look after them a great honour. A Prince is not a Prince of the Blood but a Prince of the Drum and his status is determined by which Drum. They all had separate names and significance and can never be replaced... (Mutesa 1967:193).

On June 10, 1966, President Obote declared the dissolution of the government of Buganda and ordered the Province to be divided into four parts. Simultaneously, the other three kingdoms within modern Uganda, Bunyoro, Nkore and Tooro were also dissolved.

March 2, 1988
G. K.

The impression that distinct and sophisticated compositon rules are at work in Kiganda music is sustained by a number of observations. The field researcher in Uganda may be struck by the fact that an expert *amadinda* player can usually reconstruct the second part *(okwawula)* of a xylophone piece, if he is given the first part *(okunaga)*, provided he knows the melody of the vocal theme contained in the instrumental layout. Although musicians in Uganda cultivate an excellent memory, it may happen to anyone that parts of a musical piece slip the mind temporarily. It is then interesting to note how the lost part is recalled. For instance, Evaristo Muyinda, one of the former Kabaka's musicians who instructed me in Kiganda music during several stays between 1959 and 1963, asked me to play him the one part he remembered, usually *okunaga*. In a few seconds of experimenting, he then tried to put between my part all possible notes that occurred to him, sometimes humming the vocal theme with it. By thinking rather of the resultant pattern to be expected from the combination he succeeded in reconstructing the missing *okwawula* part. If nothing helped he would have recourse to his *endingidi* fiddle, and try to reconstruct it out of the total pattern of the fiddle version.

Another observation is that identical or similar interlocking passages occur in quite different *amadinda* pieces. Compare *"Ssematimba ne Kikwabanga"* (Transcription No. 11, Table 10) with *"Naagenda kasana nga bulaba"* (No. 12, Table 10), or *"Wavvangaya"* (No. 8, Table 10) with *"Katulye kubye pesa"* (No. 18, Table 10) and many other items.

The third observation is that Kiganda xylophone music operates under concepts of consonance, though not a single "chord" except the octave is used, and that this quality immediately dissolves if a number of notes are deliberately changed, or if one misses the right entrance point with the second pattern.

I have long been convinced that it is not only the 2-note *okukoonera* part in *amadinda* music that is deduced from the combined basic parts, but that the latter are also structurally interdependent.

It is the primary aim of the present paper to show by what factors the individual parts in Kiganda xylophone music are predetermined and to what extent they are interdependent. This will enable us to lay down in descriptive technical terms the composition experience of the (unknown) ancient composers of Kiganda court music. Though we shall limit ourselves to xylophone music, we have to keep in mind that xylophones are merely one facet of Kiganda music and that this music is intimately connected with that of other instruments.

The presence of dinstinct composition techniques stresses the fact that in spite of its inner diversity and readiness to absorb borrowings from outside, the Kiganda musical system has not only preserved a remarkable stability over long periods but has remained essentially unitary. It has been customary to consider *amadinda* and *akadinda* music as two separate traditions. Although this is perfectly true from the narrower point of view of playing technique, there is evidence provided by the structure of the pieces themselves to show that these two xylophone traditions are not so separate and self-contained as it might appear.

This paper contains the 102 xylophone pieces that are the basis of the analysis. Most of the material was collected from two sources: Evaristo Muyinda and his numerous disciples and the group of blind musicians with whom I have regularly played at Salama, the Agricultural Training Centre of the Uganda Foundation for the Blind. The availability of this collection transcribed in easily readable cipher notation may encourage musicians and students in Uganda itself to collect many more songs and report variants.

The Historical Background

Though Buganda was "discovered" only as late as 1862, it is evident that its court music including the kind of xylophone music analysed has existed for a long time. To assess what changes the music might have undergone in the past belongs to the realm of speculation. But on the other hand some conclusions about the approximate age of particular Kiganda compositions may be drawn from references in the vocal parts to historical events. Taking into consideration that African musicians usually compose a new musical piece or song immediately after the moving event took place, this gives us a key for establishing a relative chronology of the court music repertoire which has been handed down. A song can give us a key for establishing a chronology with some probability. It is clear that a tune called *"Uganda kwefuga"* (Transcription No. 63, Table 11) was composed quite recently, probably around 1962 when Uganda became independent. Some other tunes, like *"Ekyuma"*

(No. 3, Table 10) for instance, refer to events early in this century and were composed at that time.[1]

One the other hand, a song like *"Olutalo olw'e Nsinsi"* (No. 7, Table 10) the story of a fierce battle, is perhaps a late 18th-century composition.

By carefully comparing the contents of the song texts, the style and vocabulary of the language with established facts in the history of Buganda, e.g. the genealogy of the kings, we may be led to a better understanding not only of the history of Uganda, but also of its music. Here training in ethnohistoric methodology such as laid down by Jan Vansina (1965) must be regarded as a necessary tool. My own work with various informants in Buganda has shown that the historical events connected with a particular song are often remembered even by people unspecialized in music. Charles Sekintu, Alisi Nabawesi, and Elvania Namukwaya Zirimu have helped me much in this matter. Any lacunae which they suspected were quickly remedied by making inquiries themselves among historical experts. Generally, as Joseph Kyagambiddwa (1955) has already demonstrated, all the songs are best correlated with the dynastic chronology of Buganda, beginning with the legendary Kintu, as was reported most comprehensively by Sir Apolo Kaggwa in his *"Ekitabo kya basekabaka be Buganda"* (1901). Kaggwa who held the office of *Katikkiro* (Prime Minister) between 1889 and 1926 was the first Western-educated Muganda historian. This work was translated into English by M. S. M. Kiwanuka and extensively annotated (Kiwanuka 1971).

Of course the problem has more dimensions: another custom in many African societies is to preserve the music of older songs and give them new texts; consequently in many cases (provided that no essential changes in the music took place) the tune would be older than the known text. To what extent this is so for Buganda may be seen from remarks in Roscoe (1911 : 31 – 2) that the king's harp players were able to invent new song texts on the spot "at a moment's notice." In such cases the new "improvised" songs must have been based largely on melodic material already known before.

Kiganda court music appears to have been comparatively stable. Although new instruments have been adopted all the time, an example being the *endingidi* one-string bowed lute, which was "invented in Buganda in 1907,"[2] the numerous stimuli from outside have always been integrated into the existing musical system.

The stability of the court music tradition may in part be explained sociologically. As Wachsmann has pointed out, Kiganda court music can be regarded as a rather esoteric tradition. The playing of certain instruments was restricted to the Kabaka's enclosure *(lubiri)*, such as *entenga*, the drum chime of twelve tuned "Uganda" drums, and until recently one of the xylophone traditions studied here, the *akadinda*.

Comparatively little material is available for a study of stability and change in Kiganda music. But we do know for certain that the old compositions for xylophone and other instruments have remained stable at least for the last few decades, which is not insignificant. If one compares recordings of *"Ssematimba ne Kikwabanga," "Kalagala e Bembe"* and others Hugh Tracey made in 1952 in the Kabaka's palace with what Evaristo Muyinda taught me ten years later (and still plays today), we can see the identity, to the degree of only one or two notes changed per song. Evaristo Muyinda was not in the group recorded by Hugh Tracey. Therefore we have two different testimonies of the same tradition before us.[3]

The dynastic chronology of Buganda, calculated at 30 years per generation and based on the revised genealogy of Kaggwa		
Ruler	*Generation*	*Year*
1. Kintu } 2. Chwa I	Beginning of the 14th Century.	
3. Kimera	1	C. 1314–
4. Tembo	3	1374–1404
5. Kiggala	4	1404–1434
6. Kiyimba	5	1434–1464
7. Kayima	6	1464–1494
8. Nakibinge	7	1494–1524
9. Mulondo } 10. Jemba	8	1524–1554
11. Suuna I	9	1554–1584
12. Sekamaanya } 13. Kimbugwe	10	1584–1614
14. Kateregga	11	1614–1644
15. Mutebi } 16. Juuko } 17. Kayemba	12	1644–1674
18. Tebandeke } 19. Ndawula	13	1674–1704
20. Kagulu } 21. Kikulwe } 22. Mawanda	14	1704–1734
23. Mwanga I } 24. Namugala } 25. Kyabaggu	15	1734–1764
26. Junju } 27. Semakookiro	16	1764–1794
28. Kamaanya	17	1794–1824
29. Suuna II	18	1824–1854
30. Mutesa I	19	1854–1884

Table 8. The dynastic chronology of Buganda, calculated at 30 years per generation and based on the revised genealogy of Sir Apolo Kaggwa. After Kiwanuka 1971:195. Rulers of the same generation are grouped together.

Further amplification of our knowledge of Kiganda music and xylophone playing in particular may be gained from pictorial documents. In 1904 Johnston published a photograph (taken in the last decade of the 19th Century) of two musicians playing *amadinda*. (Johnston 1904-II). On the two sides of the instrument, opposite each other, sit two players in white kanzus, each with two beaters. The instrument is a 12-key log xylophone, looking identical to those one sees today. We cannot hear the song these two musicians were playing in Johnston's picture, but we can clearly make out that they were playing in parallel octaves. We can also distinguish their playing areas and sufficient other details of importance to establish that this was the same *amadinda* style as today.

It is evident that the material dealt with in this paper comes from widespread historical periods. Although the musical pieces were collected after November 1959, they embrace material that may sometimes be generations apart. For this reason we shall be concerned here rather with lasting techniques in composition, which may be identical with whatever has been stable in this music, than with the characteristics of the musical periods that have probably existed in the history of Buganda.

Ill. 59 a – b. Two portaits of Kabaka Mutesa I (at the end of Sir Apolo Kaggwa's genealogical list amended by Kiwanuka).

(a) by Speke and Grant (1862), reproduced from Speke 1864:317

(b) A painting by Lady Stanley from a photograph by Stanley who visited Mutesa I on April 5, 1875. Reproduced from Moorehead 1973:146

Ill. 60. The oldest known photograph of *amadinda* playing. Reproduced from Johnston 1904-II:667

Ill. 61. A glance into the music house inside the *lubiri* enclosure of the King's court, where the *entaala*, partly seen in the picture, and the *entamiivu* drums to accompany it (background, right) were kept. Photographed by H. Tracey, June 1952

Transcription of Kiganda Xylophone Music

Staff notation may convey aesthetical meaning in itself, as one music student declared to me in defence of it. Therefore some people may find it lamentable to abandon it in its unmodified form, though its limited utility in African music has been demonstrated. Moses Serwadda and Hewitt Pantaleoni (Serwadda and Pantaleoni 1968) have opened up a path for the notation of *baakisimba* and other drum patterns in Buganda. For Kiganda xylophone music, however, something very simple exists and has been used by my teacher since 1961/62 as an "aide memoire." In this notation the five notes of the Kiganda tonal system are represented by the ciphers 1 to 5. With these, amplified by a few additional signs which I am introducing in this paper, virtually all xylophone music in southern Uganda can be transcribed accurately. Since our first experiments with this in Evaristo Muyinda's house in Nabbale, near Kampale in June 1962, it has proved to be a valuable asset for the conservation of the court music repertoire.

Cipher notation in Uganda may be considered an extension of an old practice, namely numbering the slats of log xylophones. For a long time this has been familiar in southern Uganda, in the Central African Republic and other places, for quickly assembling an instrument whose slats are usually stored in a hut. To write down a xylophone piece with numbers is therefore a logical development of an already established African concept.

The following example shows the notes of the two common Kiganda xylophones in conventional staff notation and in numbers. It may serve as a key to the transcriptions.

Amadinda notes: (12 keys)

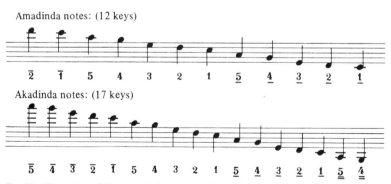

Akadinda notes: (17 keys)

Ex. 89. The notes of the *amadinda* and *akadinda* xylophones in conventional staff notation

Both notations are <u>relative</u> ones. They are not intended to convey the absolute pitches. The notes on the stave, as well as the corresponding numbers in notation refer to <u>xylophone keys</u>, and the intervals meant are those found on the Kiganda xylophones. No key or clef signature is used. In cipher notation lines above or below a cipher show the exact octave position of that note. Ciphers in the central octave (middle range) have no line. The lowest/highest octaves have two lines. We also use another important sign in this notation: the full stop. While the numbers convey the action of striking a certain xylophone key, a full stop indicates when <u>no</u> note should be struck. This notation does not consider the notion of duration, since the duration of a xylophone note on the instruments of Uganda is not altered once struck. Both symbols employed (number and full stop) have exactly the value of what I call "elementary pulses" in English; these are the smallest reference units for the musicians' orientation. Thus, both number and full stop indicate one pulse.

Another problem connected with cipher notation is that in the area concerned the concept of scale is usually one of movement from the highest to the lowest note (Wachsmann 1950 and 1957). When musicians write on their xylophones they do it this way, as I have often observed. Shall we follow this custom? I have been undecided about this for some time. It is mainly the concept of specific playing areas on the *amadinda* which made me favour the other way in the end. If we called the highest note on the *amadinda* number 1 and numbered the scale downwards, in accordance with traditional use, our system would cross the playing areas of the musicians. This would be contradictory to the structure of the music and even make the notation system unsuitable for musical analysis. The nature of the *amakoonezi* as a separate playing area and separate functional part of the music would also be veiled. Therefore I prefer to call the lowest note on the *amadinda* no. 1 and in staff notation a C. For the *akadinda* of seventeen keys I have decided (in this paper) to call the third note from the bottom number 1, here again because of the particular nature of *akadinda* playing areas. Another reason was that on the two xylophones that have been used in the Kabaka's palace for many years the *akadinda* note which I call no. 1 was the nearest in pitch to the no. 1 on the *amadinda*. Another acceptable notation in *amadinda* music would be to start on the two top notes with the ciphers $\overline{4}$ and $\overline{5}$, then move downwards with 1, 2, 3, 4, 5, <u>1</u>, <u>2</u>, <u>3</u>, <u>4</u>, <u>5</u>, down to the bottom note. But this too has more drawbacks than advantages.

Amadinda **and** *akadinda* **Tunings**

Important data about tuning procedure in Kiganda music and the nature of the tunings is found in Wachsmann 1950 and 1957. There is no doubt today that Kiganda instrumental tunings are tempered, in the sense that – in contrast to unaccompanied singing – they are no longer based on "natural" interval sizes such as "perfect" fourths and fifths (except the octave). Obviously, a compromise tuning with even intervals is being attempted on musical instruments, xylophones in particular. Whether the basic idea is a totally even division of the octave into five equal parts, however, remains to be proved. From the point of view of playing and composition techniques at least it is most convincingly so. I myself have not found any evidence that intervals are given different treatment according to which step of the scale they stand on. All intervals are treated as if in an equidistant pentatonic system, definitely at least in one of the two xylophone styles: the *amadinda*. On the other hand the actual measured tunings of Kiganda instruments often show considerable deviation from the equipentatonic mean of 240 cents, though never so far as to establish European minor thirds or seconds. On the *akadinda* musicians are usually reluctant to play any tune at arbitrary pitch levels and, it appears to me, this is not only for reasons of playing area. Evaristo Muyinda, as I have often observed, is quite decided about playing *akadinda* tunes at certain pitch levels only, and I feel preferably at a level where, by chance of minor deviations from equidistant tuning, the Kiganda-fourth sounds as near as possible to a "perfect" fourth. I feel that this observation must be mentioned.

From conversations with musicians it is also clear that in the Kiganda musical system there is nothing like a concept of minor thirds as opposed to seconds, but musicians have in mind instead a standard interval, that may be tuned wider or smaller, but is still considered to be the same interval. It is about ∓ 240 cents wide. I should like to call this standard interval a Kiganda second.

In Kiganda xylophone music an important concept is to define intervals in terms of instrumental playing, in terms of the spacing apart of xylophone slats. These "instrumental intervals" defined by distance of the beaters are freely translocated over the keyboard and still identified as the same intervals. Hence, here seems to be an interplay of two concepts in this music: (a) the notion of visual equidistance and (b) the notion of consonance, particularly with regard to (melodically laid out) fourths and fifths.

We have to realize that the concept of standard Kiganda interval is veiled by staff notation. The same Kiganda intervals may look like different ones when written in staff. For instance, what is written as $C - E$ or $D - G$ is the same interval, namely a Kiganda fourth. There is no distinction between major "thirds" and "fourths" in the Kiganda musical system. It is very important to keep this in mind when reading Kiganda music from staff. The same, of course, applies to what appears to be a distinction between "minor thirds" and "seconds", for example E−G as compared with D−E.

Herein lies one of the major deficiencies of staff notation. Cipher notation avoids this difficulty altogether since it has no implied meaning referring to interval size.

There are six intervals in Kiganda xylophone music that can be described in terms of instrumental playing. On the xylophone these are defined by distance. For the time being we shall call these intervals by their nearest European equivalents, until better terms have been found.

1. Prime (progression to the same slat)   −
2. Kiganda second
   (progression to a neighboring slat)   on average 240 cents
3. Kiganda fourth (skipping one slat)   on average 480 cents
4. Kiganda fifth (skipping two slats)   on average 720 cents
5. Kiganda seventh (skipping three slats)   on average 960 cents
6. Octave (skipping four slats)   −

The first five intervals are only used melodically in Kiganda music, the last, the octave, is the only simultaneous sound.

These intervals are represented on the xylophones as follows:

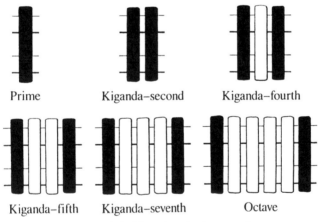

Prime   Kiganda–second   Kiganda–fourth

Kiganda–fifth   Kiganda–seventh   Octave

Ill. 62. The six intervals in Kiganda xylophone music

A Kiganda fourth is on the average 18 cents narrower than a perfect fourth. Yet it seems to have a distinctive "fourth" quality. Even if we take wide variations in this interval – as often occur in the tunings – into account, the Kiganda fourth is much further from a natural major third (386 cents) than from a perfect fourth (498 cents). Similarly with the Kiganda fifth, an interval on the average 18 cents sharp of a perfect fifth. People who have grown up in other musical traditions inevitably project their perceptual habits onto the Kiganda tonal system; Western-trained musicians, for example, often perceive the Kiganda notes in terms of an "anhemitonic" pentatonic scale, i.e. they imagine they hear something like C, D, E, G, A or C, D, F, G, B♭ etc.

Next, there is one factor in Kiganda xylophone music which reduces the six intervals we have distinguished to only three interval structures as I would propose to call this. This factor is the *miko* system, which applies to *amadinda* music. *Emiko* (plural of *omuko*), or without the initial vowel simply *miko,* are specific kinds of transposition of an *amadinda* piece, involving two conflicting procedures:

(a) transposition of a melodic phrase by steps; and

(b) octave displacement of certain constituent notes in order not to overstep the performers' restricted playing areas.[4]

Essentially, *miko* is a melodic reshuffling of the same tune "in the same pot." What was at the bottom then comes to the surface and what was on the surface goes down. The logic behind it is that musicians at the *amadinda,* while attempting to transpose a musical piece a step lower or higher on the "keyboard," have to remain within the restricted playing areas, i.e. they must not strike any slats which are not explicitly allocated to them. Through transposition the playing areas would of course also be shifted. In order to avoid this, all notes that would fall out of the fixed playing areas are displaced by an octave. Exs. 90–1 may help to explain what I mean. For example, in the well-known harp and *amadinda* song *"Olutalo olw'e Nsinsi"* ("The battle of Nsinsi", CD I/28), the *omwawuzi,* i.e. the musician playing the interlocking *okwawula* part, plays the following three notes in parallel octaves, when using the standard *muko* (cf. Transcription No. 7, Table 10).

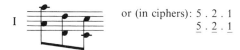

I   or (in ciphers): 5 . 2 . 1
                   5̲ . 2̲ . 1̲

Ex. 90.

If the song is to be transposed one step higher, the pattern would become: $\frac{1}{1} : \frac{3}{3} : \frac{2}{2}$ and the 1̄ in the performer's right hand would fall into the *amakoonezi,* the playing area of musician III (the *omukoonezi*), thus making it impossible for him to play his part. Therefore, the $\frac{1}{1}$ is transposed an octave down and becomes: $\frac{1}{1}$ The correct *okwawula* in *muko II* then is: $\frac{1}{1} : \frac{3}{3} : \frac{2}{2}$

Since the system is pentatonic every *amadinda* piece can appear in five different *miko.* These are the remaining four for the *okwawula* part in *"Olutalo olw'e Nsinsi":*[5]

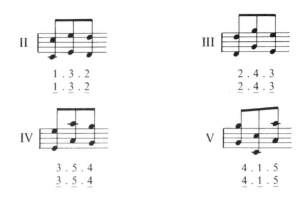

Ex. 91.

One result of this particular kind of transposition is that each *muko* of an *amadinda* piece may be appreciated almost as a different musical piece, since parts of the melodic patterns, though identical in structure, appear totally changed in shape in the transpositions (cf. Exs. 90 and 91). Another consequence is that in each *muko* a different inherent melodic-rhythmic pattern looms up from the two important bottom slats of the xylophone called *amatengezzi* (sing. *entengezzi*). Since it is the task of the third player or *omukoonezi* to duplicate this inherent note pattern two octaves higher on the two top keys (*amakoonezi*, sing. *enkoonezi*), the *okukoonera* part of each *muko* is different (CD I/29 *"Olutalo olw'e Nsinsi"*).

The *miko* system generates a concept of melody that is culture-specific. Although each of the five transpositions could be considered a different melody with regard to melodic shape, it is the same melody with regard to melodic structure. This is an important distinction to keep in mind. Octave displacement may change the melodic shape, but not the tonal structure. The patterns shown above only differ in melodic shape. It is melodic structure that matters in the composition process, while melodic shape is important to the recognition of text lines.

Consequently in the *miko* system several of the six possible intervals in Kiganda xylophone music must be considered structurally the same, for example: a descending Kiganda second is the same as an ascending Kiganda seventh (1 − 5 as compared with 1 − 5); or a descending Kiganda fourth is identical with an ascending Kiganda fifth. (1 − 4 as compared with 1 − 4). In the cipher notation this is perfectly well expressed, since the numbers remain identical in these cases.

In fact the *miko* system operates with only three interval notions: 1. prime; 2. Kiganda second *(a)* ascending *(b)* descending; 3. Kiganda fourth *(a)* ascending *(b)* descending. The octave is excluded from this classification since it has no melodic function. All the intervals within the *miko* system are thought of as equal-sized. They may be transposed throughout the range without any evidence that they are then appreciated as different. That the Kiganda tonal system should be equipentatonic is, in fact, the only working hypothesis compatible with the idea of *emiko* in *amadinda* music.

While interval structure or melodic structure is the fundamental notion to be worked on in the analysis of composition rules, melodic shape is more important as regards the question of the vocal melody being contained in the total instrumental pattern. This applies particularly to the vocal theme which is often based on the *okunaga* part. My field-work on *ennanga* harp music (Kubik 1966/67) which is related to the *amadinda* has shown that the inherent note patterns looming out of the rapidly moving total image of the instrument part represent or suggest various text phrases (cf. pp. 284–9).

In *amadinda* music the melodic shape of inherent note patterns cannot be retained in all transpositions of a piece. Octave displacement destroys individual inherent patterns in certain *miko*. Thus the "words" disappear too. The same applies to the *okunaga* part of any *amadinda* composition. In *muko* No. III (Ex. 91) of *"Olutalo olw'e Nsinsi"* (cf. Transcription No. 7, Table 10) it would be very difficult to recognize the basic words of the song which says *"Olutalo olw'e Nsinsi olwatta abantu"* ("The battle of Nsinsi killed many people"), since those very notes of the *okunaga* part that represent these words are spaced a Kiganda seventh apart. This partly explains why – in spite of the importance of the *miko* system – not all *miko* of a tune are equally popular and equally often played.

The question of absolute pitch in Buganda is of certain interest. For some time there has been a controversy over this.[6] Although *amadinda* and *akadinda* tuning models are perhaps identical in structure, it seems that they deliberately stand at different pitch levels. I have found the *akadinda* tuning model as a whole a little higher than that of the *amadinda*. By this I am not referring to the range of the xylophones, which is a phenomenon not connected with the level of the tuning models.

An example of these different levels is the measurements Hugh Tracey made in the Kabaka's palace in 1952. In the middle octave the *amadinda* tuning was 388, 344, 304, 260, 288 c.p.s. (slats nos. 6–10) while the *akadinda* was 416, 364, 312, 280 and 232 c.p.s. (slats nos. 9–13).

The two tuning models which Baganda musicians seem to have in their mind consist of a ladder of absolute pitches approaching the above vibration numbers. There is a certain amount of tolerance, but comparison of many tunings has shown this quite clearly.

Psychologically tuning is a kind of "focussing," in which the musician brings the notes he attempts on his instrument into congruence with his inner tuning model, an inner pattern of approximate pitches to which he has been trained from early youth.

More than one tuning model may be present in a particular culture. In Buganda there may be two. In practice this means that in *amadinda* tunings, which correspond to the *ennanga* harp, one can expect a note near 344 c.p.s., (172 and 688 c.p.s. respectively in the other octaves) while on the *akadinda* there will probably be a note very near 364 c.p.s. (respectively 728 and 182 c.p.s.). These "guiding" c.p.s. of 172 and 182 need not necessarily be the lowest notes of the xylophones, although this was found to be so in a few cases. Their position is quite independent of the range of the xylophone. Baganda musicians make both small and large xylophones, with high tuning and with low tuning, but this is irrelevant in this context. The *amadinda* and the *akadinda* can immediately be distinguished by the pitch levels of their tunings. This means that the actual notes of a particular xylophone can in principle start anywhere, but at some point they will always come near one of the two vibration numbers mentioned above. I found the two Kiganda "scales" to be roughly 100 cents apart, but minor fluctuations also occur. The *akadinda* tuning model, incidentally, also occurs in Busoga. The *akadinda* tunings are higher than those of the *amadinda,* "smaller" in Bantu terminology (cf. Tracey 1958 b). This may be what the prefix *ka-* really means, taking into account the magnitude concept of notes in Luganda musical terminology in which a note of normal level is called *eddoboozi;* a bass note (lit.: "big voice"), *oguloboozi;* and a high note, "small like that of a female voice" is called *akaloboozi.* This shows that the diminutive prefix *ka-* can be used to express musical "smallness".

Section 1
The amadinda

The Melodic Interdependence of the Basic Parts

Our objective in this section is to define the extent to which the two basic interlocking parts depend on each other in melodic structure. As is now widely known, *amadinda* music is performed by three musicians, two sitting opposite each other. Holding two beaters each they play two equal-spaced note series in parallel octaves, combining them in duple-division type interlocking. The third part *(okukoonera)* performed by the third player on the two top slats *(amakoonezi)* is a duplication of the inherent bass melody that can be perceived by the attentive listener looming up from the two bottom keys *(amatengezzi)* as a result of the combination of the two basic parts. A few performers in Buganda feel at liberty to occasionally leave out or alter one or two of its notes during performance. Sometimes they may play it only in its approximate shape,

Ill. 63. The *amadinda* was an instrument of important chiefs in Buganda: This was Saza Chief Kago performing together with his nephew, Danieri Seruwaniku, recorded and photographed by Hugh Tracey at Kasangati near Kampala 1952. Tracey recorded four *amadinda* pieces performed by the chief (AMA TR-138, A – 1, 2, 3, 4). Kasangati was the place were Temusewo Mukasa lived. In his report Tracey wrote: "The Ssaza Chief Kago, whom we will surely remember as one of the best informed Ganda men in local musical matters, played us his own compositions on the xylophone with the assistance of his nephew who sat opposite him" (Tracey 1953:8). Photograph: Courtesy of Hugh Tracey

especially when the other parts are constantly varied, as in the case for example in *"Ennyana ekutudde"* (No. 6, Table 10; CD I/30). This, however, does not change the fundamental concept of the *okukoonera* part as a pattern deduced from the combined basic parts. The *okukoonera* part may be disregarded in the present investigation, since it does not add structurally to the two basic parts.

But what is the relationship of the two basic parts themselves? Are they constructed at the will of the composer, or are there certain rules for setting them out? If so, is it possible that the two parts might be entirely deduced from each other as the *okukoonera* part is deduced from them?

Though court musicians still draw upon a rich musical terminology, it appears that present-day performers in Buganda cannot give a satisfactory answer as to possible rules for composition of xylophone and other music. In a sense they are merely interpreters, for almost the entire repertoire of *amadinda* music is historical. For the more esoteric *akadinda* a few new songs have been composed recently, after permission was obtained from Kabaka Mutesa II to construct this type of xylophone outside the King's enclosure. These are now mainly performed in the context of Evaristo Muyinda's concept of a "Kiganda orchestra," for example by the group of the Blind Musicians of Salama.[7]

Prescriptive rules for composition may have existed in the past. They may have been verbalized by some of the ancient composers, and followed by the majority as generally accepted norms of compositional behaviour among the musician families responsible for the court music.

The basis of the present analysis is the 50 *amadinda* songs published in Table 10 of this paper in cipher notation. Evaristo Muyinda did a final check with me so that the versions published here are to be considered what he authorized. I have also made recordings of most of them, in which Muyinda relates and explains the texts and the history of each item as well.[8] Many of the songs were recorded more than once.

A point of departure in my analysis was the intense impression transmitted to me by my teacher in his lessons that one of the essentials in *amadinda* music is a pleasing and mellow sound. Indeed, one of the striking traits of Kiganda xylophone music is an overall impression of consonance. Although no other notes than octaves are normally struck together (except in certain *ebisoko* or variations) the two basic parts always seem to be in a relationship of perfect consonance. How pronounced this really is can be proved by experiment. If the second part misses his entrance point, as often happens to a beginner, the immediate result is disagreeable dissonance. The two combined parts do not produce that mellow and pleasing consonant sound that was praised even by the first foreign visitors in Buganda, but rather an unorganized series of notes which seem to clash with one another. Musicians do not hesitate to disagree as soon as this happens, and the piece has to be started again.

But what has in fact happened? One can discover it visually if one writes any *amadinda* piece on paper so that the two parts are wrongly combined. Then you see that in the total pattern (the combination of the two basic parts) there occur many runs of Kiganda seconds (or Kiganda sevenths) as well as repetitions of the same note. It is precisely these intervals that are not preferred in melodic progression within the total pattern. Their use in *amadinda* music is limited. Practically, never more than two identical notes follow one another in the total pattern.

One the other hand there are two typical intervals that seem to govern the scene. These are the Kiganda fourth and fifth. Obviously the preference for these intervals causes the overall effect of consonance. Though tempered, Kiganda fourths and fifths have a markedly consonant quality in contrast to Kiganda seconds and sevenths.

Perhaps it is not by chance that the Muganda church music composer Joseph Kyagambiddwa (1955), who was the first Western-trained musician to take lessons in *amadinda* playing and try to write the music down, uses the term "harmonize" quite often in his book. Of course, the Baganda do not use chordal harmony, all their music being in unison and octaves. The "harmonic" or consonance experience here is essentially melodic; but there is a kind of "consecutive consonance," an important objective in this music which is expressed in the preference for certain intervals, namely Kiganda fourths and fifths, to follow one another in melodic succession. This "harmonic" effect is enhanced by the durational overlapping of the notes in this very fast music.

I have examined statistically all interval progressions occurring in the *amadinda* pieces published. The point of departure for the investigation was the *okunaga* parts of all the songs. It is this part that forms the basis of the xylophone compositions and represents an abstracted form of the vocal theme, whereas the inserted *okwawula* part is a contrasting pattern.

At first I classified all the *okunaga* parts according to their number of notes within the cycle. They are 12, 18, 24 or more. This I did because of the possibility that different rules might apply to *okunaga* patterns of different length. I found this not to be the case only at the end of the investigation.

The main work was then to discover statistically how the second or contrasting part was normally set out to fit into the first one. For this purpose I had to examine one by one all the intervals occurring in the compositions (totalling 966). The original tables are too extended to be published here,[9] unless reset in a computerized form.

Having completed this, I did a brief sampling from the point of view of the *okwawula*. This gave approximately the same proportion of intervals used in each particular context as the other way round. This shows that the "rules" I have distilled from this examination are valid reciprocally, from *okunaga* to *okwawula* and vice versa.

I have considered only the basic structure of *amadinda* patterns. No attention was given to melodic variation, first because it is comparatively rare, and secondly because in this music some variations, especially when musicians perform *okudaliza* or *okusita ebyondo* (cf. Chapter I), go deliberately against the normal interlocking relationship of the two basic parts. By temporarily suspending the accepted "rules of behaviour" tension is created. As in *embaire* xylophone music of neighbouring Busoga, variation in Kiganda xylophone music causes transient heterophony. It also deliberately violates the principle of octave relationship between the *okukoonera* part and the basic parts. I give below the results of our statistical examination. In the staff notation only one *muko* is considered. Here, *okunaga* notes are written with up-tails, the *okwawula* note that may or may not be inserted with a down-tail. In the cipher notation I have transferred the combinations discussed into all the five *miko*. Combinations not occurring in this music are crossed out. Rare combinations are marked by dotted crosses. We must keep in mind that these "rules" apply to all five *miko* transpositions. If we see, for example, that between two C's no other C may be inserted, it automatically implies that between two D's no other D may be put and so forth.

I. Non-occurring combinations (a)

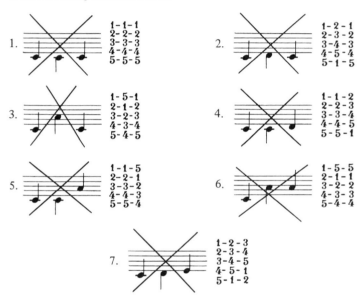

II. Rare passages (b)

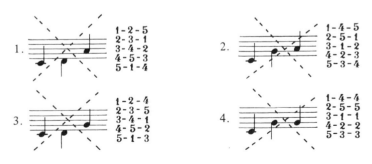

III. Preferred combinations (c)

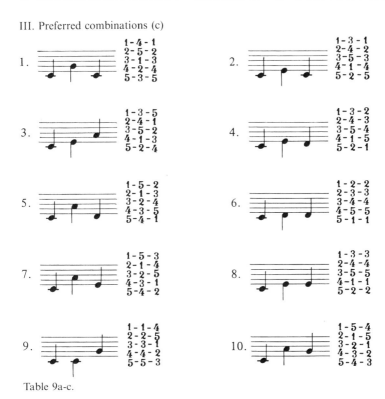

Table 9a-c.

From the above illustration we learn that there are seven non-occurring combinations in *amadinda* basic parts. We may first define these non-occurring types of interlocking in terms of instrumental performance. The first set of observations, set out below, is concerned with what happens when the melody in one of the two basic parts proceeds either to the same note (prime) or to a neighbouring note (Kiganda second). The latter progression may be either upwards or downwards, while we should not forget that in one of the *miko* you will get a Kiganda seventh instead of a Kiganda second (structurally the same interval, cf. Table 9, I/5 and 6).

From this can be abstracted the following rules of behaviour in *amadinda* music:

(1) Between two identical notes in one part the following notes are <u>not</u> used for interlocking:

    (a) the same note (giving three similar notes following each other, e.g. I/1).

    (b) either of the two adjacent notes, upwards or downwards (I/2 and 3).

(2) If two notes of one part form:
    (a) a descending Kiganda-second (= rising Kiganda-seventh), neither of these two notes is used in the other part (I/5 and 6).
    (b) a rising Kiganda-second (= descending Kiganda-seventh), the first of the two notes is not used in the other part (I/4).

    Note that the second note is very often put between, so much so that I have included this combination under the heading "Preferred Combinations" (III/6). This is an interesting case, and always takes place in one particular melodic context: it is meant to create a special *okukoonera* pattern, such as is found for instance in *"Kalagala e Bembe"* (No. 35, Table 10). It occurs in many other pieces as well. For further reference I will call this short note sequence the *Kalagala-e-bembe* particle.

Ex. 92. The *kalagala-e-bembe* particle

    (c) a rising Kiganda fourth (= descending Kiganda fifth), composers do not put the structurally intervening note in the other part, which would give an ascending run of Kiganda seconds, e.g. 1−2−3 or 5−1−2 (I/7).

These seven strictly non-occurring passages yield a total number of 7 × 5 = 35 non-occurring combinations in the whole system.

There are four further combinations under "Rare passages" (II) and finally ten under "Preferred combinations" (III).

(3) Where the first part forms a prime (two identical notes):
    (a) the preferred note in the second part is a Kiganda fourth down (= Kiganda fifth up) (III/1).
    (b) Next in preference is a Kiganda fourth up (= Kiganda fifth down) (III/2).

(4) Where the first part forms:
    (a) a descending Kiganda second (= rising Kiganda seventh), the preferred note in the second part is a Kiganda fourth up, counted from the first note (III/3).
    (b) a rising Kiganda second (= descending Kiganda-seventh), three possible notes are equally used for the second part: Kiganda fourth up, second up, and second down, all counted from the first note (III/4, 5, 6).

(5) Where the first part forms:
    (a) a rising Kiganda fourth (= descending Kiganda fifth), equally often used for the second part are: Kiganda second down, and fourth up (III/7 and 8).

(b) a descending Kiganda fourth (= rising Kiganda fifth) the preferred note is the prime (same as the first note) (III/9). Note that
the opposite form of interlocking, doubling the second note
rather than the first, is among the rare passages (II/4).

Binding rules of behaviour seem to come into play when a prime or
Kiganda second occurs in one part. In the case of a prime (cf. 3, above)
out of a total of 174 cases in my statistical tables, I had no less than 126
where the lower -fourth was used. In the case of a rising -second (under
4 b) in 85 cases I had the upper -fourth and in 62 cases the lower -second
(out of 200) which means that both forms of interlocking are acceptable.

But the most unequivocal rule of behaviour (cf. 4 a) is found with a
descending second in one part (II/3). Out of a total of 197 no less than
195 cases showed interlocking with the upper fourth. As we shall see later
this is a most important combination and almost a model example of the
fundamental importance of the Kiganda fourth as the preferred interlocking interval.

An important question now arises from this probe into the "behaviour" of *amadinda* patterns: Why are certain progressions absent and
other progressions so abundantly used?

The problem is not so clear-cut as to allow a single explanation for
every regularity we have found. It is obvious that though *okunaga* and
okwawula are dependent upon each other, this interdependence is not to
such a degree that one part could be deduced entirely from the other by
applying a single set of rules. There is always more than one possibility
for the interlocking notes, although this is further limited by factors we
have not yet touched such as the need for the vocal melody to be contained in the instrumental combination, a primary objective of the
Baganda composers.

The matter is, however, very complex and the "rules" found in the
above section are in themselves already the outcome of this complexity.
In composing Kiganda xylophone music a number of factors are at work
simultaneously. Therefore, the actual setting of the two parts against
each other is always a sort of compromise.

These factors may be isolated as follows:

(a) a desire for consonant sound and clarity of the (implied) text lines;
hence the preference for interlocking in fourths and fifths.

(b) the importance of the inherent-pattern phenomenon and the verbal
textual associations it calls forth.

(c) the desire for two or more tonal steps within a cycle, which is satisfied
by the creation of "segments of consonance."

(d) the need for the vocal melody to be contained in the instrumental
versions of a song, though it is not necessarily sung while playing.

(e) requirements of form, for example the bipartite organization of many musical pieces.

(f) the need for certain melodic "signals" (routine melodic passages) to appear in the total pattern, for example the *kalagala-e-bembe* particle or linking melodic runs.

There are many more factors all of them in interplay, producing as a result what we have experienced as the distinct "behaviour" of *amadinda* melodies. The balancing of all these requirements demanded great artistic skill and ingenuity on the part of the ancient composers, to create structures which, in a sense, are "perfect compositions", each a little universe in itself.

The preference given to Kiganda fourths (resp. Kiganda fifths) in interlocking is mainly due to two factors:

(1) that these are the only "consonant" intervals possible in a near-equipentatonic system. It is also essential to know that in this interlocking style, consonance proceeds in a zigzag fashion (in the total pattern), i. e. individual notes of either part relate to the preceding note of the other part. That is why in the composition "rules" we always count the interlocking note from the first one, when two notes are given.

(2) the necessity of establishing the inherent pattern phenomenon, and in connection with it, of enhancing the clarity of individual text lines; because the autonomous patterns looming up from the total image represent the entirety of possible text phrases. As I have outlined elsewhere (Kubik 1962c; cf. also Chapter I), this Gestalt-effect, so important in many kinds of music in sub-Saharan Africa, comes about through perceptual reorganisation by the listeners of melodic material composed in (1) predominantly disjunct intervals with (2) a perceptible internal order of multilateral pitch-relationships. Listeners then perceive rhythmic-melodic patterns which were not played by any performer, although they are contained in the structure. There is a difference between an "image as played" and an "image as heard" (cf. Kubik 1960, 1962c) and it is perhaps not coincidental that this phenomenon was first observed in the music of Buganda.[10] Within the *miko* system the largest possible interval is the Kiganda fourth (ascending and descending). Its predominant use as an interlocking interval guarantees the appearance of this audio-psychological phenomenon, which is a strong stimulus for text invention. Fourth-interlocking greatly favours the rise of independent inherent patterns heard at two or three pitch levels.

The aversion to interlocking in seconds is also explained on the same grounds. Such interlocking would cause a steady clash between consecutive seconds in this fast flowing music. It would extinguish the inherent-pattern effect and with it the possibility of hearing word phrases in the total instrumental pattern. Therefore this kind of setting is strictly avoided, except for short melodic runs as a connection between the consonance segments or particularly audible inherent melodies such as those *okukoonera* patterns where the characteristic *kalagala-e-bembe* particle occurs. There are some standard short melodic phrases which do not fall into the fourths-fifths-type interlocking, and which may be regarded as intermediate melodic runs. They connect the larger consonance segments that stand on different tonal steps. The $3-2-1$ particle is a typical example, obtained by interlocking a 3.1. progression in one part with a 2 in the other (cf. III/10). This gives a short downward run.

While ladder-type runs may be used for purely melodic (connecting) reasons, in order to link the consonance segments these runs appear always, characteristically, in a downward direction. The retrograde version of the $3-2-1$ particle, which would be $1-2-3$, is avoided (Table 9).

Like many other peoples in Africa south of the Sahara, the Baganda seem to have an aversion to ascending scalar melodies. In *amadinda* total patterns, for instance, one will never find more than two notes moving upwards in seconds. The ultimate psychological background of this widespread trait has not yet fully been assessed.

The most unexpected composition rule is reflected in the non-occurrence of more than two repeated notes. There is no argument against this on grounds of consonance, except that it would disturb the total impression of interlocking fourths-fifths, if this were the basic aim. But the "rule" is as strict as the one concerning runs of ascending seconds. Consequently the same note almost never appears more than twice in succession in the total patterns. But this rule does not appear to be valid in the xylophone style most closely related to the *amadinda*: the *embaire* of Busoga (for musical examples cf. CD I/items 2–4). The styles are so close that it has been customary in Buganda to adopt *embaire* tunes from this former tributary state and play them on the *amadinda*. *"Alifuledi"* (No. 16, Table 10) is an example in our collection, known in Busoga as *"Mobuka nkomera"* or *"Motuma nkomera."* The Kisoga *okwawula* is slightly different from the Kiganda. *Okunaga* is the same. Obviously the Baganda musicians have altered what was not in accordance with their own composition rules.

In the second xylophone style of Buganda, *akadinda*, there is also no aversion to reduplication of primes; on the contrary, *akadinda* interlocking emphasizes the prime and the Kiganda fourth, as we shall see later. Up to three repeated notes are customary in the total patterns of *akadinda* music.

What then is the explanation for this strange fact? I am convinced that it is to be found in the field of technique rather than in concepts of consonance.

It is common knowledge in Buganda that *amadinda* music and *ennanga* harp music have the same musical structure. Baganda musicians often insist that *amadinda* songs were originally played on the harp and later transferred to the xylophone (cf. Sempebwa in Kubik 1964c:157 and Chapter I). The same songs are played on these two instruments, the *okunaga* part being identical with the harpist's right hand part (also called *okunaga*) and the *okwawula* part being identical with his left hand part.

In playing, however, it makes a great difference whether this combination has to be produced by two men on the xylophone, or by only one on the harp. If these songs were originally composed for voice and harp, it is likely that the playing technique of the harp has had an influence on the structure of the music.

To pluck the same string on the harp several times with alternating hands at that enormous speed is technically very difficult and inevitably holds up the flow of the performance. Anyone who has tried to master the *ennanga* will discover this for himself.

Secondly, the Kiganda harp yields overlapping notes of longer duration than those of the *amadinda,* which increases the consonance effect, though on the harp too no notes other than octaves are played simultaneously.

Thirdly there is a special device on the harp, the rings made of lizard skin, against which the strings buzz when plucked. This has a double purpose, to give the harp its characteristic buzzing or crackling sound, and also to increase the loudness of the notes and to lengthen their duration. If one plucks the same string repeatedly this effect is bound to decrease because thereby one also damps it.

The Structure of Nuclear and Contrasting Patterns

This statistical examination of the microstructure has brought to light a number of characteristics in the technique of composing an *amadinda* tune. Now this needs amplification. The first objection that comes to mind is whether the number of possible *okwawula* notes that can be inserted might not be subject to further limitation if we examined sections of not only two, but three, four, five and more notes in the *okunaga,* in fact whole groups. Is it not likely that composition techniques in Kiganda music apply to whole phrases rather than microstructures?

Theoretically we would now have to be consistent and start examining groups of three notes to see how the contrasting part behaves. The value of such an investigation may, however, be limited, since there is no certainty that such arbitrarily chosen "groups" correspond with what Baganda musicians themselves consider to be groups.

But here we encounter a difficulty. What is a melodic group in an *amadinda* tune? Obviously *amadinda* pieces are made up of joined patterns rather than recurrent metric sections. This can be dealt with from the angle of the total pattern, as well as that of individual patterns.

A. M. Jones (in a conversation in London, 1968) suggested to me the terms nuclear and contrasting patterns for the two basic parts in *amadinda* music, to outline their traditionally accepted function.[11] The Luganda terms for these two patterns are *okunaga* and *okwawula*. Both terms are verbs. The one who plays *okunaga* is called *omunazi* (pl. *abanazi*). The one who plays *okwawula* is called *omwawuzi* (pl. *abawuzi*). Charles Sekintu, Curator of the Uganda Museum, says that Luganda musical terms are not usually used in ordinary language. Therefore it is often difficult to outline their meaning in clear terms. *"Okunaga,"* says Charles Sekintu, conveys the notion "to hit," which could mean "to start striking" the xylophone slats. The term *"okwawula"* seems to be related to *"okwawuza"* ("to divide"). *Okwawula* conveys the meaning "to separate," "to differentiate," "to link," "something between two that separates and at the same time links them, solders them together." In another context the term *okwawula* is applied in religious practice to the ordination of a priest, who as a clergyman *(omwawule)* is separated from other people.

The third term, *"okukoonera,"* conveys the meaning of striking the two top slats of the xylophone. It might be related to *"okukoona"* (to knock), says Mr. Sekintu. This could perhaps have the meaning "to make the music sound more regularly". The term *"okukoonera"* is not used in ordinary language.

The word *"amadinda"* itself is explained as follows: *"Edinda"* is <u>one</u> xylophone slat, *"amadinda"* many xylophone slats.

In other log xylophone styles of Africa, for example in south-east Africa, there are terms with similar meaning, descriptive of the task of the performers. Makonde musicians in northern Moçambique describe the task of the second player of a *dimbila* log xylophone, who plays an interlocking pattern, as *kujalula*. It might not be impossible that the terms *"kujalula"* in Shimakonde and *"okwawula"* in Luganda are etymologically related.[12]

The Luganda terms, however descriptive of the function of the individual parts, offer little indication as to their structural characteristics. Therefore I shall outline below the main characteristics of the two basic parts in *amadinda* music, based on my own observations in the field.

(1) The *okunaga* and *okwawula* parts are equal-spaced tone-rows of similar structural characteristics. This is emphasized by the fact that composition rules as applied to them are valid reciprocally. Each stroke covers two elementary pulses.

(2) In a few compositions the *okwawula* part is only a short repetitive phrase. Similarly with the *okunaga,* in very rare cases, although it is not clear whether in these cases the two parts have simply been exchanged for each other.[13]

(3) *Amadinda* patterns are of various lengths. The most important cycle numbers of individual parts are 12, 18 and 24, which yields total patterns of 24, 36 and 48, the same as we shall encounter in *akadinda* music. There are also a few patterns of odd length, which have 25 and 27 notes (see the transcriptions). One composition, *"Agenda n'omu-lungi azaawa"* (No. 50, Table 10) has 35 notes, which yields a cycle number of 70 elementary pulses.

(4) The speed of *amadinda* music is, on average, 300 M.M. for each stroke in the basic parts or 600 M.M. for the elementary pulses.

(5) Generally the *okunaga* part is the basis of the theme of the vocal part (sung in the harp versions), the *okunaga* being an abstraction of, and in unison relation with the notes of the vocal theme.

(6) The *okunaga* and *okwawula* part, though in themselves independent melodies, are a result of the technical organization of the music. It is the total pattern (combination of these two parts) that is aimed at, because it is the total pattern which contains the exact "words" of the song: the vocal theme and all text variations. Connected with the total pattern is the inherent-pattern phenomenon. These inherent note-patterns suggest words, and represent textual episodes in the song.

(7) Most *okunaga* and *okwawula* patterns are asymmetric in their inner structure, by which I mean that there are no recurrent metrical divisions, although the individual patterns are always absorbed in the overall cycle defined by the cycle number.

How do the Baganda musicians conceive these irregular tone-rows? Do they think of them as against a meter in 3/4, 4/4 or 5/4 time as for example Kyagambiddwa suggests in his transcriptions (1955)? It is difficult to ask the musicians directly. There is, however, one valuable test to find out about traditional concepts of such patterns. This is to observe how they are taught. It was enlightening to see how Evaristo Muyinda introduced his pupils to a new piece. He does not expect one to learn the whole tone-row of 18, 24 or more notes at once, nor does he proceed note by note. He always cuts the pattern into groups of notes or phrases. These groups are not metrical but generally irregular in length.

How these patterns are dissected for the purpose of teaching is an indicator of how the musician himself thinks them. I show this with an example that I remember well. When Muyinda taught me the *okunaga* part of *"Ssematimba ne Kikwabanga"* in December 1959, he split up the theme into four sections which he played to me one by one. After every single section he stopped until I had learned.

Ex. 93. Teaching the *okunaga* part of *"Ssematimba..."*

Baganda musicians obviously do not think the nuclear and contrasting patterns of *amadinda* music as "against" a meter or anything like. They think them in phrases of often changing irregular lengths. I have noticed, however, that individual musicians often have their individual groupings. For example musicians near Nkokonjeru that I visited in 1960 taught me *"Ganga alula"* but in a different phrasing from Muyinda, though the notes were the same.

Metrical divisions of the cycle do, of course, occur in Kiganda music, especially with reference to dance movement. There is a regular reference beat for listeners and dancers, and if the xylophone is accompanied with drums, the beat is struck on the *empunyi* drum. The *empunyi* strokes normally occur every sixth pulse. Besides, there are a few songs with unusual cycle numbers, such as 25, 27 and (in one case) 35: *"Agenda n'omulungi azaawa."* Here, other divisions may be used by the *empunyi*. But what is important is the principle to be found here. To perform on an *amadinda* constitutes a conceptual realm different from that of a dancer. The *amadinda* performer finds his timing in the strokes of his own part. His tone-row assumes a central position within his universe. The tone-row of his partner "falls between," "interlocks." For his partner it is the same: he also considers his tone-row as the primary reference line. And for the dancer it is the *empunyi*. Thus, the members of a performing unit each have a different standpoint relative to the whole.

(8) In many *amadinda* tunes there is a tendency towards bipartite organization, which is visible both in the individual parts and the total pattern. I only give one example but this factor is present in many xylophone pieces, sometimes being further subdivided:

|2.1.2.5.2.2.2.5.5.|2.1.2.5.2.1.2.4.4.|
Bipartite organization of *amadinda* tunes
(Example: *"Naagenda kasana nga bulaba,"*
No. 12, Table 10, *okunaga* part)

This bipartite form seems to imply a contrast idea, which is also often expressed by a shift of the tonal steps. Compare the ending of the first section in the above example which is 2.2.5.5. with that of the second section which is 1.2.4.4.

Other *amadinda* tunes have more complex forms, tripartite etc.

(9) An important characteristic of *amadinda* tunes is the presence of tonal steps. The tune always shifts from one to another in the unfolding of the composition, predominantly by steps. These tonal centres can be recognized both in the individual parts, when taken separately, and in the total pattern. Tonal steps are enhanced by the preeminence of the Kiganda fourth as an interlocking interval.

With these nine points in mind we can now set out on a wider examination of *amadinda* composition techniques, paying attention to melodic groups and other major structural features.

Ill. 64a–b. A standard drum set for accompanying *amadinda* and *akadinda* xylophone music in a popular context, i.e. outside the Kabaka's enclosure, consists of four individual drums: *Baakisimba* plays a basic ostinato pattern, *empunyi* marks the beat for the dancers, *engalabi* is the master-drum performing variation patterns, while *nankasa* is mostly used for showmanship. The latter is the only one played with sticks.

Picture (a) shows three of these drums in the Uganda Museum, Kampala, picture (b) a performance situation. The *empunyi* drummer who used only one hand to strike the beat is not seen in this picture.

(a) Kampala, March 1960; (b) At the Uganda Foundation for the Blind's Agricultural Training Centre, Salama, south of Mukono, April 1960

Typical Progressions and Consonance Segments

In all musics there are kinds of melodic movement which we may call reduplicative. By this I mean continuous melodic progression in the same direction <u>and</u> by the same interval. The simplest example is a steady progression to an equal note, a series of primes. Another is movement from step to step in the scale (upwards or downwards) – in xylophone music to the next slat. This gives a ladder-type melody. Finally such movement may be a progression of disjunct intervals of the same type, for example a cycle of fourths, upwards or downwards.

These reduplicative movements have an enormous experimental value in the structural examination of Kiganda music. For if they occur in one part they may demand similar progressions in the counterpart – or not! Whether they do or not is a criterion that may help us to assess to what extent the unwritten rules of behaviour are obligatory in a specific music. It is our objective, therefore, to find out whether reduplicative movement in one part causes definite reactions in the other.

Reduplication of the Prime

Repetitions of one note may occur both in *okunaga* and *okwawula*, apparently more often in *okunaga* though there seems to be no definite rule about it.

No one note, however, may appear more than three times in succession in either of the basic parts.[14] The only exceptions I have found are *"Balinserekerera balinsala ekyambe"* (No. 29, Table 10) and one piece that originally came from Busoga (No. 10, Table 10). Reduplications may also occur as a technique of variation (cf. *"Kawumpuli,"* No. 31, Table 10).

What does the other part do when a note is played three times in repetition? The transcriptions show that such a pattern may be interlocked either in parallel or oblique movement, the latter both ascending or descending. Only fourths and fifths must be used (in accordance with my observations earlier in this paper).

Joined Reduplications of Prime and Kiganda Fourths or Fifths

There are cases of reduplication which demand our special attention since the consonance effect is largely determined by them. I mean those instances where the reduplication of one note is followed by a reduplication of another which is in consonance relation to it (either a fourth or a fifth). For example, phrases like 1.1.4.4. etc. How does the other part then react?

Here something significant occurs. In most cases the reaction is to produce a kind of "mirror image" by using the same notes in the contrasting part but in a melodically complementary shape. This is demonstrated by the two examples below.

1. Phrase in *"Mugoowa lwatakise"* (No. 24, Table 10)

2. Phrase in *"Ab'e Bukerere balaagira emwanyi"* (No. 48, Table 10)

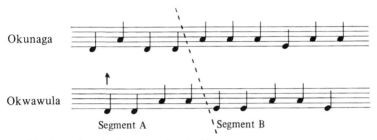

Ex. 94. Examples of mirror-type interlocking

Such passages are typical of *amadinda* music. They generate a persistent flow of consonant sound, for which reason I call them "consonance segments." In a single composition there may occur two or more such segments on different tonal steps. They may be linked by all sorts of intermediate runs, sequences, etc.

The consonance segments need not necessarily be as extensive as in the examples shown above. Sometimes they comprise only three or four notes with mirror-type interlocking. But this always suffices to express distinct tonal steps. In addition they always yield a distinct *okukoonera* pattern.

Tonal steps are an essential constituent of *amadinda* and also *akadinda* music. There is no composition in which one could say only one tonal step occurs. In many pieces there is a shift between two tonal steps, and there are a good number with three and four. Theoretically five tonal steps are possible in the *miko* system.

Reduplication in Kiganda-Seconds

(a) Descending

Melodic movement in descending seconds in *amadinda* music is regularly matched, in the contrasting part, with the upper Kiganda fourth, which starts one pulse later. Thus a parallel movement in Kiganda fourths is produced. The consonance effect of this is comparable to that of singing in parallel fourths with the difference that Kiganda consonance is interlocking. We can call this multi-part structure "interlocking parallelism in fourths".

Quite likely it is not by chance that this kind of relationship between *okunaga* and *okwawula* is so consistently used in *amadinda* music. It is a typical one that probably stands for the core of Baganda consonance concepts. It is also significant that it is connected with that kind of movement which seems to be most comfortable to Baganda musicians: a descending movement by step. I have selected an example where it is carried out over a range of more than one octave (with overstepping notes transposed by the performers).

Ex. 95. Examples of interlocking parallelism in descending fourth: *"Mugoowa lwatakise,"* No. 24, Table 10

In examining the above example we must not forget the *miko* system, otherwise the structural character of this combination may not be visible at once. That it is really interlocking parallelism can immediately be experienced, if one transposes the first note of the *okunaga* and the first three notes of the *okwawula* one octave higher.

The same kind of sequence also occurs in *akadinda* music in one of the most important *okwawula* patterns, the one called *kulya-kulya-kulya*.[15]

This type of interlocking parallelism has an interesting technical aspect. On the xylophone it appears as a kind of skipping or "span" process, in which the interlocking interval is always the next key but one. Several types of multi-part music in east Africa are based on this common technical principle, which is that the harmonizing note for a given note is found in the next note but one of the scale (cf. Chapter II).

It can almost be considered an "instrumental technique", not necessarily entailing a preference for certain intervals. When the span-process is applied by singers or players in different tone-systems in the various regions of Africa, it yields entirely different interval patterns. In a near-equipentatonic musical system such as the Kiganda one it gives parallelism in Kiganda fourths. In other areas it may give still stranger sequences of intervals. It may be present in those musics that use simultaneous harmony, but it may also be at work where consecutive or interlocking consonance is important as in southern Uganda.

(b) Ascending

What happens when reduplication in seconds occurs in ascending movement? We can hardly expect similar interlocking parallelism because this would give an ascending ladder-type melody in the total pattern. The most frequent combination I have found is the one in *"Akawologoma"* (No. 49, Table 10). In the *okwawula* part there is a five note phrase ascending in seconds. It is interlocked in the *okunaga* as shown in the following illustration.

Ex. 96. Interlocking of a ladder-type ascending pattern (in the *okwawula*)

At first this looks like another fourths interlocking, but then a sudden change occurs which yields a $3-2-1$ run in the total pattern, and it ends with a *kalagala-e-bembe* particle. Obviously the Baganda composers have tried to avoid parallelism in this case. In fact, fourth-parallelism would not have given a harmonious result, as it does in the descending form, because a fourth up from the first note is a second to the following one, as can easily be seen. This contrasts with descending fourth-parallelism, in which a̲l̲l̲ the constituent intervals (in the *miko* system) are fourths, forming a kind of fourths cycle in the total pattern. Within this musical system it would also be disagreeable if the ascending tone-row were filled out with lower Kiganda fourths. This would give interval progressions such as $1-4-2-5-3$ etc. which is a cycle of upper and lower Kiganda fourths, which does not sound very harmonious either. The best solution is the one the Baganda composers have found which is demonstrated by the above example. It is essentially this: the ascending pattern in seconds is countered with a kind of zig-zag movement in the opposing part, which creates a kind of polyphonic interlocking. Similar combinations to *"Akawologoma"* occur throughout in the *amadinda* pieces.[16]

Ascending patterns are rare even in the individual parts, and therefore I am rather hesitant to give any final conclusions on this type. What we know for certain is that when one part moves in ascending seconds the other does not do the same in parallel but interlocks mostly in counter motion.

The Song Contained in the Instrumental Versions

A most important dimension of the composition process is the relationship between instrumental parts and vocal melody. Although no singing goes with an *amadinda* performance, *amadinda* music is not "abstract" instrumental music in the Western sense. We have already learned that inherent note patterns looming up from the structure represent text lines.

Most authors and musicians in Buganda (Kyagambiddwa, Muyinda, Sempebwa, etc.) agree that music of the type heard on the *amadinda* was originally composed as harp music, and later transferred to this instrument. The harpist's pattern was

> broken up into two parts and each part is allocated to one of the (two) players of the *madinda*. The *madinda* players then produce the same song as played on the bow harp and the idea is that that should be recognizable as the song which was produced in the first instance by the voice... The primary instrument is the voice." [17]

Ennanga (harp) music, *amadinda* (xylophone) music, and the music of the royal twelve-drum instrument *entenga* form one complex within the musical traditions of the kingdom of Buganda. The same songs are performed on these three instruments, but while harp playing is always the basis and accompaniment of a voice part, *amadinda* and *entenga* are purely instrumental representations of the same songs. The "tune" (= the voice part, as sung in the harp version) can, however, be recognized in the instrumental settings.

A Muganda listener can indeed "pick out" the hidden voice part from the total image of notes played on the xylophone or the drum chime. Since the vocal part according to the rule of unison and octave concord, valid throughout Kiganda music, cannot contain other notes than those already present in the instrumental basis, an important problem remains to be solved: "In what part of the structure... can you locate the hidden notes which go to form the 'melody'?" [18]

To this question concerning the identity of the vocal part one must add two technical ones: (a) To what extent is the vocal part in *ennanga* music identical with inherent note-patterns appearing on *ennanga* and *amadinda*? (b) Is there any structural relationship between the vocal part in harp music and what appears in the *amadinda* versions as *okukoonera*?

In June 1962 I made some analytical recordings with Evaristo Muyinda. Analysis of these recordings and comparison with recordings of other famous harp players, for example Temusewo Mukasa[19] form the basis of the following observations.

The *ennanga* "is now practically extinct", writes Klaus P. Wachsmann in 1969. After the mental breakdown of the great harpist Temusewo

Mukasa there is possibly only one player left who belongs to the authentic harp tradition in Buganda, Evaristo Muyinda, who says that he was once instructed by the legendary Manyanja, whose music was unfortunately never recorded.

The instrument has been described by Wachsmann in Trowell & Wachsmann (1953:393–399). It has eight strings. The resonator corpus is an oval wooden bowl. It is covered by a membrane strained by means of leather thongs which meet on the under side of the corpus and are there attached to a small rectangular skin. Between the pegs of the harp's neck there are small movable rings consisting of banana fibre sewn into lizard skin. A small wooden wedge is inserted between ring and neck to make the fitting of the ring easier and to prevent undesired moving of the rings during play. The rings are pushed very near the vibrating strings of

Ill. 65. The late Temusewo Mukasa, who was the last *omulanga* (court harpist of the Kabaka). Photographed by Hugh Tracey in 1952

Ill. 66a – b. Details of a Kiganda harp (held by Evaristo Muyinda). Observe the ring buzzers below each peg whose squamous surfaces creates the *ennanga's* characteristic timbre, with the strings vibrating against the rings. Kampala, December 1967

the harp. When the musician plays, the strings vibrate against the squamous surface of the rings and the result is a crackling, buzzing sound. This device, like others for sound modification in African musical instruments, amplifies volume and length of notes, a lesser known fact.

The eight strings of the harp are tuned in an identical tonal system to that of the *amadinda*. The music can therefore be transcribed with the same number notation (Ill. 67).

The musician holds the harp horizontally in his lap and plucks the strings with the thumbs and indices of both hands. Ill. 67 shows the fingering pattern in *ennanga* music and the way in which the eight notes of the harp have been notated in the transcription of one harp song, found at the end of this paper. The notation is relative, it is not intended to represent the absolute pitch of the notes on the harp.

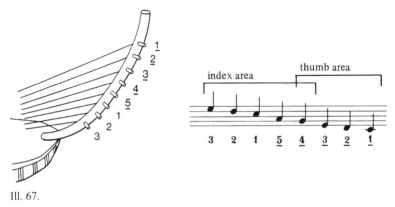

Ill. 67.

Ennanga music is performed by one singer, who accompanies himself on the harp. The music consists of three parts: *okunaga, okwawula* and *okuyimba* ("to start striking", "to differentiate", "to sing"). *Okunaga* is the harpist's right hand part, identical with the one played by the *omunazi* in the *amadinda* versions. *Okwawula* is played by the harpist's left hand. These two parts are equi-spaced series of notes combined in the interlocking way. *Okuyimba* means to sing, it is the harpist's voice part.

The structure of *ennanga* music and the exact relation between the three parts is shown under transcriptions. My choice of an example is *"Olutalo ol'we Nsinsi,"* often used by Evaristo Muyinda in lecture demonstrations, and recorded by me on numerous occasions [20] (CD I/31). It is also a very suitable song for a beginner on the harp to start with.

Joseph Kyagambiddwa, who attempted a transcription of this song in his book "African Music from the Source of the Nile," remarks about its history:

King Junju reigned from about 1780 to about 1797. In warlikeness he surpassed all his Ganda predecessors. In bravery he was second only to Kintu. Partly hating to see the once unified Ganda empire now tattered, and partly loving to fight just for fighting's sake, he made war a national business and came to regard peace as mere idleness. His achievements reached a zenith when he won the wealthy district of Buddu from Bunyoro which several of his predecessors had fought or negotiated with in vain in order to annex it to the Buganda kingdom.

The only war he ever lost was the one he did not declare. His own brother, Prince Semakokiro, revolted and marched against him with an army he had organized out of his followers.

A decisive battle was fought at Nsinsi where, after very savage fighting the King's army was defeated and routed, and he himself killed, his victorious brother becoming king of Buganda. (Semakokiro reigned from about 1797 to about 1814.) After the civil war, musicians set to work to compose the *Battle of Nsinsi* in order that posterity might learn about and commemorate the bloodiest battle that turned a number of stubborn vanquished soldiers into wanderers who later emerged as a new tribe... the *Abakunta* people (Kyagambiddwa 1955:121).

Listening to the recording of this song, the ear is at once attracted by several inherent melodic-rhythmic lines emerging from the *ennanga*. They are transcribed in the score under "aural images" (cf. Ex. 114). Comparison of the various phrases of the voice part with these inherent patterns reveals their interrelationship. The inherent patterns in the instrumental part are suggestive of certain textlines.

An instructive example is the inherent pattern II, first half. Long before the respective text phrase is sung in the tape recording, this inherent rhythm seems to "speak" the following words: *"Batulwanako ab'edda!"* Evaristo Muyinda very often introduces a new text phrase by first playing the corresponding inherent pattern into the foreground through accentuation. It can be noticed in the recording that the notes representing this text phrase are first accentuated in the harp part until the melody is firmly established as a *Gestalt*. Then it appears in the voice part.

The same happens with the phrase *"bulungi!"* which is represented melodically by the last four notes of the inherent pattern I. Shortly before singing this phrase, Muyinda accentuates, over several repetitions, the high note 3 in the harp part. As a consequence the ear becomes attracted by a melodic sequence of 1, 3, 2 and 1 which seems to "speak" the word: *"Bulungi!"*

The main theme of the song with the words *"Olutalo olw'e Nsinsi lwatta 'bantu"* is not so unequivocally represented by an inherent pattern.

Nevertheless one can hear it mysteriously looming up in the second half of inherent pattern III. This line strongly suggests the words of the main theme, although not all its notes are identical.

In this performance by Evaristo Muyinda there was no text phrase to represent any of the five *okukoonera* patterns known in the xylophone versions. One *okukoonera* can, however, be recognized as an inherent pattern in the harp part (Cf. inherent pattern I, Ex. 114). In other harp songs it often occurs that a text phrase is melodically identical with an *okukoonera* pattern. Two-note phrases are in fact likely to be so.

Summarizing we can say that various text lines in *ennanga* harp songs are usually very similar to, or identical with, inherent patterns emerging from the instrumental part. Accordingly, a Muganda listener, educated in the country's musical traditions, can pick out the hidden voice part from purely instrumental representations.

One can also observe, however, that the *okwawula* part in the harp version of *"Olutalo ol'we Nsinsi"* as performed by Muyinda on this particular occasion is slightly different from the *okwawula* of the xylophone version he taught me. Muyinda also varies this pattern in the course of the song. The score[21] gives a condensed version, in cipher notation, of Muyinda's performance. To avoid repetitions I have omitted the long instrumental interludes between the text phrases. Although the voice part in *ennanga* music is, in principle, in unison with the notes of the instrumental backing, it can be observed that some of the notes sung may be anticipated rhythmically or shifted, and there may also be a few passing notes.

We can now give a brief summary of what we have found in the composition techniques of *amadinda* and *ennanga* music.

There are considerable regularities in composition, but the final shape of a piece constitutes a compromise determined by many factors, often contradictory. Composition "rules," although prescriptive, do not have absolute validity in isolation. They may be broken. Rules may also be combined or balanced against each other.

This makes composing Kiganda music a complex and skilful art. There are, however, a few strict rules which must always be observed, such as the seven non-occurent combinations. Two very strict rules are applied from the point of view of the total pattern: that more than two identical notes should never be allowed, nor two neighbouring notes in ascending motion. *Okunaga* and *okwawula* can be considered as performers' patterns with certain structural characteristics. They aim at recreating the total image. Composition rules are to be understood primarily from the angle of the total image.

A typology of melodic movement in *amadinda* music is possible both from the point of view of the total pattern and from each of the combining parts. We have enumerated a few important ones such as (a) mirror-type combinations, (b) interlocking descending fourths sequences, and (c) various kinds of intermediate melodic runs which are always conceived in a descending direction.

An important aspect of *amadinda* music is the existence of shifts between tonal steps, evident both in the total pattern and the individual parts. Bipartite form is widespread in this music, and may be further subdivided. Individual melodic phrases may appear repeated in the total pattern at several places. The bipartite form expresses itself in many variants, for example $A + B + A + B_1$.

Amadinda tunes cause a picture-puzzle effect. Melodic and rhythmic elements in the total pattern may be perceived in various groupings and alternately felt to belong to this or that group.

The dominant type of interlocking practised in *amadinda* music is that of Kiganda fourths, both upper and lower.

Section 2
The akadinda

The Nuclear Pattern

The basis of the following investigation is the 62 *akadinda* compositions which are transcribed in cipher notation at the end of this paper (Table 11). The major part is historical songs that were played in the Kabaka's court. But as is known the *akadinda* has also been performed outside the enclosure since the 1950s, which was not its original use. It now forms part of the so-called Kiganda orchestra in which the xylophone – originally unaccompanied – now stands in the centre of an ensemble of four drums, rattles, flutes and fiddles (Kubik 1960:16).

Evaristo Muyinda is the main initiator of the Kiganda orchestra. He is also the one who originally (1957/58) trained the now popular Kiganda orchestra of the blind musicians at the Agricultural Training Centre of the Uganda Foundation for the Blind, at Salama. Since 1959 the blind have, however, continued on their own. For over ten years they have handled the *akadinda* songs they learned from Mr. Muyinda as their own endogenous tradition, without further outside instruction, and handed over the music to each fresh intake arriving to receive training in agriculture.

This fact makes Salama almost a natural scientific experiment, suitable for a study of change and stability in a tradition. It is also a place where new *akadinda* tunes have been composed in the older style and, therefore, a rare opportunity to study composition techniques live.

Most of the new compositions published here I collected from them. Usually I checked them with Evaristo Muyinda, at least those they had learned from him. But where the Salama version is different from his, I have marked this.

The new songs composed by the blind follow established composition techniques. But the blind only use two *okwawula* patterns (*"kulya-kulya"* and *"katongole"*). The text of the new songs is, for the most part, no longer connected with the Kabaka's court. Occasionally the vocal melody is also sung in the Kiganda orchestra, although the singers are

Ill. 68. The 17-key *akadinda* as it used to be, in a hut within the enclosure of the Kabaka's court. Notice the *amakundi* projections (lit. navel hernia) which prevent the slats from moving off the banana stem supports. Photo: Hugh Tracey, 1952

drowned by the battery and the xylophone, and can hardly be heard on a panorama-type recording. A few of their modern songs are attributed to Mr. Muyinda, e.g. *"Njagala okuddayo e Bukunja"* (No. 62, Table 11). As is now generally known, *akadinda* music is different in structure and playing technique from *amadinda* music. The 22-key type can be played by six musicians, three sitting opposite each other, or by five, if one of the *abanazi* takes the task of two people. The 17-key instrument can also be played by five or six people, but more often this shorter instrument is played by four or even three people. In the latter case one *omunazi* plays the *okunaga* part in parallel octaves. Two *abawuzi* sit opposite him and each plays the *okwawula* pattern an octave apart.

The *akadinda* is played in triple-division interlocking. This important interlocking model occurs in many parts of Central Africa, in fact it appears to be a fairly widespread heritage.[22] *Akadinda* music is structurally not an isolated phenomenon at all, though it may have appeared to be so. Lois Anderson, in a survey of xylophone playing in east Africa, claims to have found a parallel in another type of xylophone music in Uganda itself. "The only style which is comparable to this" she writes about the *akadinda*, "is that used by the Padhola, although an important difference is the scale structure used" (Anderson 1967:69).

An important difference between *akadinda* and *amadinda* music lies in the structure of the nuclear pattern. Another is the particular character of the *okwawula* in the *akadinda*: there are a limited number of *okwawula* patterns in the *akadinda* which are used in many tunes, whereas no such restriction exists in *amadinda* music (cf. the *akadinda* piece *"Empuuta,"* CD I/5).

These are the main characteristics of *akadinda* nuclear patterns:

(1) Like *amadinda* they are an equal-spaced series of notes.

(2) Each note covers three pulses.

(3) *Akadinda* nuclear patterns always have regular cycle numbers. The most common are 8, 12, 16. A few have 18 or 20.

(4) The average speed is 200 M.M. per note of the nuclear pattern, which gives a seed of 600 M.M. to the elementary pulses, the same as in *amadinda* music.

(5) The nuclear pattern condenses the vocal theme into a equal-spaced note series in unison relation with it. Maurice Djenda from Central African Republic, who visited Salama with me in 1967/68, feels the *akadinda* nuclear patterns as a kind of "bass" below the vocal melody. In the Kiganda orchestra the real "bass," however is the *empunyi* drum, which plays a series of regular beats coinciding with every second note in the nuclear pattern.

(6) In contrast to the *amadinda*, *akadinda* nuclear patterns have a pronounced tendency towards divisive inner rhythmic structure

(Ex. 97). Played by themselves they may often give a rather un-African impression (see also Jones 1971 b, page 140).

4 .. 4 .. 4 .. 4 .. 2 .. 2 .. 5 .. 5 .. 3 .. 3 .. 1 .. 1 ..

Ex. 97. Example of divisive rhythm in an *akadinda* basic part: *"Kisawo ..."*, No. 51, Table 11

(7) There is always one note that tends to recur regularly. I propose to call it the "guide-note." This note is of utmost importance to the composition rules. The beats of the *empunyi* drum in the Kiganda orchestra usually coincide with the guide-note in 8-note and 16-note patterns, which stresses its importance. Below I give an example of a pattern where the guide-note can be easily detected (Ex. 98).

At the beginning of a nuclear pattern the tune often jumps a fourth upwards from the guide-note. Some persons trained in Western music are strongly inclined to hear this as an up-beat and then put a barline after the guide-note, which is misleading.

2 .. 4 .. 4 .. 2 .. 1 .. 5 .. 2 .. 3 .. 3 .. 1 .. 1 .. 1 ..

Ex. 98. The guide-note in *akadinda* basic part: *"Bogerera ..."*, No. 53, Table 11

In a few songs e.g. *"Balinserekerera balinsala ekyambe"* (No. 52, Table 11) the guide-note occurs throughout, in other songs it may be left out in some places.

Studying this we make one more significant observation. In 16-note nuclear patterns the guide-note mainly occurs every 4th note. The same applies to 8-note patterns, where it may also occur every other note, e.g. in *"Matu ga njobe"* (No. 64). The situation is quite different with 12-note patterns, where it occurs mainly every third note.[23] There are a few exceptions to this rule in the present collection (e.g. *"Ganga alula"*, No. 76, Table 11).

A few compositions have no guide-note, e.g. *"Kisawo kya muwa butwa..."* (No. 51), *"Abe mbuga basengejja"* (No. 60, Table 11), *"Bijja bisamba endege"* (No. 94, Table 11) etc. All this has an effect on composition.

The guide-note may occur on any level. In most of the tunes in our collection it is note 2, but it may also be 5, 4 etc.

(8) The melodic compass of the nuclear pattern is five notes in most cases. In a good number of tunes it is four notes. In one exceptional case (*"Ssematimba ne Kikwabanga,"* No. 58, Table 11) it was six notes and in another (*"Kawuta yeggalidde,"* No. 101, Table 11) only three notes.

(9) Another striking feature of the nuclear patterns is their slightly falling melodic line regarded as a whole. In almost all compositions the ending note is lower than the starting one. The melodic peak may occur immediately after the beginning, (e.g. *"Matu ga njobe"*, No. 64, Table 11), or it may be saved for the second half of the pattern, only to fall abruptly afterwards (e.g. *"Envubu terindwa buziba,"* no. 97, Table 11).

(10) There is a pronounced tendency towards bipartite form. *"Omulwadde w'envunza..."* (no. 73, Table 11) is a typical example. The two parts are of equal length and have different tonal contents. The second section may be melodically reminiscent of the first one in some parts. Some patterns may have a tripartite form, e.g. *"Tweyanze..."* (no. 102, Table 11).

(11) The nuclear pattern also implies tonal steps, which may number from two to four. These can be recognized quite clearly by listening to the vocal theme behind the instrumental layout. Bipartite form and tonal steps may generate a kind of contrast relation between the two sections of the nuclear pattern, the second one having almost a responsorial quality.

Typology of *okwawula* Patterns

There is a limited number of fixed *okwawula* patterns in *akadinda* music. These are combined with the nuclear patterns in a certain predetermined way. Each of these patterns may appear in slight variants, that is, in a form adapted to the tonal progressions of the *okunaga* part and/or the notes of the vocal theme. The demands of consonance and text may compensate or contradict each other, which then leads to a compromise. An example of a rather far-reaching adaptation of an *okwawula* pattern is *"Omulwadde w'envunza..."* (No. 73, Table 11).

In spite of these variants the main groups can easily be distinguished. Baganda musicians usually have mnemonic devices to identify them. At Salama the two most important *okwawula* patterns are referred to as *kulya-kulya-kulya* ("to eat, to eat, to eat") and *katongole* ("small chief").[24]

Formally the *okwawula* patterns are made up of two short series of notes, one to be played with the right hand and one with the left. The two note series have equal value and interlock like two parts. They may be appreciated by musicians as separate melodies in themselves (cf. Chapter I). Staff notation tends to obscure this fact, since the right hand notes in the playing style of the Kabaka's musicians are written as quavers and the left hand ones as crotchets. But the plain fact is that both have equal accent, equal duration and equal structural importance.

When starting any of the *okwawula* patterns the first of the *abawuzi* to insert his pattern may just play the right hand notes alone. This can be clearly heard on Hugh Tracey's recordings of *akadinda* music (TR-137) in 1952. Only when the *abawuzi* are absolutely convinced that their right hand strokes are "the beat" or basic reference line and not the stroke of the *abanazi* opposite, do they add the left hand strokes. Many musicians, however, insert both patterns immediately.

The right and left hand note series are mostly a Kiganda fourth or fifth apart, which gives them a distinct consonance quality. In descending patterns the Kiganda fourth is the preferred interval, in ascending ones the Kiganda fifth.

The following is a brief typology of the most common *okwawula* patterns found in *akadinda* music. I give the basic form both in staff and cipher notation.

1. The Descending-Fourths Pattern or kulya-kulya *Pattern*

In its basic form it consists of six notes, three in each hand, which descend by steps in parallel interlocking at the distance of a Kiganda fourth. This is one of the most frequent patterns. It occurs in its basic form as well as in a number of slight adaptations. It is only used for the interlocking of 12-note *okunaga* parts.

3 5 . 2 4 . 1 3 .

Variant: 35.24.13.35.24.13.35.24.5̱3.35.24.13.

Ex. 99

2. The katongole *Pattern*

We call this four-note pattern *katongole* because its melody evokes for many musicians the syllables *ka-to-ngo-le* ("small chief"). It is a very common pattern and occurs in a few variants. It is used for 8-note and 16-note *okunaga* patterns and for a few 12-note ones as well.

Variants: (a) 24.35.
(b) 14.35.14.35.13.35.14.35.
(c) 14.35.14.35.14.35.13.35.14.35.14.35.14.35.13.35.
(d) 14.35.24.35.14.35.23.35.

Ex. 100

3. The Ascending-Fifths Pattern

This is the exact *retrograde* form of the descending-fourths pattern (see above). It becomes obvious by comparing the two patterns as they occur in the composition *"Njagala okuddayo e Bukunja"* (No. 62, Table 11) with for example *"Bijja bisamba endege"*. This relation is clearly seen in cipher notation: 41.35.24 compared with 42.53.14. The ascending fifths pattern is not found as often as the other two patterns above. We have only four pieces in our present collection.

Ex. 101

4. The "Basubira malayika" *Pattern*

We call it this, because *"Basubira malayika"*, in which it occurs, is a frequently heard tune. Though it is one of the most beautiful and interesting in Buganda, there are few compositions in which it is used.

Ex. 102

5. *The* "Akakuba-mpanga" *Pattern*

This pattern in the song *"Akakuba-mpanga n'enkoko bagenda mangu"* (No. 100, Table 11) and a related version in song No. 99, Table 11, are possibly developments of the *katongole* pattern. But it has a rather distinct quality and so I have preferred to list it separately. Its "bass" melody in the right hand is a characteristic trait. This is a very rare pattern.

3 4 . 1 3 . 2 4 . 5 3 .

Ex. 103

6. *The* "Kawuta" *Pattern*

This extraordinary *okwawula* occurs in the song *"Kawuta yeggalidde"* (No. 101), the most unusual composition in the *akadinda* repertoire. Besides fourths and fifths this pattern also has a Kiganda-seventh jump.

2 4 . 3 5 . 1 4 . 5 4 .

Ex. 104

7. *The Bow-Shaped Melody or* "Tweyanze..." *Pattern*

This is a parallel fifths pattern characterized by a bow-shaped melody. It occurs in the extraordinary composition called *"Tweyanze, tweyanze ewa Mugwanya"* (No. 102).

1 4 . 5 3 . 4 2 . 5 3 .

Variant form (as in *"Tweyanze ..."*):

14.53.42.53.14.53.42.53.14.53.43.53.

Ex. 105

Among these seven *okwawula* patterns only the first four are widely used. The most common are the first two. While we could call the first three elementary patterns, nos. 1–7 might be regarded as composed of elements found in the former. In principle all *okwawula* patterns can appear at any level though in practice this is limited by the playing areas of the *akadinda*.

Composition of *akadinda* Songs

To find out directly how the ancient composers proceeded when they created this material is no longer possible. But certain conclusions may be drawn from the behaviour of present-day musicians. I was lucky in December 1962 to be at Salama, when Amisi Sebunya (ca. 30 at that time), was just about to compose the piece *"Ab'e Salama"* ("People of Salama") together with some other blind musicians.

It took him a few days to get a satisfactory total pattern. During this period I happened to make a series of recordings, showing the various stages of the composition process. Although this may only provide limited evidence as to how the royal musicians in the Kabaka's court once composed their music, the documentation of a living process of composition is valuable in itself.

At Salama when a new tune is composed the point of departure is always a vocal melody. The composer has a firm song in his mind which he may have sung on its own for some time. In order to set it for *akadinda* he first tries to find an instrumental abstraction of his vocal theme. This is to be the *okunaga* part. It is then laid under the vocal melody like a regular equal-spaced "bass" in such a way that the instrumental notes are always in unison relation with the corresponding notes of the vocal theme.

This objective may involve the composer in various problems. The first difficulty is that the *okunaga* part should be logical in itself and predominantly divisive. The ancient composers succeeded very well in this, as testify the old songs, by comparison with some new ones that have been composed at Salama. Often the new songs have neither a pronounced guide-note nor are they divisive. This gives them a less restful, less balanced quality, even if composition techniques are applied correctly.

The first version Amisi Sebunya had for his song was an 18-note pattern. Then he decided to "stretch" the vocal melody so that it would fit a 20-note pattern (cf. No. 90, Table 11). In order to find a suitable *okunaga* part he used to assist himself by playing the entire vocal melody on the xylophone in single note or melodic style, which is an important solo style in *akadinda* music and often employed in the Kiganda orchestra. In this one man plays xylophone alone, duplicating and embellishing the vocal melody on the instrument. I have several recordings of this little known xylophone practice.[25]

When Amisi Sebunya was satisfied with the 20-note pattern, he then had to find a suitable *okwawula*. He described the composition process with the words: "First you have to find the *okunaga* part and then see whether *kulya-kulya* or *katongole* fits."

During a joint visit to Uganda with Maurice Djenda in November to January 1967/68 we stumbled on another Salama musician just in the process of composing a tune: Abusolomu Mukasa, ca. 30, who was not blind, but had worked and lived with the Salama blind for many years. He had produced some remarkable vocal music in the traditional style. Already in 1962 I had seen him participating in the composition of *akadinda* music, and if I am correct he had a share in the song *"Mpa wali yanda-yanda"* (No. 84, Table 11). Since his method is a typical one I had better relate in detail how he composed the *akadinda* piece *"Akabira kange"* (CD I/32).

One day, Abusolomu Mukasa came to the guest house where we were staying and said that he was having trouble in composing a tune. He had a new one for *akadinda;* the *okunaga* part was fine, but he had difficulty finding the right place on his own for the *okwawula* part. Certainly *katongole* would have to go with it, but he would like to try several ways of fitting it in. I followed him down to the shed where the *akadinda* was kept. We sat down each on our own side and Mukasa played and sang to me what he had already completed (Ex. 106).

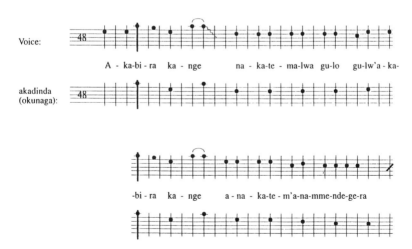

Ex. 106. Abusolomu Mukasa's song (cf. CD I/32)

We can see from the above illustration how vocal theme and *okunaga* are related. The original vocal melody is represented on the *akadinda* by an equal-spaced note series that follows it in unison. Now Mukasa asked me to play the *katongole* pattern in between. We tried it at different starting points and different levels, until he suddenly asked me to stop. He had found the right combination. The one he was in favour of obviously had the convincing quality of supplementing the *okunaga* notes in such a way that we both could hear the total pattern "sing" the words *"Akabira kange..."* Then Mukasa proposed to alter a few notes of the basic form of *okwawula* in certain places, in order to achieve greater unison with the vocal melody. The following illustration shows the complete instrumental version of Abusolomu Mukasa's tune, and the total pattern resulting from the combination of the two parts.

From comparison of the notes of the vocal theme (Ex. 106) with the total pattern (Ex. 107) it can be seen how well the "song" is contained in the instrumental version.

There are two general rules for the combination of *okunaga* and *ok-wawula* parts in *akadinda* music, one concerning the relation between (vocal) song and instrumental version, the other concerning consonance.
(a) The total pattern of the combined parts must contain the song. This often demands slight alteration of the fixed *okwawula* patterns.
(b) Each pair of notes in the *okwawula* part should as often as possible be in a consonance relationship, that is in the relationship of unison or Kiganda fourth (or fifth) with the preceding *okunaga* note.

The function ot the *okwawula* pattern is to "fill out" the *okunaga* by following the song melody (including possible variations) as closely as possible, emphasizing the tonal steps of the cycle, while at the same time providing accents to contrast with the divisive structure of the *okunaga* part.

The second rule shows that the fundamental concepts in *akadinda* music are on the whole similar to *amadinda* music, regarding fourths and fifths as consonance-enhancing intervals. But in notable contrast to the *amadinda* there is also a strong emphasis on the prime. In *akadinda* total patterns identical notes may be joined up to three times. Apparently this is even considered desirable in certain passages.

The core of *akadinda* interlocking may, therefore, be described thus: The *okunaga* note is reduplicated by the right hand *okwawula* note and contrasted by the left hand *okwawula* note which plays a Kiganda fourth up. To hold to this principle throughout all compositions would be dull and stereotypical, of course. The melodic lines of songs also demand adjustments, so many deviations occur. But at key points this core always surfaces. If faced with the problem of how to combine a fixed *okunaga* with a fixed *okwawula* (for example if one has forgotten the entrance

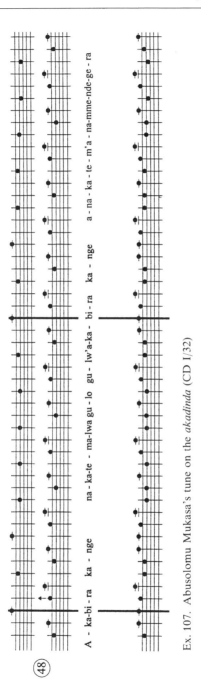

Ex. 107. Abusolomu Mukasa's tune on the *akadinda* (CD I/32)

point), these general rules may be helpful, because, of all possible combinations, only that which contains most consecutive consonances is acceptable.

We can see from the present collection that, of all known *okwawula* patterns, the two which the blind Salama musicians called *kulya-kulya-kulya* and *katongole* enjoy preferential status today. It may be a good idea therefore to try one of these two patterns with a given *okunaga*. Certainly it may be the case that a particular song demands one of the rarer *okwawula* patterns. But this can easily be discovered by the universal test of validity: once the *okwawula* is set out, one has to see whether the vocal theme is contained in the total pattern. If it is not then one has to try one of the other patterns besides *kulya-kulya* and *katongole*.

What then is the practical procedure in composition? The first thing to look at is the number of notes (form number) of a given nuclear pattern. If it has 8 or 16 notes, *katongole* has to be tried. Neither the *kulya-kulya* pattern nor the ascending-fifths pattern could be used here, because naturally they would not fit in length. The rare patterns might also work, but since the probability is small, they should only be tried if it is certain that *katongole* does not. If the nuclear pattern has 12 notes it is the descending-fourth pattern or *kulya-kulya* pattern that should be tried first, and will work in most cases. But with all 12-note *okunaga* we have to pay attention to another important distinction. If there is a guide-note we must see at what intervals it occurs. A rule of thumb is this: if the guide-note occurs every third beat of the *okunaga* pattern, the structure demands *kulya-kulya,* but if it occurs every second or fourth beat then *katongole* should be used. This explains, surprisingly at first, why *katongole* is used in the songs *"Ganga alula"* (No. 76, Table 11), *"Omusalaba"* (No. 77), *"Betunyuwa nabo omwenge"* (No. 78, Table 11) and *"Banawulira evvumbe"* (No. 79, Table 11), though they have the form number 12. Another possiblity for 12-note patterns is that the song might go better with the ascending-fifths pattern.

Further procedure is almost automatic. I now give the set of "rules" for finding an *okwawula* part to a given *okunaga* theme. As we shall see this follows regularities so strict that there is only one combination possible for each tune with any of the fixed *okwawula* patterns.

I. 12-Note okunaga *with a Guide-Note*

(a) The guide-note occurs every third beat

Both the entrance point and the level at which *kulya-kulya* should stand are found easily. First one finds the guide-note. The "rule" is that the guide-note demands to be in unison relationship with the following *okwawula* note. In the *okwawula* this will be a right-hand note, while the left-hand note should then follow suit with a Kiganda fourth up. In the following example (Ex. 108) the guide-note is shown with an up-tail. The two notes with down-tails are the *okwawula* notes that should be inserted at this point.

Ex. 108. Guide-note followed by *"kulya ..."*

There is no exception to this rule of behaviour in this particular group of *akadinda* pieces.[26] Once the correct interlocking notes following the guide-note are found, it is only a matter of seconds to deduce the whole *okwawula* pattern, because the second "rule" says that those *okwawula* notes that go with the guide-note are the middle two notes of the *kulya-kulya* pattern. In the case of Ex. 108 the complete *okwawula* pattern is therefore 35.24.13.

To make certain that this point is fully understood let us study this procedure with a full example: *"Omusango gwa balere"* (No. 55). The *okunaga* part is: 2..3..4..2..5..5..2..3..3..3..1..1.. First question: Which is the guide-note? Answer: The guide-note is the one that recurs regularly, in this case the 2. Second question: At what distance does it recur? Answer: Every three notes. Therefore we interlock with the *kulya-kulya* pattern. Now we apply the first rule, saying that the guide-note demands unison duplication. Accordingly the two *okwawula* notes following it have to be .24, because the guide-note is 2. The second rule says that the *okwawula* notes following the guide-note represent the middle *kulya*. Therefore the whole *okwawula* pattern is 35.24.13. and has to be inserted accordingly (Ex. 109).

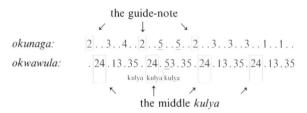

Note: 5 in the *okwawula* part (replacing 1) constitutes an adjustment to pitch 5 in the *okunaga*

Ex. 109. *"Omusango gw'abalere"* (No. 55, Table 11).
    The *akadinda* version and its structure

The final step in this procedure is to find out whether the combination contains the vocal melody. Often it will be necessary to alter the *okwawula* slightly at places in order to adapt it better to the vocal melody. In *"Omusango gwa balere"* we alter it so that 53. falls between the 5..5.. in the *okunaga,* as can be seen in the transcription above.

18-note tunes (cf. No. 61, Table 11) are treated like 12-note patterns provided that the guide-note occurs at 3-note intervals. If *kulya-kulya* does not suit the vocal theme the only other possibility would be to try its retrograde form: the ascending-fifths pattern.

(b) The guide note occurs every second or fourth beat

In this case the *katongole* pattern can be tried. It is used in the same manner as with 8-note and 16-note patterns (see below).

II. 12-Note okunaga *without a Guide-Note*

There are a number of 12-note nuclear patterns that have no guide-note but a pronounced divisive structure in compensation for it, usually grouping the notes in $2 + 2$ or $4 + 2$ sequences.[27] Here the rule for finding the *okwawula* is that the first note after the first melodic break in the *okunaga* part is to be taken as a guide-note. For example in *"Ab'e mbuga basengejja"* the note 4 is repeated four times at the beginning. Then comes a melodic break: the tune proceeds to 1. This 1 is to be taken as the guide-note. It is then interlocked by 13. in the *okwawula.* The rest of the process is identical with what has been said above.

III. 8-Note and 16-Note okunaga *with a Guide-Note*

The procedure of finding the *okwawula* is the same as with the 12-note patterns. First the guide-note must be found. Almost all compositions with the form number 8 or 16 have a guide-note. It may occur either at a 2- or a 4-note interval. In both cases the same rules can be applied.

Interlocking is slightly different, however, with the 8- and 16-note patterns, for which *katongole* should be tried. The *katongole* pattern is, unlike *kulya-kulya* not a sequence of fourths, but consists basically of two interval particles, the first a Kiganda fifth and the second a Kiganda fourth. The first particle follows the guide-note. It is inserted so that the first right-hand note starts one step <u>below</u> the guide-note (Ex. 110).

Ex. 110. Guide-note followed by *katongole*

Having got this far, there are no more real problems left. The second particle of *katongole* has to be added, which in the above example gives the full pattern 14.35.

As I have pointed out, the *katongole* pattern is often played in a slightly altered version. As with *kulya-kulya* this is caused by a desire for consonantal adjustment, as well as to suit the vocal melody. Salama musicians often prefer a contracted form of 14.35., which is 24.35. In this case the interlocking is such that the first *okwawula* note follows the guide-note in <u>unison</u>, which is quite natural because that is one step higher than the basic version.

20-note patterns generally demand *katongole* and are thus treated like 8- and 16-note patterns.

IV. 8-Note and 16-Note okunaga without a Guide-Note

This is very rare. *"Muleke atabaale"* (No. 91, Table 11) is one such item. It demands *katongole*. Usually in the present collection, such patterns without guide-note are filled out with the *"Basubira-malayika"* pattern. Since there is very little material, I cannot say whether this happens as a rule. These patterns seem to have a pronounced divisive structure.

Where *katongole* or *kulya-kulya* do not give the desired result other patterns can be tried:

(1) The <u>ascending-fifths pattern</u>. It is only employed with 12-note *okunaga*. If there is a guide-note, as in *"Nakulabudde"* (No. 92, Table 11) it appears that the middle particle should interlock it, which corresponds to the practice for the *kulya-kulya* pattern. But here one important difference seems to occur: the note to reduplicate the guide-note is in the left hand of the *okwawula,* while the right hand plays a lower Kiganda fifth to it. This is logical since this pattern is a retrograde version of *kulya-kulya.*

In divisive patterns such as *"Nantaza Lubanje"* it is also the right hand that is in unison with certain key points of the *okunaga* melody.

(2) The *"Basubira malayika"* pattern. In the present examples the pattern is inserted so that its starting point immediately follows the first note of the nuclear pattern.

If there is no guide-note and no other means of determining the *o-kwawula* entrance, one can see whether the ending and the starting note of the given *okwawula* pattern are the same (as in *kulya-kulya* and the ascending fourth pattern). If so, these two notes expect the same note in the *okunaga* between them, which gives a triple repetition in the total image. In this manner the exact entrance point may be found. The same can be observed with the *"Akakuba-mpanga"* pattern.

Summarizing our findings we may say that strict "rules" exist in *akadinda* music regarding the *okwawula*. In fact, in most musical pieces the *okwawula* part can be deduced with a fair chance of accuracy by following these rules. Both entrance point and level of the *okwawula* depend on the guide-note and at what interval it recurs, rather than on the cycle number of the *okunaga* part. It is generally the case, however, that the guide-note is not repeated throughout a nuclear pattern but remains "invisible" at certain points. Still it is very easy to find it, since it is a regularly recurring note.

Section 3
Are amadinda and akadinda Pieces Structurally Related?

Students of Kiganda xylophone music can observe that musical pieces in the two xylophone traditions often have the same title. Titles such as *"Ssematimba ne Kikwabanga," "Ennyana ekutudde," "Omusango gw'abalere," "Balinserekerera balinsala ekyambe"* and *"Ganga alula,"* to mention only those present in this collection, appear in both *amadinda* and *akadinda* music. Many more such parallels existed in the repertoire of the court musicians. From this fact an interesting question arises: Are these apparently different instrumental pieces based on different songs (that have the same title by chance), or are they identical structures arranged for performance on the two different kinds of xylophone? One of my playfellows in Kampala in 1959, Livingstone Katongole, once remarked to me about one particular *akadinda* piece: "This is the second tune that branches off from *"Ssematimba ne Kikwabanga."* How do we interpret this?

A few more observations strike us. For example, we can easily discover that musical pieces with the same title have the same number of notes in the total pattern. *"Ssematimba...," "Omusango gw'abalere," "Ganga..."* and *"Balinserekerera..."* appear with an 18-note *okunaga* on the *amadinda* and accordingly with a 12-note one on the *akadinda,* giving them in both cases a total number of 36 pulses. Those tunes with 12 notes on the *amadinda* have 8 notes on the *akadinda.*

Eventually it became clear that the total images are intended to be identical, though this is often rather difficult to discover. We can show the structural relation between *amadinda* and *akadinda* pieces of the same title with an example where the identity is obvious; the song *"Ganga alula"* (No. 19, Table 10 and No. 76, Table 11; for the *amadinda* version see also CD I/1). First we write the total image of both "branches" in staff notation, since this shows visually the direction of melodic movement.

Having done so we have to look out for any recurrent passages that may serve as key points of orientation. In the present example the notes 5 − 2 − 1 form such a passage, and we see that it occurs regularly in both the *amadinda* and *akadinda* representations. The recurrent passages are a sure indicator for finding out how the two total patterns are structurally related. We write the *amadinda* and *akadinda* settings so that the corresponding notes stand below each other. Finally, below the score we integrate notes and text of the hidden vocal part *(oluyimbo)*.

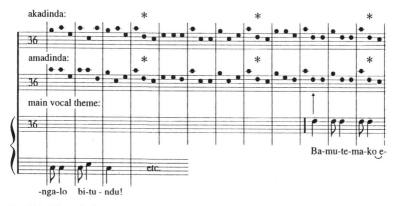

Ex. 111. The relationship between *amadinda* and *akadinda* tunes. Examples *"Ganga alula"*, No. 19, Table 10 and No. 76, Table 11

Though the two patterns do not correspond in every detail, the coincidence is enough to recognize them as the same tune. In fact, the two 36-note patterns are different only by 6 notes. But what is even more important to the Baganda musicians themselves is that the "song" (the vocal melody) be equally inherent in the total images of both versions. This can be clearly seen from Ex. 111.

The close identity of *amadinda* and *akadinda* total patterns of the same title is a fascinating aspect of the Kiganda musical system. One has to realize that it is produced with entirely different techniques. The *okwawula* parts in *akadinda* music for example are fixed patterns with little possibility of variation, and generally, composition in both xylophone traditions in Buganda is subject to strict regularities.

It will be easy for the reader to find out the relationship between the *amadinda* and *akadinda* versions of other songs as well, e.g. *"Ennyana ekutudde"* which is also quite easy, though an interesting study in itself, or the celebrated *"Ssematimba ne Kikwabanga."*

In summary we may define the relationship between *amadinda* and *akadinda* pieces:

(a) Pieces of the same title are representations of the same song, achieved with different technical means.

(b) The total patterns of the two instrumental versions coincide, though not necessarily in every single note, and of course, only in one *muko*.

(c) The degree of identity must be such that the vocal melody is contained in both versions, and can be heard out of it as an inherent structural part.

(d) Various note sections in the two versions often appear shifted against each other along the axis of elementary pulses. This causes a slight difference in the rhythm of the vocal melody in each of the two versions.

Transcriptions

The present transcriptions can be used both for musicological analysis and for playing. An explanation of the cipher notation has already been given. I do not think that musicians who would like to play this music will find any difficulty in learning their parts from the numbers, provided that they have a suitably tuned log-xylophone at hand. Several distinct performance styles and ways of accentuation exist in Kiganda xylophone music, of which I have already given a brief account (cf. Chapter I). These styles of playing have technical names in Luganda and may be employed successively in a single performance.

The accepted way of performing Kiganda xylophone music is to repeat the combining parts over and over. Slight variation in the impact of the notes, a change in accentuation, phrasing, etc. are vital to this music and give it an almost "psychedelic" quality, where all sort of inherent patterns seem to puzzle up from the total image, which often makes it impossible for a listener to discover who plays which note. We know now that these inherent note-patterns have a text function. They "speak" and evoke verbal associations for the Baganda musicians. Various parts of the texts of the songs on which these instrumental compositions are always based are suggested by inherent note patterns. This comes to light in harp music, where the same instrumental patterns are played as on the *amadinda* but where the vocal part is also performed.

In addition to subtle variations achieved by accentuation and phrasing, or even leaving out a few notes as in the performance style called *okusita ebyondo* ("to erect corners"), melodic variation may also be employed in some cases. There are a few compositions where it is always used, for example *"Ekyuma ekya Bora," "Ennyana ekutudde"* etc., and there are others where it never occurs.

Melodic variations *(ebisoko)* in Kiganda music also have a text function. The purpose of playing instrumental *ebisoko* is to suggest other words by the new inherent melodic-rhythmic patterns which emerge from the total image as a result of the slight change of its structure. However, Kiganda xylophone music is composed, even in the variations. When a musician plays *ebisoko,* he will draw on a reservoir of variant patterns in his mind and insert them in the correct places, thus temporarily substituting sections of the basic parts. The share of "free" improvisation is normally very small.

Variation techniques in Kiganda xylophone music resemble those of neighbouring Busoga. The variant notes need not necessarily be consonant with the other parts. Also they do not have an immediate effect on the third part in *amadinda* music, or on the lower octave duplications in *akadinda* music. Often the audible result of variation is that of dissonances which bend to raise the tension. A slight heterophonic effect is a frequent outcome. If the same variant pattern is repeated over long periods in *amadinda* music the third player *(omukoonezi)* may feel tempted to follow the new pattern that arises from the *amatengezzi.* But he may also duplicate it only approximately.[28]

The *okukoonera* part itself may also be slightly varied. Sometimes it only follows the *amatengezzi* pattern approximately; it may stop temporarily or a few notes may be left out to increase tension. But all this is employed in moderation, not excessively.

I have not included the *okukoonera* part in the transcriptions (except in the demonstration example of the *miko* system, *"Olutalo olw'e Nsinsi",* Ex. 113), because it is deduced from the two lowest notes and does not add any new structural element to the composition.

In the transcriptions, I only mark the entrance point with an asterisk. This is to be taken as a suggestion. Musicians often start it at other points though the one I have marked is frequent. Normally the *okukoonera* part is itself constructed in two, three or more phrases which develop logically. The starting point should preferably be in accordance with this inner logic of development.

The performer may wish to know which hand plays which note in the *okukoonera.* Here the general rule is that it should be an alternate motion of left and right hand, even if this means that the hands have to cross sometimes.

Another basic rule is that slat number $\bar{2}$ belongs to the right hand, slat number $\bar{1}$ to the left. The actual playing of *okukoonera* is usually a compromise between these two rules. Below there are two examples of the motor patterns in *okukoonera,* in which both principles can be seen. "r" and "l" mean right and left hand beats.

1. Okukoonera of *"Ennyana ekutudde"* (No. 6)

```
  l  r l  r l  r      l  r l  r l  r
  1 . 2 2 . 1 1 . 2 . . . 1 . 2 1 . 1 1 . 2 . . .
```

2. Okukoonera of *"Mwanga alimpa"* (No. 5)

```
  l     r  l  r   r  l r  l  r
  1 . . . 2 . 1 . 2 . . 2 . 1 2 . 2 . 1 . . . . .
```

Ex. 112. 1. *Okukoonera* of *"Ennyana ekutudde"*, No. 6, Table 10, CD I/30
2. *Okukoonera* of *"Mwanga alimpa"*, No. 5, Table 10

A certain amount of misunderstanding has been caused by the *miko*. The *miko* are a system of great theoretical importance in Kiganda music, but of well-defined and limited practical importance. In the present transcriptions of *amadinda* music I have only given the particular *muko* that is most frequently played.

Only one *muko* is played in a single performance. Individual players may have their preferences, but it is not customary to change from one to another *muko* within the same performance.

Usually one or two *miko* per song are popular. *"Ssematimba ne Kikwabanga," "Omusango gw'abalere," "Walugembe eyava e Kkunywa," "Katego,"* to mention only a few examples, are well known in at least two *miko*. There is a natural restriction over uncontrolled use of the transpositions, because the vocal melody does not come out equally well in every *muko*. For demonstration purposes, for instance in a lecture etc. Evaristo Muyinda and his musicians are glad to "show" all *miko* of a tune, but normally they will prefer the one they are used to (cf. CD I/29).

As far as we know *miko* are only used in *amadinda* music. In *akadinda* music a piece can be played one step higher or lower without bothering about playing areas, because the *akadinda,* especially the 22-note variety, is large enough. *Miko*-style transposition of the *okwawula* part would, however, be impossible, because the *okwawula,* in itself an interlocking structure, could hardly be octave-transposed in bits without destroying its motor structure. Nevertheless one night in June 1962 Evaristo Muyinda explained to me what he considered to be the *miko* of the *akadinda*. This refers to possible changes in the *okunaga* part only, where a few notes may be octave-transposed. This is then called another *"muko"*.

In *akadinda* music there may also be variations which I have marked accordingly in the transcriptions. It is usually one of the top players that is entitled to vary, and the other players need not necessarily follow him in the lower octaves. This also leads to heterophony.

In the transcriptions I have listed the *amadinda* pieces by the number of notes in the basic parts, while the *akadinda* pieces are given in the order of the different *okwawula* patterns. When several versions of a piece were collected this is mentioned specially. Slight melodic variations are written under the respective notes that can be varied. If the variations are meant to form a group, this is marked by a horizontal bracket embracing this group. A particular form of variation is development of the theme. This occurs for example in *"Ekyuma ekya Bora"* (No. 3, Table 10) and *"Ennyana ekutudde"* (No. 6, Table 10).

For the sake of simplicity I have dropped octave duplications. But one should remember that the basic parts in *amadinda* are performed in parallel octaves, and in *akadinda* in three parallel octaves. An arrow means the entrance point of the second part. Like that of the *okukoonera,* marked by an asterisk, this should be taken as a suggestion. A few musicians prefer to enter at some other place. If they do they enter with the appropriate note, of course.

Two pieces in this collection have no title. The musicians who taught me were unable to give me one. Perhaps it will be possible to identify these tunes some time.

Pieces of apparently recent date are marked by the letter M, following the translation of the title. Most of these "modern" tunes refer to events unconnected with the Kabaka's court.

All *amadinda* compositions published here were collected from royal musicians, particularly Evaristo Muyinda, except Nos. 10 and 16 which I learned from Basoga visitors to the Uganda Museum. Among the *akadinda* pieces in Table 11, the following were collected from royal musicians: Nos. 51–53, 55–61, 64–69, 71–72, 74–76, 92–102. The following were collected from musicians at the Agricultural Training Centre of the Foundation for the Blind, Salama: Nos. 54, 62–63, 70, 73, 77–91.

MUKO I

```
                 *
         L       R    L        R   L        R   L R      L R
okukoonera  . 1 . . . 2 . 1 . . . 2 . 1 . . . 2 . 1 2 . 2 2
okunaga (24) 4 . 3 . 4 . 3 . 3 . 3 . 4 . 3 . 4 . 4 . 2 . 2 .
okwawula    . 1 . 5 . 2 . 1 . 5 . 2 . 1 . 5 . 2 . 1 . 5 . 2
                                                    ↑
```

MUKO II

```
            *
            R   L       R   L       R   L       R   L
okukoonera  . 2 . 1 . . . 2 . 1 . . . 2 . 1 . . . 2 . 1 . .
okunaga (24) 5 . 4 . 5 . 4 . 4 . 4 . 5 . 4 . 5 . 5 . 3 . 3 .
okwawula    . 2 . 1 . 3 . 2 . 1 . 3 . 2 . 1 . 3 . 2 . 1 . 3
                                            ↑
```

MUKO III

```
        L     R L        . R      L     R L   L       *R
okukoonera  1 . . 2 1 . . . 2 . . 1 . 2 1 . 1 . . 2 . .
okunaga (24) 1 . 5 . 1 . 5 . 5 . 5 . 1 . 5 . 1 . 1 . 4 . 4 .
okwawula    . 3 . 2 . 4 . 3 . 2 . 4 . 3 . 2 . 4 . 3 . 2 . 4
                                        ↑
```

MUKO IV

```
        *
        R   L   R   L   R   L   R   L   R   R
okukoonera  2 . 1 . 2 . 1 . 1 . 1 . 2 . 1 . 2 . 2 . . . . .
okunaga (24) 2 . 1 . 2 . 1 . 1 . 1 . 2 . 1 . 2 . 2 . 5 . 5 .
okwawula    . 4 . 3 . 5 . 4 . 3 . 5 . 4 . 3 . 5 . 4 . 3 . 5
                                        ↑
```

MUKO V

```
            *
            R       L R   L   R L      R       L       R   L R
okukoonera  . . 2 . . 1 2 . 2 . 2 1 . . 2 . . 1 . . 1 . 1 1
okunaga (24) 3 . 2 . 3 . 2 . 2 . 2 . 3 . 2 . 3 . 3 . 1 . 1 .
okwawula    . 5 . 4 . 1 . 5 . 4 . 1 . 5 . 4 . 1 . 5 . 4 . 1
                                                ↑
```

Ex. 113. The *amadinda* version of *"Olutalo olw'e Nsinsi"* in its five *miko* (as demonstrated by Evaristo Muyinda). Recorded June 1962/Kubik, tape at Nabbale, near Kampala. Phonogrammarchiv Vienna (cf. CD I/29)

Note: *Okunaga* and *okwawula* parts to be performed in octave duplication
↑   point of entrance for the *okwawula* part
*   point of entrance for the *okukoonera* part
R   struck with right-hand beater
L   struck with left-hand beater

The next *muko* transposition closes the cycle and brings us back into *muko* I

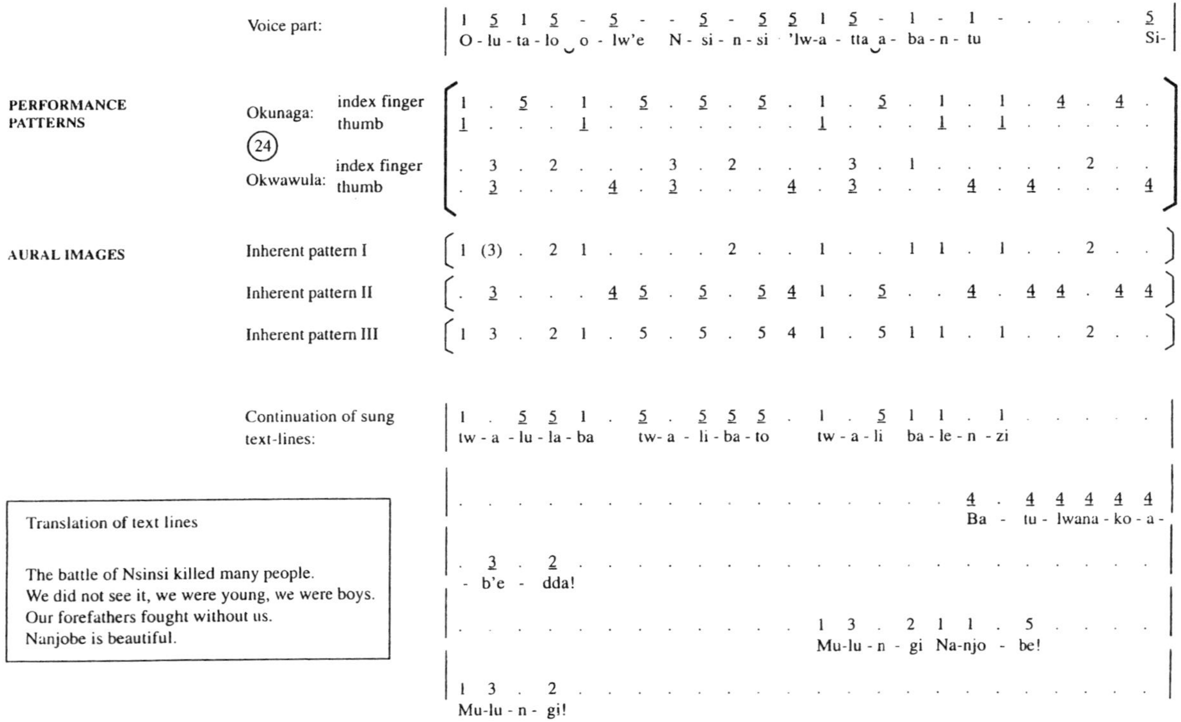

Voice part:

PERFORMANCE PATTERNS

Okunaga: index finger / thumb (24)

Okwawula: index finger / thumb

AURAL IMAGES

Inherent pattern I

Inherent pattern II

Inherent pattern III

Continuation of sung text-lines:

Voice text (sung syllables):
O - lu - ta - lo o - lw'e N - si - n - si 'lw-a - tta a - ba - n - tu Si-

tw - a - lu - la - ba tw- a - li - ba - to tw- a - li ba - le - n - zi

- b'e - dda! Ba - lu - lwana - ko - a -

Mu-lu - n - gi! Mu-lu - n - gi Na-njo - be!

Translation of text lines

The battle of Nsinsi killed many people.
We did not see it, we were young, we were boys.
Our forefathers fought without us.
Nanjobe is beautiful.

Ex. 114. *"Olutalo olw'e Nsinsi"* ("The battle of Nsinsi"). Harp song performed by Evaristo Muyinda. Recording: Kubik/Orig. Tape No. 34/1 at Nabbale near Kampala, June 1962 (cf. CD I/31).

Table 10.   Amadinda Pieces

Group I (12 notes)

1. *Banno bakoola ng'osiga* ("Your friends are pruning, but you are sowing")

   Ok.   4.3⌐4.1.3.3.4.2.3.4.2.1.
   Okw. 5.3.3.5.5.3.5.2.3.5.1.1.

2. *Ndyegulira ekkadde* ("I will buy myself an old woman")

   Ok.   2.1.2.2.2.5.2.1.1⌐2.3.5.
   Okw. 5.4.2.

3. *Ekyuma ekya Bora* ("The swinging machine of Bora")

   Ok.   4⌐3.2.3.3.2.4.3.2.3.3.2.
   Okw. 5.5.4.1.5.1.5.5.1.1.5.1.

   Development of the *okunaga:*
   a)   4.5.1.1.3.2.4.5.2.3.3.2.
   b)   4.5.1.1.3.2.4.4.2.3.3.2.
   c)   4.5.2.4.3.2.4.3.2.3.3.2.

4. *Abana ba Kalemba* or *Besibye bulungi* ("The children of Kalemba – they are smartly dressed")

   Ok.   4.3⌐4.4.2.2.4.3.2.4.2.1.
   Okw. 5.2.2.5.2.1.5.2.2.5.1.1.
   |1.3|

5. *Segomba ngoye Mwanga alimpa* ("I don't pine for clothes, Mwanga will give me")

   Ok.   5.4.5⌐5.3.3.5.4.3.5.2.1.
   Okw. 3.3.1.3.2.1.2.3.4.2.2.1.

6. *Ennyana ekutudde* ("The calf has broken loose") (CD I/30)

   Ok.   5.5.3.5.2.1.5.5.3.3.1.1⌐
   Okw. 1.2.4.

   Variations of the *okwawula:*
   a)   1.2.3.2.3.4.1.2.3.1.1.4.
   b)   1.2.3.1.2.4.1.2.3.1.1.4.

   Variation of the *okunaga:*
         5.1.3.5.2.1.5.1.3.3.1.1.

7. *Olutalo olw'e Nsinsi* ("The battle of Nsinsi") (CD I/28–9)

   Ok.   4.3.4.3.3.3.4.3.4.4.2⌐2.
   Okw. 5.2.1.

   Variation of the *okwawula:*
         5.2.1.5.2.1.5.2.1.4.2.2.

8. *Wavvangaya* (proper name)

Ok. 4.3.4.3.3↓2.4.3.4.3.3.1.
Okw. 5.2̇.1.

9. *Omunyoro atunda nandere* ("The Munyoro sells *nandere* fish")

Ok. 5.4.3.5.4.3.5.4.3↓4.4.2.
Okw. 2.2.1.2.2.1.2.3.1̇.2.1.1.

10. Title unknown[29]

Ok. 5.5.5↓5.4.3.5.4.2.5.4.3.
Okw. 3.2̇.1.

Group II (18 notes)

11. *Ssematimba ne Kikwabanga* ("Ssematimba and Kikwabanga")

Ok. 4.5.2.3.3.5.2̇.1.2.5.2↓2.1.4.4.2.1.1.
Okw. 5.4.3.2.4.4.4.1.1.4.3.1.2.3.4.3.2.2.

12. *Naagenda kasana nga bulaba* ("We will leave when it is daylight")

Ok. 2.1.2.5.2.2.2.5.5.2.1.2.5.2.1.2.4↓4.
Okw. 2̇.3.4.3.2.2.4.5.5.2.3.4.3.2.3.4.5.4.

13. *Omusango gw'abalere* ("The case of the flute players")

Ok. 2̇.1.2.5.2↓2.1.5.5.2.1.2.3.4.5.1.4.4.
Okw. 5.4.3.2.5.4.3.1.5.2.4.3.2.4.4.3.2.2.

14. *Omuwa butwa wakyejo* ("The poison-giver is daring")

Ok. 3.4.4.2.4.4.3↓4.1.3.4.3.1.3.2.4.2.2.
Okw. 5.3.4.5.2̇.3.3.5.2.2.4.1.5.2.4.4.1.1.

15. *Mwasansa* (name)

Ok. 4↓3.2̇.
Okw. 5.5.5.1.5.1.1.4.4.1.5.2.3.5.1.1.4.4.

16. *Alifuledi* (name)[30]

Ok. 4.3.4.3.5↓5.5.3.4.2.2.2.4.3.4.4.3.1.
Okw. 3.3.1.5.2.4.4.2.1.5.1.1.5.2.1.5.2̇.1.

17. *Omutamanya n'gamba* ("The ignorant one")

Ok. 4↓5.5.2̇.3.3.5.2.1.4.5.1.3.4.4.1.3.2.
Okw. 5.3.4.3.1.3.3.4.5.1.4.5.4.2.4.4.5.1.

18. *Katulye kubye pesa* ("Let's spend our money", i.e. eat well)

Ok. 4.3.4.3.3.2.4.3.5.5.3.4.3.3.2.4.3.1↓
Okw. 1.1.5.2.1.5.1.5.5.2.5.5.2̇.1.5.1.5.5.
     5.

19. *Ganga alula* ("Ganga had a narrow escape") (CD I/1)
    Ok.   5⌡3.5.4.3.2.3.2.1.4.3.2.4.2.2.4.2.2.
    Okw. 5.5.2̇.1.5.1.3.5.1.1.5.1.3.5.2.2.5.1.

20. *Balagana enkonge* ("Those who warn each other of danger today")
    Ok.   3.4.4.2.3.4.3.1.2.1.3.3.1.2.1.4.1⌡1.
    Okw. 4.5.4.2̇.3.3.2.1.2.5.4.3.1.2.5.4.1.1.
          3.   3.

21. *Byasi byabuna olugudo* ("Bullets all over the road")
    Ok.   4.3⌡2̇.4.3.2.3.2.2.4.3.2.3.3.1.2.3.1.
    Okw. 5.5.1.4.4.1.5.5.1.5.4.1.3.3.1.5.1.1.

22. *Ab'e Busoga beggala ngabo* ("The people of Busoga use shields for doors")[31]
    Ok.   4.4⌡5.2̇.4.4.5.2.2.4.4.5.1.2.3.5.1.1.
    Okw. 3.4.4.1.3.4.4.2.1.3.2.4.1.2.1.4.1.1.

23. *Nanjobe* (proper name)
    Ok.   5.5.4⌡5.1̇.1.3.5.4.1.1.1.3.5.4.3.2.2.
          4.   4.
    Okw. 5.3.4.5.3.2.1.3.4.5.3.2.1.2.5.1.3.2.

24. *Mugoowa lwatakise* ("When Mugoowa has not reported to court")
    Ok.   5.5.5.3.3.2.3.3.1.3.3.2.1.5.4.5.1⌡2.
    Okw. 5.4.3.3.5.1̇.5.4.1.3.3.1.5.4.3.2.1.3.

25. *Gulemye Mpangala* (name of a chief)
    Ok.   5.5.3.2̇.4.5.1.2.3.3⌡1.1.3.2.3.5.1.2.
    Okw. 5.4.5.4.4.1.3.5.4.3.4.5.2.2.2.4.4.1.

26. *Mawanda segwanga* ("Mawanda the great")
    Ok.   4⌡3.4.4.3.4.3.3.4.5.3.5.5.1.4.2.2.1.
    Okw. 5.5.2̇.5.5.2.5.5.2.5.5.2.5.5.1.5.5.2.

27. *Ebigambo ebibulire bitta enyumba* ("Reported words ruin families")
    Ok.   4.3.5.5.3.4.4.2.2.4.2⌡1.4.3.3.4.3.1.
    Okw. 5.2.1.5.1.1.5.2.1.5.2̇.1.5.2.1.5.2.1.

28. *Walugembe eyava e Kkunywa* ("Walugembe who came from Kkunywa")
    Ok.   5.5⌡1.3.5.5.1.3.3.5.5.1.2.3.4.1.2.2.
    Okw. 4.5.5.2.4.5.5.3.2.4.3.5.2.3.2.5.2.2̇.

29. *Omujooni: Balinserekerera balinsala ekyambe* ("Poor as I am, they will brutal-
    ly murder me")
    Ok.   5.5.4.4.2.3.4.1.1.4.4.4.4.2.3.4.1.2⌡
    Okw. 2.2.2.1.3.5.2.1.3.5.2.2.1.3.5.2̇.1.4.
                         4.

30. *Lutaaya yesse yekka* ("Lutaaya has killed himself")

Ok.   2.3.4.3.3.4.2.1.1.2.3.4.2.2.4.2↓1.1.

Okw. 5.4.3.5.2.1.5.2.1.5.4.3.5.2.1.5.2.2.

31. *Kawumpuli* ("The plague")

Ok.   1.2.3.2.2.3.2.1.4.1.2.3.1.1.4.1↓1.4.

Okw. 4.5.2.4.1.5.4.1.5.4.5.2.4.1.5.4.1.1.

       ⌊5.5.5.5.5.5.⌋

32. *Abalung'ana be baleta engoye* ("It was the Arabs who brought cloth")

Ok.   4.4↓2.3.2.2.4.5.2.3.3.3.2.3.1.1.3.2.

Okw. 5.4.1.

Group III (24 notes)

33. *Atalabanga mundu agende Buleega* ("One who has never seen a gun should go to Buleega")

Ok.   4.3↓4.1.3.2.1.3.3.1.2.1.4.3.4.1.3.2.1.2.2.1.2.1.

Okw. 5.3.4.5.4.3.5.3.3.5.1.1.5.3.4.5.4.2.5.4.3.5.1.1.

34. *Ezali embikke kasagazi kawunga* ("The plantations which were well-cared for are now waste")

Ok.   1.3.5.1.1.3.5.1.1.3.4.4.1.3.5.1.5.3.5.5.1.3.4↓4.

Okw. 2.4.5.1.2.4.5.1.2.4.5.5.2.4.5.1.2.4.1.5.2.4.5.5.

      ⌊1.   1.   1.1.   5.⌋

35. *Kalagala e Bembe* ("Kalagala of Bembe")[32]

Ok.   5.4.1.3.2.1.5.4.1.2.2.2.5.4.1.3.2.1.5.4.1.4.1↓1.

Okw. 4.3.2.3.4.5.4.3.2.3.2.5.5.2.2.3.4.5.4.3.2.3.1.1.

36. *Semakokiro ne Jjunju* ("Semakokiro and Jjunju")

Ok.   3.5.5.2.4.3.1.5.4.3.1.1.4.3.4↓4.4.2.5.2.2.5.1.2.

Okw. 2.2.1.2.2.5.2.2.5.1.5.3.5.5.1.2.3.2.1.5.4.1.1.4.

37. *Agawuluguma ennyanja* ("What rumbles in the lake")

Ok.   5.4.3.2.4.4.3.2.5.4.1.1.4.3.2.1.3.3.3.2↓5.4.2.2.

Okw. 1.2.1.5.2.2.1.5.4.2.1.5.1.2.1.4.1.1.5.4.3.1.1.5.

38. *Akaalo kekamu* ("In the same village live the ruthless ones")

Ok.   5.4.4.2.4.3.4.5.4.4.4↓1.1.4.3.3.1.5.4.2.3.2.5.2.2.

Okw. 4.4.5.2.1.3.3.2.3.4.1.2.2.5.1.3.2.4.4.1.5.3.2.1.

      1.

39. *Afa talamusa* ("The dead do not give greeting")

Ok.   5↓5.1.3.5.5.1.3.2.5.1.3.4.5.1.3.4.4.1.3.2.5.1.3.

Okw. 2.4.5.5.2.4.5.5.2.2.5.5.2.4.5.4.2.4.4.5.2.2.5.5.

40. Okuzanyira ku nyanja kutunda mwoyo ("To play by the lake is to sell one's spirit")

Ok. 4.3.4.2.4.4$^\downarrow$2.3.5.1.1.1.4.3.5.1.2.1.4.3.5.5.2.1.

Okw. 4.4.2.1.4.4.5.1.3.2.5.4.5.1.3.$\overset{*}{2}$.2.4.5.1.1.4.4.2

41. Ngabo Maanya eziriwangula Mugerere ("The shields of Kamanya will conquer Mugerere")

Ok. 5.4.3.1.1.4.3.4$^\downarrow$4.4.2.5.2.2.5.1.2.4.5.5.$\overset{*}{2}$.4.3.1.

Okw. 2.2.1.2.2.5.2.2.5.1.5.3.5.5.1.2.3.2.1.5.4.1.1.4.

42. Ensiriba ya munange Katego ("The charm of my friend Katego")

Ok. 5.4$^\downarrow$2.1.5.2.3.3.5.2.1.1.4.5.4.2.1.2.4.4.2.1.2.2.

Okw. 3.4.3.4.3.1.3.3.4.4.1.1.$\overset{*}{2}$.3.4.5.4.2.3.4.2.5.2.2. 4.

43. Atakulubeere ("He who will not assist you")

Ok. 5.4.5.1.2.3.4.4.3.3$^\downarrow$2.2.5.4.5.1.2.3.4.4.2.5.2.2.

Okw. 5.4.2.2.1.2.3.5.$\overset{*}{2}$.2.1.2.5.4.2.2.1.1.3.4.2.2.1.1.

44. Nkejje namuwanula ("The largest nkejje-fish on the rack")

Ok. 5.4.5.4.3.1.4.4.2.4.4.1.5.1.4.1.1.5.1.2.1.3.3.1$^\downarrow$

Okw. 3.$\overset{*}{2}$.2.2.1.2.3.2.4.4.1.2.3.3.1.1.4.3.4.5.4.3.1.2.

45. Kansimbe omuggo awali Kibuka ("Let me plant my stick where Kibuka is")

Ok. 3.5.$\overset{*}{2}$.4.3.5.2.2.3.5.1.1.3.5.2.4$^\downarrow$3.4.2.4.3.5.1.1.

Okw. 1.1.4.4.1.2.1.4.1.1.4.5.1.2.2.5.1.2.1.4.1.1.4.5.

46. Omukazi omunafu agayigga na ngabo ("The idle woman has to talk through her garden with a shield")

Ok. 1.3.3.4.1.2.3.4.1.2.2.4.1$^\downarrow$2.2.4.1.2.3.4.1.3.3.4.

Okw. 3.5.1.1.3.5.2.3.3.5.$\overset{*}{2}$.3.3.5.1.1.3.5.2.3.2.5.2.2.

Group IV (over 24 notes)

47. Bakebezi bali e Kitende ("The sly ones are at Kitende"). 25 notes[33]

Ok. 3.4.4.1.3.2.3.4.5.2.3.3.1.1.4.5.2.4.4.1.3.2.2.5.1$^\downarrow$
|5.5.5.|

Okw. 5.5.$\overset{*}{2}$.3.4.5.4.1.3.4.3.1.5.4.1.1.4.4.2.3.4.5.5.2.2. 3.

48. Ab'e Bukerere balaagira emwanyi ("The people of Bukerere live on coffee"). 27 notes

Ok. 5$^\downarrow$5.5.3.5.5.4.5.1.3.3.4.5.1.4.4.5.1.3.3.4.5.1.2.5.2.2.

Okw. 3.3.5.5.3.$\overset{*}{2}$.1.4.3.5.2.1.4.4.2.1.4.3.5.2.1.2.5.2.2.5.5.

49. *Akawologoma* ("The small lion"). 27 notes

Ok. 5.3.3.5.4.5.3.2.3.1.4.1.1.4.3.2⸍3.1.4.2.2.4.3.4.2.1.2.
Okw. 1.2.3.4.4.4.1.2.3.4.5.4.5.5.5.2.3.4.1.1.5.1.1.4.1.1.5.
                          3.

50. *Agenda n'omulungi azaawa* ("He who goes with the beautiful one loses himself"). 35 notes

Ok.   3.2.3.3.1.5.2.2.3.2.5.4.1.5.1.1.1.3.3.1.1.4.3.
Okw. 1.2.3.3.2.3.3.3.5.3.1.3.3.2.5.4.5.1.2.3.3.1.4.
Ok.   2.5.4.3.2⸍5.4.1.5.3.1.1.
Okw. 4.1.5.1.4.1.1.5.1.2.1.5.

Table 11. Akadinda Pieces

Group I (*Kulya-kulya* pattern)

51. *Kisawo kya muwa butwa kiwedemu emwanyi* ("The bag of a poison-giver has no more coffee beans")

Ok. 4⸍.4..4..4..2..2..5..5..3..3..1..1..
Okw. 35.24.13.35.24.13.35.24.13.35.14.13.

52. *Omujooni: Balinserekerera balinsala ekyambe* ("Poor as I am, they will brutally murder me")

Ok. 2..4..4..2..3..3..2..4..4..2..1..5⸍.
        5   5
Okw. 35.24.13.35.24.13.35.24.13.35.24.53.

53. *Bogerera mwogerere* ("One has to speak for him")

Ok. 2..4..4..2..1..5..2..3..3..1..1..1⸍.
Okw. 35.24.13.

54. *Omugenyi agenda Kyandanda* ("The guest is leaving")

Ok. 4..4..4⸍.2..1..1..2..3..3..2..5..5..
Okw. 35.24.13.35.24.13.35.24.53.35.24.13.

55. *Omusango gw'abalere* ("The case of the flute players")

Ok. 2..3..4..2..5..5↓.2..3..3..3..1..1..
Okw. 35.24.13.35.24.13.35.24.13.35.24.53.

56. *Mwekume abatambala bajja* ("Beware, the Batambala are coming")

Ok. 1..3..4↓.1..3..3..1..3..4..1..1..1..
Okw. 24.13.52.

Variation of *okwawula:* 24.13.52.24.13.42.24.13.52.14.13.42.

57. *Nkada bamuyitanga mukadde* ("They took Nkada for an old woman")

Ok. 4..4..2..5..5..2..4..4↓.2..3..3..1..
Okw. 35.24.13.35.24.13.35.24.53.35.24.13.
     |34.23.|

58. *Abasiba embuzi* or *Ssematimba ne Kikwabanga* ("Those who rear goats – Ssematimba and Kikwabanga")

Ok. 5..5↓.4..2..2..4..5..1..1..5..3..3..
Okw. 24.13.52.

Many variations of the *okwawula;* for example:
24.12.52.24.13.51.24.13.52.13.13.52.

59. *Sala akalagala kuliko emmamba ye* ("Bring a young banana leaf for his lung-fish")

Ok. 5..4..3..5..2..2↓.5..4..3..5..1..1..
Okw. 13.52.41.

Extended version of *okwawula:* 13.52.41.13.51.41.13.52.41.13.52.41.

60. *Ab'e mbuga basengejja* ("People at the Chief's residence are filtering")

Ok. 4..4..4..4↓.1..1..3..3..2..2..1..1..
Okw. 24.13.52.24.13.52.24.13.52.24.13.42.

61. *Wakayayu azinide ebuko analya ki?* ("Wakayayu has danced at his in-laws, what will he eat?")

Ok. 2..4..4..2..3..3↓.2..1..5..2..1..5..3..3..3..2..1..5..
Okw. 35.24.53.35.24.53.35.23.13.35.24.53.35.24.13.35.24.13.
                                4.

62. *Njagala okuddayo e Bukunja* ("I want to go back to Bukunja")

Ok. 3..4..4..3..1..1↓.3..2..5..3..2..2..
Okw. 4Ī.35.24.3Ī.35.24.4Ī.35.24.4Ī.35.14.

63. *Uganda kwefuga* ("Uganda Independence")

Ok. 4..4..4↓.2..1..5..1..1..5..2..1..5..
Okw. 35.24.13.

Variant pattern of *okwawula* by Mr. Waida, Salama:
35.24.13.35.24.13.35.24.13.35.24.14.

Group II (*Katongole*-pattern)

64. *Matu ga njobe* ("The ears of the water-buck")[34]

    Ok. 2..4..2..5..2..3..1ᶦ.1..
    Okw. 14.35.14.35.14.35.13.35.

65. *Nzige buzige si rusejera* ("Grown-up locusts are not young ones")[35]

    Ok. 2ᶦ.4..2..2..1..1..2..5..
    Okw. 14.35.

66. *Yabba nandere* ("He stole *Nandere* fish")

    Ok. 2ᶦ.4..1..1..2..3..1..1..
    Okw. 14.35.14.35.13.35.14.35.

    Important variation of the *okwawula:* 13.35.13.35.13.33.14.35.

67. *Omusango gw'ennyama* ("The case of the meat")

    Ok. 5..5..4..1..1..2..3..2ᶦ.
    Okw. 24.35.24.35.13.35.24.35.
         ⌊1   1   1⌋

68. *Omunyoro atunda nandere* ("The Munyoro sells *Nandere* fish")[36]

    Ok. 2ᶦ.4..2..5..2..3..1..1..
    Okw. 24.35.

    Variation of *okwawula:*
    24.35.24.35.23.35.14.35.

    Many musicians prefer this *okwawula:*
    14.35.14.35.13.35.14.35.

69. *Ennyana ekutudde* ("The calf has broken loose")

    Ok. 2ᶦ.4..1..1..2..3..1..1..
    Okw. 14.35.14.35.23.35.14.35.
                   1.

    Variation of *okunaga:*
    2..4..4..4..2..3..1..1..

70. *Bawala luga* (= nickname for a cruel person)

    Ok. 4..4..4..2..5..2..4..2ᶦ.
    Okw. 14.35.24.35.14.35.23.35.

71. *Yalambula amasaza* ("He toured the counties")

    Ok. 2..4..4..4ᶦ.2..2..5..5..2..3..3..3..2..2..1..1..
    Okw. 35.24.35.14.34.13.35.13.35.14.35.14.35.14.34.14.

    Variations of the *okwawula:*[37]
    a) 35.24.35.14.35.14.35.13.35.14.35.14.35.14.34.14.
    b) 25.24.25.14.35.14.34.13.35.24.35.14.35.24.34.14.

72. *Webale kujja Nakatanza* ("It is good you have come, Nakatanza")

Ok.   2..3..2..5..2⌐.2..1..5..2..3..2..5..2..2..1..1..
Okw. 14.35.14.35.13.35.14.35.14.25.13.35.13.35.14.35.
   2   2   2   2   2   2

73. *Omulwadde w'envunza analaba obuyinja* ("Stones will hurt the feet of one with jiggers")

Ok.   2..4..4..4⌐.2..2..1..1..2..3..3..3..2..1..5..5..
              4
Okw. 35.24.35.14.35.13.35.13.35.14.35.53.35.24.35.14.

74. *Singa namera byoya yinga mbuse* ("If I had wings I could fly")

Ok.   2..4..4..4..2..3..2..5..3..5..5..5..2..3..2⌐.5..
Okw. 14.35.14.35.14.35.13.35.14.35.14.35.14.35.13.35.

75. *Walulumba ekyakukendula enkende kki?* ("Wasp, what made your waist so narrow?")

Ok.   2..4..4..4..2..1..1..1..2⌐.3..3..3..2. .5..5..5..
Okw. 24.35.24.35.24.35.24.35.24.35.24.35.24.35.14.35.

Another version of the *okwawula:*
13.35.13.35.14.35.14.35.14.35.14.35.14.35.14.35.

76. *Ganga alula* ("Ganga had a narrow escape")

Ok.   2⌐.4..2..2..2..5..1..5..2..3..1..1..
           |5..5..4..|
Okw. 14.35.24.25.14.35.54.35.13.35.14.35.

77. *Omusalaba* ("The cross"). M.[38]

Ok.   4..1..1..1..3..1..1..5..5..1..2..1⌐.
Okw. 13.24.13.24.13.24.13.24.53.24.12.24.

78. *Betunyuwa nabo omwenge* ("Those with whom we share the beer"). M.

Ok.   4..4..4..1..2..1..5⌐.1..3..2..1..1..
   |3..3..5..|
Okw. 24.13.24.13.24.13.24.14.24.12.24.53.
                5

79. *Banawulira evvumbe* ("They will smell the aroma"). M.[39]

Ok.   4⌐.3..4..4..2..1..2..2..4..3..1..1..
Okw. 14.35.

80. *Ennyanja ye Rwaje* ("The lake of Rwaje")

Ok.   3⌐.4..4..4..3..2..2..2..3..5..5..1..3..1..1..1..
Okw. 34.4Ī.34.4Ī.25.4Ī.25.4Ī.35.4Ī.15.4Ī.35.4Ī.25.4Ī
   2   2   2

81. *Baabirya bisooboza* ("They ate the beans at the leaf stage")
   Ok. 3⌐.3..1..1..2..1..4..4..2..2..2..1..5..5..1..5..
   Okw. 14.35.14.35.24.35.24.35.24.35.24.35.24.35.14.35.

82. *Kyalale* ("Raleigh bicycle"). M.
   Ok. 3⌐.5..3..3..3..1..2..2..5..5..2..2..3..4..3..1..
   Okw. 25.4ī.25.4ī.25.4ī.25.4ī.25.4ī.25.4ī.24.4ī.25.4ī.

83. *Nali simanyi nga ndiwona esasi* ("I did not expect to survive the bull")
   Ok. 2..2..4..4..2..3..1..1..2⌐.2..2..5..2..3..1..1..
   Okw. 24.35.14.35.23.35.14.35.24.35.24.35.24.35.14.35.

84. *Mpa wali yanda-yanda* ("Nobody will dance for me when I am dead"). M.
   Ok. 2..4⌐.3..3..3..4..1..1..2..4..4..3..2..2..5..5..
   Okw. 35.14.

85. *Kataza miti* ("*Kataza* tree")
   Ok. 2⌐.4..2..3..3..2..1..1..2..4..2..1..1..1..5..5..
   Okw. 14.35.14.35.14.35.54.35.14.35.14.35.14.35.14.35.

86. *Omukanya bulo atuyanye* ("The eater of millet has perspired")
   Ok. 1..4⌐.4..2..1..2..1..1..1..4..4..2..1..2..5..5..
   Okw. 14.35.

87. *Empuuta nagirya* ("I ate Mpuuta fish") (CD I/5)
   Ok. 4..4⌐.3..2..2..3..5..5..3..3..2..1..1..2..1..1..
   Okw. 53.24.

88. *Muno omwa baba* ("In this house of my grandfather")
   Ok. 3..3..3..1..3..4..3⌐.1..3..2..1..5..3..5..5..5..
   Okw. 35.4ī.

89. Title unknown
   Ok. 1⌐.3..1..2..2..2..5..5..1..3..1..4..4..4..4..
   Okw. 13.24.13.24.13.24.53.24.13.24.53.24.53.24.53.24.

90. *Ab'e Salama* ("People of Salama"). M.
   Ok. 2..4..4..4..3..3..3..2..1..1..2..4..4..4..2⌐.2..2..1..5..5..
   Okw. 14.35.

91. *Muleke atabaale* ("let him do as he pleases"). M.
   Ok. 4..4..4..4..1..1..1..4..3⌐.3..3..3..5..1..5..1..5..1..2..2..
   Okw. 53.24.

Group III

92. *Nakulabudde* ("I warned you")
   Ok. 4..5..5..4..2..2..4..3..1..4..2..2⌐.
   Okw. 53.14.25.

93. *Nantaza Lubanje* (proper name)

    Ok.   5..5..5..5..3..1..2..1..4..4..3↓.3..
    Okw. 53.14.25.

94. *Bijja bisamba endege* ("They come rattling the anklet bells")

    Ok.   4..4..4..1↓.1..1..3..3..3..2..2..2..
    Okw. 42.53.14.

95. *Omunyoro atikkira engule* ("The Munyoro wears the crown")

    Ok.   3..3..3..3..1..1..3..3..2..2..5..5↓.
    Okw. 42.53.14.

Group IV

96. *Mukadde mwangu* ("The fast old one")

    Ok.   4↓.4..1..1..3..3..2..5..
    Okw. 52.14.14.35.

97. *Envubu terindwa buziba* ("One does not wait for a hippo in deep waters")

    Ok.   4..4..4..4..2↓.3..2..3..5..5..5..5..3..1..1..1..
    Okw. 42.14.14.35.

98. *Basubira malayika* ("They hope for an angel")

    Ok.   5↓.5..2..2..4..4..3..1..
    Okw. 53.25.25.4Ī.

Other patterns

99. *Kirema embuzi okulya* ("What the goat cannot eat")[40]

    Ok.   4..4..2..5..5..3↓.2..1..
    Okw. 42.24.53.14.

100. *Akakuba-mpanga n'enkoko bagenda mangu* ("The bird of prey and the chikken disappear fast")

    Ok.   4..4..2..5..3↓.3..3..1..
    Okw. 34.13.24.53.

101. *Kawuta yeggalidde* ("Kawuta has shut himself up")

    Ok.   2↓.1..2..1..2..1..2..5..
    Okw. 24.35.14.54.

102. *Tweyanze, tweyanze ewa Mugwanya* ("We pay homage at Mugwanya")

    Ok.   4..Ī..Ī..Ī↓.4..Ī..5..5..4..3..3..3..
    Okw. 14.53.42.53.14.53.42.53.14.53.43.53.

Appendix: Biographical note on Evaristo Muyinda

Evaristo Muyinda was born in 1914 in Nabbale, near Kampala, Uganda, which is still his home today. At the age of two he lost his father. At nine he began to learn the Kiganda xylophones *amadinda* and *akadinda*. From the early 1940s he was a Kabaka's musician within the *akadinda* ensemble.

His carreer took an unexpected turn when Klaus Wachsmann, then Curator of the Uganda Museum recruted him at the age of 35 years to become chief music demonstrator at the Museum.

From 1949 onwards he was Wachsmann's research assistant for many years. In this capacity he demonstrated Kiganda music regularly not only for visitors of the Museum, but also during lectures at Makerere University College, Kampala and elsewhere. From 1950 on he taught the performance techniques and repertoire of various Kiganda instruments at schools.

Gradually he developed great expertise, particularly on the *endingidi* (one-string bowed lute), *entongoli* (lyre) and *enderre* (notched flute), as well as various drums, notably the small *nankasa* (conical drum played with sticks) performed in show manner. He gave public concerts throughout the 1950s with groups of his own and published several 78 r.p.m. records with local record companies, in Kampala, notably the titles: *"Omunya"* and *"Akainja."* He was also recorded by Hugh Tracey in 1952 for the Gallotone label.[41] It was during that time that he began to develop his idea of a Kiganda grand orchestra that would unite all the instruments known in Buganda's traditions.

No doubt, Klaus Wachsmann had considerable influence upon Evaristo Muyinda, encouraging him in various directions. I possess the following notes by Wachsmann concerning the early stages of Evaristo Muyinda's experience on the *ennanga* (arched harp):

> When he became involved in the demonstrations at the Uganda Museum, he hardly knew how to play. He never was a Kabaka's *omulanga* by any stretch of the imagination. ... M. was a Kabaka's musician in the *akadinda* team. When I brought him in as a music demonstrator at the Museum he enlarged his repertoire to include the harp. (M. was never Head Attendant).[42] I encouraged him to try his hand on the *ennanga,* and I persuaded Temusewo Mukasa, the last of the true *abalanga,* to guide Muyinda's study. I had worked with Temusewo for many years since 1937 and I was in a position to broach the subject of Muyinda's training to him, and Temusewo reluctantly agreed. However, I gathered that Temusewo did not keep his part of the bargain, which is perfectly normal for a traditional musician of Temusewo's standing.[43]

During the 1950s, on Klaus Wachsmann's suggestion, Joseph Kyagambiddwa, the Muganda church music composer, became a student of Evaristo Muyinda in *amadinda* playing and Kiganda music theory. In a sense, Evaristo Muyinda is co-author of Kyagambiddwa's book "African Music from the Source of the Nile" (1955) which could not have been written without the latter's explanation of song-texts (often literally translated by Kyagambiddwa from interviews with Muyinda) and his teaching of a large repertoire of *amadinda* pieces.

In the years 1957 to 1959 Muyinda organized the *akadinda* ensemble of the Blind Musicians of Salama at the Agricultural Training Centre for the Blind, Salama, south of Mukono. The *akadinda* ensemble became something like an institution with the performers coming and going, because a blind trainee did not usually stay at the school longer than about a year before completing his course and returning home.

In the period between November and April 1959/60, on various occasions in 1961 to 1963, and finally in December 1967/January 1968 Evaristo Muyinda was my tutor in xylophone music.

I remember that when I first heard the name Muyinda at Namagunga Catholic Mission, soon after my arrival in Uganda on November 23, 1959, and when it was suggested by Father Lycklama that I might approach him to be my teacher, he was portrayed as a "modern musician."

In 1964 Lois Anderson, a student of Klaus Wachsmann received her first instructions from him from which resulted her thesis (Anderson 1968) at the University of California, Los Angeles. In the late 1960s, with the active participation of Miles Lee, radio producer at the Uganda Broadcasting station, a national dance troup named "Heart Beat of Africa" was organized, in which Evaristo Muyinda was to play a prominent role. With "Heart Beat of Africa" he travelled on extensive tours to the United States of America, to Japan, India, England and West Germany.

In 1967/68 he worked in close cooperation with Peter Cooke as a teacher of Kiganda musical instruments and dance at Kyambogo Teachers' Training College, near Kampala, where duplicate sets of the Kabaka's previously destroyed *akadinda* xylophone and the *entenga* drums were constructed. Due to the political turmoil in Uganda during the 1970s I last met Muyinda in Kampala in 1972, then lost contact with him for over a decade. Rumours had it that he was murdered by Idi Amin's henchmen.

In the early 1980s I began to make inquiries through friends in Kampala about his fate and whereabouts. When it turned out that he was alive and working as usually at the Uganda Museum, I discussed the matter with Artur Simon, Museum für Völkerkunde, West-Berlin and we devised a plan to bring Muyinda to Europe for a concert and interviews.

This was successful and in summer 1983 we met Muyinda at the airport in West-Berlin. He was now 69 years old.

On June 21, 1983, he appeared solo in front of an enthusiastic audience in the garden of the Museum für Völkerkunde, having already performed in Bayreuth on June 18 at Iwalewa-Haus. Muyinda's visit was the beginning of a second career. The tour of Germany obviously had a positive psychological effect on him. On the same occasion he was also extensively recorded and interviewed at the Museum in Berlin (cf. Wegner 1984) and he constructed and tuned an *amadinda,* activities which all enhanced his optimism. After his return to Kampala, his daughter Marie Francis Muyinda wrote to me (letter dated Kampala 20/8/1983): "…He came back on the 11th July with a strange nice younger complexion…"

A year later (1984) Muyinda again toured Germany, once more on the invitation of the Museum für Völkerkunde, now accompanied by two (younger) former Kabaka's musicians, Ludoviko Sserwanga, born 1939, and Hadisoni Kiyaga, born 1945. A concert under the title "Court music from Buganda (Uganda)" took place on June 28, 1984.

More recently Evaristo Muyinda took part with a group of fourteen musicians and dancers in the "Festival of Traditional Music 87 Bantu" organized by the International Institute for Comparative Music Studies, West-Berlin. This Festival was a joint project of the Extra-European Arts Committee, the Holland Festival, the Royal Tropical Institute (Amsterdam), the Maison de la Culture du Monde (Paris) and the Centro di Ricerca per il Teatro (Milan), and supported by the Ministry of External Affairs Bonn.

CHAPTER V
Concepts About Movement and Sound in the Eastern Angolan Culture Area

What I have termed the "eastern Angolan culture area" (cf. Map 8) corresponds linguistically with Malcolm Guthrie's Zone K/Group 10 in his tentative classification of the Bantu languages (Guthrie 1948:52). It includes, among others, the following languages: Chokwe, Luvale (Lwena), and the so-called Ngangela dialect cluster with Mbwela, Nkhangala, Mbunda, Luchazi, Lwimbi, Ngondzelo and other related languages. Ethnographically and culturally, this area coincides with George Peter Murdock's population cluster 13, which he calls "Lunda" (Murdock 1969:9), suggesting the historical roots of this group of peoples. In its major part it covers most of the eastern half of Angola, extending somewhat into northwestern Zambia and southern parts of Zaïre.

The research data published here was obtained mainly during fieldwork carried out by the author in Angola in 1965, particularly in the Kwitu and Kwanavale river areas of Kwandu-Kuvangu Province (cf. Map 9) supplemented by some data obtained in northwestern Zambia in 1971 and thereafter. The initial Angolan fieldwork was supported by a research grant of the Junta de Investigações do Ultramar, Lisboa; the Zambian fieldwork was financed by the Fonds zur Förderung der Wissenschaftlichen Forschung, Wien (Project No. 1395), and carried out during the author's affiliation to the Institute for African Studies, University of Zambia, Lusaka. Follow-up studies were undertaken in Angola in 1979, 1981 and 1982, and in Zambia in 1973, 77/78, 1979 and 1987.

This large chapter consists of three sections which originally were separate papers. The topics are however, related to each other to an extent that these papers give us three different looks at the same culture and its processes of enculturation. Each glance has its own specific accents and subject matter, but together, I believe the three section combine to give a sort of stereo-vision of this culture area.

March 10, 1989
G. K.

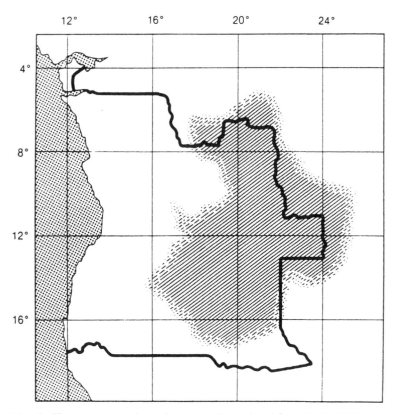

Map 8. The eastern Angolan culture area. Reproduced from Kubik 1982b:[19]

Section I
Musical Enculturation[1]

As is the case in most Bantu languages, there are no terms in those of eastern Angola whose semantic fields could be considered congruent with that of the Latin word musica and its derivatives in European languages, nor are there any words exactly equivalent to "dance" or "games". It is not easy to find a general term for "musical instruments" either, although native speakers sometimes construct one to satisfy translation needs or insistent questions by foreigners. The sound-producing utensils are normally called only by their specific designations.

In the languages of the Ngangela dialect continuum, musical terminology includes the key terms of Table 12.

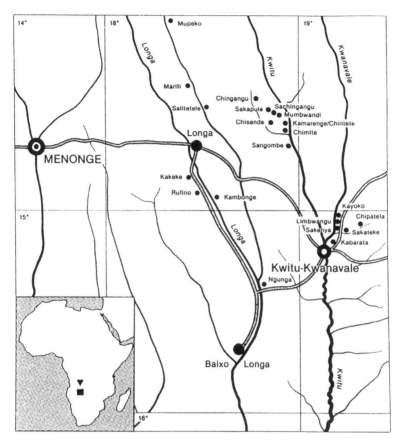

Map 9. Region of recordings and field research in south-eastern Angola 1965.
Reproduced from Kubik 1982b:[19]

With one exception (see Table 13), "age-sets" or "age-groups" are
distinguished in the Ngangela dialect continuum irrespective of sex, each
with particular social connotations, i.e. particular expectancies of social
behaviour and a specific place for the individual within the society. These
age-groups are not rigidly delimitated against each other, but may over-
lap under certain circumstances. Age is not counted by years as in Western societies; thus it may occur that a person who belongs to a later
age-set, for example, because he/she has passed through certain initiation
ceremonies, may actually be younger with regard to the unrecorded
birthdates than some belonging to an earlier one.

kwimba	– "to sing (with the human voice)"; this includes specialized actions of sound producing, such as kwimba chintovi ("to blow" the leaf of a muvulya tree).
kusika	– "to play an instrument"; for example, kusika ngoma ("to perform on a drum"), kusika chisanzi ("to play a lamellophone"), etc. Besides these there are specialized terms such as kukuwa mingongi ("to strike the concussion sticks") as in a circumcision school (cf. Kubik 1977 : 260–2). One can also say kusika muluzi ("to whistle"), although kukumba muluzi seems to be more common.[2]
kuhandeka	– "to speak." Birds do not "sing", but "speak". However, birds' talk is appreciated as including pitch modifications according to the principles of semantic and grammatical tone in the eastern Angolan languages. Hence one says, mwekuhandeka tuzila ("how the birds talk").
kutanga	– "to recite"; kutangesa – "to make recite", "to teach reciting". A text, often of historical content, is recited under the guidance of a drum.[3] This action also includes pitch sequences, and some parts would be considered as "song" by a casual observer.
mwaso (pl. mi-)	– "a song"; any sound-producing action suggesting text lines. There are many subcategories of this term, for example mwaso wa chisimo ("story song"). Subcategories also include myaso yakumukanda ("songs of the boys' circumcision school") or even further subdivisions such as myaso ya Kawali ("the songs of Kawali", i.e. songs of a type associated with dance movements as in the famous song about "Kawali", a mythical figure in the circumcision school).
lizi lyakama	– a "deep voice" (literally a "big voice"), a deep sound.
lizi lyalindend	– a "high voice" (literally a "small voice"), a high sound.
kutendeka	– "to sing with a high voice".
kukokolola	– "to sing with a deep voice".
kukeleka	– "to tune a musical instrument".
kulema ngoma	– "to stretch a skin on a drum".
chipwali (pl. vi-)	– a long goblet-shaped drum; the standard drum type in eastern Angolan villages.
ntangi	– a deep-tuned note on an instrument; (or) the deep-tuned specimen within a set of instruments of the same kind (such as a drum set etc.).
chimpululu	– a middle-tuned note on an instrument; (or) the middle-tuned specimen within a set.
mundengu	– a high-tuned note or an instrument; (or) the high-tuned specimen within a set.
kukina or kuchina	– (in some dialects) – "to dance", "to move the body" (or parts of it) in an organized, dance-like motion. Used as a generic term, it is then further delineated; for example one can say, wekukina koka, "he/she performs the koka motion", i.e. a jerky movement of the pelvis while standing on

	the spot, also called *koka na koka. Vukina* is the noun, often denoting any kind of dance. However, in some areas *kukina* is used in a narrower sense, denoting a specific set of movement patterns. Ngangela dance terminology includes countless terms for specific patterns, each clearly defined, for example: *kuhunga, kundekula* (or *kawali*), *vutotola, chizukula, linyanga, kakese, katonda, chiyanda, lungu, mutenya, chikoka, vanthongwe* etc.[4]
kuheha	– "to play"; for example the board game *(milavalava)*;[5] this term can never be used in connection with "musical instruments". *Kuheha* also denotes any kind of playful action by children and teenagers.
shombe	– a term borrowed possibly from non-Ngangela languages; now used as a generic term for dance-games of various formations including song, as performed by children and teenagers. *Vanike vekuheha na kwimba myaso* ("children/ teenagers play and sing songs").

Table 12. Key terms of music terminology in the languages of the Ngangela dialect continuum

The terms reported in Table 13 above may also be used comparatively; for example, *mukuluntu* also means elder brother or sister, e.g. in the contrastive expressions *mukuluntu wange* ("my elder brother/sister") and *ntsongo yange* ("my younger brother/sister). In a similar manner the term *kanike* may be applied by elders, comparatively, even to a twenty-five year old person.

Obviously, certain activities aiming at or including the production of sound are associated with certain age-sets. Thus, it is often stated by adherents to the culture that this or that activity is an affair of *vanike,* to which may be added a descriptive term indicating whether these are "males" or "females" *(vanike vayala* or *vanike vampwevo).* It is interesting that there is no independent single term for "boys" or "girls", in contrast to many other Bantu languages. In the Ngangela languages such a concept can only be expressed by adding "male" or "female" to the age-group term, or in some contexts by using descriptive or substitute terminology, such as *mwanampwevo* ("a young woman"). The term *vanike* can be used in a narrower or wider sense. Sometimes it refers to small children prior to the obligatory initiation ceremonies, sometimes it includes teenagers up to 17 or 18 years (youngsters who in an English social environment nowadays would not agree to be called "children").

With regard to sound-producing activities of the age-set of *vanike,* it can be noticed in eastern Angola that boys are customarily (or expected to be) much more active and dominating in this field. Girls rarely become "musically" active before puberty. It is not by chance, therefore, that our data predominantly covers boys' activities.

Age-group terminology	Expected educational standards
Kakeke (pl. *tu-*) – an infant, a very small child; also referred to as *nkemba* (pl. *va-*). This stage lasts up to about three years of age.	Under mother's care, until weaning and first walking experience.
Kanike (pl. *va-*) – a child approximately to completion of puberty, i.e. ca. 15 to 17 years.	Prior to formal, institutionalized education this age-set engages in countless activities, such as storytelling, riddling, games, music/dance, making of toys, making of various sound-producing devices. All this is part of informal learning. Formal education (begins earlier for boys, and later for girls): a) passage through the *mukanda* circumcision school for boys, which lasts several months; b) passage through the *chikula* puberty school for girls after appearance of the first menstruation.
Mukwenze (pl. *va-*) for a male; *mwanampwevo* (pl. *va-*) for a female; – a young person, approximately between 16 and 25 years of age.	Passage through higher grades of formal education (not obligatory). a) Institutions for young men: 1. *vandumbu* initation, i.e. into the knowledge of the voices of the dead kings. This usually takes place between ca. 15 and 16 years, but can also be performed earlier. 2. *mungongi* initation, i.e. admission into a secret society for men usually between 16 and 20 years. b) Institutions for older girls and women: 1. *makisi avampwevo* ("the masks of women"), i.e. initiation into the masked association of women as a counterweight against those of men. 2. *tuwema* ("the flames"). Initiation into a secret society for women.
Mukuluntu (pl. *va-*) – person of mature age, usually above 25 years.	Responsibility in many social, political, and religious areas. Acquisition of esoteric knowledge. Among the men informal learning of an ideographic script *(tusona)*.
Kasinakazi (pl. *tu-*) – an old person, physical characteristic: white hair (*vwele*).	Acquisition of esoteric knowledge. Entrustment with highest social, political and religious roles.

Table 13. Age-group terminology in Mbwela, one of the "Ngangela" languages with expected educational standards

A. Sound-Producing Activities as Part of Entertainment and Informal Education

1. Activities Open to All for Active Participation Regardless of Sex or Age

The most important of these is the telling of *visimo* (sing. *chisimo*), – chantefables, stories containing a song to be sung by the storyteller and responded to by the assembled community ranging from small children to grandparents. Storytelling is a non-professional activity in this area, i.e. it is unspecialized and unpaid, although there are distinguished experts among all age groups. Anyone is entitled to tell a story *(kuta chisimo)* if he knows one, as our collection demonstrates. Some very young children may have a gift for storytelling.

> *Chisimo* (chantefable) told by Kayoko, m., 6 years old. Title: Vanana Somili ("Mother Somili"). Ethnic group: – Nkhangala. Language: Nkhangala/Mbwela. Recorded at Chingangu, area of the administration post Longa, Distrito Cuando-Cubango, October 1965[6] (CD I/33).

This was one of two stories I recorded of Kayoko, aged 6, who was an expert in other musical or sound-producing realms as well. A content analysis of the text translated below, and many other *visimo* recorded in the area, has shown that there are no stories specially designed for "children". Ngangela society does not consider "children" to be intellectually less capable than adults; there is also no concept that would regard some narrative material as "unsuitable" for "minors", although there are ritual texts (outside the realm of *visimo*) considered unsuitable, not for "children", but for (all) non-initiates. Adherents to the culture, regardless of age, are expected to grasp intuitively the symbolism in the stories as it shimmers through, for example in Kayoko's *chisimo:*[7]

> A young man set out to find a woman for marriage. After a long and fruitless search he arrived at a lonely village, where he found a young woman who had stayed in her house all her life. Since she was born she had never left the house. The man asked her whether she wanted to marry him and she replied, "Yes! Let us go!"
>
> On their journey to the young man's village, the woman suddenly stood still in front of a tree and asked, "What is this?" Her husband answered, "This is a tree." – "What is the name of this tree?" – The man explained it to her. Every moment the woman stopped to ask, because she had never seen such things, as she had stayed in the house all her life. The man began to sing:

Vanana Somili	Mother Somili
Kwana vyuma kwihula	Asking continuously about things
Kandende ngamwene	If she had only seen a little bit
Vyose vyuma vyakwihula	All the things, she is asking about

As they proceeded with their journey, the woman continued to ask about the name of every single object they encountered on their way. She wondered about the little red seeds of some bushes called *vinthundu;* she also asked about *vimpundya,* another edible fruit. "What is this?" And then she asked about *vimaho* – the leaves of a certain tree.

When they arrived at the house of the husband, the man said, "This is the footboard *(echi ni chipamba)* at the entrance." They entered the house. They slept. The next morning they went to see the husband's relatives. On the way there they met a big python *(mboma)* in the bush. The woman did not know that this was a dangerous snake and, therefore, did not avoid it. As usual she asked, "What is this?" And the python killed her. Now the husband had to recompensate her parents for the loss of their daughter.

2. Activities Regarded as Age-Specific and as Customarily Associated with
vanike

There is a wide variety of activities to be encountered among young boys, some of them categorized as "songs" *(myaso)* and/or "dance" *(vukina),* some as *kuheha* ("playing"), some others, however, are not included in any of these categories and are merely referred to by their proper names.

Luvimbi (two types), children's instruments performed by Kufuna, ca. 16, Kayoko, ca. 6, and another boy. Ethnic group: – Nkhangala. Language: Nkhangala/Mbwela. Recorded at Chingangu, area of the administration post Longa, Distrito Cuando-Cubango, October 1965[8] (CD I/items 34, 35 and 36).

Luvimbi (sing.) is a generic term applied to sound-producing instruments of two kinds used by children in this area to make sounds/noises not usually considered part of any "song" *(mwaso),* for the sake of personal entertainment. There are two types of *luvimbi;* in both cases leaves of a tree are brought to vibrate, and thus produce a sound.

These instruments are usually made by boys for the fun of it during brief hunting excursions to the bushes in the vicinity of the village or when returning from a bathing and water-fetching trip to the river. The first type, shown by Kufuna, aged ca. 16, is manufactured in a minute by cutting a thin tree branch, about 15 cm long, peeling off the bark and splitting one end. An ordinary leaf, apparently from any kind of tree or shrub, is cut to the shape of the blade of a small pocket-knife with one end pointed, and then inserted into the split (Illustration 69). The instrument is then approached to the player's lips horizontally, with the end of the split, which is also in horizontal position, pointing to the left. Holding the stick with his right hand in this manner, the performer blows with a gentle pressure at the split containing the loose leaf. The leaf begins to vibrate, and the result is a rather shrill and obtrusive sound. The pitch can be changed by inserting the leaf more or less deeply into the slit. If it is inserted deeper, the sound becomes higher. I did not observe, however, that any of the performers made an organized "musical" use of this device. The *mavimbi* (pl.) were not tuned by intention, even when the boys began to play them in concert.

Ill. 69. The first type of *luvimbi* as played in Chingangu, northeast of Longa, southeastern Angola, October 1965

After this demonstration, a second type of *luvimbi* was shown to me by Kayoko, aged six, the boy who had told the story. He slung two fresh leaves, apparently also from any kind of tree, around the inner side of the second and third fingers of his left hand, in the manner depicted in the Illustrations 70 and 71. Then he approached his hand vertically to his mouth and blew lightly at the tiny slit between the loosely held leaves.

Eventually the boys gave a "concert" with the two types of *luvimbi,* a third boy joining them. Although they were not considering their performance as transmitting a particular "song", it is remarkable that the universal African responsorial principle soon became evident as an organizing factor.

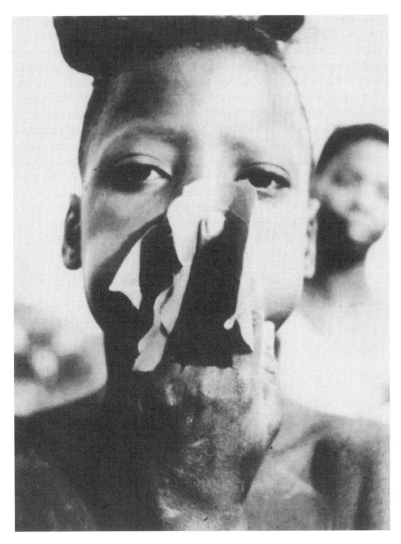

Among the -Luvale and -Luchazi in Kabompo District, northwestern Zambia, a similar device is known as *chintovi* (pl. *vi-*). This is a fresh leaf taken from the *muvulya* tree (bot. Diplorrhynchus mossambicensis), rolled up, and then put into the boy's mouth like a cigar. Gentle blowing produces a sound which can be modified by inserting the rolled leaf more or less deeply into one's mouth. The demonstrator, Mose Kamwocha, m., ca. 13, described his performance as: *tukwimba chintovi cha muti muvulya* ("we are singing *chintovi* of the *muvulya* tree"). He emphasized that the leaf must be fresh, otherwise it would not work.[9]

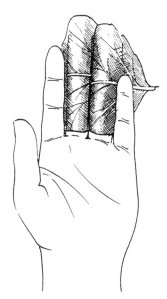

Ill. 70 and 71. The second type of *luvimbi* shown by Kayoko, aged approximately 6, as played in Chingangu, southeastern Angola, October 1965. Front and back view of the hand holding two freshly plucked leaves.

Kambulumbumba (musical bow) performed collectively by three children, Kayoko, ca. 6, Vimbanda, ca. 8 and Litwayi, ca. 12 years. Ethnic group: Nkhangala. Language: -Nkhangala/Mbwela. Place and date as above[10] (CD I/37).

It was not by chance that I recorded so many different activities of young boys on the same day in the same village. Once the children had sensed my interest by recording the *visimo* of Kayoko, the whole peer group offered to show me more of their sound-producing world. Their interest in listening to the recorded results was, of course, a further stimulus.

Kambulumbumba – the word means literally "a small musical bow" – was in the present case, an ordinary hunting bow *(vuta)* turned into a musical instrument. The Vankhangala boys may have adopted the idea of using a hunting bow for musical purposes from the autochtonous inhabitants of southeastern Angola, the !Kung' (San-speakers) of whom very small bands were still surviving in the Kwandu-Kuvangu Province in 1965. During long food-gathering trips the !Kung' customarily employ a hunting bow either as a mouth-bow (with a noose added to divide the string) or a gourd-resonated bow, in which case a *likolo* ("bush orange") serves as a resonator.[11] The term *kambulumbumba,* however, is Bantu, and is probably onomatopoeic. *Ka-* is a diminutive prefix. *Mbulumbumba* is the usual designation for a calabash-resonated musical bow in south-western Angola among the -Nkhumbi, -Handa and related peoples. The idea to play the hunting bow in the manner documented here is also Bantu and not San. The children at Chingangu treated the bow like a one-string (idiochord-)zither, as known in many musical cultures of central Africa.[12]

The stave of the bow is made from the wood of the *mukuve* tree (bot. Cryptosepalum pseudotaxus); the only string is twisted from antelope skin. For the performance the stave of the bow is placed on the sand floor, with some sand shoveled up at the sides, and firmly held down by the middle boy (Vimbanda). With its single undivided string *(lungusa)* the stave forms a vertical plane.

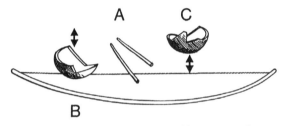

Ill. 72. Playing positions, musical functions and instruments for sound production and manipulation of the three musicians of the *kambulumbumba*. Chingangu, southeastern Angola, October 1965

Three performers act upon the single string collectively, each with a specific task (Illustration 72). This kind of "labour division" is evidently a further Bantu (and not San) cultural trait. Vimbanda (performer A) strikes the strings with two sticks in an alternate left-right movement. Although his series of strokes, at first glance, seems to be uniformous and equispacial, a closer analysis reveals that the strokes are differently accented, which is also suggested by the didactic mnemonic syllables used for teaching the pattern. The small Kayoko (performer B) is sitting obliquely opposite performer A and produces a counter-rhythm by approaching a broken piece of calabash, held in his right hand, with its outer surface to the string at the moment of every third stroke of performer A. The vibration of the string touches the calabash, resulting in a loud and "crackling" sound. The task of performer C (Litwayi), sitting on the left-hand side of Vimbanda and holding another piece of calabash in his right hand, is to stop the string from time to time at a certain point. In this manner a second note, approximately a fourth higher, is obtained.

According to the boys, a performance on the *kambulumbumba* suggests only one song, whose text is the name of the instrument itself:

Ill. 73. Kayoko, Vimbanda and Litwayi (from left to right) performing on the *kambulumbumba*. Chingangu village, October 1965

kambulumbumba, kambulumbumba, kambulumbumba, kambulumbumba,

¯   ¯   ¯   ¯   ¯   ¯   ¯   ¯   ¯   ¯   ¯   ¯   ¯   ¯   ¯   ¯   ¯   ¯   ¯

While the result of the action is considered as "song" *(mwaso)*, each boy is acutely aware of the kinetic and timbre-melodic aspects of his particular part. Player A (Vimbanda) told me afterwards that he associated the following syllables with his alternate left-right strokes of the sticks (CD I/38):

De ke le ŋge ke le, de ke ŋge ne ke le.

Through such mnemonic patterns the foundation is laid in children for later expertise in African music. As I pointed out elsewhere (Kubik 1972 b), mnemonic patterns are part of a system of "oral notation" which transmits, through phonetic units, the rhythm and accent structure of the patterns to be performed. At an early age children in eastern Angola (and elsewhere) develop an acute ear for such mnemonics and an ability to convert them at short notice between different perceptual or conceptual realms: from auditive into motional/kinetic and the reverse, even into visual patterning. The mnemonic syllables used by a boy while learning his pattern of strokes are also an invaluable aid to the scientific observer trying to discover how a pattern is structured and where its accents are. In the present case, a first analysis already reveals that the syllables beginning with the plosive (and thereby accent-suggesting) sound *k* occur every third stroke, thus implying a certain structure of the pattern. However, it is evident that this is not a simple "triple rhythm"; in fact, the first and second parts of the total stick pattern of 12 strokes are slightly different in their timing. This is suggested by the subtle change of the mnemonic pattern from *ke-le-ŋge* to *ke-ŋge-ne* suggesting that the distances between the left-right alternate strokes are now minutely different. A complex internal polyrhythm is actually hidden in the apparently simple motional pattern of Vibanda.

I was interested in finding out to what extent the conceptualization of this pattern is shared by others in the same area, and asked the *likembe-* (lamellophone-) player Kufuna Kandonga to perform it for me in isolation on an object and then pronounce the mnemonics again. The result was that it is identical.[13]

Mwekuhandeka tuzila (how the birds' talk imitated by Mose Kamwocha, m., born 1958. Ethnic group: -Luvale/-Lunda. Language: Luchazi. Village: Chikenge, Kabompo District, N.W. Province, Zambia[14] (CD I/39).

Young boys are experts in interpreting verbally the sounds produced by birds. In this culture area children develop an acute sensitivity towards pitch alterations as meaningful processes by their learning of a tonal language. Consequently, involuntary verbal associations to any kind of sound sequence, whether produced by man, animals or mechanical devices, such as a train speeding over the rails, occur in abundance. Everything in nature seems to "talk" – words or ideophonic syllables –, and any (instrumental) melody is sooner or later verbalized by the audience. The languages of eastern Angola are not tonal to the same extent that some languages of the Kwa family in West Africa are, but semantic and grammatical tone is a crucial feature in many instances. In addition, strictly conventionalized behaviour with regard to the flow of intonation in individual sentences is expected.

The word phrases projected by man into "birds' talk" vary from one dialect group to another, often within the distance of a few villages.[15] They are always rhythmically and melodically organized, reflecting closely the sound patterns produced by the birds. Some of the patterns appear to be sung, such as, for example, the pattern Mose Kamwocha associated with the bird *mungandzi*. A high incidence of ideophones is evident in these phrases. Some of them cannot be translated, while others transmit a verbal message in relation to man and his environment.

Livembe (a kind of dove)	. . . *Kukwe Sakasweka kukwe!* ("Kukwe! Father of Kasweka, kukwe!")
Mungandzi (a black bird)	. . . *Nyamwile, fwaku fwaku, hatangwa hatangwa hembo lya mukwenu fwaku fwaku muchinenewe, hwehwehwehwe.* ("Mrs. Nyamwile, fwaku fwaku,[16] every day in the village of your friends, fwaku fwaku, run away! Hwe hwe hwe hwe!")
Ndantsampwa (a small, rather fat bird)	. . . *mem'angy'owo!* ($^-$ – _) ("My water, there it is!"[17])

Some birds may "speak" more than one phrase. The bird *munthembo*, according to Mose Kamwocha (cf. CD I/39) speaks these words:

Munthembo wekuhandeka ngweni: Muvi chilya vwenge, ndavi chilukula mutima. (8×) Mukemwo mwekuhandeka munthembo omwo. – Munthembo nawa wekuhandeka ngweni: njinengila muchitapu chatuʒy'e swi lovi swi lovi (3×) swi lovi swi lovi chapititi lovi swi lovi . . . (etc.) . . . Mwekuhandeka munthembo nawa, ngweni [kuzola] tunengila muchitapu chatuzi, tunengila swi lovi twatuhuka, tunengila twatuhuka, tunengila twatuhuka. Kunahu.

("The bird *munthembo* speaks as follows: An [iron] arrow eats up the penis, a wooden arrow-head knocks down the heart. (8 ×). In this way *munthembo* speaks. – *Munthembo* also speaks the following: I have entered a clay-pit of shit, in and out, in and out (3 ×), in and out, in and out *chapititi,* in and out, . . . (etc.) . . . This is how *munthembo* also speaks, saying [Mose is laughing] we have entered a clay-pit of shit, we have entered in and out, we have come out, we have entered, we have come out, we have entered, we have come out. That's all.")

Muvi is a pointed arrow of iron. *Ndavi* is a wooden arrow-head. It is such rounded, blunt arrowheads that are used for bird hunting. When a bird is hit by this kind of arrow, explained Mose, it falls down, but without showing a wound. "The bird *munthembo* says that a pointed arrow comes for the penis, but a wooden arrow-head knocks down the heart" (. . . *muvi kuhitula vwenge, vunoni ndavi yekulukula mutima*).

Mose did not explain the symbolism in this phrase, but it is noteworthy that the term *vwenge* for "penis" is especially used between members of the same age-set in a *mukanda* circumcision school instead of another more common term. Although Mose could not explain the use of the prefix *chi-* in the word *"chilya",* he said it transmitted the idea of *"wekulya"* (he/she/it eats). "To eat" often has sexual meaning. As I understand this phrase, it could refer to two different approaches to love, the aggressive style, symbolized by the arrow, which is out for sexual pleasure, and the other, soft approach, which hits the heart. In any case, the discussion of such subjects is common among graduates from the *mukanda*. (See also below).

Age-specific "musical" activities of children and teenagers include many more types, too numerous for all to be discussed here. *Shombe* is the term applied to many dance-games with songs attracting both boys and girls. More specifically, in southeastern Angola, among the -Mbwela, -Nkhangala and the -Chokwe, there is *kamundonda,* a dance-game performed on moonlit nights by either girls alone,[18] or boys and girls jointly, forming two front rows.[19] The participants are between thirteen and eighteen years old. Related to the *kamundonda* dance-game is *kandouwa,* also performed by teenagers with young adults participating occasionally.[20] The informal nature of these activities implies that it is not necessary for all boys or girls within a certain age-set to participate, in contrast to the obligatory or compulsory aspects of formal education.

Across the border, in northwestern Zambia, some new forms of adolescent entertainment have developed. A string instrument called *mbanjo* (from American: "banjo"), unknown formerly in the eastern Angolan culture area, has been popular since the 1950s among 10- to 15-year-old boys. It is usually a three- to four-stringed instrument showing some affinities with the Namibian *ramkie* (cf. Rycroft 1980). It swept into Northwestern Province, Zambia, with imported South African music during the Jive and *kwela* craze of the 1950s and was quickly adapted to local musical styles. Today, factory-manufactured banjos are no longer available in most parts of southern Africa. What is called banjo is now an entirely homemade instrument manufactured by young boys with great care and devotion. It is the custom that if a boy such as Petulu from Chikenge has passed the *mukanda* circumcision school, he will begin to demonstrate his newly obtained status and individuality by carving a banjo for himself, learning to perform on it, and singing and playing solo along the roadside (Illustration 74). At the age of 16 or 17 he will outgrow this stage and either abandon music altogether or learn to perform on other instruments.

In this manner the "banjo" has become what may be called here an age-set instrument, i.e. it is linked to the transient subculture of a certain age group.[21] The skill shown by some of these enterprising teenagers was the subject some time ago of an article in the Zambian youth magazine "Orbit" (anon. 1974). Some of these boys also organize performance groups, such as the "Kasazi Boys' Jazz," comprising three boys and one girl, at Lutali river, Kabompo District, documented by Moya Aliya Malamusi and myself in 1979.[22]

Ill. 74. Petulu and friend performing on a home-made "banjo" (*mbanjo*), today an "age-set instrument" among 10- to 15-year old boys in Zambia. Chikenge village, Kabompo District, N.W. Province, Zambia, August 1971

The homemade banjo as an age-set denominator is a tradition which the Eastern Angolan culture area now has in common with most of the territory of Zambia, and much of Zimbabwe and Malaŵi. In Northwestern Angola on the other hand (as I recorded in 1982 in Malanji Province) "guitars", also homemade, have assumed similar functions among young boys.

Many of the informal sound-producing activities are associated with individual talent. During my fieldwork in Angola I was introduced on several occasions to young people who were said to have extraordinary talents or expertise. Chief Kayoko (in a village north of Kwitu-Kwanavale in southeastern Angola) once introduced me to two youngsters, Andriano and Alberto, both ca. 14 from the village Sacheleka. They were known in the whole area for singing songs of various types in a duet using head-voices.[23] They were also experts in performing *kachacha* and *muselemeka* dance rhythms on the three long goblet-shaped drums *(vipwali)* known individually as *ntangi, chimpululu,* and *mundengu,* and, when played as a "chime" by one person, as *tumboi.*

In the same village, there was Terceiro, only five years old, from Chief Kayoko's family, who used to perform on a small "children's" drum *(ngoma ya vanike)* built especially for him. It was obvious that Chief

Kayoko was interested in having his children and grand-children to be well-versed in drumming. *Machakili machakili* and other basic drum patterns were performed extremely well by his five-year old [24] (CD I/40). A parallel case was the seven-year-old son of the master drummer Musezi Nyambwamba, ca. 60, the little Ingwe (literally: "Leopard"). He used to play a membrane drum *(ngoma)* while his father performed on the slit-drum *(chinkuvu)*. Obviously his son was being trained to be his future successor.[25]

Drum patterns are taught and identified by mnemonic syllables or verbal mnemonics for example: *machakili machakili* or *kuvamba kuli masika* or *kapapili njamba* etc. Occasionally these, besides others, have become the names of the patterns and associated dance forms themselves.[26]

B. Sound-Producing Activities as Part of Formal Education

These activities are linked to certain educational institutions. They are age-specific, although the teaching personnel may share in some of them, and some are even open to participation to all members of the same sex. There are separate initiation schools for boys and for girls.

Mukanda is an incisive marker in the life of a male individual in this culture area. Although the term *kanike* (pl. *vanike*) includes children who have "been to" and others who have "not yet been to" the circumcision school, pre- and post-*mukanda* activities differ to a great extent. What is learned and performed inside the school by the initiates (*tundanda* in the Ngangela languages, *tundanji* in Chokwe and Luvale) is totally controlled by the ritual context.

While in seclusion, the young boys – after their circumcision – take part in the following music/dance activities which are part of the curriculum of a *mukanda:*[27]

(1) *Kukuwa mingongi* – performance of the secret concussion sticks together with their teachers and male visitors from the village. The pattern is the basis for the general *myaso yakumukanda (mukanda* songs) sung in three to four harmonious parts, sometimes all night long.

(2) *Kutangesa* – recitations steered by one *ntangi* drum. The young boys learn long texts of historical content which they are to perform during the return ceremony to the village.

(3) Dance songs to go with the movement patterns *kuhunga* and *kundekula,* also practised for the coming-out ceremony. These songs are didactic in content.[28]

Released from the *mukanda,* the graduates then assume new tasks as "small guardians" or "helper-guardians" *(tulombola-ntito)* in any of the

Ill. 75. The boy Malesu with a small drum made for him while in seclusion in the
mukanda circumcision school. Sangombe village, Mumbezi river, Kabompo District, N.W. Province, Zambia, October 1971

mikanda schools that are started in subsequent years in the area with new
boys to be circumcised. During these post-graduate years as teenagers
some of the boys may learn to use yet one more sound-producing instrument: the bull-roarer *(ndumba-mwelela)*. Its use in Angola during initiation in order to frighten the initiates, who are secluded, by its strange
sound is widespread, also outside the eastern Angolan culture area. In
mukanda initiation it is not universally used among the "Ngangela"-
speakers, but it seems to appear quite regularly among the -Luvale and
their neighbours during a ritual episode called *kulonda ntsimba* ("the
climbing of the genet cat").[29]

Sometimes a special drum about half the size of the ordinary village
chipwali, may be given to an initiate for learning drum patterns while he
is still inside *mukanda.* I was able to observe this in October 1971 at the
village Sangombe, a sparsely populated area north of Chikenge in

Kabompo District, Zambia, where a *mukanda* was going on for only one child, Malesu, ca. 8 years old. Being the only "inmate" of the circumcision school, with a team of teachers and guardians assigned to take care of him, he seemed to enjoy preferential treatment in various ways. The small drum was called *yantsongo,* referring to its tuning (Illustration 75).

The institution for girls, parallel to *mukanda,* is called *chikula* in southeastern Angola among the -Mbwela, and is characterized by the symbolic name *litungu lya nyamuso* among the -Luchazi of Kabompo District in northwestern Zambia. *Litungu* is the pyramid-shaped grass shelter at the edge of the village, where the female initiate *(mwali)* receives her instructions. Nyamuso, in its basic meaning, denotes a large insect, alluding to the female initiate.

Music/dance activities of the girl while in seclusion, and especially during the coming-out ceremony, show close parallels to those of the boys. The two girls, one very small, one about 17 years old and already engaged, who were released from seclusion on June 24, 1979 in the village of Chikenge, Kabompo District, Zambia, performed *kachacha* dance movements and a recitation *(kutangesa)* in front of the drums played by men.[30] In *chikula* ceremonies in southeastern Angola, which are said to be a Lunda introduction, the women "drum" upon the orifices of large calabashes during the secret instruction outside the village.

Although young girls share in some of the musical life of a village at an early age and learn work rhythms and movement patterns from their mothers, such as *kuhunga,* winnowing millet with a certain type of flat basket, called *lisehwa,* the foundation for music/dance activities of females is laid during the initiation rites. During her work the woman holds her small oval basket in her hand and performs a swinging movement, forming circles in contrary motion with each hand. In later life women are not less active musically than men, although they play fewer musical instruments. Besides community songs, in which everyone shares, and storytelling, a major realm for women's music in the eastern Angolan culture area is the women's "secret societies", such as *makisi a vampwevo* (the "masks" of the women) or *tuwema* (the "flames"), during which – in absolute darkness – the singing young women produce by a device that is kept secret a shower of sparks frightening to men (CD I/41).

Section 2
Patterns of Body Movement in Mbwela/Nkhangala Boys' Initiation

The *mukanda* institution is known by this name throughout the eastern Angolan culture area. It can be described as a boys' initiation and circumcision school and is the most important educational institution among -Luvale, -Chokwe, -Nkhangala, -Mbwela, -Mbunda, -Luchazi and other groups. All of these groups are closely related culturally and linguistically and share common historical links.

I first studied *mukanda* in Angola, where I worked in the southeast among Mbwela-, Nkhangala- and Chokwe-speaking groups living along the upper Kwitu River and its tributaries in what is now called Kwandu-Kuvangu Province (cf. Map 9), and in the northeast near Kazombo ("Cazombo" on Portuguese maps) among the -Luvale. This field work was conducted between July and December 1965. Further study of *mukanda* was made in 1971, 1973, 1979, and 1987, when I was engaged in field work in Northwestern Province, Zambia, among Luchazi-speaking communities. The present discussion is mainly based on recordings, films and information collected in southeastern Angola in 1965, where I examined four different *mikanda* (cf. Table 14). Data from my later work on *mikanda* (= plural of *mukanda*) from the Zambian side of the border is included in some places for comparison and amplification.

Mukanda of village headman	Number and age of novices		Rites in which I assisted
Sakateke	6	ca. 5–10	1. *kukusha mpoko* (to wash the knife) 2. *kulundulula mukanda* (to remove the *mukanda*)
Limbwangu	4	ca. 6–10	*kulundulula mukanda*
Chintete	16	ca. 6–15	– –
Sakapula	2	ca. 8–10	*kulundulula mukanda*

Table 14. *Mikanda* documented in southeastern Angola, 1965

I have given detailed accounts elsewhere of the social and cultural aspects of *mukanda* in southeastern Angola (Kubik 1971 b, 1974 a, 1982 a and 1982 b), of the meaning and cultural context of the associated *makisi* mask complex (Kubik 1969 b, 1971 b and 1985), music education (Kubik 1973 a), and of the songs of the initiates (Kubik 1969 b, 1971 b, 1982 b). Accounts by other authors describing *mukanda* as a ritual include those of Victor Turner for the Lunda-Ndembu (Turner 1953, 1967), C.M.N.

White (1961) for the -Luvale, Hermann Baumann (1932) for the -Chokwe, Martinho van Koolwijk (1963a and b) for the western -Ngangela, and other scattered accounts.

My own preoccupation with *mukanda* developed in Angola, as part of an integrated study of enculturation and socialization as a participating field researcher. I learned the Mbwela language and began to go through the rites of Mbwela youth. Besides *mukanda*, which is recognized by the people as the first stage in formal education, I had to pass two further stages: *vandumbu* (cf. Kubik 1971b) and *mungongi*[31].

Mukanda is considered by Mbwela communities to be a necessary intervention in a male human's life to make him aware of his future roles. *Mukanda* does not instantly transform a "child" (*kanike*) into a "man," as has sometimes been suggested in the literature, but into a socially better adapted individual.

In this section of Chapter V I consider among other aspects the relation of the initiates' songs and body movements to some of the psychosocial processes in *mukanda* initiation. At the same time, I will also introduce a system of transcription for body movement structures.

In Mbwela and related languages, the word *mukanda* denotes (a) the rectangular enclosure outside a village where the newly circumcised boys are kept in seclusion for four to five months and (b) the institution as such, with its associated activities.

The season for *mukanda* coincides with the dry season, which is approximately from April or May to October or November. The age of the initiates ranges from six to ten, though occasionally some boys may be older.

Organization of *mukanda*

The initiator of a *mukanda* in a given year is called *chizika-mukanda*. Arrangements for *mukanda* can only be made when a sufficient number of boys in a village or a cluster of neighboring villages has reached the desired age. Then, some time in April, May, June or July of that year, the would-be *chizika-mukanda* publicly declares that his protégé (to whom he may be a physical father, the maternal uncle or another male authority) is ready for circumcision. If nobody in the community objects he begins to look out for possible partners in other families, until a minimum group of boys, between three and six in most cases, has been recruited. Then begin the definite preparations, and guardians and teachers are appointed.

With the day of starting *mukanda* drawing closer, the event is announced. A masked dancer (*likisi*) appears the night before, and the women dance in the village, while the boys are being prepared. The act of circumcision is carried out the next morning. It takes place at the edge of the village in front of a piece from a termite hill and a forked structure of wood referred to as *lusumba*. After the operation, while the newly circumcised boys rest in the shade, their guardians and teachers begin to construct a lodge in the forest, not far from the place referred to as *ha lusumba*. Here the boys will stay in seclusion for the next five to six months. After the healing of the wound, they are no longer strictly confined to the lodge, but at day-time they can move freely around in the vicinity, on "expeditions" through the forest areas and to the river. But they have to avoid meeting women on their paths and are not allowed to walk in direction to the village.

The *chizika-mukanda* remains the chief authority responsible for discipline and progress in the lodge during the whole seclusion period, up to the ceremonial return of the initiates to their village. Of comparable high authority is the *chikenzi* (circumciser) who is a specialist. The craft of a circumciser is transmitted from generation to generation often within certain families. Although the *chikenzi*'s intervention is terminated with the successful operation, he is then a regular visitor to the lodge and he shares in the rites marking transition from one stage to the next.

The most important role inside *mukanda* is that of the *chilombola* (pl. *vilombola*), i.e. the guardian of a *kandanda* (initiate; singular of *tundanda*). Usually a *chilombola* is recruited from the male relatives of a newly circumcised boy. He may be a cousin, elder brother, or a more distant relative of the boy. He is never the father or mother's brother. Every initiate has his personal guardian, and in addition there are one or more assisting guardians called *tulombola-ntito*. The latter are youths, brothers, cousins, even friends, who are often just a few years older than the initiates. The *vilombola* are remunerated by the mothers of the boys. In addition a specialist teacher of songs and recitations may be employed.

The mothers of the initiates (*vanyatundanda*) are responsible for sending food to the boys secluded in the *mukanda*. From a certain stage on masked dancers, who are guardians in disguise, appear regularly in the village and collect gifts from women to support the school (CD I/42). The appearance of masked dancers ensures the women that the children in the lodge are fine. The women respond together to the singing of the masked figures; they cheer at them or run away pretending fear, according to the kind of mask, or they mirror their dance movements (cf. Kubik 1969b, 1971b). When there is communal singing in the lodge during the night, the boys' mothers are expected to stay up in the villages, sometimes all night, and show their appreciation with *vingunda* (or *zingunda*), i.e. joyous ululations, which are produced by striking the mouth with the open hand.

In the eastern Angolan culture area a *mukanda* passes through several stages. Transition of the initiates from one to the next stage is marked by certain rites or events. In Mbwela they are named as follows:

(1) *kuswama mukanda* ("'hiding' the *mukanda* lodge"). This expression refers to the opening of a *mukanda*, immediately after the circumcision operation. The initiates enter their first stage of instruction.

(2) *kulonda ntsimba* ("climbing the genet cat"). A rite which marks the end of the first stage and transition to the second stage. It is organized when the wounds of all the initiates in the lodge have healed.

(3) *kukusha mpoko* ("washing the knife"). In this rite the knife of the circumciser is symbolically "washed." The initiates enter the third stage – a period of intensive instruction.

(4) *kulundulula mukanda* ("to 'uproot' the *mukanda*"). The lodge is burnt and the initiates are returning to their village as graduates of the *mukanda*.

In the first stage of *mukanda*, the initiates are said to be "still at the leaves" (*vachili hamefo*): the penis is wrapped in a soft leaf, and the main task of the guardian is to replace the leaf each morning after cleaning the wound with traditional medicine. As soon as the wound is healed, about two to three weeks after the operation, a period of intensive instruction begins. At this stage, much emphasis is placed on discipline and cooperation. Knowledge about nature is acquired by the initiates while roaming in groups near the *mukanda* during the day, as they set traps, shoot birds with bows and arrows, and fish. In the *mukanda* itself, some elements of craftsmanship are learned, such as the plaiting and twisting of plants and strips of bark for making dance costumes. Traditional technology is emphasized more, however, in subsequent years, when the initiates return to *mukanda* in new roles.

Nonverbal interaction is as important as verbal instruction in the *mukanda*. There is a specific category of songs referred to as *myaso yatundanda* ("songs of the initiates"), which are performed only by the initiates and are accompanied by dance movements. An analysis of the content and symbolism of these songs shows concern with the internalization of new modes of behavior that will be expected of graduates of the *mukanda*. While it is particularly the initiates' behavior towards their mothers that changes, new behavior towards sisters, fathers, maternal uncles, guardians and other members of the village community must also be learned. "Difficult" children may be given more verbal instruction than is usual by the guardians. This was especially marked in the case of a mentally retarded child in a *mukanda* that I studied at the village of Mikula (Katuva River), northwestern Zambia, in 1971.

Another category of songs is performed by male visitors, guardians and initiates to the accompaniment of concussion sticks. These sessions of communal singing in the *mukanda* during the night are referred to as *kukuwa mingongi* (see also CD I/19, Chapter III). Some of the songs are didactic and recall important historical events or relate taboos (*vizila*, sing. *chizila*) to be observed by the *tundanda* and others in the *mukanda*. Examples of such taboos include the eating of certain kinds of food and entering the *mukanda* through the guardian's gate, rather than through the gate for the *tundanda*.

All these rules function as a set of behavioral prescriptions aimed at maintaining a precarious and rather fragile psychic balance among those involved in the *mukanda*. This is particularly true during the first period, which is considered dangerous. I was aware of the enormous tension during this period when I stayed and lived in the lodge and assumed some of the roles. As the tension gradually diminished with the successful healing of the initiates' wounds and their "getting better" in many ways, the taboos became less numerous and were less rigidly enforced. Some taboos extend, however, beyond the *mukanda* period for years later.

Body Movement and the Psychology of *mukanda*

Certainly, music and dance instruction is in itself an important objective of the *mukanda* in southeast Angolan societies, and the results of the five months' instruction are lavishly displayed before the women on the day of the initiates' return to the village. But such instruction is also a part of a general system of education.

Some dance patterns are linked structurally with other patterns of body movement, such as those associated with beating bark cloth or winnowing. These links cross boundaries of age and sex groups, in that a dance pattern of the initiates may appear in a structurally similar form in women's work, and this may be recognized by the people. Furthermore, the movement patterns do not stand in isolation but are part of a movement style that even transcends, in some aspects, ethnic and linguistic boundaries.

A movement pattern of initiates called *kundekula*, for example, is known not only in southeastern Angola, but also among the -Luchazi and -Luvale of northwestern Zambia. There it is known as *kawali*, after the name of the most famous song that accompanies the body movement. There is a link between body movement and song in that certain songs always go with certain movements. Other movement patterns, such as a certain combination of strokes on the concussion sticks, transgress the area occupied by the *mukanda*-practicing populations in their geographical distribution.

Some dance patterns are specifically for the initiates and do not occur in performances unconnected with the *mukanda* school. Dances from the village are not performed in the lodge, though they may be performed in the village during the chief rites of *mukanda*, such as *kukusha mpoko* or *chikula*, in which the women dance *chilunga* to the drums. On the other hand, in the northwestern corner of Ngangela-speaking eastern Angola, *kachacha* patterns have penetrated *mukanda*, including the striking of the characteristic 16-pulse timeline pattern on the body of the deep-tuned drum (*ntangi*). In a synch-sound film I made of a dance practice of *tundanda* initiates in a Luchazi *mukanda* at Lutali River (Zambezi District, northwestern Zambia), the accompaniment for the *kawali* dance pattern was plain *kachacha*.[32] This may be due to the fact that the rhythmic foundation of the *kawali*-type of songs is very close to *kachacha*, even in southeastern Angola. Also relevant is the fact that, in the area where I filmed, there is a strong Luvale cultural influence upon the VaLuchazi.

During the teaching sessions in *mukanda*, which take place almost daily, the *tundanda* experience relief from the stress and sorrow caused by their isolation from their mothers and seclusion in a camp in the forest. Dancing makes them "not think of their mothers."

Such relief seems to come about in two ways. First of all, stick or dance patterns associated with the status of initiates are always performed in a group, never alone. Even in the rare case of a *mukanda* with only one initiate – one of which I documented in Zambia at Sangombe's village (north of Chikenge) in 1971 – other boys from the village came regularly to help him perform in a group. In the case I documented, Malesu, the boy depicted in Section I with his small drum (cf. p. 347), was the only *kandanda* ("initiate;" sing. of *tundanda*). Though there are many *mikanda* with two boys, particularly when the village is small and the area sparsely populated, two initiates are also not considered sufficient for a satisfactory performance.

The number two is emphasized during the first stage of the *mukanda*: the boys generally sleep in pairs and the cage-like sleeping devices are constructed to allow for this. The intense relationship between an initiate and his guardian during the first stage of the *mukanda* (when the wound is not yet healed) is another dual set-up that is later eased. After the feast *kulonda ntsimba* (see below), the paired sleeping devices are burnt, and all the boys sleep together and act more and more as a group. The increasing emphasis on the group as soon as the initiates "get better," obviously absorbs a great deal of the same inner forces that once bound each boy to his mother.

The sensation of relief from the stress of the *mukanda* also arises from another source – the movement patterns themselves, which seem, from their structural content, to exert feelings of relief. Before discussing this, however, it may be beneficial to first give a brief summary of the results of our psychological work on *mukanda* in the eastern Angolan culture area. This is based on a sample of 30 *mikanda* studied on numerous field trips to the area between 1965 and 1987.

For the study of *mukanda* in psychological terms, I employed a combination of three methods. The first was an intra-cultural approach as a participant observer. After the initial experience in Angola in 1965, I assumed various roles in later field work, such as the role of assistant guardian in the *mukanda* of Malesu at Sangombe, in 1971. The second method was the application of a psycho-analytical interpretive framework based on Sigmund Freud's theory of the unconscious (cf. Freud 1955), with the reservation, however, that the Oedipus complex is not a central theme in a matrilineal society. The third approach was to study *mukanda* in the context of enculturation and socialization processes and the various institutions existing for those objectives.

In a work such as this, which deals mainly with music, it is not possible to go into great detail about the depth psychology of *mukanda*. However, *mukanda* is neither a music and dance school nor is it merely an institution for carrying out circumcision. It has a most important psychological dimension. Among the peoples described here, the absence of the foreskin is considered a "passport" to manhood. A man who never went to *mukanda* is regarded as equivalent to a woman or a child. But the operation itself is essentially a symbolic act, though hygienic and other reasons may be given by rationalizing informants. It is part of a symbol syndrome which aims at a complex set of educational and personality-forming processes. Herein lie essential differences with Islamic circumcision, which is not historically related to *mukanda*.

One of the most important aims of the *mukanda* school is connected with the matrilineal structure of Mbwela/Nkhangala society, where men often marry into the villages of their wives and where men as a whole traditionally feel threatened by the women. Small boys are extremely dependent upon their mothers. A cohesive group of adult men must claim back their future members and devise means of breaking the strong attachment of male children to both their physical mothers and to the mothers. The latter constitute the female group in a household and are all addressed with the same word, *vanana*. Mother-fixation is a threat to the coherence of the male sub-section of the larger society, particularly when it is organized matrilineally. The men's society must assert itself – it must frighten the women (with the masks), and it must have its own secrets and its own exclusive niches in daily life, just as the women have theirs.[33]

Hence, when male children reach the so-called latency period,[34] using Sigmund Freud's term, the moment is seen as a chance to reclaim the boy and sever relations with the womenfolk (Mwondela n.d. [ca. 1971]:6). Various African societies have, of course, developed different methods of breaking the mother-attachment of pre-puberty males. Either it is broken abruptly in the form of a drama, as in *mukanda* (with all its accompanying activities, such as music, dance, masquerade, etc.), or else gradually. In all cases, the aim is to educate the young male child to become independent of the women and to counter possible identification with his mother, which could lead to the assumption of "female roles." The prepuce with its smegma (*vusinu, vwandza*) symbolizes the female part in a male child's psyche, that which is to be "eliminated" or repressed by the *mukanda* intervention. It is not surprising, therefore, that homosexuality at an adult age is extremely rare among the *mukanda*-practicing people.

For the reasons discussed, *mukanda* is not to be misunderstood as a "puberty rite;" it is a pre-puberty educational and personality-forming institution. After the conclusion of *mukanda*, the initiates now returning to normal life in the village are not considered "adults," but only youngsters on the path to adulthood. The graduate will no longer live in his mother's house – this is, obviously, most important. He will live either in a house built for him or with a male relative, preferably with the maternal uncle, who has authority greater than that of the physical father. He could also live together with other boys who are graduates of *mukanda*, thus confirming age-set solidarity. The relationship to his mother, after *mukanda*, is not broken. He still feels love towards his mother, but this love is combined with psychological distance.

During the months of the seclusion period, the psychological transformation process within each of the young males is achieved through various techniques. To mark the beginning of the first "traumatic" period, the boys are removed from the village and pass through the traumatic (and intentionally dramatized) experience of circumcision at the edge of the village. This short act marks the breach with their "mothers" who are not permitted to approach the scene. Then, with the subsequent "banning" into the forest, libido, in Sigmund Freud's terminology, is gradually transferred to another object: the *chilombola*, or individual guardian, who becomes a kind of mother substitute. This is confirmed not only by direct observation of interactions between the two, but by many conversations I had with the participants.[35] It is interesting that the *chilombola* – like in a classical psychoanalytical situation – develops counter-transference, i.e. he becomes emotionally attached to the child, assuming a role which is something like a synthesis of "guardian," "father," "brother," "mother" and "doctor." He treats the circumcision wound with medical plants, and generally looks after "his" child's need. A *chilombola* always sleeps in the *mukanda* and must not have sexual intercourse with his wife during the period of seclusion. But the transference by the *kandanda* (initiate) and counter-transference by the *chilombola* (guardian) that now develops must be dissolved after some time, although it remains to some degree throughout their lives. This is expressed, for example, in various taboos and in the reverence a former *kandanda* feels towards his former *chilombola* all his life.

Mother-attachment, now transferred, is subsequently split up between various persons. Gradually, with the healing of the wound, the *chilombola* retreats, and at the same time the *kandanda* realizes that he is not alone, but that there are comrades with whom he has passed through the same fate. This recognition is the basis of a gradually forming identification process with those other *tundanda* in whom he discovers his own ego. The libido is then more and more projected upon the "comrades."

Only in rare cases does mother-attachment persist and develop into mother-fixation, which results in initiates that are considered to be problem children, as I was able to observe in great detail with the boy Injini at the village of Mikula, Katuva River, northwestern Zambia, in 1971. During all the months of seclusion in *mukanda*, Injini did almost nothing but cry. The child suffered from a severe neurosis which the male community tried to cure with its own means. He reached adulthood, but died later as a young man, as I was told during my most recent visit to the area in 1987.

Dramatical actions or psycho-dramas are organized in *mukanda* to promote the relatively rapid processes of psychological adjustment the boys must go through. One of these dramas is called *kutsimpwa makisi* (literally: "to be initiated into the masks") as recorded in my cinéfilm No. F7 from Sakateke village, August 1965). During this rite the initiates have to crawl, under mortal fear, through a "tunnel" formed by the masks lining up with their legs spread wide. After that they are told the secret of the masks.

Another action drama is the "dying of an initiate." I did not see this myself, but it was reported to me in great detail by Kufuna Kandonga from Chisende village in November 1965 (cf. Kubik 1971:679). In this action drama during a rite of the second stage of *mukanda*, the boys are told that they will be killed with an arrow. They are told to line up outside the *mukanda* and then, one by one, move towards the "tree of the dead" (*muti wa vakulu*) planted in the center of every Mbwela *mukanda*. Arriving at the "tree," the leader of the rite, with an arrow in one hand and a pot of red paint in the other, whispers to the initiate, "You embrace the tree and fall down like a dead person." The boy acts this out. The man puts red paint on the boy's breast and the arrow near his body. When the next boy enters through the gate, he sees his comrade in his "blood" on the ground and believes that he has been killed. The same process is then repeated until all the boys are through. The movements of entering, embracing the "tree" and falling down are acted out like a drama.

After the healing of the wounds, the *tundanda* are organized as a group, within which the first who is circumcised (*sakambungu*) takes a leadership role. During their excursions (during which they learn skills such as how to set traps and shoot birds), as well as during dance rehearsals and the learning of recitation (*kutangesa*), the *tundanda* now appear almost as a single body. A strong sense of group cohesion develops, and a deep sense of solidarity. These affective relationships continue

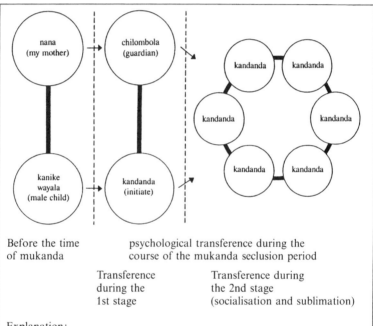

Before the time of mukanda

psychological transference during the course of the mukanda seclusion period

Transference during the 1st stage

Transference during the 2nd stage (socialisation and sublimation)

Explanation:

1st stage: the period immediately after circumcision (= removal of the prepuce as something female, dirty); act of circumcision also dramatized as the dying of the initiate, symbolizing the death of his infantile psyche. Mother-attachment is transferred to the *chilombola* (guardian).

2nd stage: splitting up of the *chilombola – tundanda* dual relationship and its ultimate sublimation. Transference to the group of "comrades of fate," the *tundanda*, in the sense of a collective, reciprocal transference among boys of the same age set. Remnants of this transference remain throughout one's life.

Table 15. On the psychology of *mukanda* initiation: transference and sublimation of mother-attachment of a male child in the various stages of the *mukanda* seclusion period

into the post-*mukanda* life to embrace the menfolk as a whole; feelings of comradeship and respect for one another come to be considered essential virtues of social interaction.

Table 15 summarizes what developmental changes are generated by the *mukanda* experience in the initiates, interpreted from the viewpoint of psychoanalytical theory.

A key to understanding the psychological meaning of *mukanda* can also be found in certain oral texts. At Chimite village, a remote place up the Kwitu river in southeastern Angola, I collected in 1965 a myth of origin of *mukanda* whose content is revealing. It seems to be the only aetiological myth about *mukanda* which has been collected among Ngangela-speaking peoples to date. Prata, an associate of Chief Chimite, told me on September 23, 1965:

> This is how *mukanda* started. Once there lived a brother with his sister together. The name of the sister was Senda. The name of the brother was Mwene Nyumbu. At that time all people were *vilima* (uncircumcised). The sister insulted her brother by saying: You have smegma (*vusinu*) under your foreskin! This was a terrible offence. Mwene Nyumbu went for a knife and cut his prepuce with his own hand. When his brothers saw him they saved his life. They carried him to the forest (*musenge*) and constructed an enclosure, a round enclosure. This was the first *mukanda*. The brothers were feeling ashamed to cure the wound in front of the women. There, in the *mukanda*, they began to treat the wound. The other men said: What shall we do to that woman that insulted Mwene Nyumbu? – Let us make masks. And they began to make the masks *mpumpu* and *kanganzi*. These masks do not beat the women. Therefore, they invented *dhinyampha*, to beat the women very hard so that they would become scared and never offend any man any longer. The mask *mpumpu* represents Mwene Nyumbu.

Prata added:

> And for that reason we take the oath of *mwongwa-luvanda* in the *mukanda*. Mwene Nyumbu said: I am here the *mwene* (king), and I am naked. Anyone who reveals what can be seen in the *mukanda* must die. These masks are mine! Nobody may betray this secret to the women, for if anyone did they would lose their fear and become irreverent.

A legendary king, Mwene Nyumbu, is depicted in this myth as the founder of the circumcision school. *Mukanda* began with the act of self-circumcision. After his sister Senda to whom he was possibly married had insulted him with reference to his prepuce by saying *"Vusinu vwove!"* ("Your [dirty] smegma!"), Mwene Nyumbu circumcised himself.

Here, it must be explained that brother-sister marriage did occur in Lunda ruling families, and this has often been pointed out in the ethnographic literature. In matrilineal societies such as those of eastern Angola it even has a deeper meaning demonstrating what people fear as one of the possible results of a male child's fixation to female members of his extended family. From the men's viewpoint incest is seen as the worst scenario in the power struggle, by which the women's power and superiority would be sealed until a grown-up man could be insulted in the most hurting manner, as Senda did to Mwene Nyumbu.

Analysis of Song Texts

As much as oral traditions cast light on the psychological meaning of *mukanda* so do the songs of the initiates. A *mukanda* curriculum consists of a culturally tested repertoire of techniques designed to achieve a lasting change in an individual's patterns of behavior. Song and dance instruction, both in content and form, is one of the vehicles used to achieve these adaptations. With regard to song texts, a content analysis is revealing. Below are the texts in Mbwela of four frequently heard *myaso yatundanda* ("songs of the initiates"), which they sing while practicing the dance patterns *kuhunga* and *kundekula*[36] (CD I/43).

1 – Song for kuhunga

Leader:	*Ndo, ndo, ndo, nana yow'e* (repeated several times)
Chorus:	*Ndo* (repeated several times)
L.:	*Ndo, ndo, ndo* (repeated several times)
Ch.:	*Nana yow'e ndo.*
	Mba!
	Mba! Mba! Mba! Mba! Mba!
Ch. (variant):	*Nana nay'e ndo.*
Leader:	*Ndo*[37], *ndo, ndo,* my mother is over there.[38]
Chorus:	*Ndo.*
L.:	*Ndo, ndo, ndo.*
Ch.:	My mother is over there, *ndo.*
	Mba!
	Mba! Mba! Mba! Mba! Mba!
Ch. (variant):	My mother has gone, *ndo!*

2 – Song for kundekula

Kawaly'ee! Nana yow'e èéè! (2x)
Kawali. Mwanandonga!
Njichikatale vanana kwimbo.
Kawaly'ee! Nana yow'e èéè!

Kawali ee! My mother is over there, *èéè!* (2x)
Kawali Mwanandonga![39]
Let me go and see my mother there in the village.
Kawali ee! My mother is over there, *èéè!*

3 – Song for kundekula

Watunga ndzivw'e. (2x)
Watunga ndzivw'e kundonga,
mukuku waSakampanda
watunga ndzivw'e.
Watunga ndzivw'e kundonga,
Nana yow'e!

He built a house *e!* (2x)
He built a house *e!* at the river
the *mukuku*-bird of Sakampanda,
he built a house *e!*
He built a house *e!* at the river.
My mother is over there, *e!*

4 – Song for kundekula

Nani[40] lingendzo!
Nany'e! Lingendzo lyaNtumba!
Katolo tatuye!
Katolo tatuye kwimbo tukaliwana!
Nani lingendzo!

Woe! The big bell!
Woe! The big bell of Ntumba![41]
Katolo, let us go!
Katolo, let us go to the village, we shall meet!
Woe! The big bell!

In these songs, which are only to be sung by *tundanda*, there is symbolic expression of what the boys would really like to do at this stage of seclusion and of what they fear. The isolation from one's mother is the traumatic experience of the *kandanda* and therefore, the word *nana* ("my mother") is central and appears in many of the songs. The sentence *Nana yow'e* ("My mother is over there." "My mother is far away.") is contained in three of the four song texts transcribed here (1, 2 and 3).

In the song *"Ndo, ndo, ndo, nana yow'e,"* the mother is the basic theme of the text and mention of her also occurs in the *kawali* song. These two songs are considered to be the most important ones for *tundanda* in the circumcision school of the Ngangela-speaking peoples of eastern Angola. The songs are known from the Kwitu River area up to Kabompo District in the Northwestern Province of Zambia and the texts are identical in both areas. Songs such as these contain the key to understanding the psychology of the socialization process in *mukanda*.

Fortunato Pereira Gonçalves, born in 1933, of the administration of Kwitu-Kwanavale, gave the following interpretation of the song of Kawali:

> Kawali was a boy who had gone to the *mukanda*. And his mother, who remained in the village, continued to cry all the time. The men said: "Kawali! His mother is going to weep." And Kawali said: "I could go and see my mother in the village!" So the men invented a song.[42]

Independently of Fortunato, the young Mose Kamwocha, born 1957, a boy from northwestern Zambia who had graduated from the *mukanda* at Chikenge village, Kabompo District, in 1969, interpreted the song of Kawali as follows:

> There was a *kandanda* long ago, his name was Kawali. The people made him suffer very much. So then that Kawali began to sing his song, saying: "Kawali e, my mother is there in the village. Myself, I am here in the *mukanda* and I suffer very much, while my mother is in the village." These are thoughts of myself, Mose. The elders did not tell me. But it is my own thinking.[43]

Mose's interpretation conforms with that of Fortunato in its basic content. Mose's village, Chikenge, is 560 km in a straight air line from Kwitu-Kwanavale. Although he said that these were his personal ideas about the song of Kawali, the substantial agreement between the two testimonies shows how well the deeper meaning of the didactic songs in a *mukanda* school is understood by the *tundanda*, even without much verbal explanation by the *vilombola* and the music/dance teachers.

The song of Kawali is satirical, referring to the case of a *kandanda* who was unable to detach himself from his mother. Whether Kawali was a real or ficticious person is difficult to determine. If he was a real person, he must have lived in the remote past, as this song is too widespread to be considered a recent creation. But since then, this *kandanda* named Kawali has become an archetypal figure: the boy who could not detach himself from his mother, and the mother, who was herself unwilling to break her ties to the child, as demonstrated by her crying in the village.[44]

Satirical songs such as this one are didactic and have a psychologically transforming impact on the boys in the *mukanda*. The underlying technique is that the song expresses precisely the secret desire of all *tundanda*: to return to their mothers in the village. But by the "public" mentioning of such a desire in a song of mockery about a mythical *kandanda* who was unable to rid himself of his infantile desire, the individual initiate is gradually pushed towards assuming the mocking attitude. His old "Ego," now to be overcome, is projected on the archetypal figure of Kawali. The timeless desires of all *tundanda* are projected on a symbolic figure and thus more easily extracted from the psyche. By song and motoric participation in the activities within the new community of initiates of approximately the same age, the process of internalizing the new attitude is greatly promoted.

Song 3 seems to have a meaning similar to that of the first two songs. Mose Kamwocha thinks the following about it:

> *Mukuku* is a bird of the river (*kazila wakundonga*). Perhaps it means: I have built my house (nest) in the bush and my mother is far away. Like the *mukuku*-bird, a *kandanda* also lives outside the village, far away from mother (Zambia notes 1971).

Song 4 was interpreted by Mose as follows:

> There were two children, perhaps they saw a mask (*likisi*) and called out: *"Nani! Tutine lingendzo!"* ("Woe! Let us run away from the big bell!").

Some masked characters carry a bell, with which they announce their arrival.[45] Children who have not yet been to the *mukanda* are immensely afraid of the masks. Song 4 contains a condensed description of the infantile stage, before initiation into the knowledge of masks.

These songs are coordinated with movement patterns that are also performed in a group. The emphasis on group identity, group attachment and solidarity is also seen in the organization of everyday life during the seclusion period. The initiates eat together the same food each day, and from special plates whose appearance is a secret of the *mukanda*. Many other objects of the *mukanda* are also secret, such as the sleeping devices, the ritual fire, the concussion sticks, the "tree" and the masks. Later, when they finally return to the village, the initiates walk about together and share the same festive dance dress and body paint. This does not mean that age-group experience in a male individual's life starts with *mukanda*, for younger children also play in peer groups, but in *mukanda*, the age-group assumes a more exclusive role. These activities provide great relief from the emotional tension felt by the initiates during this period.

In the ASA[46] Conference on the "Anthropology of the Body", organized by John Blacking in Belfast in 1975, the psychical and possible somatic effects of music were discussed; there, I presented some of the findings I discuss here. My analysis of data from Angola, as well as from other areas of Africa, suggests that music by itself (i.e. the performance or perception of music, applied in isolation) cannot generate or release any psychologically altered states or stimulate therapeutical effects. If a person is not psychologically prepared to reach an altered state of mind, or to accept therapeutical intervention, he or she remains indifferent and totally unaffected by the musical stimulus. Even if the person is forced to join in the performance, their performance will lack any particular verve. But if a person has experienced, or is taught by group members to expect, a psychological effect from a certain music and/or dance activity [47], then they can "use" music to reach precisely that altered state of mind they are striving to reach.

A drug has its standard effects, but music will enhance only those modifications of behavior that are expected by the individual or group, from the effects of war songs upon warriors or work songs upon workers to the effects of the initiation songs and dance movements upon the initiates. However, these aural and motional patterns are not psychologically neutral either. A key to an understanding of their function in life-crisis rituals such as *mukanda* may be found in their complex regularity. In the analytical psychology of Carl Gustav Jung, it is considered that structures of strong inner coherence have a compensatory effect in states of severe tension (Jung 1974). A structure of great inner order, such as the "mandala" figures described by Jung, may be produced spontaneously by individuals in a state of psychic disorder. Jung's examples are drawn from the visual realm, but the same applies to the aural.

If such states are provoked by ritual, the ritual itself must contain patterns and symbols to which the individual can take recourse and which may help to trigger off the necessary process of psychic reintegration. VaMbwela people acknowledge that there is a danger of *kuzaluka* ("to run mad") during the *mukanda* rites if certain interdictions are not observed. Just as taboos are barriers designed to avert the danger of psychic and social disintegration, some of the movement patterns function in a similar way. Because of their complex and harmonious inner order, such movement patterns serve in *mukanda* as a form of compensation for the transient emotional disorder, characterized by fear and anxiety.

Mbwela/Nkhangala culture thus provides external structures of a compelling logic that must be absorbed physically by the initiates, through participatory movement. The movement patterns to be learned are structurally regular. Many combinations in Mbwela boys' initiation music are made up of interpolations between two and three, built up to form compound units defined by the numbers six and twelve. The formal layout of dance figures is also determined by regular constellations emphasizing the numbers 3, 4, 6, 8, 9, 12, and 16.

This is, of course, not unusual in the context of African music. However, as I have suggested, therapeutical or other effects are not linked to a particular structure of such patterns, but rather to their general qualities of complexity, inner logic and harmonious order. There are *muka-nda*-specific movements, but in their structural aspects they are not different from movement in non-*mukanda* music.

Through the playing of stick patterns in the group and performing *kuhunga* and *kundekula* (as well as other dance patterns), life in the camp – away from the mothers – becomes an acceptable routine for the *tundanda*. Not only do they identify with their new roles in the group, but each individual, perhaps on an unconscious level, is also deeply affected by the coercive inner order of the patterns learned.

Patterns of Body Movement in Musical Performance

One of the first musical activities of the young boys in the *mukanda* is to learn concussion stick patterns. They are urged to do this during the first stage following circumcision, when they are "still at the leaves," as this stage is described in symbolic language. At sunrise and sunset the initiates assemble by the long fire-place whose real name is one of the secrets of the *mukanda* never to be revealed to the women. No associates of *mukanda* may jump over this fire-place under penalty of later impotence. Each *kandanda* holds a stick of about 20 to 25 cm long in each hand. Striking the sticks together, they sing symbolic songs of welcome to the rising sun and songs of farewell to the setting sun.

The most important communal activity during *mukanda* is the performance of songs inside the lodge at night. Men and youths from the village form a circle looking towards the fire and perform the "songs of the *mukanda*" (*myaso yakumukanda*) in multi-part voice combinations (compare also: CD I/19, Chapter III). The initiates are obliged to participate in these sessions, which are referred to as *kukuwa mingongi*. Each performer holds two concussion sticks (*mingongi*), which are secret instruments of the *mukanda*. Women and uncircumcised boys in the village must not see them. They are told that the initiates have their legs cut by magic and beat the calf bones together or, alternatively, that the sticks are bones from dead corpses in the cemetery. One of the promises extracted from the boys at the end of the seclusion period during the oath of *mwongwa-luvanda* is never to reveal that the *mingongi* are just wooden sticks. The *mingongi* are made by the guardians, and on the closing day of *mukanda* they are burnt together with all the other secret things inside the lodge, the "tree of the dead," some masks, and so on.

Besides *mingongi*, other secret instruments are the *tutanga* (sing. *katanga*). These are wooden slats vertically suspended from a string that runs through a tiny hole near the upper edge of the slat. The player holds his *katanga* in the left hand. The beating stick, which is usually one of the

Ill. 76. Position of striking a *katanga*

mingongi, is held in the right hand, and with it, the player strikes the slat in the middle (Illustration 76).

The name *tutanga* was not used in all of the four *mikanda* I studied in southeastern Angola in 1965; I only heard it at Sakateke. Nor was it current in *mikanda* among the -Luvale living near Cazombo, whom I visited in December 1965, nor in any of the *mikanda* I studied later (1971 – 1987) across the border on Zambian territory among -Luchazi, -Luvale and -Chokwe peoples. Thus, the term seems to be specifically linked to isolated groups in southeastern Angola. In the other *mikanda*, vertically held slats were used, but they were less elaborately shaped (as compared with Illustration 76) and just called *mingongi*. *Mingongi* and *tutanga* are interesting examples of instruments that would never be seen by field workers unless they stayed in the lodge; in addition, neither of these instruments would ever appear in any archaeological record.

During performance, the *mingongi* are not struck together in the same way by all players. The players organize themselves into groups that strike different patterns, which they combine while singing the songs of *mukanda* (Ill. 78).

The following is a description of the music in terms of body movement rather than sounds. In Mbwela there is a generic term designating dance-like body movement, namely the verb *kukina* – the noun is *vukina* – and there are many specific terms describing various dance movements. There are the words meaning "song", *mwaso* (pl. *myaso*), ("to sing"), *kwimba*, ("to play an instrument [*kusika*]), and a rich vocabulary refer-ring to specific "musical" actions.

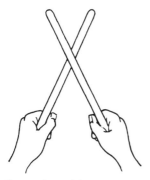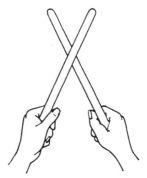

Ill. 77. Concussion stick patterns and their combinations (viewed from above)
Key to transcription:

Righthand stick hits the   Lefthand stick hits the
left from above   right from above
(Transcription symbol: A)   (Transcription symbol: B)

As is often the case in African music, there is a difference between a listener's auditory impression and a performer's motor concept of sound patterns. Ill. 78 would be appreciated by listeners as a pattern covering six elementary pulses (cycle 6), while for the players, the total pattern repeats every 12 pulses (cycle 12).

The basic stick pattern is allocated to the initiates (Group I in the transcription). Though others may play the initiates' pattern, I have never seen initiates play the stick patterns of the other performers. Subsequent discussions with informants give the following explanations: (a) theirs is the easiest pattern to play, and (b) it conforms with the *tundanda* status to play the basic pattern.

The sticks are struck in a slow, up-and-down duple motion (cf. Illustration 77): first a down-stroke of the right stick, hitting the rising left stick from above, and then a down-stroke of the left stick, hitting the right stick from above; the two sticks meet about halfway. The meter of the songs is related to the *tundanda*'s stick pattern. While the initiates play the basic duple pattern, a group of men and older boys produces the same movement pattern a little faster, so that the strokes of the two groups combine in a two-against-three relationship (cf. transcription, Illustration 78). After six strokes of group II and four strokes of group I, the two movement patterns meet. The third group performs a pattern that <u>sounds</u> identical with that of group II, but is <u>produced</u> differently. While groups I and II play down-up-down-up with each stick in contrary motion, group III strikes up-down-down with the right stick and consequently, down-up-up with the left stick, performing a pattern in threes.

The lefthand stick is hit by the righthand stick on the first stroke from below and on the second and third strokes from above; one could also

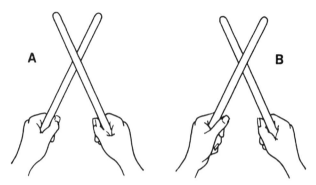

Ill. 78. Transcription of *kuwuwa mingongi*

Group I (*tundanda*):	12	A . . B . . A . . B . .
Group II (men and youths):		A . B . A . B . A . B .
Group III (men and youths):		B . A . A . B . A . A .
Individual men playing *tutanga*:	(I)	x x . x x . x x . x x .
	(II)	. . x . . x . . x . . x

Note: "x" is a stroke. The points are "empty" pulses along the time line. They are filled in by portions of the song melody

say, the righthand stick is hit by the left on the first stroke from above, and on the two subsequent ones from below. In transcription we use two symbols only: A (right stick hits left stick from above) and B (left stick hits right stick from above). Both sticks move, however, completely evenly.

This combination is then further expanded by the addition of patterns struck on the vertically suspended wooden slats (*tutanga*). The *tutanga* patterns are fast strokes that interlock with the other patterns. *Tutanga* are never played by the *tundanda*, only by older boys and men. In these sessions the initiates learn to perform their basic strokes against the other staggered strokes and also to keep time throughout the song.

In the symbolic ceremony of *kulonda ntsimba* ("the climbing of the genet cat"), which takes place after the wound has healed, the initiates are compared with climbing genet cats. At this time, they are allowed for the first time in weeks to take a bath in the river. After this ceremony, a new phase of instruction begins. From then on, teaching is strictly formal, that is, a situation in which a clear distinction can be made between a body of teachers (in this case, the guardians and dance instructors) and pupils, with the two meeting on a regular basis.

One kind of formal instruction in *mukanda* involves the teaching of recitations (*kutangesa* or *kutanga*). Their arrangement takes the form of an alternation between drum beats and the reciting voices of the boys. During an evening teaching session, the initiates usually practice *kutanga* before dance instruction. One low-pitched long drum (*ntangi*) is used by

Ill. 79. Instruction of *kuhunga* inside the *mukanda*. The small Malesu is being taught by his chief guardian, who demonstrates the movement pattern and explains it verbally, often using mnemonic syllables and correcting the *kandanda*'s mistakes. Sangombe village, north of Chikenge, Kabompo District, Zambia, September 25, 1971

the instructor. The texts of the recitations are symbolic and also rather long, in order to train the initiates' memory.

For dance instruction, three single-skinned long drums are needed, the *vipwali* (sing. *chipwali*). These drums are played by the instructors and are not secret instruments, but are brought over from the village, where they are also used in other dances not connected with this institution. Tuned with tuning paste, these drums are used in sets of three and are played with the hands. The individual drum names are *ntangi* for the instrument with a "big voice" (*lizi lyakama*), which is also used for the recitations, *chimpululu* for the middle-voiced (*lizi lyamukatikati*) drum, and *mundengu* for the one with a "small voice" (*lizi lyalindende*).

The boys put on dance skirts made of the reddish *ndzombo* fibres of the inner bark of bot. Syrygium guineense. These skirts are made for them in the *mukanda* by elder brothers before the feast of *kulonda ntsimba*, and the initiates wear them for the first time after the ritual bath in the river. People in the *mukanda* say: "Now they will begin to learn *kuhunga*," a dance movement.

Until the end of the period of initiation, the *tundanda* learn and practise various movements and dances that they perform in public during the final feast of the *mukanda*, when they return to the village. The most common and typical movements for this period are called *kuhunga* and *kundekula*, verbs that refer to the character of the movements. These are linked with two types of songs of the initiates which are called *myaso yakuhungisa* ("songs to make *kuhunga*") and *myaso yaKawali* ("songs of Kawali").

Kuhunga means "to winnow," an action suggested by the pattern performed by the *tundanda* with the pelvis; it reminds onlookers of the women's work of winnowing a basket full of bulrush millet (*masangu*). People say that the initiates' dance pattern alludes to the women's winnowing, though the movement patterns are not completely identical. *Kuhunga* is not only practised by *tundanda*, but also by certain masks (for example, *chikũza*), and by girls at the end of their initiation school.

The motional structure of *kuhunga* may be described as a fast left-right twisting of the pelvis <u>without</u> shifting the pelvis' center. The right hip is turned forward, while the left is turned backwards simultaneously. Then the same occurs in reverse order. This is performed at great speed, each motional action corresponding in its time value with one elementary pulse. This can be illustrated in a sketch much more clearly than through words:

Ill. 80. The movements of the pelvis (reproduced from Kubik 1982b:[10])

Phase I and II of the pattern follow each other so rapidly that the *ndzombo* skirt swings out from the centrifugal force. The dancers hold their arms in front of them, bent at the elbows. Their feet perform pedaling movements, while they remain on the ground, and in one part of the dance, the dancers skip one behind the other in a counter-clockwise direction.

The arms are lifted and the elbows are bent at right angles and held away from the body. Arms, head and shoulders are kept still in this position. The dancer holds his rattle stick in his hand and turns his hips while the point of his navel traces a short left-right movement: ⌒ and ⌒ . To observe the movement of one's navel is really the key to understanding and learning this pattern correctly.

The dancer's legs and knees are kept flexible and perform a complementary movement. When the left heel is raised, the pelvis is turned so that the right hip moves forward and the left backward, with the center of the abdomen remaining stationary. The dance skirt swings counterclockwise to the left. Next, the left leg is stretched and at the same time the right heel is raised. The left hip now seems to move forward, and right backward, with the pelvis appearing twisted towards the left in relation to the torso, and the dance skirt swings back clockwise.

This is most clearly seen in movie films on those occasions when the initiates put on ornamental patterns of white and red body paint. This paint is applied during the last rehearsal, which takes place a few days before the return to the village, and on the great day of return. The patterns of paint are structured in a way that highlights and emphasizes the dance movement to be performed. They make the movement centers of the body more conspicuous, so that body motion is transformed into a vivid display of contracting and pulsating ornamental motion.

While doing *kuhunga*, the boys may move forward with tiny steps but usually, they stay on one spot. An analysis of a filmed segment of the leg-and-foot work shows a "pedaling" pattern, in which the dancer lifts his heels alternately. Lifting the heel goes with bending the knee. This quick heel lifting, together with simultaneous displacement of body weight from one foot to another, is necessary to allow the turns of the pelvis to occur (cf. transcription). Shoulders are not moved in this dance pattern, though the upper torso vibrates a little as a result of the pelvis' turns. Torso and arms remain rather immobile. This comparative immobility emphasizes the propeller-like swinging-out of the dance skirt.

Kuhunga is a duple motion: left-right, left-right, but it is superimposed on a triple pattern of the drums. When the dance skirt swings out, one notices a soft, regular sound produced by the shaking of the fibres – at least with experienced dancers. People say the dance skirt sounds something like: *ka-cha-ka-cha-ka-cha*, etc.

In the *mukanda*, sound patterns such as *ka-cha* etc. play an important role as teaching devices. They may be mnemonic syllables or semantic speech. In dance instruction they are used by the teacher to characterize movement patterns and to correct the initiates' mistakes. These mnemonics are a kind of oral notation comparable to what is found in other parts of Africa and in India. There are also, verbal patterns employed in the *mukanda* which go with patterns of body movement or drumming. For example: *kuvamba kuli masika*, a drum pattern that accompanies novices' dances, means: "in the lodge there is coldness." The timbre and movement structure of this phrase is directly related to the drum pattern; the drum "speaks" these words. This kind of verbal association occurs among speakers of tonal languages when they hear pitch patterns. One of several possible verbal associations fits the drum pattern so well that it becomes a kind of label for this pattern. In this case, the verbal content is an appropriate comment because temperatures in July and August may well reach zero degrees in exceptionally cold years in southeastern Angola, and the stay in the lodge can become very uncomfortable for the initiates and their guardians.

Kuhunga is considered to be the most important dance pattern of the initiates and is always mentioned first in conversation, while *kundekula* is second in importance. The dance skirt is designed for *kuhunga*, but is also used in *kundekula*. The guardians, as well as the dance master, take great care to improve the performance standards of their pupils. Conversation, criticism and discussion reflect their values and attitudes: for example, in a Zambian *mukanda* at Chikenge, one initiate was known as *Kaliselwa* ("Little Cloud"), because he was so excellent in performing *kuhunga*. A good dancer, say the people, should make the dance skirt swing out continuously in perpetual motion so that it seems to stand still like a "little cloud" (Ill. 80).

The rhythmic structure of *kuhunga* is based on a cycle number of 12 elementary pulses, which are grouped as triplets. While the drums perform this "triple rhythm," the *tundanda* twist their pelvises in a duple movement that creates tension, arising from the contrast between $4 \times 3 = 12$ elementary pulses (drum rhythm) and $6 \times 2 = 12$ (pelvic movement) (Ill. 84).

The movement pattern *kundekula* (also often called *kawali*) is the second pattern characteristic of boys' initiation music in Mbwela/Nkhangala culture. Its structure is different from that of *kuhunga*, as it is based on a cycle number of 16 pulses. The basic motional components of *kundekula* are circular ("rolling") movements of the shoulders and two-part steps with the leg-and-foot complex, during which the dancer basically remains stationary.

The *tundanda* form a circle, facing the center, limbs relaxed, knees bent. Then the leg-and-foot complex is moved in the following manner:
(1) Left leg (and foot) slightly lifted off the ground.
(2) Foot turned a little outward.
(3) Leg stretched.
(4) Foot put forward on the ground without displacement of body weight.
(5) Leg (and foot) lifted again.
(6) Foot placed back into initial position (compare Illustrations 84 and 86).
(7) Displacement of body weight.

The same is done with the right leg. In this way, left and right foot are put forward alternately. Simultaneously, the dancers perform the rolling shoulder motion in such a way that the shoulders always take opposite positions (one up – the other down, one behind – the other in front), like the pedals of a bicycle that were being pumped backwards. It is a constant, circular motion. This is combined with a periodical retraction and release of the shoulder blades.

When one looks at the dancing boys from behind, one could believe that shoulders, shoulder blades and back were made of rubber, especially with the application of the body paint – so elastic does this movement appear when it is well performed. Interaction between legs, feet, shoulders and shoulder blades can be shown in a transcription (Ill. 85).

From time to time, the initiates stop this pattern, tap the ground with their rattle sticks several times and move on a little further, counterclockwise, stepping sideways. While doing so, they continue facing one another, looking towards the center of the circle.

Another pattern called *chikoka* is occasionally performed in *mukanda*. This pattern is based on the *kundekula* movement, which is stopped from time to time and interspersed with brief episodes of skipping forward, legs and feet kept close together. Then there is *vutotola*, a movement style named after the mask *katotola*, whose movement patterns the initiates imitate. *Vutotola* is danced by the initiates at the end of one particular kind of *kutanga* recitation. The basic dance patterns *kuhunga* and *kundekula* may be displayed in various formations in which the initiates are seen in kneeling position, front support position, and also forming other figures.

The above analysis refers particularly to performances witnessed in southeastern Angola; the transcriptions at the end of this section were taken from a silent film of the coming-out ceremony at the village of Limbwangu near Kayoko in 1965. But the *mikanda* described here do not vary significantly from those held throughout a much larger region. In 1979 I made a synch-sound film of a Luchazi *mukanda* at Lutali River,

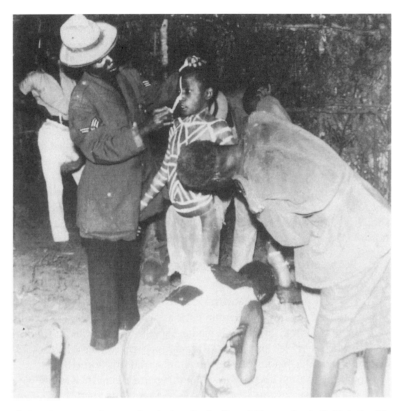

Ill. 81. *Kusona* – the art of painting the bodies of the *tundanda* (initiates) with *mphemba* (white kaolin) and *mukundu* (red ocher) in the night before their return to the village. At the *mukanda* of Sakatete, Kwanavale River area, September 1965. Archive No. F 494

Zambezi District, Zambia, a few dozen kilometers across the Angolan border[48]. What can be seen in this film, with the *tundanda* practicing *kuhunga* and *kawali* (the other term for *kundekula*), is basically identical with what I recorded some 500 km further southeast in 1965.

On the final day of *mukanda*, the initiates return to the village and the lodge is burnt, together with the secret musical instruments, some of the masks, the "tree of the dead," and the plates containing medicine that are attached to it. Surrounded by their mothers and all the villagers, the initiates form various dance figures, such as lines, circles, squares, etc. They then begin to display the patterns *kuhunga*, *kundekula* and others, while singing the didactic songs of the *mukanda* that they have learned during seclusion. This is accompanied by the three long drums, played by men. The women become very excited during the performance: some

Ill. 82. Performance of *kuhunga* during the coming-out ceremony at the village of Limbwangu, area of Soma Kayoko, north of Kwitu-Kwanavale, southeastern Angola, August 24, 1965

respond by imitating the dance pattern of the boys for a few moments, some throw groundnuts at the dancing initiates, and others bring gifts in large baskets for the initiates and their guardians.

Instruction and learning does not come to an end with the closure of a *mukanda* school and the return of the boys to their village. A year or two later, another *mukanda* is established nearby and the former initiates, who are now graduates, return to it and assume other roles. When they are sufficiently grown-up to wear mask costumes, new dance patterns and pantomimes are learned. Each mask has its own distinct repertoire of dance movements and theatrical behavior – for example, *mutenya* is a rotating pelvis motion with sexual meaning, and *kátonda* the name for jerky hip thrusts. These patterns are part of the movement repertory of the comic mask called *chileya* (literally: "the fool"), a kind of jester or court fool who is very popular, especially among the women. *Chileya* uses the "female" pelvis motion to parody women, to the delight of both the women and all other onlookers (cf. CD I/42).

Ill. 83. Performance of *kundekula* during the coming-out ceremony at the village of Limbwangu, area of Soma Kayoko, north of Kwitu-Kwanavale, south-eastern Angola, August 24, 1965

When a boy ultimately starts to learn masked dancing at the age of sixteen or seventeen, he already has a good movement repertoire because of earlier instruction received in the *mukanda* and his subsequent observation. For example, *kuhunga* also occurs in the dance style and theatrical pantomime of certain masks. The Chokwe-originated *chikunza* that represents the ancient Chokwe king Kanyika, and *kalelwa*, representing his assistant, dance *kuhunga*, though the leg part of the pattern is different from the initiates' version. There is also a mask called *kandanda*, which represents an archetypal image of an initiate who died in the camp. Usually it is a boy (though he must be a graduate of the *mukanda*) who wears this mask costume. The *kandanda* mask behaves exactly like an initiate of the lodge and performs the patterns *kuhunga* and *kundekula*.

Transcription and Analyses

Applying a frame-by-frame transcription system from silent film (cf. Kubik 1965c, 1972c) that was originally developed for the motion analysis of African instrumental performances, it is possible to look at dance movement in Africa from a modified angle. The objective of frame-by-frame transcription is not to add a new system of dance notation to those already existing, such as Laban and Benesh notation[49], which claim universal applicability. Notation like that we are using in the following transcription aims at analyzing movement patterns structurally, that is, in their internal numerical relationships, in contrast to a descriptive assessment of movement in space. Taking the dance practice of initiates in *mukanda* schools within one delineated culture area as an example, I have employed a repertoire of symbols with variable meanings to analyze two different motional patterns used.

These dance notations are not prescriptive in the sense of the dance notation systems normally used; that is to say, they are not designed for the teaching of dance through a notational system. Rather, they have purely analytical objectives. The basic idea is to seize the motional content of movement patterns in their time dimension. Such notation can then be linearly related to musical notation.

During field work it is necessary first to isolate and define the intra-culturally conceptualized motional centers, preferably with the help of the dancers themselves. These are then named accordingly in the local language, for example (in translation) shoulders, shoulder blades, pelvis, etc. Next comes the assessment of the motional sequence (cycle) within each center, which has to be split up for analytical purposes into recognizable kinemes, i.e. the smallest intra-culturally significant motional units. In a film, the kinemes can be discovered through slow-motion viewing of a cinematographic record of a dance by isolating the so-called "corner points" or "points of inflexion" of a motional sequence[50]. Through these terms we understand those moments within the motional cycle, reached by a single moving agent, at which the kinetic energy invested by the dancer is exhausted or, in other words, when it has reached zero intensity. In order to continue movement, often combined with an abrupt change of direction in the spatial performance by the moving agent, the dancer must supply new muscle energy.

Corner points are something like marks at the end of a segment of movement. They are visible on movie film: a change in or complete reversal of the direction of movement follows after a short stand-still or running-down phase.

With the exception of uninterrupted or flowing, circular movements (such as in *mutenya*, a slow pelvis circle performed by girls during the female initiation ceremonies in eastern Angola), it is possible to isolate the corner points relatively quickly on film or through participatory observation in the field. The body can be divided up into parts that have constant energy flow and those that are segmented.

In the case of *mutenya*, in which no corner points exist, one may mark a starting point for repetition anywhere during the circle, preferably in coordination with pivot points in the drum accompaniment. On the other hand, in a simple work pattern such as hammering bast in a traditional circumcision school, there are just two such corner points – the impact point of the hammer (the moment when the hammer hits the barkcloth) and the vertex (i.e. the highest point in space attained by the lifted hammer). This is a two-dimensional movement. In eastern Angola and many other areas of central Africa, dance movement is usually three-dimensional. In these cases there may exist three or more corner points or points of inflexion for each motional center.

A kineme is a motional segment that flows into a corner point. Each kineme must be given an abstract graphic symbol for identification. With the aid of a schematic drawing of corner points or certain frames reproduced from the film, a key for the graphic symbols is established. For transcription, ordinary graph paper is used. The horizontal lines represent the motional centers activated in a particular dance; the vertical lines indicate the frames of the film and should be numbered continuously. Any visually distinctive sign can serve as a transcription symbol for a kineme, such as + , x, /, !, o, ●, (,), ▲, ▼, -, □, ■, etc. These signs are to be understood as emic, i.e. they are significant within one culture and not meant to be standard symbols of a universalistic dance notation. They can also change their meaning from one dance to the next, although it is convenient to maintain the same symbols within one dance culture. In transcription from film, we mark each kineme the moment it is completed, that is to say, the moment the investment of energy by the dancer has returned to zero intensity and a corner point is discernible in the film. The totality of transcribed symbols makes the rhythmic-motional relationships within the dance pattern visible. When musical instruments are used – provided that they are visible in the film – a basic instrumental pattern (for example, a beat-representing drum), hand clapping or one of the asymmetric African time-line patterns can be transcribed as well. This establishes a link between the dance and the music.

Most of the initiates' movement patterns can be analyzed through frame-by-frame transcription. In the largely three-dimensional movements of the dancers and in complex work patterns, several corner points can usually be discerned. Before transcription, it is necessary to discover all corner points in a movement pattern by watching a movie film in slow motion and drawing up an inventory. Then each corner point or corner position must be defined verbally and in some cases represented with an illustration – either with a characteristic photograph or, even better, with the appropriate frames reproduced out of the film. Later, frame-by-frame transcription may be used in order to represent the structure of the movement pattern on a graph.

Dancer's position:

Headdress

Ndzombo skirt

Transcription from 8 mm. film, black and white, X/D/l (short extract) 16 frames/sec. Place and date: Limbwangu, August 24, 1965.

Symbols: < pelvis turned clockwise with left hip
(corner points)   reaching a forward position:
            > pelvis turned counterclockwise with right hip reaching a
              forward position:
            ▲ left heel raised, knee bent
            ■ left leg stretched, body weight on left foot
            △ right heel raised, knee bent
            □ right leg stretched, body weight on
              right foot

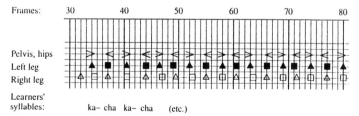

Ill. 84. Illustration and transcription of *kuhunga*

For example, in *kuhunga*, the two corner points of the movement center called "left knee" are 1) knee bent and 2) leg stretched. Through frame-by-frame analysis, we now look for the time sequence in which these "positions" occur. We see, for instance, that the bending knee reaches its identifying moment approximately every sixth frame of the film. The stretching of the leg does as well, but the movements of the two legs are related in opposition to one another (cf. transcription).

In the graph transcription, the corner points of all motion centers are marked systematically at crossing points of the vertical lines of the graph paper that stand for the frames of the film and the horizontal lines that stand for motion centers or body areas. The key to each symbol is the illustration of the respective corner point position that goes with the sheet of graph notation, or a verbal explanation of the symbols used. In this way the temporal organization of movement patterns can be represented very accurately in a graph transcription, and thus make clear their inner structure.

(a) Analysis of leg and foot movements, 8 mm. film, black and white, X 4/B/ll, frame-by-frame transcription, 16 frames/sec. Place and date: Limbwangu, August 24, 1965.

Symbols: ● impact of left foot (put on the ground)
(corner points)   ○ impact of right foot (put on the ground)

●——|
Impact   foot rests on the ground   lifting off

\ foot turned outward to the left
/ foot turned outward to the right
| foot put into straight position

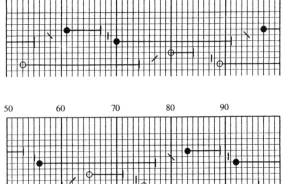

Frames:
  Left foot put forward:
  Initial position:
  Right foot put forward:
  Initial position:

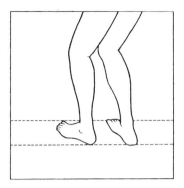 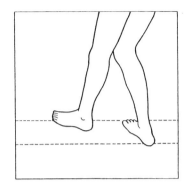

Kundekula step: initial position
(left foot)

Kundekula step: position 4
(left foot)

(b) Combination of movement patterns of various body parts in *kundekula*: leg-and-foot complex, shoulders and arms, shoulder blades and back. Transcription (extract) from 8 mm. film, black and white, X 4/B/7, Limbwangu, August 24, 1965.

Additional symbols: ᴀ▲ vertex in circular shoulder movement (the highest point). Right and left symbol.

ᴠ▼ bottom position in circular shoulder movement (the lowest point). Right and left symbol.
(Both shoulders move backwards in tracing circles.)

⊂ contraction of shoulder blades, stomach put slightly forward, pelvis thrust backward

⊃ release of shoulder blades, stomach contracted, pelvis forward, back appears broad and stooped

⦿ placement of body weight onto left foot
⦿ placement of body weight onto right foot

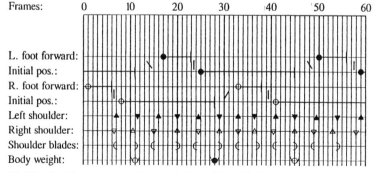

Ill. 85a–b. Illustration and transcription of *kundekula*

Section 3
Likembe Tunings and Musical Concepts of an Adolescent Kachokwe: Kufuna Kandonga

The following is an analysis of the sonic concepts and musical behavior of a post-*mukanda* adolescent, Kufuna Kandonga, who was about 15 years old at the time of study, 1965. On the basis of his musical terminology, his tuning process and other observations, I will formulate some conclusions about his *likembe* tunings and his music. All this is related to the wider realm of Mbwela/Nkhangala and Chokwe musical concepts and the history of the *likembe* in central Africa.

Kufuna Kandonga traveled with me in southeastern Angola in 1965. He lost his life in the late 1970s as a civilian victim of the prolonged armed conflict in Angola.[51]

Some General Remarks on the *likembe* in Central Africa

The name *likembe* is associated with a distinctive type of box-resonated lamellophone of Zaïrean (Congolese) origin which is known in vast areas of central Africa. It is characterized by the following organological traits:

(1) A box-shaped resonator.

(2) A distinctive cut-out section in the back, projecting from the top end of the hollowed-out box.[52] Thus, the soundboard of a *likembe* is longer than its resonating box. Instrument makers usually begin by cutting out this top section.

(3) The box is hollowed out, usually from the left side, but in many cases from both. Before closing the resonating chamber with thin strips of wood, the maker usually inserts a few small pieces of glass, one or two bottle tops or small stones to create additional vibration when the instrument is played.

(4) The iron bridge is usually ⊔-shaped. The backrest is a flat, longish piece of hard wood and is not attached to the soundboard. It is held in position solely by the pressure of the lamellae.

(5) A special characteristic of this instrument is the attachment of the straining bar to the soundboard between bridge and backrest to hold fast the iron lamellae: a series of small holes is burned through the soundboard from the back along the innermost edge of the cut-out section. Wire is threaded through these holes and slung along the straining bar on the front of the soundboard in order to hold it firm. This method also explains why, in this particular kind of lamellophone, the soundboard must project beyond the resonator, for

only in this way is the back of the soundboard accessible to pierce the holes. The holes lie outside the box.

(6) Usually a *likembe* has from 8 to 12 lamellae, which are made of forged iron. Umbrella stays were a commonly used material in Angola in the 1960s. The width of each lamella varies little throughout its length in contrast to some other types of lamellophone[53], on which the ends of the lamellae may be broadened. Sometimes those of the *likembe* tend to be slightly thinner at their playing ends. Usually the ends are also filed smooth by the maker in order not to hurt the player's thumbs.

(7) Iron ring buzzers are threaded onto some or all of the lamellae. The instrument makers (who are usually identical with the players) often calculate carefully the distribution of these buzzers over the keyboard because one of the purposes of the buzzers is to group certain notes together and so create preconceived accentuation patterns in the music. In Angolan *makembe* (pl.) the buzzers are often attached to the deep notes.

(8) Two sound holes are burned into the resonator, one in the end pointing to the player as he holds his instrument, the other into the back of the resonator. By alternately opening and closing the back hole with the left middle finger, the player can modify the timbre of individual tones and produce vibrato and wow effects. The middle finger movement on this sound hole is considered the most difficult part of *likembe* playing technique. Often the middle finger moves in a counter rhythm to the motor patterns of the two thumbs.

(9) The layout of the notes tends to be left-right alternating in pitch, with the lowest frequencies in the middle of the keyboard. In many instruments a further deep note is found on the right side, from the player's point of view.

The word *likembe* is known throughout central Africa today. It is known as far as western and northern Uganda and the southern Sudan and occurs in varied local adaptations according to the nature of the languages into which it was introduced. For example, the Mpyɛmɔ people in the southwestern corner of the Central African Republic and in southeastern Cameroon use the form *kembe*. The original *li*-prefix was not adopted because it does not occur in the Mpyɛmɔ language. The instrument was reportedly introduced to that area by workers returning from Congo-Brazzaville along the Sangha River[54].

Among the Azande of southern Sudan, another adaption of the word is reported. It was called *ɽekembe* (with a flapped r) in 1930, according to A.N. Tucker (personal communication). Among the Acooli of northern Uganda it is called *lukeme*, which is a further phonetic deformation of the original Zaïrean word, resulting from the adaptation of name and instrument by speakers of a Nilotic language in Uganda.

The most likely area of origin and dispersal of this kind of lamellophone seems to be the region of the Lower Congo River. My guess is that it is a relatively recent (possibly early 19th century) offshoot of the family of African lamellophones. Maes, in an article on the Congo, called it "type fluvial" and wrote:

> ou bien cette forme de sanza provient du Bas-Congo et a été transportée à l'intérieur du Congo par les indigènes aux services des premiers coloniaux, ou bien son berceau se trouve dans la région des Bangala, tribu où nous avons recruté la grande majorité des soldats de l'armée indigène de la première periode de notre pénétration... (Maes 1921:557–8).

Laurenty (1962:205) also believes that "Bakongo et Bangala furent probablement les vecteurs de ce genre de sanza à travers le Congo."

In the decade before the First World War, the *likembe* was established along the Congo River (among the Kongo, Mfinu and Teke) and up-river as far as Kisangani (ex-Stanleyville). It was known among the Loi and Mbuja. The *likembe* had also spread along the Ubangi River, where it was collected several times from Ngbaka musicians in the years 1911–13, and also from the Ngbandi.[55] In the northeast this instrument had already penetrated Uganda via the West Nile District, and in southern parts of Zaïre it was found in the Kasai at that time.

As a travel instrument used by porters, workers and colonial servants, the *likembe* spread rapidly at the end of the 19th century with the increase in traveling during the final stages of Western exploration and colonization of the interior of central Africa. This process accelerated even further with the introduction of migratory labor in Zaïre. Often the *likembe* was the only companion of the solitary traveler to the mines and to the industrial and urban centers.

In Angola the *likembe* was still spreading in popularity in 1965 when I started my field research there. I saw it being played then in eastern, southeastern and northeastern parts of Angola by -Chokwe, -Luvale, -Mbwela, -Luchazi and -Nkhangala musicians. I also found it used by the !Kung' near Longa (then: Cuando-Cubango District), who had adopted it from Bantu-speaking neighbors. Several standard songs played by Mbwela-speaking musicians in the southeast, such as *"Yani manguchata kumufweta,"* had texts in Chokwe, a clear indication of the direction from which the instrument and its music were imported into southeastern Angola.

Fortunato Pereira Gonçalves of Kwitu-Kwanavale, one of my friends and companions during my travels in the region of the Kwitu River, defined the *likembe* as an instrument "with a box resonator and played

while walking on a long journey[56]." Like elsewhere in central Africa, the
likembe in Angola was an instrument of the emerging working class and,
as such, it was also inter-ethnic. In southeastern Angola in 1965 it was
mainly played by casual laborers, usually between about 14 and 30 years
of age. At Longa I recorded five *likembe* players of whom two were
Vambwela, one was Kaluchazi, one Kachokwe and one !Kung' in a
group of about twenty workers employed by a local Portuguese agricultural merchant. Other *likembe* players I met in the region had either
worked in some other part of Angola on Portuguese-owned estates or
had been in the mines in South Africa (*ku Njoni,* i.e. in Johannesburg).
One player, Tololi Mbundu, aged 30, whom I met and recorded at Chief
Kabarata's village, 9 km northeast of Kwitu-Kwanavale, had an exceptional repertoire. Besides many songs in the local Ngangela dialect, he
played *"Ilanga la shona,"* a South African guitar song of the late 1940s
that he had transferred to his *likembe.*

Kufuna Kandonga also said that the *likembe* was an instrument played
by young people. This was certainly true for southeastern Angola in
1965, when the *likembe* was considered one of the recent fashions. Kufuna also told me the following story about the appearance of the *likembe*
at Longa:

> *Muchapata* and *chisanzi chandoma* were the first (lamellophones)
> in the region, and also *lungandu. Likembe* was at first in Kwitu-
> Kwanavale. At the time of the Chef de Posto Mutalanima at
> Longa, that was 10 or 15 years ago, the *likembe* was brought here.
> It was the *vantu vambunga* who brought it. Musisi, a man from the
> village of Soma Kakeke (a Chokwe settlement about 15 km south
> of Longa) went to Kwitu (meaning the administration post of
> Kwitu-Kwanavale) and brought the *likembe* from there.[57]

According to this oral tradition, it would appear that *likembe* was in
the Longa area not much earlier than about 1950, and that it came from
the east – from Kwitu-Kwanavale – where it had probably arrived from
eastern or northeastern Angola (CD I/44, *"Mwandumba Kalunga").*

I did not see any guitars being played in the area of Longa and
Kwitu-Kwanavale in 1965. The guitar, which had begun to replace the
likembe as an instrument for personal entertainment in Zaïre soon after
World War II, was virtually unknown in southeastern Angola at that
time.

Biographical Notes on Kufuna Kandonga

Kufuna Mwozi Kandonga was born in the village of Soma (Chief)
Kayoko, north of the administration post Kwitu-Kwanavale[58]. During

my Angolan field research (July to December 1965), he was based in the village of Soma Chisende, northeast of Longa, in the same district. In his matrilineage, he was a Kachokwe, but he was brought up in a predominantly Mbwela/Nkhangala-speaking community. His colloquial language was Mbwela and he used it even in villages with a predominantly Chokwe population. Once we went to Mariti (a Chokwe village north of Longa) and he was harshly rebuked by elderly men in the *ndzango*, the assembly place for men in the center of a village, for speaking Mbwela. They had recognized him as a Kachokwe by the shape of his front teeth, which were cut to a point.

Kufuna lost his father when he was very small, but his mother was still alive in 1965. He lived with his maternal uncle at Chisende when I arrived there in October. Shortly before that time he had worked for a year on a Portuguese coffee plantation in central Angola, together with two other boys of the same age from Chisende: Chimutwe and Kufuna Milonga. There he learned the Angolan vernacular language Umbundu and some Portuguese. He once even reached Luanda, he told me.

He learned *likembe* at a place called Kuhilili from a man named Titima Vutale, to whom he paid 30 Escudos for the instruction. From him Kufuna learned the well-known pieces *"Malova mundonga"* and *"Zambelela ngenzi mulikembe."* After that, Vutale left again for Johannesburg to work in the mines, Kufuna explained.

Likembe playing was an important element in Kufuna's life. Once he said to me: "If I gave up the *likembe*, I would play with the vagina of a woman instead, or even with my mother!." For him, *likembe* playing had an important psycho-cathartic function at his adolescent stage, as well as a socializing one. At Chisende, Kufuna was the leader of a small group of boys who were always active together and shared the *likembe* music (CD I/45 *"Manguchata kumufweta"*). They were: Kufuna Kandonga himself, who played the *likembe*, Tololi Masozi Chimutwe, who usually struck the 16-pulse time-line pattern called *kachacha* with two sticks on the front of the *likembe*, the small Ndeleiji Kahilu Vikuni vyaSoma, who was learning the *likembe* and Kufuna Milonga. All of these boys were about 13 to 15 years old and had completed the traditional *mukanda* school. None of them had gone to a Western-type school.

During my stay at Chisende, one frequent form of amusement of this group was to mimic the movement style and the verbal behavior of the Portuguese supervisor on the coffee plantation where they had worked, who always used to urge them to work faster.

From October to December 1965 Kufuna was my constant companion during long excursions on foot to remote villages in the region. He even accompanied me to camps of the !Kung' (San) people.

Musical Terms and the Tuning Layout of the *likembe*

In the Mbwela/Nkhangala language as spoken in the area of Kufuna's home, *chisanzi* is a category embracing all kinds of lamellophones. This term was even extended to include my Uher tape recorder. Kufuna's type of lamellophone was called *chisanzi chalikembe*, or simply *likembe*. The other types of lamellophones found in the area were known under the following names:

(1) *chisanzi chandingo* in Mbwela or *chisanzi chandoma* in Chokwe, a board lamellophone with a gourd resonator;

(2) *chisanzi chalungandu* in Mbwela or *mandumbwa* in Chokwe, a board lamellophone with a gourd resonator and with the lamellae arranged in two ranks; and

(3) *chisanzi chamuchapata*, or just *muchapata*, in Chokwe, a lamellophone with a bell-shaped resonator. While the first two types of instruments listed here were considered proper Ngangela/Mbwela instruments (though Chokwe musicians also used to play them), *muchapata* was known as a Chokwe import of long ago.

In Kufuna's village, Chisende, there was a strong lamellophone tradition. The most respected musician was Sachiteta, about 70 years old in 1965, who was a marvelous performer on the *muchapata* and one of the last players left in the area.

The wood used for the body of all four types of *chisanzi* usually comes from the *mukula* tree (*Pterocarpus angolensis*). Kufuna said it was difficult to find a big piece of *mukula* wood around Chisende to make a *likembe* as large as his own. Often the wood has to be collected from far away, as was the case when he made a *likembe* for me.

Kufuna called the various parts of his instrument as follows: *vingeya* (sing. *ngeya*) = the lamellae; *manjota* = the buzzing rings around some of the lamellae[59]. Inside the instrument (*mu ntima yachisanzi*) there are various buzzers such as small stones, bottle tops, small pieces of glass, etc. All of these are called *ndendulu*. They vibrate and provide a percussive "accompaniment" effect during the playing of the instrument. The timbre of the vibration can be modified by the player by changing the way he holds the *likembe*. The buzzers then slide away to a different corner of the box resonator and the timbre spectrum of the sympathetic resonance is changed. These buzzers are also called *manjota*.

For the box resonator, a square piece of *mukula* wood is hollowed out from the sides. The two side openings are each closed with a cover (*chifwiko*), usually a thin (about 4 mm) and longish little board cut from the soft wood of a eucalyptus tree (*kalipi*). The joints are then glued with black wax (*vulongo*). No nails are used in this area. Musicians do not usually leave their instruments in direct sunlight, as the wax melts easily.

Ill. 86. *Likembe* (box-resonated lamellophone, with 10 notes, and vibrato hole in the back). The instrument on the right is Kufuna Kandonga's *likembe*, the one on the left a specimen purchased at the village of Mupeku. The soundboard of Kufuna's instrument measured 20 × 12.5 cm. Not including the projecting top part of the soundboard, the box resonator then measured 16 × 12.5 × 2.5 cm. The body of this *likembe* was slightly curved in its length. The wood of the hollowed box was about 4 mm thick. The diameter of the back hole was 1.5 cm. The width of the lamellae decreased from ca. 5 mm at the top ends to ca. 2 mm at the playing ends. The buzzers (*manjota*) were attached only to the four lowest notes to amplify the sound and also to lengthen their duration. The soundboard was decorated with burned-in reliefs in Chokwe fashion. At Mupeku, November 1965

A sound hole is burned into the back of the *likembe*. Kufuna did not name it specifically, just calling it *mpako*, which is "a hole in a piece of wood." The sound coming out of this hole was referred to as *mwukú*. Kufuna did not define this term further. Rev. Emil Pearson, in his

Ill. 87. Kufuna Kandonga at the village of Sakonvoyo (kuMboyombacho), one of our many stops during the journey in Cuando-Cubango District, October 1965. This photograph shows Kufuna in one of his favorite playing positions. This position is the characteristic "seated" manner of playing the *likembe* and is very common in central and eastern Africa. The left hand is passed under the left leg. Both hands hold the instrument just above the ground, which functions as a sound reflector. On other occasions I saw Kufuna playing it from the other side, passing the right hand under the right leg. Once he even played with both hands under both legs, but that was his "show" style and not his regular playing position.

Ngangela-English dictionary, translates *mûku* as "breath" (Pearson 1970:227).

A sound hole is most important in the technique of *likembe* playing and the most difficult part to learn. In compositions such as *"Zambelela ngenzi mulikembe,"* which are based on a cycle of 12 pulse units, the

Ill. 88. Kufuna shows the technique of closing and opening the sound hole on the back of the *likembe* with the left middle finger. Note the characteristic shape of a *likembe*, with the cut-out top part and the series of holes pierced through the soundboard for threading wire to fasten the straining bar. The chain visible in this picture is for carrying the instrument. On other instruments in Kufuna's area, a string was used instead of the chain. At the village of Mupeku, November 1965

player's left middle finger performs quick alternate open-close movements on the sound hole as fast as the elementary pulsation of the music. The basic technique of using the back hole is this, according to Kufuna: "When a thumb strikes *ntangi* (a deep tone), the hole must be closed, when it strikes *mundengu* (a high tone), it is opened."[60]

The *likembe* is tuned by pulling the metal lamellae to different lengths over the iron bridge, which is called *lyambeji*. Black wax is never used for tuning, in contrast to the *ndingo* and *lungandu* lamellophones.

The tuning layout of the notes on Kufuna's *likembe* is shown in Ex. 115. I have numbered the lamellae from left to right from the point of view of the person playing, and not from a musical or scalar point of view. Ex. 115 shows a typical arrangement of notes on a *likembe* of southeastern Angola, such as Kufuna's, the playing area of each thumb, and how he named the notes:

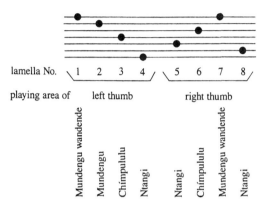

Ex. 115. The tuning layout of Kufuna Kandonga's *likembe*

The tonal range of Kufuna's *likembe* was exactly one octave. This is represented by the outer lines in Ex. 115. Within the octave (lamellae 4 : 7) there were six different tones. The two highest notes (lamellae 1 and 7) were tuned in unison for technical reasons: Kufuna wanted to have an identical high note in the playing areas of both thumbs in order to use this note in certain combinations of simultaneous (harmonic) sound. As to the two deepest notes, one lay in the playing area of the left thumb (No. 4), and the other in that of the right thumb (No. 8). Ring buzzers were attached to those four low notes which formed the most frequent combinations of simultaneous sound in Kufuna's music, lamellae Nos. 4 + 5 and Nos. 8 + 3. The sound of these basic notes was thus amplified. Kufuna explained that both the *manjota* (ring buzzers) and the movements of the left middle finger on the back hole were particularly effective with the deep tones.

The naming of tones in the Mbwela language is based on the concept of pitch regions and not on that of individual notes of a scale. Kufuna and others distinguished three pitch levels:

(1) *ntangi* (= a deep tone),
(2) *chímpululu* (= a middle tone),
(3) *mundengu* (= a high tone).

The same terms are used for the three individual members of a *vipwali* drum set, tuned at different pitches. The various sections of the two cheeks of a slit drum (*chinkuvu*) are also named in the same way, according to the pitch they give. On the *likembe*, the three lowest-tuned lamellae (4, 5 and 8) were referred to as *ntangi* by Kufuna, No. 3 and 6 as *chimpululu*, No. 2 was called *mundengu* and No. 1 and 7 were each called *mundengu wandende* (literally: "small *mundengu*"). Other players in the area used close variants of this terminology.

The designations "small" for what is called a "high" tone in English, and "large" for a deep tone are familiar from many areas of Africa, and these concepts are also essential in the music of the Vambwela, Valuchazi, Tuchokwe and related groups. According to Fortunato Pereira Gonçalves, a comparable terminology is used in Mbwela vocal music. *Kutendeka* means *kwimba lizi lyalindende* (to sing with a small, i.e. a high voice); *kukokolola* means *kwimba lizi lyakama* (to sing with a big, i.e. a low voice). If one wants a group of people to sing in parts, one may say in Mbwela: *Muli nakwimba lizi limolika, mwapande kwimba ou nalizi lyendi ou nalizi lyendi!* ("You are singing all the same voice, you should sing this one with his own voice and that one with his own voice").

The Mbwela categories are not, however, congruent in their semantic fields with those notions in Western music expressing ideas of chordal part-singing. The sentence above can provoke a demonstration of harmonic multi-part music, but on another occasion it can elicit singing in parallel octaves. Only unison singing is excluded when everyone should sing his "own voice." I have tested this idea on several occasions. When someone sang *lizi lyalindende*, I would ask his partner to sing *lizi lyakama* together with him. On several occasions the result was indeed a "second voice" in thirds or fifths (or fourths), but other individuals, according to the range of their voices, just sang the tune an octave lower. "To sing everyone his own voice" means to Mbwela-speaking peoples that the same tune should be sung at different pitch levels according to the individual range of the voices of men, women and children, though not at random levels. Although it is not explicitly stated in the terminology, the implication is that these different pitch levels should combine at such distances that the resulting voice combinations should be recognized by the people as sounding good. For the Ngangela group of peoples in eastern Angola, this means the distances of what in Western music would be called thirds, fifths (or fourths) and octaves, though the size of the first three intervals are not identical with those found on Western instruments (cf. below). "Thirds," "fifths" ("fourths"), "octaves" and their combinations are all accepted as equally good-sounding, that is, harmonious intervals in multi-part music.

Kufuna's Tuning Process

Kukeleka is the Mbwela/Nkhangala term meaning "to tune a musical instrument." *Kukeleka chisanzi* means "to tune the *chisanzi*" and *likembe lyove vakeleka* can be translated, "they are tuning your *likembe*." The word *kweseka* ("to try") can be used to describe the actions of someone who does not really know how to tune an instrument.

Kufuna's tuning proceeds along the line of a clearly perceived inner tuning model. On one occasion I observed him do the following: When tuning, he started definitely from the bottom. But he proceeded like this: first he tuned lamella No. 4 against 8, then No. 4 against 3 in a sort of fourth. Then he played the tone row 4 + 8 + 5 + 3, while tuning No. 5. Then he played 4 + 8 + 5 + 3 + 6 and finally the whole scale stepwise up and down[61].

On another occasion I again observed him tuning: He started with No. 4 then he tuned No. 8 and then he played melodically 4 + 8 + 5 + 3; then he tuned lamellae Nos. 4 and 5 together, No. 8 with 3 and No. 5 with No. 6; finally he played in upwards movement the tone row 4 + 8 + 5 + 3 + 6 melodically. Suddenly he disliked the tuning of his initial *ngeya* (lamella No. 4). He played the series 4 + 3 + 2, then he checked No. 2 against No. 6, making No. 6 once again lower. No. 5 and 6 were also tuned to each other in a 'third'.[62]

I was able to confirm on several occasions that the starting point of Kufuna's tuning process was always lamella No. 4, from which he proceeded to 8 and then to 3.

The prevailing trend in Kufuna's tuning process also became evident from his checking procedure. For one thing, he constantly examined what I would call a scale, proceeding from the largest (lowest) to the smallest (highest) note. Secondly, he checked certain determined intervals by using a kind of spanning movement, always jumping one note of the scale.

At the beginning of each *likembe* song, he used to play a characteristic melodic phrase. To an occasional observer, it might appear to be a kind of introduction. Though it may be legitimate to apply that label, it had some other distinctive quality and usually appeared in a very similar form at the beginning of all of Kufuna's compositions. Kufuna did not give any verbal explanation regarding this matter, but it is clear that this phrase, apart from being an "introduction," was a device for a last check of the tuning.

Kufuna's tuning check phrase, as I would call it (Ex. 116), reveals very clearly the two main ideas guiding him when he tuned his instrument: (1) the idea of a scale, conceived as proceeding from the largest to the smallest note, and

(2) the idea of certain harmonic sounds, here played in "arpeggio" in a zigzag downward movement.

Start of song

Ex. 116. Tuning check phrase as introduction to the song *"Yani manguchata kumufweta"* (Recording B 10451)

My First Reactions to Kufuna's Tunings

Diary note at Chisende village, October 17, 1965:
I had requested some people in the village to make a new *likembe* for me exactly the same size as Kufuna's. So they asked for Kufuna's *likembe* as a model. During the work, however, they put it out of tune. When his *likembe* was returned to us, Kufuna appeared to be irritated, because of the discord. Then he tuned his *likembe* anew, but what came out was very strange. For me it was another scale, different from the one I had been familiar with from his playing... He said: "Now the *likembe* is tuned well again!" and started to play the same tunes he had always played such as "Litombi" and others. For me this "new scale" was characterized by the fact that two notes, namely lamellae 2 and 8, appeared to be about a semitone lower than before in the context of this scale; the whole tuning now sounded to me as if in a minor key. I must say that it was very hard for my ear to adjust to "hearing" from now on all the *likembe* tunes which I had learned from Kufuna in 'minor,' in this "new scale." Kufuna himself played with his usual zeal, without saying a word that anything had perhaps changed.

For me this reorientation was so difficult that I took Kufuna's *likembe* secretly while he went to bring our food from the village and tuned it back to the "old tuning." Then I began to play "Litombi" and other pieces which I had learned from him with an innocent air, walking up and down while I saw Kufuna slowly coming back. Kufuna smiled with an expression of surprise and called to me in Portuguese: Isso! (That's it!) He instantly began to rock with his shoulders while I continued playing the *likembe*. Immediately after this he took the instrument and now played himself without giving the slightest hint that he had noticed any change.

This "adventure" has cost me a lot of headaches. The new "minor scale" sounded to me completely consonant, and the "old scale" with a note I perceived as between F and F sharp (lamella No. 3) also sounded consonant.

Diary note at Chisende village, October 26, 1965:
As regards the tuning of the *likembe* I now have definite indications that the "F sharp" (lamella No. 3) in the scale is deeper than a (relative) F sharp and lies somewhere between F and F sharp. Because once I tuned the *likembe* to a perfect F sharp, but Kufuna immediately intervened and said this was a wrong tuning. Then he tuned my F sharp slightly deeper at once.

Diary note at Mariti village, October 29, 1965 (referring to my previous observations):
One day I noticed that he was not happy with the scale as I had tuned it, the one containing the F sharp (the interval of a major third between lamellae No. 8 and 3). He began to change the tuning; this took a long time. At a certain stage during this process that "minor scale" came out again. But this time apparently it did not satisfy him. Then he put the octaves out of tune ... (Author's translation of the original diary notes in German).

A self-analysis of my first reactions towards Angolan tunings in 1965 reveals a familiar pattern.[63] What I had perceived as different tunings on the two occasions, the first with a note between F and F sharp (relative pitches), the second in a minor key with an approximate semitone between lamellae No. 4 and 8, was appreciated by Kufuna, without any doubt, as the same tuning. Subjectively, therefore, he had not changed his tuning pattern at all on October 17, when he had retuned his *likembe* and I had suddenly perceived it all in a minor key. It only appeared to me to be a different tuning from his previous one because we reacted to the objective tonal material from two different (learned) viewpoints of tonal and scalar recognition. As in the field of color perception and classification, to quote an example from an area better known in cross-cultural studies, I had distinguished as two categories, "green" and "blue," from what for him was a tolerable variation within one. This was a result of our musical enculturation during childhood within two different musical cultures.

Kufuna never showed any sign that he conceived of more than precisely one tuning pattern for his *likembe*. He always tuned his instrument to the same hexatonic scale, though with certain objectively measurable fluctuations in the intervals. These fluctuations, however, occurred within a clearly delimited margin of tolerance that was intra-culturally acceptable to him.

The "changes" in Kufuna's tunings that I had perceived over a period of some weeks were, therefore, merely a result of my projection of the Western tone system onto his tonal material. For him, these slight modifications were irrelevant because they did not destroy the identity of his scalar morpheme.

The Measurements

I observed Kufuna Kandonga's tuning process over a period of six weeks in 1965 as we traveled together in southeastern Angola; Kufuna carried his *likembe* with him on this trip.[64] In recording the tunings in the field, I followed the method recommended by the late A.M. Jones of the School of Oriental and African Studies, London. I set the recorder going and sounded a pitch pipe giving A = 440 c.p.s. I then played each note of Kufuna's *likembe* myself, in order from left to right (from the player's point of view as indicated by the numbers in Ex. 115 above), several times on each note. The tape recorder was not stopped until the recording was completed (cf. also Jones 1970:122–4).

A.M. Jones later measured the tones from my tape recordings, via an intermediate copy on disc, with a stroboconn at the School of Oriental and African Studies, for which I am indeed grateful to him. The conclusions about the nature of Kufuna Kandonga's tunings are my own.

Table 16 shows Kufuna's *likembe* tunings, recorded on five different occasions between October 15 and November 26, 1965. Since Kufuna accompanied me on a journey with his instrument, two of the tunings were not recorded in his home village but in Mupeku, a Luchazi village some 80 km north of Longa.

Lamella No.	B10450 Chisende, 10/15/65			B10618 Chisende, 11/1/65		
	c.p.s.	cents	cents interval	c.p.s.	cents	cents interval
1	416	350	9	424	380	15
7	414	341	323	420	365	341
2	343.5	18	165	345	24	176
6	312.4	1053	164	311.5	1048	136
3	284	889	161	288	912	178
5	259	728	187	260	734	213
8	232.3	541	183	230	521	146
4	209	358		211	375	

Table 16a

B10622 Chisende 11/4/65			B10497 Mupeku 11/24/65			B10500 Mupeku 11/26/65		
c.p.s.	cents	cents interv.	c.p.s.	cents	cents interv.	c.p.s.	cents	cents interv.
435	427		412	331		411	328	
433	419	8	404.5	300	31	410	323	5
354	68	351	333	1163	337	334.3	1170	353
328	1136	132	298	971	192	300.6	986	184
296	962	174	270.3	802	169	270.3	802	184
275	834	128	250	668	134	252	680	122
239	591	243	223	469	199	224.7	483	197
222	463	128	201.5	294	175	202.6	303	180

Table 16b.[65]

The tunings were recorded under the following circumstances:

B 10450 (October 15) was recorded immediately after the boys had performed the song *"Litombi"* rather enthusiastically for my first tape recording with them, in the house where we all stayed at Chisende village.

B 10618 (November 1) was recorded in the same house, after Kufuna had played and sung several of his pieces solo. When he finished the last song, I took his *likembe* and sounded the lamellae to record the tuning.

B 10622 (November 4): Kufuna had just finished recording a large part of his repertoire, sixteen songs at that time. After recording, I told him that I wanted to put the tuning on tape, as I had done before. He declined and said that he first wanted to retune his *likembe*. When he finished, he gave it to me with the words: *Njinahaka lizi lyalindende* ("I have put small voice," i.e. I have tuned it at a high level). This is the tuning I recorded here, and not the one in which he had played the sixteen songs. On that occasion I wrote in my diary: "This is another tuning, higher than the previous one." The tuning pattern had not changed, only the tuning level. It is also worth noting that Kufuna did not record any more songs after he had retuned his *likembe*.

B 10497 (November 24) was recorded in Mupeku, one of the stops on our journey. I took the tuning after Kufuna had played one song. There were no other people present in the house. After I had put the tuning on tape, he played six more songs without changing it.

B 10500 (November 26): Two days later, at Mupeku, I again took his tuning after a very inspired solo session (CD I/46). On this day he was so absorbed with playing that he did not even want to stop. At the beginning of this session he had said to me joyfully: *"Maná njiku-lingileko ntsongo yange!"* (Wait, I do that for you, my young brother!)

Whenever I wanted to stop the recording, presuming that he was playing the last item, he said: "Not yet, let me do another one!"

The last two tunings taken at Mupeku (B 10497 and B 10500) may be considered identical except for one note. Kufuna did not, most probably, touch his tuning during the two day interval, except that he adjusted the unison between lamellae No. 1 and 7 before the second tuning was recorded. In the first recording (B 10497 on November 24), the two unison notes were out of tune by no less than 31 cents. This was probably a result of an ailment that his *likembe* had developed when we were still at Chisende. On my original tape No. R 74 there is a recording session with Kufuna dated November 17th which had to be interrupted for that reason. In recording No. B 10646/g, his lamella No. 1 slipped out of its position towards the left in the course of playing and caused an audible rise in the note's pitch. This *ngeya* did not get better in the following recording (B 10647) either.

It is quite likely that this "ailment" was not entirely cured when we arrived at Mupeku, where I recorded the next tuning in the chronological series (B 10497). This would explain the deviation of 31 cents. Subsequently, Kufuna must have adjusted or repaired this lamella, with the result that the difference between the sounds of lamellae No. 1 and 7, which were supposed to be in unison, was down to 5 cents in the recording on November 26th (B 10500).

Evaluation of the Measurements

The five different tunings show a rather coherent picture:

(1) Tuning Level and "Absolute Pitch"

Kufuna's *likembe* was a relatively low-tuned instrument, compared with most of the other *makembe* I recorded in Longa, Kabarata and other villages. The basic note fluctuated between the values 209, 211, 222, 201.5 and 202.6 c.p.s. on different days. This is not a very wide margin, except for the 222 c.p.s. in B 10622, which Kufuna himself regarded as higher pitched. According to his statement about B 10622 (*Njinahaka lizi lyalindende*), Kufuna obviously recognized the overall level of his tuning to be different from the other tunings he had recorded before. His verbal statement is interesting because it implies that, in his pitch consciousness, a rise of the tuning level by less than a Western semitone is recognized as a change of the "largeness" of the instrument's voice, that is, in the overall pitch level. The difference between tuning B 10622 and the previous tuning (B 10618) expressed in cents is as follows:

B 10618 cents	Difference (in cents)	B 10622 cents
380	47	427
365	54	419
24	44	68
1048	88	1136
912	50	962
734	100	834
521	70	591
375	88	463

Table 17

Since B 10618 is the highest of the four low tunings, a comparison with B 10622 gives us an idea of the minimum difference in pitch necessary for Kufuna to consider two tunings to be different in their overall pitch level. From the cents figures in Table 17, it can be assumed that this minimum difference is between about 50 to 100 cents, about half the value of a standard interval of his scale (cf. below). Kufuna possesses absolute pitch within this margin of tolerance.

(2) Unisons

Lamellae No. 1 and 7 are tuned in unison. On the five occasions recorded, they were 9, 15, 8, 31 and 5 cents apart, with lamella no. 1 always being higher. Though Kufuna did not give any verbal statement as to the subjective accuracy of his unisons, his behavior indicated that the 31 cents of B 10497 were out of his margin of tolerance for unisons. He would not have corrected it down to 5 cents if he thought it was all right.

(3) Octaves

The octave between lamellae No. 4 and 7 deviated from true octaves (1200 cents) by the following values: − 17, − 10, − 44, + 6 and + 20 cents. The widest variation (− 44 cents) occurred on the day he had tuned his *likembe* "small voice." Since it also combined with an unusually narrow interval (of only 128 cents) between the two lowest notes (Nos. 4 and 8), I believe that lamella No. 4 (222 c.p.s.) might have gone too high on this particular occasion. If we tentatively added 44 cents to the bottom interval, it would become 172 cents instead of 128 and the octaves would be true. Of course, it is fruitless to speculate on whether or not one lamella was badly tuned in B 10622 without playing it back to Kufuna and asking his opinion. But there are four indications that B 10622 may be at least partly a poor tuning by Kufuna's standards:

(1) He tuned especially for recording the scale and did not play a single song afterwards.

(2) An octave of only 1156 cents is definitely out of tune according to Kufuna's acute hearing.

(3) The intervallic structure of this particular tuning is very uneven as compared with his other tunings.

(4) He did not usually tune his *likembe* at "small voice," so it may have been just a serendipitous idea after all. The next time I recorded his tuning (B 10497), he was back at a low pitch level.

(4) The Nature of Kufuna Kandonga's Tunings

At a first glance, the cents figures of Table 16 seem to display a pattern that might be interpreted as a "gapped" equiheptatonic tuning (cf. Jones 1971 b: 24–55). Kufuna's *likembe* tunings contain six notes within the octave; between his sixth and his octave there is a large step about twice the size of the standard interval of his scale. This gap is not found in any of the other *likembe* tunings I recorded in southeastern Angola. Some other players had a tuning layout identical to Kufuna's except for lamella No. 7, which was tuned to the note missing in Kufuna's layout. No. 1 and 7 were not in unison on those instruments.

The gapped interval in Kufuna's tunings was 323, 341, 351, 337, and 353 cents on the different days, which are values clearly in the region of equiheptatonic (neutral) thirds (342.8 cents).

(5) Interdependence of Certain Pitches

The interval between lamellae Nos. 8 and 5, however, showed a constant and striking tendency towards deviation from the equiheptatonic standard interval of 171.4 cents. Lamella No. 5 is tuned slightly higher than its position in an equiheptatonic scale would demand.

In this context another fact strikes the observer: the total interdependence of the intervals between lamellae Nos. 4 and 8, compared with Nos. 8 and 5. When one of the two adjacent intervals becomes larger, the other shrinks by about the same value. This pattern was very characteristic throughout the six weeks: 187/183; 213/146/; 243/128; 199/175; 197/180. This confirms that Kufuna tunes not only by comparing neighboring notes with each other, by step, but also "by jump," skipping one note of the scale. This means, however, checking thirds whose cents figures are the sum of the pairs shown above. If we add those figures, two by two, we find that the resulting thirds showed very stable values over the period of six weeks, in contrast to their intervallic components: 370, 359, 371, 374 and 377 cents.

(6) Simultaneous Sounds and Patterns of Consonance

Further evaluation of the measurements can only be pursued taking into consideration Kufuna's behavior in the tuning process and the structure of his music. Which are the most frequent simultaneous sounds in Kufuna's music?

Kufuna started his tuning process with lamella No. 4, then No. 8, but he never struck these two together. According to the measurements, this basic interval was always smaller than a Western whole tone but never as small as a semitone. It fluctuated between the values 183, 146, 128, 175 and 180 cents during the six weeks. The next lamella to be tuned was No. 3, which he appeared to approach from No. 4. To a Western observer it would sound like a fourth, sometimes like an augmented fourth. The cents values were: 531, 537, 499, 508 and 499. The two notes cannot be sounded together because they are both in the playing area of the left thumb.

In his music, Kufuna only sounded simultaneously those lamellae which are enumerated in the following Table 18.

Simultaneous striking of lamellae no.	B10450 10/15/65 cents	B10618 11/1/65 cents	B10622 11/4/65 cents	B10497 11/24/65 cents	B10500 11/26/65 cents
4 + 5	370	359	371	374	377
8 + 3	348	391	371	333	319
4 + 6	695	673	673	677	683
8 + 2	677	703	677	694	687
5 + 1	822	846	793	863	848
6 + 1	497	532	491	560	542
4 + 7	1183	1190	1156	1206	1220

Table 18

His basic consonances were the thirds of lamellae Nos. 4 + 5 and 8 + 3, and the fifths of Nos. 4 + 6 and 8 + 2. These were the most frequently heard simultaneous sounds in his *likembe* music. It is obvious that he was guided in the tuning process by the expectation of these particular consonances. In the vocal parts that he sang in duet with his friend Chimutwe to the *likembe*, the same combinations occur. The vocal parallel thirds duplicated those of lamellae Nos. 4 + 5 and 8 + 3.

(7) Tonal Blocks

All the simultaneous sounds were grouped into two tonal-harmonic blocks which were built up on two roots (lamellae Nos. 4 and 8) crossing the separate playing areas of the left and right thumbs. All of Kufuna's *likembe* pieces made use of root progressions between these two blocks.[66]

The notes dependent on each root are found in the opposite playing area; this is for technical reasons. Together with the first root (lamellae No. 4), Kufuna used to sound simultaneously No. 5 (giving a third), No. 6 (a fifth) or No. 7 (an octave). Together with the second root (lamella No. 8), he played No. 3 (giving a third), or No. 2 (a fifth). More rarely the combinations 5 + 1 or 6 + 1 occurred. Entirely excluded from the system were the following combinations: lamellae No. 4 + 8, 1 + 8, 3 + 5, 3 + 6, 3 + 7, 2 + 5, 2 + 6, and 2 + 7. Though it would be technically possible, these lamellae were never struck together.

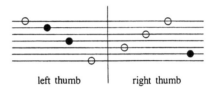

left thumb | right thumb

Ex. 117. Tonal-harmonic blocks in Kufuna's *likembe* music.
Only lamellae of the opposite playing areas are sounded together. Those marked with rings only go with rings, those with dots only with dots.

In central Africa the presence of two tonal blocks forming some kind of triad over two roots normally signals a relationship, however remote, with mouth bow harmonies (i.e. two fundamentals and partials exploited up to partial 6 over both roots).[67] In lamellophone tunings of eastern Angola, however, the situation is complex. Without denying the possibility of any such relationship, those "mouth bow harmonies" must have long been "tempered" in the instrumental tunings of eastern Angola.

(8) Equal-Step Principle and Consonance: the Compromise

If one considers not only the cents intervals between the steps of Kufuna's tunings, such as in Table 15, but also those of the notes sounded together, some further elucidation can be reached. The values of Kufuna's thirds (lamellae Nos. 4 + 5 and 8 + 3) are most frequently around 370 cents. The third between lamellae Nos. 4 and 5 was very stable, showing the values 370, 359, 371, 374 and 377 cents. As to the third of lamellae 8 + 3, there was a tendency to tune it slightly narrower. The fluctuations were also greater with this third, which had the following cents figures: 348, 391, 371, 333 and 319.

There is a clear tendency in Kufuna's tunings to tune the third between lamellae 4 + 5 larger than a theoretical equiheptatonic third (342.8 cents), but smaller than a natural third (386 cents). From my overall experience with Mbwela/Nkhangala music, it appears that this is one of the expressions of a basic compromise at work in the tonal-harmonic system of various communities within Guthrie's zone K in southeastern and eastern Angola. It is also evident in chorus singing (cf. Chapter III). The concept of a heptatonic scale, proceeding in identical steps from the largest (deepest) to the smallest (highest) note, if it plays a role at all here, must be constantly adjusted against the equally important concept of harmonic consonance.

In contrast to the thirds in Kufuna's tunings, the fifths 4 + 6 and 8 + 2 are virtually equiheptatonic. The ideal equiheptatonic fifth is 685.6 cents. Against natural fifths (of 702 cents), equiheptatonic ones are only about 15 cents narrower, while equiheptatonic thirds (342.8 cents) deviate from natural thirds (386 cents) by no less than approximately 43 cents, a very audible difference. Among populations such as those in eastern Angola, whose music is based on harmonic part-singing, the need for harmonic correction in combining "equiheptatonic intervals" must be greater, therefore, with thirds than with fifths. Equiheptatonic fifths are as near to perfect fifths as are the major thirds on a Western piano (400 cents) to natural thirds. For a harmonically sensitive people such as the -Mbwela, -Luchazi, -Chokwe and others in eastern Angola, equiheptatonic fifths may be harmonically marginally acceptable. In addition, one can observe in Mbwela chorus singing and in the tuning of instruments such as lamellophones that the neutral thirds, structurally inherent in a non-modal heptatonic system, are as often as possible intonated halfway towards perfect (natural) thirds. This is why a value of about 370 cents plays such an important role in Kufuna's tunings.

With *likembe* this compromise is achieved in the tuning process. The objective of producing harmonic sounds and at the same time even, non-modal pitch sequences is not at all easy to reach. Kufuna, who was an excellent musician, sometimes took a surprisingly long time to tune his *likembe* until he was satisfied with the sounds and their combinations. The absence of a seventh note in his tunings may be in itself at least partly an expression of this compromise.

Summary

In his *likembe* tunings, Kufuna appears to be aiming at a compromise between two conflicting principles:
(a) the idea of a non-modal, even heptatonic scale, starting with the lowest note, with the seventh note missing in his case, and
(b) the idea of consonant sounds in thirds and fifths over two roots (lamellae No. 4 and 8) which are tuned approximately an equiheptatonic second apart. These roots and their co-notes form two opposing tonal-harmonic blocks. Progression between these two blocks is an important characteristic of his music and that of other lamellophone players in the region.

During the tuning process, the first idea manifests itself in Kufuna's scalar checking movements, while the second idea asserts itself in his frequent checking of the thirds. In addition, Kufuna is aware of an absolute pitch level in his *likembe* tuning pattern.

* * *

Note on Some of the Recordings Illustrating Chapter V

My Angolan recordings 1965 were originally archived in Luanda at the Instituto de Investigação Científica de Angola. Those archival copies made in January 1966 in my presence have, however, disappeared. Since the post-independence turmoils of 1975, their whereabouts have been unknown. The same collection was fortunately also copied at the Phonogrammarchiv of the Austrian Academy of Sciences[68]. The numbers by which Kufuna Kandonga's recordings have been identified are those of the Vienna Phonogrammarchiv. In 1980, while the double album *Mukanda na makisi* (MC11), was being prepared in the Museum für Völkerkunde Berlin (cf. Kubik 1982b), a sound engineer discovered that the recording head of my tape recorder in 1965 had not been adjusted properly; consequently, adjustments had to be made on the recording head of the tape recorder for high fidelity copies to be made. After this discovery, excellent copies of what until then appeared to be poorly recorded material were made of the entire collection. These are stored in the Abteilung Musikethnologie of the Museum für Völkerkunde Berlin.

Notes

Introduction

[1] Cf. the discussions of this topic during the 1950s, esp. Grimaud 1956.

[2] Cf. Paul Oliver 1970 with regard to the "roots" of the Blues in the Sudanic Belt of West Africa, i.e. Lomax "Western Sudan" and "Moslem Sudan;" David Evans 1970, 1981, on African-American instrumental traditions; Kazadi wa Mukuna 1979; G. Kubik 1979a, 1986a, 1990, 1991b, and Pinto (ed.) 1986, 1988 and 1991 with regard to Bantu traits in Afro-Brazilian music.

[3] Letter from Klaus Wachsmann, October 30, 1980.

[4] Grupo Victoria, 40–5844 (Southern Music Publishing Co.), His Master's Voice G.V.31.

[5] Cf. Lamellophone solo, "Esanzi," Pathé Cpt 6824, PA 2554 (S) "Danse des Piroguiers Badouma," Mission Ogooué-Congo. Enregistreé par A. Didier. Recueilli par G. Rouget. 78 r.p.m.

[6] Cf. for example Azuka Tuburu's work on dance among the Igbo of Nigeria (Tuburu 1987).

[7] Compare the results of Lomax' Choreometrics scheme, Lomax et al. 1969.

[8] Note from a conversation in 1972.

[9] Cf. Lomax 1968, Dauer 1969b, Günther 1969, etc.; and John Baily's report on the ICTM Colloquium on Film and Video (Baily 1988).

[10] Cf. Günther 1969, Dauer 1967b.

[11] Cf. Ferreira 1968; Phiri 1982; Kubik 1987a (with Moya Aliya Malamusi).

[12] Cf. Aniakor 1978, Kubik et al. 1989:62–3.

[13] Kubik 1961a, repr. 1983; Johnston 1973/74.

[14] In some cultures the beat is felt in the right hand strokes, in others in the left.

[15] Conversation with Paul Kavyu, Nairobi 1976.

[16] Cf. Djenda 1968c, Kubik 1983:374.

Chapter I

[1] Cf. Posnansky 1969; and personal notes during a joint visit to Bigo with Merrick Posnansky in March 1960.

[2] Cf. Wachsmann 1971 and Kubik et al. 1982:31–2.

[3] Speke 1863:309, 324f., 347.

[4] Buganda = name of the country
Uganda = Kiswahili adaptation of the name "Buganda", later extended to cover the territory which became a British protectorate, and has been independent since October 9, 1962.
Baganda (pl.) = the people of Buganda, (sing.: Muganda).
Luganda = the language
Kiganda = things concerning the Baganda and their country, e.g. Kiganda music.

[5] Botanical name: Markhamia platycalix.

[6] Lusoga and Luganda; botanical name: *Vitex Fischeri*.

[7] I owe much information on Baganda culture and religion to Charles Sekintu who also spent many hours with me translating Muyinda's musical terminology.

[8] Cf. the transcription in Kubik 1960:24; and Chapter IV: *amadinda* piece No. 33, Table 10.

406 · Notes

9 In Buganda I played on *akadinda* instruments in Kireka and Salama (Uganda Foundation for the Blind), on *amadinda* sets in Nabbale (my teacher's home), in Salama, in a village near Nkokonjeru, and in Kampala (Uganda Museum); in Busoga on two *embaire* sets from different makers at Bumanya (Saza Bulmaoji).

10 To study this more scientifically I made recordings at intervals of a number of weeks of the pentatonic *budongo* tunings by Waiswa Lubogo (Orig. Tapes A24, R12 – R15, 1962).

11 I have recorded two different kinds of *embaire* music in northern Busoga. One kind (the one described in this paper) being rather like *amadinda* music, and the other kind reminding me of xylophone playing I have heard in Bunyoro. This style is not built on isorhythmic basic melodies, but uses 'broken rhythms' which interlock in a different way (Orig. Tape R18/1963).

12 Information from Alisi Nabawesi, Kampala 1962.

13 Parts A and B are to be played in parallel octaves. In the score the higher octave has been omitted.

14 Rec. Orig.-Tape No. R 18, January 2, 1963.

15 Parts A and B are to be played in parallel octaves. In the score the lower octave duplication has been omitted.

16 Orig. Tapes No. 5/II/4, 7/I/2, 10/II/2, 1959/60.

17 Octave duplications have been dropped in this score to make reading easier.

18 Transcribed from Orig. Tape No. R24, side 1, item 1, recording Hillegeist/Kubik 1963.

19 English translation by Livingstone Katongole who was one of my playmates on the *amadinda*.

20 Interview with Charles Sekintu, Kampala, 1962.

21 Cf. AMA-TR 137 record.

22 Cf. transcription of "*Basubira malayika*" (Example 10).

23 AMA records TR 137, Hugh Tracey 1950.

24 Cf. description in Kyagambiddwa 1955:116.

25 Orig. Tapes No. A 3, December 1961.

Chapter II

1 Figures provided by Armin Prinz, personal communication, 1988.
2 Cf. the Rev. Canon E. C. Gore of the Church Missionary Society.
3 Conversation March 28, 1988.
4 Cf. the collections of the Musée Royal de l'Afrique Centrale in Tervuren, Belgium, or the Musikinstrumentenmuseum/Münchener Stadtmuseum, Munich, Germany. Cf. Laurenty 1960.
5 Evans-Pritchard 1928, 1932, 1962–65, etc.
6 Recorded interview with A. N. Tucker on July 21, 1974, including performances. Orig. Tapes L 115–117, duration ca. one hour.
7 Kremser 1982, Haller & Kremser 1975.
8 Cf. recordings of Gananga, m., ca. 24 years old, No. B 5097, Phonogrammarchiv Vienna.
9 Cf. my letters to Hugh Tracey in *African Music* 3(2):43–47 [1963].
10 My research trip to the Azande became possible by permission of the Ministère de l'Intérieur et de l'Information in Bangui. I particularly thank Monsieur Christian Toléqué of the Commission de Contrôle du Service de l'Information, and Monsieur Victor Teteya, Director of the Radiodiffusion Nationale Cen-

trafricaine, who very much facilitated my project. I am most grateful also to the technicians of the radio station, who repeatedly helped me out of trouble with my tape recorder.

My sincere thanks go to the Azande harp players, especially to Maurice Gambassi, Jérôme Assas, Jérôme Sournac, Samuel Ouzana and Mockys Dieudonné Yves, who taught me how to play the Azande harp and helped me as interpreters. In addition I am grateful to David Kamoundé, who transcribed most of the songs recorded in Zande.

My warm recognition goes to the fathers of the Catholic Missions at Zemio, Rafai and Bangassou, who lodged me whenever I happened to stay in these places. I particularly should like to thank Father Piet van Horne, S.S.Sp., who kindly translated some of the songs into French.

Finally, I thank my unknown friends in the villages of the Central African Republic, who willingly housed me on my way and helped me forth.

[11] Orig.-Tape No. R 42/I/4; April 5, 1964.

[12] Orig.-Tape No. R 41/II/6.

[13] Orig.-Tape No. R 42/I/3.

[14] His famous song is called "Ouzana" and about himself. See the scores.

[15] The Azande *likembe* player whom I recorded in Bondo, Zaïre, in 1960, played a kind of music which I would describe as largely "Bantu"-influenced. His music had a pronounced inherent rhythm (I.R.) effect. The *likembe* tune was transcribed in Kubik 1962c: 37–8.

[16] Cf. the text of *"Limbyayo,"* Ex. 33 in the transcriptions.

[17] Cf. for example the song *"Nzanginza mu dukporani yo"* ("The Harp is in our Village"), Exs. 31 and 32 at the end of this chapter.

[18] In the 1950s Hugh Tracey recorded a Zande harpist in Congo (Zaïre) who steadily sang the phrase *"Gitari na Congo,"* obviously referring to his harp as guitar. Record: LF 1171, Music of Africa Series, No. 6, Side 2, Zande/Bandiya tribe.

[19] In 1964 this was a difficult riddle to solve, since this playing technique was exclusively linked, also among the Azande to gourd-resonated xylophones such as the *longo* which I recorded at Mabou, near Djema (Orig.-Tape No. R 46/A/5). But many years later the problem was solved. Manfred Kremser, working among the Azande in Zaïre in 1974, recorded a gourd-resonated xylophone called *manza* and stated that it was the exclusive property of the ruling family of the *avungara* (Kremser 1982:297). Therefore the instrument played at Zemio's court was certainly *manza* in its social context and playing technique, but either the technology or the materials for making such an elaborate instrument was lacking by 1964 and so they simply placed five slats of wood over banana stems, as with the *kponingbo*.

[20] Measurements kindly made by the Reverend A. M. Jones, School of Oriental and African Studies, London, with a Stroboconn, from my original tape recordings.

[21] *Wili* is sometimes pronounced *wiri, vili* etc.

[22] Cf. measurements in Table 2–3.

[23] Cf. measurements in Table 2.

[24] Cf. also analytical recording Phonogrammarchiv Vienna B 8777.

[25] Measurements by the Reverend A. M. Jones, London, with a Stroboconn.

[26] I had lost my pitch-pipe.

[27] Difficult to measure, said A. M. Jones.

[28] In Zemio I recorded an elderly blind musician, who held the harp horizontally. This was the only case, but the country is vast and I do not know anywhere

408 · *Notes*

near all the harp players. Occasionally one may find a player of the "vertical" harp, singing a song that is popular with "horizontal" harp players and vice versa. Historical and contemporary harp traditions in Azande country are not in a relationship of antagonism.

29 Original French translation as given to me by my interpreters:
Quelque chose un peu, c'est du travail.
Il faut jouer de la guitare et chanter sa chanson.
Les vielles choses sont le travail.

30 Cf. the melodic variations of the refrain in bars 3, 14, 15, 20 and 21.

31 Cf. Example 31 in the scores (transcriptions).

32 Unless the instrumental backing itself is changed to fit the various text themes. Slight changes are quite frequent. Compare particularly *"Nakepengele,"* Example 36, bars 7 and 8; *"Limbyayo,"* Ex. 33, bar 11; *"Agbe ni nduandu ngboro,"* Ex. 35, bar 24 and *"Tade so zo koue M.E.S.A.N.,"* Ex. 45, bars 6, 7 and 15. Such changes should not be mistaken for "variation."

33 Compare for example how Ouzana gets his second and third theme in *"Agbe ni nduandu ngboro,"* Ex. 35; particularly the words *Ako! Ako ai!* and *ku ndawayo.*

34 This is not the only singing style in the performance, just one episode.

35 This is not valid for pieces of Banda provenance.

36 Some variations in *"Agbe ni nduandu ngboro"* (Example 35) are an exception.

37 Cf. the full score in Example 32.

38 Dancing Time No. 8, 420034 PE. Sir Victor Uwaifo, "Guitar Boy and Mamywater." Philips West African Records.

39 In an appraisal written for an American publisher.

40 Cf. Ouzana's title *"Gba duleo,"* rendered by Laku Heke as *"Ngbadule o."*

Chapter III

1 Cf. Chapter V, Section 3.

2 Cf. Chapter II on Kiganda and Chapter III on Zande music.

3 Cf. Recordings in the Abteilung Musikethnologie, Museum für Völkerkunde, Berlin, and field notes Kubik/1977.

4 E. g. in southern Uganda and the south-west corner of the Central African Republic.

5 E. g. in the lower Zambezi valley, Moçambique, in Manding' xylophones of Guinée (cf. Rouget 1969), and in *kora* tunings.

6 Cf. Example 61, *"Kitandoli matala."*

7 Cf., for example, my recordings of a *matuli* dance among the Wapangwa (B 7361, Phonogrammarchiv Vienna – extract published on the first of the accompanying music cassettes of Simon [ed.] 1983) and the song *"Dendulu"* in Kikisi published on CD I/13.

8 Cf. Example 62 *"Mphezi-mphezi"* (CD I/14).

9 Cf. the closing of *"Kitandoli matala"* in Example 61.

10 "Tonal-gebundener" Parallelismus (Schneider 1934, 1951:45).

11 Cf. my recordings B 8813/Karre and B 8814–17/Buru in the Phonogrammarchiv Vienna Exp. Kubik 1963–64.

12 At this point I should like to express my gratitude to the former Second President of the Austrian National Assembly, the late Friedrich Hillegeist, for kindly supporting our work in East and south-eastern Africa, August 7, 1961 – January 10, 1963, with the means for the purchase of a vehicle.

[13] Most of my early Tanzanian recordings (1960 and 1962) on which this section is based have been copied and placed in the Phonogrammarchiv of the Austrian Academy of Sciences, Vienna. Cf. Catalogue Nos. B 4824–4856 and Nos. B 7236 – 7424.

[14] Cf. recording B 7265, Phonogrammarchiv Vienna. Published on the first of the accompanying music cassettes of Simon (ed.) 1983.

[15] Cf. recording B 7372 of the *izeze* player Mdachi, Phonogrammarchiv Vienna.

[16] The recordings were made by Philipp Donner, Institute of Workers' Music in Helsinki.

[17] Cf. recording B 7287, Phonogrammarchiv Vienna. One of Mirindi's musical pieces was recently published on the first of the accompanying music cassettes of Simon (ed.) 1983.

[18] The similarity of this name with that of a people in northern Moçambique and southern Tanzania is coincidental.

[19] Recording Phonogrammarchiv Vienna B 8755.

[20] In contrast to, for example, variation in *embaire* music of southern Uganda. Cf. Chapter I.

[21] Cf. Example 65 and CD I/17.

[22] Cf. also the melodic variations played by the bow on CD I/17.

[23] It should be no surprise that the term *ŋgɔmbi* is applied to the harp among the Fang', and to the stick-zither among other ethnic groups of West-Central Africa, such as the Makua in Congo. It expresses a feeling of identity regarding these different string traditions.

[24] Recording Phonogrammarchiv Vienna, B 7015.

[25] Cf. my recordings Orig. Tape A 16 at Namagembe, south of Itigi, April 1962.

[26] Recordings by Hugh Tracey, AMA Sound of Africa Series.

[27] Unpublished recordings by Henry Anyumba Owuor, Nairobi. The collection of his own recordings since 1956 is the largest and most comprehensive one ever made by an individual of his own ethnic group in Africa. It is stored privately in Nairobi.

[28] Field notes in southern Cameroon 1964 and 1966.

[29] Plainly audible in the Bongili recorded example, Orig. Tape 57/II.

[30] Cf. Edward Bowdich's description of harmony among the Asante of Ghana, 1819.

[31] Pechuël-Loesche 1907:115. Translated by the author. The German original reads: "Aber genaueres Aufmerken lehrt, dass die Stimmen, in verschiedener Tonhöhe einsetzend, sich durchschnittlich parallel bewegen, dass leitereigene Akkorde die Hauptrolle spielen. ... Da den meisten Stücken der straffe Aufbau mangelt, haben die Mitwirkenden sie nicht fest im Gedächtnis. ... Sie setzen falsch ein, tasten nach den Tönen, gleiten hin und her, nehmen tempo rubato, fallen auf Zwischentöne, die wir gar nicht in Noten schreiben können. ... Das gibt ein Gemisch von Schwebungen, gefälligen Akkordfolgen, greulichen Missklängen, wie man es daheim in Dorfschenken und Spinnstuben zu hören bekommt. Eben wegen dieser Unsicherheit der Sänger bleibt es meistens zweifelhaft, ob ein Stück in Moll oder in Dur zu nehmen ist. Das Tongeschlecht scheint den Leuten gleichgültig zu sein. Deshalb kann man nicht gut sagen, Moll sei oft nur ein missratenes Dur, und umgekehrt. Der nämliche Satz erklingt stundenlang bald so, bald so, und, wie bereits erwähnt, zugleich auch derartig abweichend in Tonfolge und melodischem Akzent, dass man nicht weiss, was man aufschreiben soll."

[32] Example 59 and CD I/19.

[33] Cf. Djenda & Kubik 1971 and Kubik 1983:395–400.

34 Cf. the E♭ in Example 60a. I have been asked by an attentive reader: "If you start with C, then D♭, why do you choose to go to E♭ as the next note of the scale? Why not E? E is already present over the C, so why not use it?" The answer is: If the lower voice proceeded to E the strict parallelism of the two voices in major thirds would be broken; because E would form a minor third with the G intoned by the upper voice.

35 Example 66, CD I/21.

36 I could equally have transcribed this song using E♭, D♭, C.

37 Cf. also the complete text transcription in Kubik 1987b:64–7.

38 A recording of the mass, sung by the students of Madunda Middle School, Rudewa District, Iringa Region, in March 1960 is found in the Phonogramm-archiv Vienna, Nos. B 4835–4836. The "Gloria" has been published on the first of the accompanying music cassettes of Simon (ed.) 1983.

39 An extract of this performance was published on the first of the accompanying music cassettes of Simon (ed.) 1983.

40 This paper is based on research in Angola and Zambia. My Angolan research was carried out in 1965 with financial assistance from the Junta de Investiga-ções do Ultramar, Lisboa (Portugal), and in 1982 in the context of an official invitation by the Secretaria de Estado da Cultura, Luanda, to hold a six-week seminar with fieldwork on "Introdução á metodologia das pesquisas culturais" at the Departamento Nacional de Folklore, Luanda. My research work in Zambia in 1971, 1973, 1977/78, and 1979 was carried out as an affiliate of the Institute for African Studies of the University of Zambia, with research grants from the Foundation for the Advancement of Scientific Research, Vienna, Project Nos. 1395, 2792, and 4210.

41 This process has now reached genocidal proportions in southern Angola where San-speakers have been systematically exterminated during a war that has been going on since the early 1970s with no end in sight (cf. Souindoula 1982 and Kubik 1984a).

42 "Khoisanid" and "Khoisan:" these are blanket terms which were introduced into the literature by L. Schultze (1928) to embrace the racial stock of the non-negroid population of southern Africa. The terms derive from khoi-khoin by which the pastoral Hottentots called themselves and san, applied by the Hottentots to the so-called Bushmen hunter-gatherers.

43 According to an oral tradition I collected from Soba Sangombe in the Kwitu-Kwanavale river area, Province Kwandu-Kuvangu, south-eastern Angola, in 1965, the custom of lengthening the labia minora was inaugurated by a certain Ngangela chief after sexual experience with !Kung' girls. Some data on chikula female initiation among the -Nkhangala and -Mbwela at Soba Kayoko's vil-lage, ca. 25 km north of the administration post Kwitu-Kwanavale can be found in my fieldnotes 1965 accompanying Orig. Tape 77, Phonogrammarchiv Vienna.

44 Recordings at Chikenge, Kabompo District, Zambia, November 21, 1971. Orig. Tape L 27/I/2, Phonogrammarchiv Vienna.

45 Personal communication by Luka Kangamba, 1977.

46 Personal communication by Moya Aliya Malamusi, Chileka, Malaŵi, 1979.

47 According to Moya Aliya Malamusi, June 9, 1982.

48 For illustrations cf. Kubik 1975/76 and 1987a.

49 Fieldnotes Kubik/Angola 1965, at village Mambondwe, area of Quilengues/ Dinde.

50 Cf. England 1964, 1967; Kubik 1970b, 1987a.

51 Cf. "Therekantalo," Nsenga music. CD I/22.

[52] Cf. Kirby 1932, 1934; England 1964, 1967.
[53] For further discussion cf. also Rycroft 1966, 1967, 1980, 1981/82; Kubik 1984b, 1985.
[54] Institute of Workers' Music, Mannerheimintie 40 C 74, SF-00100 Helsinki, Finnland.
[55] Recordings Kubik, Angolan research 1965, Phonogrammarchiv Vienna B 10663–10671, B 10507–10515.
[56] Cf. complete list in Kubik 1970a:67–8.
[57] Cf. table of measured bow tunings in Kubik 1987a.
[58] As demonstrated in England's song transcription (England 1967:60).
[59] The first item discussed in Rycroft's assessment of Westphal's material *"G!anwa"* (1978:17). Rycroft renders it in this transposition: (E$^\flat$) C A$^\flat$ G F E$^\flat$.
[60] Letter from A. M. Jones, October 6, 1964.
[61] This is not a quotation from some informant, but a thought experiment in narrative style.
[62] Cf. also Marjory Davidson's account disussed further below.
[63] *Silimba* music was recorded by Moya Aliya Malamusi in northwestern Zambia in 1979 and 1987 (research project P 6316 G, Kubik/Malamusi, in cooperation with the Institute for African Studies, University of Zambia; recordings September 1987). Cf. CD I/25.
[64] A. Tracey 1961:50, 1970:40, 1972:90–104.
[65] Orig. Tape 76/II/9.
[66] Orig. Tape 76/II/14.

Chapter IV

[1] Klaus Wachsmann, personal communication, London 1963.
[2] Klaus Wachsmann, personal communication, London 1963.
[3] Hugh Tracey's recordings are available on the Sound of Africa Series, published by the International Library of African Music, I.S.E.R. Rhodes University, Grahamstown 6140, South Africa. Cf. especially AMA TR-137.
[4] Cf. Illustration 22 in Chapter I.
[5] Complete transcriptions of all five *miko* transpositions of *"Olutalo olw'e Nsinsi"* in cipher notation are found in the transcription section of this chapter (p. 312)
[6] Kyagambiddwa 1955; Wachsmann 1956c; Jones 1971b.
[7] Cf. recordings Kubik 1960, 1961–1963, 1967/68, Phonogrammarchiv Vienna and cinematographic shots, private collection Kubik, Vienna.
[8] Cf. Orig. Tape 120–121.
[9] It would be possible today (1990) to reexamine the material regarding both regularities and liberties in composition with the help of a suitable computer programme. For future research I would also suggest arranging the entire repertoire of court music compositions transcribed so far according to analysis of the song texts, so that they are linked with the genealogical list of the *basekabaka*, the dead kings (cf. above). It would be interesting to see whether such a "relative chronology" reveals any sort of patterns in composition style.
[10] Inherent note-patterns (inherent rhythms, inherent melodic-rhythmic lines) can be defined as autonomous patterns which only exist as an aural image and are not played as such by the performers. This is a gestalt-psychological phenomenon which is prominent in certain kinds of African music. The inherent

patterns can be traced back structurally to the total pattern of the notes of a piece of music.

[11] Cf. also his rendering of my transcription of *"Olutalo olw'e Nsinsi"* (Jones 1971b:270), in which he speaks of the *okunaga* part as the nuclear theme.

[12] Field notes Moçambique, near Mamaua, 20 km from Mueda. Oct. 26, 1962.

[13] Cf. No. 15 of the *amadinda* pieces.

[14] This must not be confused with the total pattern of *amadinda* pieces, where the same note may only occur twice in succession.

[15] Cf. Section 2: The akadinda.

[16] Cf. for example *"Agenda n'omulungi azaawa"* (No. 50) where the *kalagala-e-bembe* particle occurs at the beginning of such a phrase.

[17] Sempebwa in the discussion part in Chapter I.

[18] Cf. Mr. Sempebwa in the above-mentioned discussion.

[19] Cf. Hugh Tracey's recordings published on the AMA "Sound of Africa" series TR-138.

[20] Orig. Tape No. 34/1, stored in the Phonogrammarchiv in Vienna.

[21] Cf. the transcription part of this chapter.

[22] Cf. also the Introduction.

[23] Cf. the above Example 90.

[24] Cf. also Chapter I, pp. 74–5.

[25] Cf. *baakisimba* dance song, rec. November 1959, on the record "The Blind Musicians of Salama," A.I.T. Records (Kenya) Ltd., Nairobi GKA No. 2.

[26] Cf. Nos. 52–57, 59, and 61–63 under Group I.

[27] Cf. *"Kisawo kya muwa butwa ... "* (No. 51) and *"Ab'e mbuga basengejja"* (No. 60).

[28] This seems to happen in *"Ekyuma"* (No. 3).

[29] This song is said to have originated in Busoga.

[30] This song is known in Busoga as *"Mobuka nkomera."*

[31] On one occasion Evaristo Muyinda taught me this tune saying it was *"Walugembe eyava e Kkunywa."* Cf. No. 28. This may have been an error.

[32] This song is also known under the name *"Nandikuwadde ennyanja e kalide"* ("I would have been generous, but the lake has dried up"). In this case Evaristo Muyinda prefers to have two notes in the *okunaga* part changed: 5.4.1.3.2.5.5.4.1.2.2.2.5.4.1.3.2.4.4.4.1.4.4.1.1..

[33] The melodic variants in the two parts can be employed during some repetitions of the 25-note cycle.

[34] The notes of this song, as Evaristo Muyinda taught me, are practically identical with those of *"Omunyoro atunda nandere"* (No. 68).

[35] The Blind Musicians of Salama play the *okwawula* at the Agricultural Training Center as 24.35. Some people call this song *"Endwadde ya kabotongo"* ("The disease of syphilis").

[36] This title was recently changed to *"Omusajja atunda nandere"* ("The man sells *nandere* fish").

[37] These variations can also be mixed to form new variant patterns.

[38] The above version of *okwawula* is that of the Salama Blind; Evaristo Muyinda's version was slightly different: 5̲3.24.5̲3.24.5̲3.23.5̲3.24.5̲3.24.5̲3.24

[39] A few musicians play *okwawula* as 24.35.̲

[40] On another occasion Evaristo Muyinda taught me exactly the same patterns under the title *"Kiri ku luggi"* ("That which is outside the door").

[41] TOM TOM TR 335 *"Ekigambo Kilungi Nyo,"* Evaristo N. Muyinda and Party.

[42] Referring to a letter by Merrick Posnansky to the editor of *"African Music"* [2(4)/1961] in which Muyinda is called "Head attendant" of the Uganda Museum.

[43] Klaus Wachsmann, February 9, 1978.

Chapter V

[1] Enculturation = growing into a culture through education processes; the slow absorption of culture-specific forms of behaviour, thought systems and learnable practices by young people in a society (cf. Kubik 1982a:73–75).

[2] Cf. various recordings, Angola 1965/Kubik, stored in the Abteilung Musikethnologie, Museum für Völkerkunde, Berlin.

[3] Cf. examples on the record Kubik 1982b.

[4] Cf. analytical dance demonstration films, Reel No. 4 by Kufuna Kandonga, m., aged 15, at Chisende, Province Kwandu-Kuvangu, Angola, November 1965; and Reel No. 15 by Mose Kamwocha, m., aged 13, and friends, at Chikenge, Kabompo District, Zambia, November 1971.

[5] Cf. Kubik 1982a.

[6] Orig.-Tape No. B 66/1/3.

[7] Translated from Mbwela/Nkhangala by the author.

[8] Orig.-Tape No. R 66/II/3–6.

[9] Orig.-Tape No. L 30/II/1–4, December 23, 1971.

[10] Orig.-Tape No. R 66/II/7–8.

[11] Cf. Kubik 1987a:114–115, 119.

[12] Field-notes M. Djenda/G. Kubik in the Central African Republic and Gabon 1966.

[13] Cf. Orig.-Tape No. 75/I/5, at Kumboyombacho, southeastern Angola, November 1965.

[14] Orig.-Tape Nos. L 16/I/7, September 13, 1971 and L 24/II/12–13, November 5, 1971.

[15] Cf. for comparison: Emil Pearson's documentation, 1977:133.

[16] *Fwaku* is an ideophone and portraits the birds with its rich hair coming along proudly.

[17] This bird is calling the rain. It begins to sing when the rain is near (Note November 25, 1971).

[18] Cf. Orig.-Tape No. 71/3.

[19] Orig.-Tape No. R 68/I/3 and II.

[20] Orig.-Tape 74/II/5 at Mariti, north of Longa.

[21] With regard to a socio-anthropological definition of the term "age-set" see Bock 1974:158.

[22] Cf. Malamusi 1984:198.

[23] Orig.-Tape 65/II/4–7 at Kayoko, September 1965.

[24] Orig.-Tape 65/II/11.

[25] Orig.-Tape 57/I/10, at Chief Kakeke's village, ca. 15 km south of Longa, Province Kwandu-Kuvangu, southeastern Angola, August 1965.

[26] Conversation with elders at Sangombe and Mikula, Kabompo District, N.W. Province, Zambia, September 1971.

[27] For details, cf. also the following section.

[28] See motion film analysis of these patterns in Kubik 1977:253–74.

[29] Orig.-Tape No. L 16, Sangombe, Kabompo District, September 1971.

[30] Orig.-Tape No. A 75/I and II, motion film, synch-sound No. 27.

31 Field data yet unpublished.
32 Ciné Film No. 32/1979, Zambia.
33 Examples of female institutions include *chikula* or *litungu lya nyamuso* initiation, the *makisi a vampwevo* (or "masks" of the women) and *tuwema*, the flames.
34 Some readers may not be famliliar with psychoanalytical theory. I am therefore including the following dictionary definitions of some terms used here (cf. Drever [13]1972):

   transference ... "also used generally, of the passing of an affective attitude or colouring from one object or person to another object or person connected by association in the experience of an individual person" (p. 302).

   libido ... "Term, used by psychoanalysts originally, in its usual sense of sexual desire, but later, in the most general sense of vital impulse of 'energy'; the sexual meaning is, however, retained in particular connexions ..., or in discussion of the stages of *libido development* from the pregenital phase to complete *psychosexual* organization" (p. 156).

   latency period ... "In psychoanalytic literature, a period of sexual development between the age of 4 or 5 and the beginning of adolescence, separating infantile from normal sexuality" (p. 154).

   fixation ... "Employed in three distinct technical senses: ... (3) of interest or emotional attitude, by analytical schools, to designate the attachment, generally interpreted psychosexually, to an early stage of development, or object at such stage, with difficulty in forming new attachments, developing new interests, or establishing new adaptations" (p.98).

   projection ... "... by the psychoanalysts, the attributing unconsciously to other people, usually as a defence against unpleasant feelings in ourselves, such as a feeling of *guilt*, or *inferiority feeling*, of thoughts, feelings, and acts towards us, by means of which we justify ourselves in our own eyes" (p. 255).
35 Field notes Kubik 1965 and 1971.
36 Recordings published on the double album *Mukanda na makisi*, Museum Collection MC 11, Abteilung Musikethnologie, Museum für Völkerkunde, Berlin, item B3, recorded at the village of Sakateke, August 16, 1965.
37 *Ndo* and *mba* are ideophones. Emil Pearson (1970:253) writes: *ndo*, ideo. thud, tap. For the related Luvale language Horton (1949:153) gives the meanings: *ndo* – thumping, meeting together, destruction; *mba* – denotes falling with a thud.
38 In the sense of: My mother is far away.
39 It is not certain that the initiates sing *Mwanandonga* which is probably another name of the boy Kawali. It means tributary of a river, literally "child river." Even when using headphones the spot is difficult to discern on the tape recording. In the recordings from other *mikanda*, the word *mwanandonga* is definitely used.
40 Exclamation of fear or terror.
41 "Ntumba" is a female personal name.
42 *Kauali é um rapaz que tinha ido para* mukanda. *E a sua mãe que ficou no quimbo, andava sempre a chorar. Os homens foram dizer: "Kauali, a sua mãe anda a chorar". E Kauali disse: "Eu podia ir ver a minha mãe no quimbo." Os homens inventaram uma cantiga.* Angola notes 1965.
43 *Kwakele kandanda halaza, lizina lyeni Kawali. Vakele nakuvayandesa chikuma. Kaha vunoni uze Kawali waputukile nakwimba nwaso weni ngweni 'Kawali e, vanana vovo kwimbo. Ange njili kuno kumukanda nakuyanda chikuma. Vunoni vanana vovo kwimbo.' Kusinganyeka muvwongo vwa Mose. Vakuluntu kavan-*

jilekele. Vunoni kusinganyeka cha Mose. Zambia notes 1971. Trans. from Luchazi by the author.
[44] Compare also Fortunato's interpretation.
[45] Compare recording A1 of the *kalelwa* mask (record *Mukanda na makisi,* MC 11).
[46] Association of Social Anthropologists, London.
[47] Cf. Azande harp music, Chapter II.
[48] Orig.-Film No. 32.
[49] Cf. discussion in Blacking 1977.
[50] Cf. Kubik 1972c:35, 1977:270.
[51] Personal communication by António Chipango in Luanda, March 1982.
[52] Cf. the back view of the *likembe,* Ill. 89.
[53] For example *chisanzi chandingo* in southeastern Angola.
[54] Field notes C.A.R. 1966.
[55] Cf. the details of the collection in the Musée Royal de l'Afrique Centrale, Tervuren, and the sources indicated in Laurenty 1962.
[56] Note at Kabarata village, August 1965.
[57] Note, October 1965.
[58] Then: Cuito-Cuanavale, Cuando-Cubango District, southeastern Angola.
[59] On Kufuna's instrument, they were only on the four lowest lamellae, Nos. 3, 4, 5 and 8; cf. Illustration 86.
[60] For the note names, cf. Ex. 115 below.
[61] Diary note at Mariti, October 21, 1965.
[62] Diary note at Chingangu on our way home to Chisende, October 1965.
[63] Cf. our discussion of Pechuël-Loesche's reaction to vocal music of the Bafioti (1907) in Chapter III.
[64] On five different occasions I recorded his tunings on an UHER Report S tape recorder, at 19 cm/sec, half-track, with an AKG D 19 microphone.
[65] The measurements in cents and c.p.s. were kindly provided by the Rev. Dr. A.M. Jones, London. The cents figures are from the Stroboconn. The c.p.s. figures are given to the nearest whole number.
[66] For the term "root progression," cf. Blacking 1959.
[67] Cf. also Chapter III.
[68] Phonogrammarchiv of the Austrian Academy of Sciences, Liebiggasse 5, A-1010 Vienna. Cf. Catalogue 1970 under B 10069–10671:11–45.

Bibliography

Abraham, Roy Clive
  1958   *Dictionary of Modern Yoruba*. London: University of London Press.
Achike, James
  n.d.   *Die Trommel in Afrika*. Wien: Afro-Asiatisches Institut.
Adagala, Kavetsa
  1981   "Language and Literature in Kenya Primary Schools: Lulogooline tsing'ano
          tsya Valogooli." *Review of Ethnology* 7(16-18):121-42.
Agawu, V. Kofi
  1986   "'Gi Dumu', 'Nyekpadudo', and the Study of West African Rhythm."
          Ethnomusicology 30(1):64-83.
Akpabot, Samuel
  1971   "Standard Drum Patterns in Nigeria." *African Music* 5(1):37-9.
  1973   "A Re-Assessment of Some Popular Theories on African Music." In *Proceed-
          ings of the Lusaka International Music Conference June 15-22, 1971*. Lusaka:
          Institute for African Studies, n. p.
  1975   *Ibibio Music in Nigerian Culture*. Michigan: Michigan State University Press.
  1975/76 "The Talking Drums of Nigeria." *African Music* 5(4):36-40.
Alaja-Browne, Afolabi
  1985   *Juju Music: A Study of its Social History and Style*. Ph.D. dissertation. Pitts-
          burgh: University of Pittsburgh.
Alexandre, Pierre
  1974   "Introduction to a Fang Oral Art Genre: Gabon and Cameroon Mvet." *Bulle-
          tin of the School of Oriental and African Studies* 37:1-7.
Almeida, António de
  1956   "La macronymphie chez les femmes indigènes de l'Angola." In *Comptes
          rendues de l'Association des Anatomistes*, XLIIIe Réunion. Lisbon, 131-50.
Amu, Ephraim
  1934   "How to Study African Rhythm." *Teacher's Journal* (Gold Coast) 6:33-4, 121-
          4.
Anderson, Lois Ann
  1967   "The African Xylophone." *African Arts/Arts d'Afrique* 1:46-9.
  1968   *The Miko Modal System in Kiganda Xylophone Music*. 2 vols. Ph.D. disserta-
          tion. University of California, Los Angeles.
  1977   "The Entenga Tuned Drum Ensemble." In *Essays for a Humanist. An Offering
          to Klaus Wachsmann*. New York: The Town House Press, 1-57.
  1984   "Multi-Part Relationships in Xylophone and Tuned-Drum Traditions in
          Buganda." *Selected Reports in Ethnomusicology* 5 (Studies in African Mu-
          sic):120-44.
Aniakor, Chike
  1978   "Omabe Festival." *Nigeria Magazine* 126-7:3-12.
Aning, Ben A.
  1969   "Wangara Xylophone and its Music." In *Papers in African Studies* 3:57-63.
Ankermann, Bernhard
  1901   "Die afrikanischen Musikinstrumente." *Ethnologisches Notizblatt* 3(1):I-X, 1-
          132, Table I-III. (Reprint 1976, Leipzig: Zentralantiquariat.)

anon.
1974   "Success Stories: Banjo Maker Francis Mwanza - How He Does it." *Orbit* (The
       Magazine for Young Zambians) 3(3):12.
Arom, Simha
1967   "Instruments de musique particuliers à certaines ethnies de la République
       Centrafricaine." *Journal of the International Folk Music Council* 19:104-8.
1969   "Essai d'une notation des monodies à des fins d'analyse." *Revue de
       Musicologie* 55(2):172-216.
1974   "Une méthode pour la transcription de polyphonies et polyrythmies de tradi-
       tion orales." *Revue de Musicologie* 59(2):165-90.
1976   "The Use of Play-Back Techniques in the Study of Oral Polyphonies."
       Ethnomusicology 20(3):483-519.
1985   *Polyphonies et polyrythmies instrumentales d'Afrique Centrale: Structure et
       méthodologie.* Société d'Études Linguistiques et Anthropologiques de France.
       2 vols. Paris: Centre National de la Recherche Scientifique.
1990   "La 'mémoire collective' dans les musiques traditionelles d'Afrique Centrale."
       Revue de Musicologie 76(2):149-62.
1991   "A Synthesizer in the Central African Bush: a Method of Interactive Explora-
       tion of Musical Scales." *Hamburger Jahrbuch für Musikwissenscahft* 11 (Für
       Györgi Ligeti. Die Referate des Ligeti-Kongresses Hamburg 1988), 163-78.
Arom, Simha & France Cloarec-Heiss
1976   "Le langage tambouriné des Banda-Linda (République Centrafricaine)." In
       Théories et méthodes en linguistique africaine. Communications au 11ème
       Congrès de la Société de Linguistique d'Afrique Occidentale, Yaoundé, avril
       1974. Luc Bouquiaux, ed. Bibliothèque de la SELAF, 54-55. Paris: SELAF -
       ORSTOM, 113-69.
Avorgbedor, Daniel
1985   "The Transmission, Preservation, and Realisation of Song Texts: A Psycho-
       Musical Approach." In *Cross Rhythms.* Occasional Papers in African Folk-
       lore/Music. Daniel Avorgbedor & Kwesi Yankah, eds. Bloomington: Indiana
       University, Trickster Press, 67-92.
1987   "The Construction and Manipulation of Temporal Structures in *Yeve* Cult Mu-
       sic: A Multi-Dimensional Approach." *African Music* 6(4):4-18.
Baily, John
1985   "Music Structure and Human Movement." In *Musical Structure and Cognition.*
       Peter Howell, Ian Cross & Robert West, eds. London: Academic Press, 237-58.
1988   "ICTM Colloquium on Film and Video." *Yearbook for Traditional Music*
       20:193-8.
1989   "Film Making as Musical Ethnography." *The World of Music* 31(3):3-20.
1990   "Music Performance, Motor Structure, and Cognitive Models." In *VII. Euro-
       pean Seminar in Ethnomusicology: Pre-publication of the Conference Papers.*
       Berlin: International Institute for Comparative Music Studies and Documen-
       tation, 33-45.
Ballantine, Christopher
1965   "The Polyrhythmic Foundation of Tswana Pipe Melody." *African Music*
       3(4):52-67.
1991   "Concert and Dance: The Foundations of Black Jazz in South Africa between
       the Twenties and Early Forties." *Popular Music* 10(2):121-45.
Bareis, Urban
1991   "Formen neo-traditioneller Musik in Kpando, Ghana." In *Populäre Musik in
       Afrika.* Veröffentlichungen des Museums für Völkerkunde Berlin. Neue Folge

53, Abteilung Musikethnologie VIII. Veit Erlmann, ed. Berlin: Staatliche Museen Preußischer Kulturbesitz, 59-108.

Bascom, William
1958   "Main Problems of Stability and Change in Tradition." *African Music* 2(1):6-10.

Bastin, Marie-Louise
1961   *Art decoratif Tshokwe.* Lisbon: DIAMANG.
1983   "Instruments de musique, chants et danses des Tshokwe (region de Dundo, district de la Lunda, Angola)." *African Musicology* 1(1):45-66.
1992   "Musical Instruments, Songs and Dances of the Chokwe (Dundo Region, Lunda District, Angola)." *African Music* 7(2):23-44.

Baumann, Hermann
1930   *Tänze der Frischbeschnittenen. N.O.-Angola.* Cinefilm, 4 min. C 122. Institute for Scientific Cinematography.
1932   "Die Mannbarkeitsfeiern bei den Tsokwe (N.O. Angola; West Afrika) und ihren Nachbarn." *Baessler-Archiv* 15:1-54.

Baumann, Max Peter
1993   "Listening as an Emic/Etic Process in the Context of Observation and Inquiry." *The World of Music* 35(1):34-62.

Beier, Ulli
1954a   "The Talking Drums of the Yoruba." *African Music* 1(1):29-31.
1954b   "Yoruba Folk Operas." *African Music* 1(1):32-4.
1956   "Yoruba Vocal Music." *African Music* 1(3):23-8.
1980   *Neue Kunst in Afrika.* Das Buch zur Ausstellung im Mittelrhein. Landesmuseum Mainz. Berlin: Dietrich Reimer.

Beier, Ulli & Gerald Moore
1974   "Literature." In *Encyclopaedia Britannica.* 15th edition. Vol. 13. Helen Hemingway Banton, ed. Chicago: Encyclopaedia Britannica, 237-41.

Ben-Amos, Dan
1975   *Sweet Words. Storytelling Events in Benin.* Philadelphia: Institute for the Study of Human Issues, Inc.

Bender, Wolfgang
1985   *Sweet Mother. Moderne afrikanische Musik.* München: Trickster.

Bender, Wolfgang (ed.)
1989   *Perspectives on African Music.* Bayreuth African Studies Series 9. Bayreuth: Bayreuth University.

Benseler, Arthur
1973   "Beobachtungen zur Kwela-Musik 1960 bis 1963." *Jazzforschung-Jazz Research* 5:119-26.
1973/74 "Beobachtungen zur Kwela-Musik 1960 bis 1963." *Jazzforschung - Jazz Research* 5:119-26.

Berliner, Paul
1975   "The Vocal Styles Accompanying the Mbira Dza Vadzimu." *Zambezia* ?:103-4.
1975/76 "Music and Spirit Posession at a Shona Bira." *African Music* 5(4):130-9.
1976   "The Poetic Song Texts Accompanying the Mbira dza vadzimu." *Ethnomusicology* 20(3):451-81.
1978   *The Soul of Mbira: Music and Traditions of the Shona People of Zimbabwe.* Berkeley: University of California Press.
1993   *Thinking in Jazz. The Infinite Art of Improvisation.* Chicago Studies in Ethnomusicology. Chicago: The University of Chicago Press.

Blacking, John
  1955a   "Eight Flute Tunes from Butembo, East Belgian Congo - An Analysis in Two Parts, Musical and Physical." *African Music* 1(2):24-52.
  1955b   "Some Notes on a Theory of African Rhythm Advanced by Erich von Hornbostel." *African Music* 1(2):12-20.
  1959   "Problems of Pitch, Pattern and Harmony in the Ocarina Music of the Venda." *African Music* 2(2):15-23.
  1961   "Patterns of Nsenga *kalimba* Music." *African Music* 2(4):26-43.
  1962   "Musical Expeditions of the Venda." *African Music* 3(1):54-78.
  1965a   "Music in Uganda." *African Music* 3(4):14-7.
  1965b   "The Role of Music in the Culture of the Venda of the Northern Transvaal." In *Studies in Ethnomusicology* 2. M. Kolinski, ed. New York: Oak Publications, 20-53.
  1967   *Venda Children's Songs: A Study of Ethnomusicological Analysis.* Johannesburg: Witwatersrand University Press.
  1969a   *Process and Product in Human Society.* Inaugural Lecture. Johannesburg: Witwatersrand University Press.
  1969b   "Songs, Dances, Mimes and Symbolism of Venda Girls' Initiation Schools." *African Studies* 28 (1-4):3-35, 69-118, 149-200, 215-66.
  1970a   "Deep and Surface Structures in Venda Music." *DYN* - The Journal of the Durham University Anthropological Society 1:69-98.
  1970b   "Tonal Organization in the Music of Two Venda Initiation Schools." *Ethnomusicology* 14(1):1-56.
  1973a   "Fieldwork in African Music." *Review of Ethnology* 3(23):177-83.
  1973b   *How Musical is Man?* Seattle, London: University of Washington Press.
  1977   "Some Problems of Theory and Method in the Study of Musical Change." *Yearbook of the International Folk Music Council* 9:1-26.
  1986   "Identifying Processes of Musical Change." *The World of Music* 28(1):3-15.
  1989   "Challenging the Myth of Ethnic Music: First Performance of a New Song in an African Oral Tradition 1961." *Yearbook for Traditional Music* 21:17-24.
Blacking, John (ed.)
  1977   *The Anthropology of the Body.* A.S.A. Monograph 15. London: Academic Press.
Blacking, John & Joann W. Kealiinohomoku (eds.)
  1979   *The Performing Arts. Music and Dance.* The Hague: Mouton.
Blench, Roger
  1987   "Idoma Musical Instruments." *African Music* 6(4):42-52.
Blesh, Rudi
  1946   *Shining Trumpets. A History of Jazz.* London, New York: Cassell & Company Ltd.
Bock, Philip K.
  1974   *Modern Cultural Anthropology. An Introduction.* New York: Alfred A. Knopf.
Boone, Olga
  1936   *Les Xylophones du Congo Belge.* Annales du Musée du Congo Belge 3(3):69-144.
Bowdich, Thomas Edward
  1819   *Mission from Cape Coast Castle to Ashantee.* London: John Murray.
Brandel, Rose
  1959   "The African Hemiola Style." *Ethnomusicology* 3(3):106-17.
  1961   *The Music of Central Africa: An Ethnomusicological Study.* The Hague: Martinus Nijhoff.

Brandl, Rudolf Maria
    1969   *Märchenlieder aus dem Ituri-Wald. Die Lieder aus den Erzählungen der Waldneger und Pygmäen von der Kongo-Expedition.* P.DDr. Anton Vorbichler SVD in den Jahren 1958/59. Ph.D. Dissertation. Wien.
    1975   "Preislied auf 'Willi Naba' und 'Annemaria'." Anmerkungen zur Transkription. *Ethnologische Zeitschrift Zürich* (Festschrift W. Staude) 1:9-15.
Bregman, Albert S.
    1990   *Auditory Scene Analysis: The Perceptual Organization of Sound.* Cambridge: MIT Press.
Bregman, Albert S. & Jeffrey Campbell
    1971   "Primary Auditory Stream Segregation and Perception of Order in Rapid Sequences of Tones." *Journal of Experimental Psychology* 89(2):244-9.
Bright, William
    1963   "Language and Music: Areas for Cooperation." *Ethnomusicology* 7(1):26-32.
Brown, Ernest
    1983   "Drums on the Water: the Kuomboka Ceremony of the Lozi of Zambia." *African Musicology* 1(1):65-80.
Camp, Charles M. & Bruno Nettl
    1955   "The Musical Bow in Southern Africa." *Anthropos* 50:65-80.
Capello, H. & R. Ivens
    1881   *De Benguella ás terras de Iácca: Descripção de uma viagem na Africa Central e Occidental.* Expedição organisada nos anos de 1877 - 1880. 2 vols. Lisbon: Imprensa Nacional.
Carrington, John F.
    1949   *Talking Drums of Africa.* London: Carey Kingsgate Press.
Casati, Gaetano
    1891   *Zehn Jahre in Aequatoria und die Rückkehr mit Emin Pascha.* 2 vols. Bamberg: C. C. Buchner.
Cavazzi, Giovanni Antonio
    1687   *Istórica Descrizione dé 'Tré' Regni: Congo, Matamba et Angola.* Bologna: Giacomo Monti.
Cazeneuve, Jean
    1967   *L'Ethnologie.* Encyclopédie Larousse de poche. Paris: Librairie Larousse.
Chernoff, John Miller
    1979   *African Rhythm and African Sensibility: Aesthetics and Social Action in African Musical Idioms.* Chicago: University of Chicago Press.
Chilivumbo, Alifeyo B.
    1972   "Vimbuza or Mashawe: A Mystic Therapy." *African Music* 5(2):6-9.
Chinyeka, Kayombo ka
    1973   *Vihandyeka vya mana - Sayings of Wisdom.* Acta Ethnologica et Linguistica 30. Series Africana 8. Wien: E. Stiglmayr.
Chowning, John M.
    1991   "Music from Machines: Perceptual Fushion and Auditory Perspective - for Ligeti." *Hamburger Jahrbuch für Musikwissenschaft* 11 (Für Györgi Ligeti. Die Referate des Ligeti-Kongresses Hamburg 1988): 231-43.
Collins, John
    1985   *African Pop Roots.* Berkshire: W. Foulsham & Co. Ltd.
    1986   *E. T. Mensah. The King of Highlife.* London: Off the Record Press.
    1987   "Jazz Feedback to Africa." *American Music* 5(2):176-193.
    1989   "The Early History of West African Highlife Music." *Popular Music* 8(3):221-30.

Cooke, Peter
1970   "Ganda Xylophone Music: Another Approach." *African Music* 4(4):62-80.
1971   "Ludaya - A Transverse Flute from Eastern Uganda." *Yearbook of the International Folk Music Council* 3:79-90.
1991   "Report on Pitch Perception Experiment Carried out in Buganda and Busoga (Uganda) August 1990." Info of the *ICTM Study Group on Computer Aided Research,* 33:2-6.
1992   "Report on Pitch Perception Experiments Carried out in Buganda and Busoga (Uganda)." *African Music* 7(2):119-25.
Coplan, David
1978   "Go to My Town, Cape Coast! The Social History of Ghanaian Highlife." In *Eight Urban Musical Cultures: Tradition and Change.* Bruno Nettl, ed. Urbana: University of Illinois Press, 96-114.
1979-80   "Marabi Culture: Continuity and Transformation in African Music in Johannesburg, 1929 - 1940." *African Urban Studies:*49-75.
1982a   "The Emergence of an African Working-Class Culture." In *Industrialisation and Social Change in South Africa.* S. Marks & R. Rathbone, eds. London: Longman, 358-75.
1982b   "The Urbanisation of African Music: Some Theoretical Observations." *Popular Music* 2:112-29.
1985   *In Township Tonight! South Africa's Black City Music and Theatre.* Johannesburg: Ravan Press.
Corcoran, D. W. J.
1971   *Pattern Recognition.* Harmondsworth: Penguin.
Csikszentmihalyi, Mihalyi
1974   *Flow: Studies of Enjoyment.* Chicago: University of Chicago Press.
1990   *Flow: The Psychology of Optimal Experience.* New York: Harper and Row Press.
Csikszentmihalyi, Mihalyi & Isabella Selega (eds.)
1988   *Optimal Experience: Psychological Studies of Flow in Consciousness.* New York: Cambridge University Press.
Curtis, Natalie
1920   *Songs and Tales From the Dark Continent.* New York: Schirmer.
Czurda, Margarete
1953   "Beziehungen zwischen Lautcharakter und Sinneseindrücken." *Wiener Archiv für Psychologe, Psychiatrie und Neurologie* 3:73-84.
Dampierre, Éric de
1963   *Poètes Nzakara.* Classiques Africain. Institut d'Ethnologie. Université de Paris, Julliard. Paris: Dampierre and Institut d'Ethnologie.
1982   "Sons aînés, sons cadets: Les sanza d'Ebézagui." *Revue de Musicologie* 68(1-2):325-9.
1991   *Harpes Zandé.* Domaine musicologique. Paris: Klincksieck.
Dampierre, Éric de (ed.)
1994   *Harpes et harpistes du Haut-Oubangui.* Ateliers 14. Mission sociologique du Haut-Oubangui. Laboratoire d'ethnologie et de sociologie comparative. Société d'ethnologie. Université de Paris X. Nanterre: Labethno.
Dark, Philip & Matthew Hill
1972   "Musical Instruments on Benin Plaques." In *Essays on Music and History in Africa.* Klaus Wachsmann, ed. Evanston: Northwestern University Press, 67-78.

Dargie, David
  1988   *Xhosa Music. Its Techniques and Instruments, with a Collection of Songs.* Cape
          Town & Johannesburg: David Philip.
  1991   "Umngqokolo: Xhosa Overtone Singing and the Song Nondel'ekhaya." *African Music* 7(1):33-47.
Darkwa, Asante
  1980   "New Horizons in Music and Worship in Ghana." *African Urban Studies* 8:63-70.
  1982   "The Marakwets and Keiyo in Music: A Socio-Cultural Study." *Black Perspective in Music* 10(2):149-66.
Dauer, Alfons M.
  1955   "Grundlagen und Entwicklung des Jazz." *Jazz Podium* 4:7-8; 5:5-6; 6:7; 7:7 and 10; 9:7-8; 10:11-2.
  1958   *Der Jazz. Seine Ursprünge und seine Entwicklung.* Eisenach, Kassel: Erich Röth.
  1966a   "Afrikanische Musik und völkerkundlicher Tonfilm. Ein Beitrag zur Methodik der Transkription." *Research Film* 5(5):439-56. Reprinted 1983 in *Musik in Afrika. 20 Beiträge zur Kenntnis traditioneller afrikanischer Musikkulturen.* Artur Simon, ed. Veröffentlichungen des Museums für Völkerkunde Berlin. Neue Folge 40. Abteilung Musikethnologie IV. Berlin: Staatliche Museen Preußischer Kulturbesitz, 129-201.
  1966b   "Musik-Landschaften in Afrika." *Afrika heute*, Sonderbeilage 23.
  1967a   "Lieder der Gonja. Musik- und Textanalyse. Nebst einigen methodischen Bemerkungen." *Zeitschrift für Ethnologie* 92(2):200-38.
  1967b   "Stil und Technik im afrikanischen Tanz. Betrachtungen zu den Weltfestspielen afrikanischer Kunst in Dakar 1966." *Afrika heute*, Sonderbeilage 24. Reprinted 1983 in *Musik in Afrika. 20 Beiträge zur Kenntnis traditioneller afrikanischer Musikkulturen.* Artur Simon, ed. Veröffentlichungen des Museums für Völkerkunde Berlin. Neue Folge 40, Abteilung Musikethnologie IV. Berlin: Staatliche Museen Preußischer Kulturbesitz, 217-33.
  1969a   "Kinesis und Katharsis. Prologemena zur Deutung afrikanischer Rhythmik." *Afrika heute* 20 (Sonderbeilage): 1-12.
  1969b   "Zum Bewegungsverhalten afrikanischer Tänzer." *Research Film* 6(6):517-26. Reprinted 1983 in *Musik in Afrika. 20 Beiträge zur Kenntnis traditioneller afrikanischer Musikkulturen.* Artur Simon, ed. Veröffentlichungen des Museums für Völkerkunde. Neue Folge 40, Abteilung Musikethnologie IV. Berlin: Staatliche Museen Preußischer Kulturbesitz, 234-8.
  1969c   "Research Film in Ethnomusicology - Aims and Achievements." *Yearbook of the International Folk Music Council* 1:226-33.
  1985   *Tradition afrikanischer Blasorchester und Entstehung des Jazz.* Graz: Akademische Druck- und Verlagsanstalt.
  1988a   "Derler 1: Ein System zur Klassifikation von Rhythmen. Musiktheoretische und musikhistorische Aspekte." *Jazzforschung - Jazz Research* 20:117-54.
  1988b   "Gibt es einen Weltrhythmus?" *Österreichische Musikzeitschrift* 7-8:390-4.
Dauer, Alfons M.; Bauch, G.; Goemann, C. & C. Otte
  1969   "Synchrone Dokumentations-Tonfilmaufnahmen auf Expeditionen durch Kameramannschaften in Zusammenarbeit mit völkerkundlichen Fachwissenschaftlern." *Research Film* 6(5):396-411.
Davidson, Basil
  1967   *African Kingdoms.* London: Time-Life.

Davidson, Marjory
1970   "Some Music for the Lala *kankobele*." *African Music* 4(4):103-13.
1973/4 "Some Patterns of Rhythm and Harmony in Kalumbu Music." *African Music* 5(3):70-6.
DeVale, Sue Carole
1984   "Prolegomena to a Study of Harp and Voice Sounds in Uganda: A Graphic System for the Notation of Texture." *Selected Reports in Ethnomusicology* 5:284-315.
Dias, Margot
1966   "Os instrumentos musicais de Moçambique." *Geographica* 2(6):2-17.
1986   *Os instrumentos musicais de Moçambique*. Instituto de Investigação Cientifica Tropical. Lisbon: Centro de Antropologia Cultural.
Djedje, Jacqueline Cogdell
1982   "The Concept of Patronage: An Examination of Hausa and Dagomba One-String Fiddle Traditions." *Journal of African Studies* 9(3):116-27.
1984   "The Interplay of Melodic Phrases: An Analysis of Dagomba and Hausa One-String Fiddle Music." *Selected Reports in Ethnomusicology* 5:81-118.
Djedje, Jacqueline Cogdell & William G. Carter (eds.)
1989   *African Musicology: Current Trends. A Festschrift presented to J. H. Kwabena Nketia*. Vols. 1 and 2. Los Angeles: University of California Crossroads Press.
Djenda, Maurice
1966/7 "Les anciennes danses des Mpyèmò." *African Music* 4(1):40-6.
1968a   "Ein Todesfall - Todeszeremonien und Divination der Mpyemo." *Afrika heute* 7:104-7.
1968b   "L'arc-en-terre des Gbaya-Bokoto." *African Music* 4(2):44-6.
1968c   "Les pygmées de la Haute Sangha." *Geographica* 4(14):26-43.
1968d   "Moderne Musik in Malawi: Stile, Instrumente und Musiker." *Afrika heute* 15:217-8.
1969   "Die Musik der Asena. Ergebnisse meiner Musikstudien in Malawi." *Afrika heute* 3:37-9.
1992-93 "De la disparition des éléments culturels chez les Mpyemõ — Observations participantes." *Bulletin of the International Committee on Urgent Anthropological and Ethnological Research* 34-35:149-60.
Djenda, Maurice & Gerhard Kubik
1969   *Instruments de Musique Mpyɛmõ. Organologie, nomenclature et techniques d'execution*. Unpublished manuscript.
1971   "Traditions orales littéraires Mpyɛmɔ̃, recueillies en République Centrafricaine et au Cameroun, 1964 - 1969." *Bulletin of the International Committee on Urgent Anthropological and Ethnological Research* 13:13-55.
Donner, Philip
1983   "The Frame of Reference of Music - Two Realities." *Suomen Antropologi* 4:184-97.
Donner, Philip (ed.)
1984   "Nipe nikupe - perustietoa Tansanian musiikista ja kulttuurista." *Musiikin Suunta* 3:3-59.
Dorson, Richard M. (ed.)
1972   *African Folklore*. New York: Anchor Books, Doubleday.
Dowling, W. Jay
1973   "The Perception of Interleaved Melodies." *Cognitive Psychology* 5:322-37.

Drever, James
[13] 1972   *A Dictionary of Psychology.* Harmondsworth: Penguin Reference Books. First edition: 1952.
Duerden, Dennis
1974   *African Art. An Introduction.* London: Hamlyn.
Duran, Lucy
1989   "Key to N'dour: The Roots of the Senegalese Star." *Popular Music* 8(3) October:275-84.
Ehrenfels, Christian von
1890   "Über Gestaltsqualitäten." *Vierteljahresschrift zur wissenschaftlichen Philosophie* 114(3):249-92.
Ehret, Bethwell A.
1974   *Ethiopians and East Africans. The Problem of Contacts.* Nairobi Historical Studies 3. Nairobi: East African Publishing House.
Ehret, Christopher
1981   "Languages and Peoples." In *Cultural Atlas of Africa.* Jocelyn Murray, ed. Oxford: Elsevier Publishers, Phaidon Press, 24-30.
Ekman, Paul
1976   "Movements with Precise Meanings." *Journal of Communication* 26(3):14-26.
Ekman, Paul & Wallace V. Friesen
1969   "The Repertoire of Nonverbal Behaviour: Categories, Origins, Usage and Coding." *Semiotica* 1(1):49-98.
Ekwueme, Laz E. N.
1973/4   "African Music in Christian Liturgy: the Igbo Experiment." *African Music* 5(3):12-33.
1975/6   "Structural Levels of Rhythm and Form in African Music - with Particular Reference to the West Coast." *African Music* 5(4):27-35.
1980   "Analysis and Analytic Techniques in African Music. A Theory of Melodic Scales." *African Music* 6(1):89-106.
Elliott, Jorge
1979   "The Relationship Between Painting and Scripts." In *The Visual Arts. Plastic and Graphic.* Justine M. Cordwell, ed. The Hague: Mouton, 609-30.
England, Nicholas
1964   "Symposium on Transcription and Analysis. A Hukwe Song with Musical Bow." *Ethnomusicology* 8(3):223-77.
1967   "Bushman Counterpoint." *Journal of the International Folk Music Council* 19:58-66.
Eno-Belinga, Martin Samuel
1966   *Littérature et musique populaire en Afrique Noire.* Ouvrage couronné au 1er Festival Mondial des Arts Nègres. Paris: Cujas.
1969   "Musique traditionelle et musique moderne au Cameroun." *Bulletin of the International Committee on Urgent Anthropological and Ethnological Research* 11:83-90.
1970   *Découverte des chantefables Beti - Bulu - Fang du Cameroun.* Collection: Langues et littératures de l'Afrique Noire VII. Paris: Klincksieck.
1977   "Relations géométriques entre la tradition orale africaine et l'audiovisuel." *Communication au Coll. "Audiovisuel et Choc des Cultures," 23-26 Février 1977.* L'Institut National de l'Audiovisuel. Manuscript.
1979   "L'épopée camerounaise - Le Mvet." *Abbia* (Yaoundé) 34-37:176-213.

Erlmann, Veit
1983 "Notes on Musical Instruments Among the Fulani of Diamare (North Cameroon)." *African Music* 6(3):16-41.
1985 "Black Political Song in South Africa — Some Research Perspectives." *Popular Music Perspectives* 2:187-209.
1989a "A Conversation with Joseph Shabalala of Ladysmith Black Mambazo. Aspects of African Performers' Life Stories." *The World of Music* 31(1):31-58.
1989b "'Horses in the Race Course': The Domestication of Ingoma Dancing in South Africa 1929-39." *Popular Music* 8(3):259-73.
1990 "Migration and Performance: Zulu Migrant Workers' *isicathamiya* Performance in South Africa, 1890-1950." *Ethnomusicology* 34(2) Spring-Summer:199-220.
1991 *African Stars: Studies in Black South African Performance.* Chicago Studies in Ethnomusicology. Chicago: University of Chicago Press.
Erlmann, Veit (ed.)
1991 *Populäre Musik in Afrika.* Veröffentlichungen des Museums für Völkerkunde Berlin. Neue Folge 53, Abteilung Musikethnologie VIII. Berlin: Staatliche Museen Preußischer Kulturbesitz.
Ervedosa, Carlos
1980 *Arqueologia angolana.* Luanda: Ministério da Educação.
Euba, Akin
1967 "Multiple Pitch Lines in Yoruba Choral Music." *Journal of the International Folk Music Council* 19:66-71.
1970a "Music Adapts to a Changed World." *Africa Report* 15(8):24-7.
1970b "New Idioms of Music Drama Among the Yoruba: An Introductory Study." *Yearbook of the International Folk Music Council* 2:92-107.
1971 "Islamic Musical Culture Among the Yoruba: A Preliminary Survey." In *Essays on Music and History in Africa.* Klaus Wachsmann, ed. Evanston: Northwestern University Press, 171-81.
1972 "Creative Potential and Propagation of African Traditional Music." In *African Music Meeting in Yaounde (Cameroon), 23-27 February 1970 organized by UNESCO, Paris.* UNESCO: La Revue Musicale, 119-25.
1974 *Dùndún Music of the Yorùbá.* Unpublished Ph.D. dissertation. University of Ghana.
1977 "Ìlù Èṣù (Drumming for Èṣù): Analysis of a Dùndún Performance." In *Essays for a Humanist. An Offering to Klaus Wachsmann.* New York: The Town House Press, 121-45.
1988a "Der afrikanische Komponist in Europa. Die Herausforderung des Bi-Kulturalismus". *Österreichische Musikzeitschrift* 7-8:404-7.
1988b *Essays on Music in Africa.* Bayreuth: IWALEWA-Haus.
1990 *Yoruba drumming: The Dùndún Tradition.* Bayreuth African Studies. Bayreuth: E. Breitinger, Bayreuth University.
Evans, David
1970 "Afro-American One-Stringed Instruments." *Western Folklore* 29(4):229-45.
1976 "Review of Gerhard Kubik: The Kachamba Brothers' Band ..." *Jazzforschung - Jazz Research* 8:235-6.
1978a "Field Work with Blues Singers: The Unitentionally Induced Natural Context." *Southern Folklore Quarterly* 42:9-16.
1978b "Structure and Meaning in the Folk Blues." In: *The Study of American Folklore.* Jan Harold Brunvand, ed. New York: W. W. Norton, 421-47.

1981   "Black American Music as a Symbol of Identity." *Jazz Research* 13:105-16.
Evans-Pritchard, Edward Evan
    1928   "The Dance (Azande)." *Africa* 4(1):464-2.
    1932   "The Zande Corporation of Witch-Doctors." *Journal of the Royal Anthropological Institute* 62:302, 315, 317-20.
    1962-65 "Some Zande Texts." *Kush* 10:289-314; 11:273-301; 12:251-81; 13:213-40.
Fagunwa, Daniel Orùwolé
    1949a   *Igbó Olódùmarè*. Edinburgh: Thomas Nelson and Sons.
    1949b   *Irèké Oníbùdó*. Edinburgh: Thomas Nelson and Sons.
Feld, Steven
    1984   "Sound Structure as Social Structure." *Ethnomusicology* 28(3):383-409.
Ferreira, António Rita
    1968   "The Nyau Brotherhood Among the Mozambique Cewa." *South African Journal of Sciences* 64:20-4.
Fiagbedzi, Nissio
    1977   *The Music of the Anlo-Ewe: Its Historical Background, Cultural Matrix and Style*. Ph.D. dissertation. Los Angeles: U. C. L. A.
    1980a   "A Preliminary Inquiry into Inherent Rhythms in Anlo Dance Drumming." *Journal of the Performing Arts (Legon)* 1(1):83-92. School of Performing Arts, Legon, Accra.
    1980b   "On Signing and Symbolism in Music. The Evidence from among an African People." *Journal of Performing Arts* 1(1).
Födermayr, Franz
    1966/7   "The Arabian Influence in the Tuareg Music." *African Music* 4(1):25-37.
    1969   "Lieder der Bäle-Bilia." *Mitteilungen der Anthropologischen Gesellschaft in Wien* 99:64-76, Plates I-IX.
    1970   "Zur Ololyge in Afrika." In *Musik als Gestalt und Erlebnis*. Festschrift Walter Graf zum 65. Geburtstag. E. Schenk, ed. Wien: Hermann Böhlaus Nachf., 57-65.
    1971   *Zur gesanglichen Stimmgebung in der außereuropäischen Musik. Ein Beitrag zur Methodik der vergleichenden Musikwissenschaft*. E. Stiglmayr, ed. Acta Ethnologica et Linguistica 24, Series Musicologia 1. Wien: Stiglmayr.
Fortune, George
    1962   *Ideophones in Shona*. London: Oxford University Press.
Frake, Charles O.
    1963   "The Ethnographic Study of Cognitive Systems." In *Anthropology and Human Behaviour*. T. Gladwin & W. C. Sturtevant, eds. Washington: Anthropological Society, 72-85, 91-3.
França, J. Camarate
    1953   "As gravuras rupestres do Tchitundo-hulo (Deserto de Moçâmedes)." *Mensário Administrativo* [Luanda] 65/66:5-44, additional pages with 20 tables.
Freud, Sigmund
    1955   *The Psychological Works of Sigmund Freud*. Standard Edition. London: Hogarth Press.
Froger, François
    1698   *Relations d'un voyage fait en 1695 - 1697 aux côtes d'Afrique*. Paris: Nic Le Gros.
Gansemans, Jos
    1973/4   "Recherche ethnomusicologique au Rwanda." *African Music* 5(3):65-9.
    1978   *La musique et son rôle dans la vie sociale et rituelle Luba*. Tervuren: Musée Royal de l'Afrique Centrale.

1980   *Les instruments de musique Luba (Shaba, Zaire).* Tervuren: Musée Royal de
        l'Afrique Centrale.
1988   *Les instruments de musique du Rwanda: étude ethnomusicologique.* Symbolae
        Facultatis Litterarum et Philosophiae Lovaniensis, Series A, Vol. 16.
        Louvain, Belgium: Leuven University Press.
Gansemans, Jos & Barbara Schmidt-Wrenger
1986   *Musikgeschichte in Bildern: Zentralafrika.* Bd. 1, Lieferung 12. Leipzig:
        Deutscher Verlag für Musik.
Garfias, Robert
1979-80 "The Role of Dreams and Spirit Possession in the Mbira Dza Vadzimu Music
        of the Shona People of Zimbabwe." *Journal of Altered States of Consciousness*
        5(3):211-34.
1983   "The Marimba of Mexico and Central America." *Latin American Music Re-
        view* 4(2) Fall/Winter:203-28.
Gavazzi, Milovan
1969   "Zur dringenden ethnographischen Filmdokumentation." *Bulletin of the In-
        ternational Committee on Urgent Anthropological and Ethnological Research*
        11:127-31.
Gbadamosi, Bakare & Ulli Beier
1959   *Yoruba Poetry.* Ibadan: General Publications Section, Ministry of Education.
Giorgetti, Filiberto
1951   *Note de musica Zande. Con trascrizioni musicali di uccelli, tainburi, xilòfoni e
        canti Zande.* Museum Combonianum No. 5. Verona: Missioni Africane.
1957   *Musica Africana. Sua tècnica e acùstica.* Museum Combonianum 10. Bologna:
        Editrice Nigrizia.
1965   "Zande Harp Music. Observations on 'Harp Music of the Azande and Related
        Peoples in the Central African Republic' by Gerhard Kubik (African Music
        3(3))." *African Music* 3(4):74-6.
Goodenough, Ward H.
1957   "Cultural Anthropology and Linguistics." In *Report on the Seventh Annual
        Round Table Meeting on Linguistics and Language Study.* Paul Garvin, ed.
        Georgetown: Georgetown University.
Gore, E. C.
1926   *A Zande Grammar.* London: The Sheldon Press.
Gottlieb, Robert
1986   "Musical Scales of the Sudan as Found Among the Gumuz, Berta, and
        Ingessana Peoples." *The World of Music* 28(2):56-76.
Gourlay, Ken A.
1982   "Long Trumpets in Northern Nigeria - in History and Today." *African Music*
        6(2):48-72.
Graf, Walter
1969   "Zum Faktor des Schöpferischen in der Musik der schriftlosen Völker".
        Mitteilungen der Anthropologischen Gesellschaft in Wien 99:53-63.
1980   *Vergleichende Musikwissenschaft. Ausgewählte Aufsätze.* Franz Födermayr, ed.
        Acta Ethnologica et Linguistica 50. Wien: E. Stiglmayr.
Greenberg, Joseph H.
1966   *The Languages of Africa.* Research Center for the Language Sciences, Indiana
        University. Bloomington: Indiana University Press.
Grimaud, Yvette
1956   "Note sur la musique vocale des Bochiman !Kung' et des pygmées Babinga."
        Colloques de Wégimont 13:105-26.

Günther, Helmut
    1969   *Grundphänomene und Grundbegriffe des afrikanischen und afro-amerikanischen Tanzes*. Beiträge zur Jazzforschung/Studies in Jazz Research 1. Graz: Universal Edition.

Günther, Robert
    1964   *Musik in Rwanda*. Serie IN-80, Sciences Humaines 50. Tervuren: Musée Royal de l'Afrique Centrale.

Guthrie, Malcolm
    1948   *The Classification of the Bantu Languages*. London: Oxford University Press.

Gwenge, John
    1965   *Kukula ndi Mwambo*. Limbe: Malawi Publications and Literature Bureau.

Haller, Sabine & Manfred Kremser
    1975   "Danse et thérapeutique chez les Azande." *Bulletin of the International Committee on Urgent Anthropological and Ethnological Research* 17:65-78.

Hamelberger, E.
    1951   "Ecrit sur le sable." *Annales Spiritaines* 61:123-6.
    1952   "A escrita na areia." *Portugal em Africa* 9:323-30.

Hampton, Barbara L.
    1978   "The Contiguity Factor in Ga Music." *The Black Perspective in Music* 6(1): 32-48.
    1979/80   "A Revised Analytical Approach to Musical Processes in Urban Africa." *African Urban Studies* 6:1-16.
    1982   "Music and Ritual Symbolism in the Ga Funeral." *Yearbook for Traditional Music* 14:75-105.

Hansen, Deidre Doris
    1981   *The Music of the Xhosa Speaking People*. Ph.D. dissertation. Faculty of Arts. University of Witwatersrand.

Hartel, Uwe
    1969   *Laut und Sinn in der Sprache der Suaheli*. Ph.D. dissertation. University of Vienna.

Heise, George A. & George A. Miller
    1951   "An Experimental Study of Auditory Patterns." *American Journal of Psychology* 64(1):68-77.

Herskovits, Melville J.
    1938a   *Acculturation. The Study of Culture Contact*. New York: J. J. Augustin.
    1938b   *Dahomey*. 2 vols. New York: J. J. Augustin.
    1941   *The Myth of the Negro Past*. New York: Harper and Brothers.
    1948   *Man and His Works*. New York: Alfred Knopf.
    1972   "Cultural Relativism and Cultural Values." In Melville J. Herskovits, *Cultural Relativism. Perspectives in Cultural Pluralism*. Frances Herskovits, ed. New York: Random House.

Herzog, George
    1949   "Canon in West African Xylophone Melodies." *Journal of the American Musicological Society* 2(3):196-7.

Hodder, Ian
    1989   *The Meaning of Things. Material Culture and Symbolic Expression*. One World Archaeology. London: Unwin Hyman.

Hood, Mantle
    1960   "The Challenge of 'Bi-Musicality'." *Ethnomusicology* 4(2):55-9.
    1966   "Sléndro and Pelog Redefined." *Selected Reports* 1(1):28-48.
    1971   *The Ethnomusicologist*. New York: McGraw Hill.

Hornbostel, Erich Moritz von
1911   "Über ein akustisches Kriterium für Kulturzusammenhänge." *Zeitschrift für Ethnologie* 43:601-15.
1928   "African Negro Music." *Africa* 1(1):30-62.
Horton, A. E.
1949   *A Grammar of Luvale*. Bantu Grammatical Archives, ed. by C. M. Doke. Johannesburg: Witwatersrand University Press.
Husmann, Heinrich
1936   "Marimba und Sansa der Sambesikultur." *Zeitschrift für Ethnologie* 68(1-3):197-210.
Hussein, Ebrahim
1980   "Traditional African Theatre." In *The East African Experience. Essays on English and Swahili Literature*. 2nd Jahnheinz-Jahn-Symposium. Ulla Schild, ed. Mainzer Afrika Studien. Berlin: Dietrich Reimer, 35-53.
Instituto Nacional de Línguas
1980   *Histórico sobre a criação dos alfabetos em línguas nacionais*. MPLA/Partido do Trabalho. Luanda: Departamento de Investigação Científica Aplicada.
Jackson, Irene V. (ed.)
1985a   *More than Dancing: Essays on Afro-American Music and Musicians*. Westport, CT: Greenwood Press.
1985b   *More than Drumming: Essays of African and Afro-Latin Music and Musicians*. Westport, CT: Greenwood Press.
Jeffreys, M. D. W.
1961   "Negro Influences in Indonesia." *African Music* 2(4):10-6.
Jaritz, W.
1983   *Über Bahnen auf Billardtischen oder: Eine mathematische Untersuchung von Ideogrammen angolanischer Herkunft*. Mathematisch-Statistische Sektion, Bericht Nr.207. Graz: Research Centre.
Johnson, Frederick (ed.)
⁶1955   *A Standard Swahili - English Dictionary* (founded on Madan's Swahili - English Dictionary). Ed. by the Inter-Territorial Language Committee for the East African Dependencies, under the direction of the Late Frederick Johnson. Oxford University Press. London: Geoffrey Cumberlege. First edition 1939.
Johnston, Sir Harry H.
1904   *The Uganda Protectorate*. 2 vols. London: Hutchinson & Co.
Johnston, Thomas F.
1970   "Xizambi Friction-Bow Music of the Shangana-Tsonga." *African Music* 4(4):81-95.
1971   "Shangana-Tsonga Drum and Bow Rhythms." *African Music* 5(1):59-72.
1973/4 "Mohambi Xylophone Music of the Shangana-Tsonga." *African Music* 5(3):86-93.
1987   "Children's Music of the Shangana-Tsonga." *African Music* 6(4):126-43.
Jones, Arthur M.
1934   "African Drumming - A Study of the Combination of Rhythms in African Music." *Bantu Studies* 8(1):1-16.
1937   "The Study of African Musical Rhythm." *Bantu Studies* 11:295-316.
1945   "African Music: The Mganda Dance." *African Studies* 4(4):180-8.
1949   *African Music in Northern Rhodesia and Some Other Places*. The Occasional Papers of the Rhodes Livingstone Museum 4. Manchester: Manchester University Press.

1950   "The Kalimba of the Lala Tribe, N. Rhodesia." *Africa* 20:324-34.
1951   "Blue Notes and Hot Rhythm. Some Notes on Africanisms in Jazz, Both Melodic and Rhythmic." *African Music Society Newsletter* 1(4):9-12.
1954a   "African Rhythm." *Africa* 24(1):26-47.
1954b   "East and West, North and South - the Homogeneity of African Music South of the Sahara." *African Music* 1(1):57-62.
1956   "A Simple Tonometer." *Nature* 177:242.
1958   "On Transcribing African Music." *African Music* 2(1):11-4.
1959a   "Indonesia and Africa: The Xylophone as a Culture Indicator." *Journal of the Royal Anthropological Institute* 89(2):155-68.
1959b   *Studies in African Music.* 2 vols. London: Oxford University Press.
1962   "Venda Note Names." *African Music* 3(1):49-53.
1963   "Experiment with a Xylophone Key." *African Music* 3(2):6-10.
1964   "African Metrical Lyrics." *African Music* 3(3):6-14.
1970   "On Using the Stroboconn." *African Music* 4(4):122-3.
1971a   "Africa and Indonesia: an Ancient Colonial Era." In *Essays on Music and History in Africa and Asia.* K. P. Wachsmann, ed. Evanston: Northwestern University Press, 81-92.
1971b   *Africa and Indonesia. The Evidence of the Xylophone and Other Musical and Cultural Factors.* Leiden: E. J. Brill.
1972   "Elephantiasis and Music." *African Music* 5(2):46-9.
1973/4a Letters to the Editor. *African Music* 5(3):96-7.
1973/4b "Luo Music and its Rhythm." *African Music* 5(3):43-54.
1974   "The Singing of a Swahili Epic." *Review of Ethnology* 4(3):17-32.
1975/6 "Swahili Epic Poetry: a Musical Study." *African Music* 5(4):105-29.
1976   *African Hymnody in Christian Worship. A History of the Development of African Music in Christian Worship.* Gwelo: Mambo Press.
1978a   "Review of 'Les mendzaŋ des Chanteurs de Yaoundé' by Pie-Claude Ngumu." *Review of Ethnology* 5(2-3):23-4.
1978b   "'Stretched Octaves' in XylophonenTuning." *Review of Ethnology* 6(16):121-4.
1978c   "Unusual Music for a Swahili Epic." *Afrika und Übersee* 60(4):295-309.
1980   "Panpipes and Equiheptatonic Pitch." *African Music* 6(1):62-9.
Jones, Arthur M. & L. Kombe
1952   *The Icila Dance, Old Style. A Study in African Music and Dance of the Lala Tribe of Northern Rhodesia.* Roodepoort: African Music Society.
Joseph, Rosemary
1983   "Zulu Women's Music." *African Music* 6(3):53-87.
Jung, Carl Gustav
1950   *Gestaltungen des Unbewußten.* Psychologische Abhandlungen 7. Zürich: Rascher Verlag.
1974   *Man and his Symbols.* London: Jupiter Books.
Junker, Wilhelm
1890-2 *Travels in Africa 1875-1886.* 3 vols. London: Chapman Hall.
Kaduma, G. Z.
1972   *A Theatrical Description of Five Tanzanian Dances.* Dar es Salaam. Unpublished manuscript.
Kaggwa, Sir Apolo
1901   *Basekabaka be Buganda.* (2nd ed., 1912; 3rd ed., 1927. Reprinted 1953, 1971.) Kampala: Uganda Bookshop. Translated by M. S. M. Kiwanuka under the title *The Kings of Buganda.* Nairobi: East African Publishing House.

1905   *Ekitabo kye empisa za Baganda*. Kampala. Reprint 1934, London: Sheldon Press.
1908   *Ekitabo ky'ebika bya Baganda*. Mengo: Uganda Bookshop and Uganda Society.
1912   *Ekitabo kya basekabaka be Buganda*. 2nd edition London: Luzac & Co.

Kakoma, George W.
1972   "Musical Traditions of East Africa." In: African Music Meeting in Yaounde (Cameroon), 23-27 February 1970, organized by UNESCO. Paris: La Revue Musicale, 77-88.

Kamwendo, Frank & Mike Kamwendo
1987   "Daniel James Kachamba. The Giant Lives On." *Quest* 3(3):34-7.

Kashoki, Mubanga E.
1972   "The Socio-Cultural Setting of Verbal Play: A Description of Some Riddles among the Bemba." *Review of Ethnology* 3(15):113-9.

Katamba, Francis & Peter Cooke
1987   "Ssematimba ne Kikwabanga: The Music and Poetry of a Ganda Historical Song." *The World of Music* 29(2):49-68.

Kauffman, Robert
1969   "Some Aspects of Aesthetics in the Shona Music of Rhodesia." *Ethnomusicology* 13(3):507-11.
1970   *Multi-Part Relationships in the Shona Music of Rhodesia*. Ph.D. dissertation. University of California, Los Angeles.
1972   "Shona Urban Music and the Problem of Acculturation." *Yearbook of the International Folk Music Council* 4:47-56.
1979   "Tactility as an Aesthetic Consideration in African Music." In *The Performing Arts*. J. Blacking & J. W. Kealiinohomoku, eds. The Hague: Mouton, 251-3.
1979-80   "Tradition and Innovation in the Urban Music of Zimbabwe." *African Urban Studies* 6:41-8.
1980   "African Rhythm: a Reassessment." *Ethnomusicology* 24(3):393-415.
1984   "Multipart Relationships in Shona Vocal Music." In *Studies in African Music. Selected Reports in Ethnomusicology* 5. J. H. Kwabena Nketia & Jacqueline D. Djedje, eds. Los Angeles: Program in Ethnomusicology, University of California, 145-59.

Kavyu, Paul
1978   "Some Kamba Dance Songs." *Review of Ethnology* 5(5-7):33-49.
1986   *Drum Music of Akamba*. Studien zur Musik Afrikas 2. Hohenschäftlarn: Klaus Renner.

Kazadi wa Mukuna
1971   "Congo Music: Africa's Favorite Beat." *Africa Report* 16(4):25-7.
1973   "Trends in Nineteenth and Twentieth Century Music in the Congo-Zaire." In *Musikkulturen Asiens, Afrikas und Ozeaniens im 19. Jahrhundert*. Robert Günther, ed. Regensburg: Gustav Bosse, 267-84.
1976   O contacto musical transatlântico: Contribuição Bantu na música popular brasileira. Ph.D. dissertation. University of São Paulo.
1979   "The Origin of Zairean Modern Music: A Socio-Economic Aspect." *African Urban Studies* 6:31-9.
1992   "The Genesis of Urban Music in Zaïre." African Music 7(2):72-84.

Kebede, Ashenafi
1979-80   "Musical Innovation and Acculturation in Ethiopian Culture." *African Urban Studies* 6:77-88.
1982   *Roots of Black Music. The Vocal, Instrumental and Dance Heritage of Africa and Black America*. New Jersey: Prentice Hall Inc.

Keil, Charles
1979   *Tiv Song. The Sociology of Art in a Classless Society.* Chicago: The University of Chicago Press.
King, Anthony
1960   "Employment of the 'Standard Pattern' in Yoruba Music." *African Music* 2(3):51-4.
1961   *Yoruba Sacred Music from Ekiti.* Ibadan: Ibadan University Press.
1972   "The Construction and Tuning of the *Kora.*" *African Language Studies* 13:113-36.
Kirby, Percival Robson
1926   "Some Problems of Primitive Harmony and Polyphony with Special Reference to Bantu Practice." *South African Journal of Science* 23:951-70.
1930   "A Study of Negro Harmony." *Musical Quarterly* 16(4):404-14.
1932   "The Recognition and Practical Use of the Harmonics of Stretched Strings by the Bantu of South Africa." *Bantu Studies* 6(1):30-46.
1933   "The Reed-Flute Ensembles of South Africa." *Journal of the Royal Anthropological Institute* 63:313-88.
1934   *The Musical Instruments of the Native Races of South Africa.* London: Oxford University Press. (2nd ed. 1965, Johannesburg: Witwatersrand University Press.)
1936   "The Musical Practices of the /?Auni and ≠Khomani Bushmen." *Bantu Studies* 10(4):373-431.
1961   "Physical Phenomena Which Appear to Have Determined the Bases and Development of an Harmonic Sense Among Bushmen, Hottentot and Bantu." *African Music* 2(4):6-9.
Kishilo w'Itunga
1976   "Structure des chansons des Lega de Mwenga." *Revue Zaïroise des Arts* 1:7-22.
1987   "Une analyse de la 'Messe Katangaise' de Joseph Kiwele." *African Music* 6(4):108-25.
1989   *Musiques des Balega du Kivu. Contribution à l'étude de la variabilité des fonctions et des structures des "nyimbo" traditionels du Zaïre.* Ph.D. dissertation. Louvain la Neuve: Université Catholique de Louvain.
Kiwanuka, M. S. M.
1971   *The Kings of Buganda, by Sir Apolo Kaggwa.* Historical Texts of Eastern and Central Africa I. Nairobi: East African Publishing House.
Kiwanuka, Semakula
1971   *The History of Buganda. From the Foundation of the Kingdom to 1900.* London: Longman.
Klein, Christopher
1990   *Messekompositionen in Afrika. Ein Beitrag zur Geschichte und Typologie der katholischen Kirchenmusik Afrikas.* Arbeiten aus dem Mainzer Institut für Ethnologie und Afrika-Studien 3. Göttingen: Edition Re.
Knappert, Jan
1971   *Swahili Islamic Poetry.* 3 vols. Leiden: Brill.
Knight, Roderic
1971   "Towards a Notation and Tablature for the Kora, and its Application to Other Instruments." *African Music* 5(1): 23-36.
1972   Letters to the Editor. *African Music* 5(2):112-3.
1974   "Mandinka Drumming." *African Music* 7(4):24-35.
1982   "Manding/Fula Relations - as Reflected in the Manding Song Repertoire." *African Music* 6(2):37-47.

1991   *Vibrato Octaves: Tunings and Modes of the Made Balo and Kora.* Baltimore: SEMPOD Laboratory, Department of Music, University of Maryland, Baltimore County.

Knoll, M.; Kugler, J.; Höfer, O. & S. D. Lawder
1963   "Effects of Chemical Stimulation of Electrically Induced Phosphenes on Their Band-Width Shape, Number and Intensity." *Confina Neurologica* 23:201-26.

Koetting, James
1970   "Analysis and Notation of West African Drum Ensemble Music." *Selected Reports* 1(3):115-46.
1979/80   "The Organization and Functioning of Migrant Kasena Flute and Drum Ensembles in Nima/Accra." *African Urban Studies* 6:17-30.
1985   "Assessing Meter in Kasena Jongo." *Sonus* 5(2): 11-9.
1986   "What Do We Know about African Rhythm?" *Ethnomusicology* 30(1):58-63.

Koffka, Kurt
1935   *Principles of Gestalt Psychology.* London: K. Paul, Trench, Trubner and Co. New York: Harcourt, Brace & Company.

Kolb, Peter
1719   *Caput Bonae Spei Hodiernum: das ist, Vollständige Beschreibung des africanischen Vorgebürges der Guten Hoffnung.* Nuremberg: Peter Conrad Monath.

Kolinski, Mieczyslaw
n.d.   *Die Musik Westafrikas.* Unpublished manuscript. (Deposited in the Department of Anthropology, Northwestern University, Evanston.)
1973   "A Cross-Cultural Approach to Metro-Rhythmic Patterns." *Ethnomusicology* 17(3):494-506.

Koma-Koma, W. P.
1965   *M'ganda kapena Malipenga.* Limbe: Malawi Publications and Literature Bureau.

Koolwijk, Martinho van
1964a   "Entre os Ganguelas. I. Circuncisão dos Rapazes." *Portugal em Africa* 20(117):5-21.
1964b   "Entre os Ganguelas. II. Festa da inciação das raparigas." *Portugal em Africa* 20(119):23-41.

Kremser, Manfred
1982   "Die Musikinstrumente der Azande. Ein Beitrag zur Musikgeschichte Zentrafrikas." In *Bericht über den fünfzehnten österreichischen Historikertag in Salzburg.* Referate und Protokoll der Sektion 7: Historische Volks- und Völkerkunde. Wien: Verband Österreichischer Geschichtsvereine, 295-300.

Kruger, Jaco
1989   "Rediscovering the Venda Ground-Bow." *Ethnomusicology* 33(3) Fall:391-404.

Kubik, Gerhard
1959   "Der Metronomsinn, oder: A feeling for the Beat." *Jazz Podium* 8(6):140-1.
1960   "The Structure of Kiganda Xylophone Music." *African Music* 2(3):6-30. Corrigenda in *African Music* 4(4):136-7 [1970].
1961a   "Musikgestaltung in Afrika." *Neues Afrika* 3(5):195-200.
1961b   "Musikinstrumente und Tänze der Wapangwa in Tanganyika." *Mitteilungen der Anthropologischen Gesellschaft in Wien* 91:144-7.
1961c   "Spuren des Blues (Ein Bericht aus Nigerien)." *Jazz Podium* 10(6):157-60.
1962a   "Beziehungen zwischen Musik und Sprache in Afrika." *Neues Afrika* 1:33-7.
1962b   "Review of Rose Brandel: The Music of Central Africa." *African Music* 3(1):116-8.

1962c   "The Phenomenon of Inherent Rhythms in East and Central African Instru-
         mental Music." *African Music* 3(1):33-42. Corrigenda in *African Music*
         4(4):136-7 [1970].

1963   "Was ist Jazzrhythmus? Bemerkungen zu Dr. Dauer's Aufsatz." *Jazz Podium*
         12(5):110-3.

1964a   "Harp Music of the Azande and Related Peoples in the Central African Re-
         public." *African Music* 3(3):37-76.

1964b   "Recording and Studying Music in Northern Mozambique." *African Music*
         3(3):77-100. Corrigenda in *African Music* 4(4):136-7 [1970].

1964c   "Xylophone Playing in Southern Uganda." *The Journal of the Royal Anthropo-
         logical Institute* 94(2):138-59.

1965a   "Märchen für Yoruba-Kinder." *Der ideale Partner* 4(2):14-5.

1965b   "Neue Musikformen in Schwarzafrika. Psychologische und musikethno-
         logische Grundlagen." Sonderbeilage zur Zeitschrift *Afrika heute* 4:1-16.

1965c   "Transcription of Mangwilo Xylophone Music from Film Strips." *African Mu-
         sic* 3(4): Corrigenda in *African Music* 4(4):136-7 [1970].

1966   "Die Popularität von Musikarten im Afrika südlich der Sahara." *Afrika heute*
         15:370-5.

1967a   "La musique en République Centrafricaine." *Afrika* 8(1):43-7.

1967b   "The Traditional Music of Tanzania." *Afrika* 8(2):29-32.

1968a   "Àló - Yoruba Story Songs. Excerpts from Material Collected in Nigeria." *Afri-
         can Music* 4(2):10-32.

1968b   "Ethnomusicological Research in Southern Parts of Malawi." *The Society of
         Malawi Journal* 21(1):20-32.

1968c   *Mehrstimmigkeit und Tonsysteme in Zentral- und Ostafrika.* Österreichische
         Akademie der Wissenschaften. Wien: Hermann Böhlaus Nachfolger.

1969a   "Composition Techniques in Kiganda Xylophone Music." *African Music*
         4(3):22-72. Corrigenda in *African Music* 4(4):136-7 [1970].

1969b   "Masks of the Mbwela." *Geographica* 5(20):2-19.

1970a   "Aufbau und Struktur der Amadinda-Musik von Buganda." In *Festschrift
         Walter Graf zum 65. Geburtstag.* E. Schenk, ed. Wien: Hermann Böhlaus
         Nachfolger, 107-37.

1970b   *Musica Traditional e Aculturada dos !Kung' de Angola.* Estudos de Antro-
         pologia Cultural 4. Lisbon: Junta de Investigações do Ultramar.

1971a   "Carl Mauch's Mbira Musical Transcriptions of 1872." *Review of Ethnology*
         3(10):73-80. Reprinted in: *Ethnohistory in Vienna.* Karl Wernhart, ed. Edition
         Herodot. Forum 9. Aachen: Rader, 165-72.

1971b   Die Institution mukanda und assoziierte Einrichtungen bei den Vambwela/
         Vankangela und verwandten Ethnien in Südostangola. Field Research Docu-
         ment, August - December 1965. Ph.D. dissertation. University of Vienna.

1971c   "Zur inneren Kritik ethnographischer Feldberichte aus der kolonialen
         Periode." *Wiener Ethnohistorische Blätter* 2:31-41.

1971/2   "Die Verarbeitung von Kwela, Jazz und Pop in der modernen Musik von Ma-
         lawi." *Jazzforschung - Jazz Research* 3/4:51-115.

1972a   "Letter to Peter Cooke." Letter to the Editor. *African Music* 5(2):114-5.

1972b   "Oral Notation of Some West and Central African Time-Line Patterns." *Re-
         view of Ethnology* 3(22):169-76.

1972c   "Transcription of African Music from Silent Film: Theory and Methods." *Afri-
         can Music* 5(2):28-39.

1973a   "Music and Dance Education in *Mukanda* Schools of Mbwela and Nkangela

Communities." In *Proceedings of the Lusaka Music Conference* June 15-22, 1971. Institute for African Studies, University of Zambia. Lusaka: Institute for African Studies, n. p.

1973b "Verstehen in afrikanischen Musikkulturen." In *Musik und Verstehen. Aufsätze zur semiotischen Theorie, Ästhetik und Soziologie der musikalischen Rezeption.* P. Faltin & H.-P. Reinecke, eds. Köln: Arno Volk, 171-88.

1974a "Sozialisierungsprozeß und Gesänge der Initianden in *mukanda*-Schulen (Südost-Angola)." In *Memoriam António Jorge Dias.* Vol. 1. Lisbon: Junta de Investigações do Ultramar, 247-70.

1974b *The Kachamba Brothers' Band - A Study of Neo-Traditional Music in Malaŵi.* Zambian Paper No. 9. Lusaka: Institute for African Studies, University of Zambia.

1975a "Aufnahme und Auswertung von Kinematogrammen malawischer Musik." *Wissenschaftlicher Film* 16:44-52.

1975b "Kulturelle und sprachliche Feldforschungen in Nordwest-Zambia, 1971 und 1973." *Bulletin of the International Committee on Urgent Anthropological and Ethnological Research* 17:87-115.

1975c "Notation de la musique africaine." *Abbia* (Yaoundé) 29-30:211-23.

1975/6 "Musical Bows in South-Western Angola, 1965." *African Music* 5(4):98-104.

1976 "Daniel Kachamba's Solo Guitar Music - Notes on the Sound Films E 2136 and E 2137, Encyclopaedia Cinematographica, Göttingen." *Jazzforschung-Jazz Research* 8:159-95.

1977 "Patterns of Body Movement in the Music of Boys' Initiation in South-East Angola." In *The Anthropology of the Body.* John Blacking, ed. Monograph 15. London: Academic Press, 253-74.

1978a "Boys' Circumcision School of the Yao - A Cinematographic Documentation atChief Makanjila's Village in Malaŵi, 1967." *Review of Ethnology* 6(1-7):1-37.

1978b "Donald Kachamba's Kwela Music: Malawi Twist." Film E 2328, Encyclopaedia Cinematographica. *Publikationen zu Wissenschaftlichen Filmen* 8(29):3-20.

1978c "Donald Kachamba's Kwela Music: Simanjemanje, Chachacha." Film E 2329, Encyclopaedia Cinematographica. *Publikationen zu Wissenschaftlichen Filmen* 8(30):3-21.

1978d Review of Emil Pearson's "People of the Aurora." *Review of Ethnology* 5(11-14):108-12.

1979a *Angolan Traits in Black Music, Games and Dances of Brazil. A Study of African Cultural Extensions Overseas.* Estudos de Antropologia Cultural 10. Lisbon: Junta de Investigações do Ultramar.

1979b "Pattern Perception and Recognition in African Music." In *The Performing Arts.* John Blacking & Joann W. Kealiinohomoku, eds. The Hague: Mouton, 221-49.

1979/80 "Donald Kachamba's Montage Recordings: Aspects of Urban Music History in Malawi." *African Urban Studies* 6:89-122.

1980a "Angola" (vol. 10:431-5). "Cameroon" (vol. 3:647-9). "Kwela." (vol. 10:329-30) "Lamellapohone." (vol. 10:401-7) "Malaŵi." (vol. 11:550-4) "Marimba." (vol. 11:681-3) "Mvet." (vol. 13:3) "Tanzania" (vol. 18:567-71). In *The New Grove Dictionary of Music and Musicians.* Stanley Sadie, ed. London: Macmillan.

1980b "Likembe Tunings of Kufuna Kandonga (Angola)." *African Music* 6(1):70-88.

1981a "Extensionen afrikanischer Kulturen in Brasilien." *Wiener Ethnohistorische Blätter* 21:3-75; 22: 3-77.

1981b   "Music and Dance." In *Cultural Atlas of Africa*. Jocelyn Murray, ed. Oxford: Elsevier, 90-7.

1981c   "Neo-Traditional Music in East Africa Since 1945." *Popular Music* 1:83-104.

1982a   "Erziehungssysteme in ost- und zentralafrikanischen Kulturen - Forschungsansätze, -methoden und -ergebnisse." *Mitteilungen der Anthropologischen Gesellschaft in Wien* 112:72-87.

1982b   *Mukanda na Makisi - Circumcision School and Masks*. Record Museum Collection MC 11. Museum für Völkerkunde Berlin. Berlin: Staatliche Museen Preußischer Kulturbesitz.

1983   "Kognitive Grundlagen der afrikanischen Musik." In *Musik in Afrika. 20 Beiträge zur Kenntnis traditioneller afrikanischer Musikkulturen.* Veröffentlichungen des Museums für Völkerkunde Berlin. Neue Folge 40, Abteilung Musikethnologie IV. Artur Simon, ed. Berlin: Staatliche Museen Preußischer Kulturbesitz, 327-400.

1984a   "Das Khoisan-Erbe im Süden von Angola, dargestellt anhand ethnographischer, linguistischer und musikologischer Fakten." *Wiener Ethnohistorische Blätter* 27:125-55.

1984b   "Einige Grundbegriffe und -konzepte der afrikanischen Musikforschung." *Jahrbuch für musikalische Volks- und Völkerkunde* 11:57-102.

1985   "African Tone-Systems - A Reassessement." *Yearbook for Traditional Music* 17:31-63.

1986a   "Afrikanische Musikkulturen in Brasilien - Candomblé: ein religiöser Synkretismus?" In *Welt Musik Brasilien. Einführung in Musiktraditionen Brasiliens.* Tiago de Oliveira Pinto, ed. Internationales Institut für vergleichende Musikstudien und Dokumentation Berlin. Mainz: Schott, 121-47.

1986b   "Hubert Kponton (1905-1982), Erfinder, Künstler und Begründer eines ethnographischen Privatmuseums in Lome, Togo." In *Festschrift Anne-Marie Schweeger-Hefel. Archiv für Völkerkunde* 40. Wien: Museum für Völkerkunde, 157-71.

1986c   "Stability and Change in African Musical Traditions." *The World of Music* 28(1):44-69.

1987a   "Das Khoisan-Erbe im Süden von Angola: Bewegungsformen, Bogenharmonik und tonale Ordnung in der Musik der !Kung' und benachbarter Bantu-Populationen." In *Afrikanische Musikkulturen.* Erich Stockmann, ed. Berlin: Verlag Neue Musik, 82-196.

1987b   *Malaŵian Music - A Framework for Analysis*. Zomba: Centre for Social Research, University of Malaŵi. Limbe: Montfort Press (author assisted by Moya A. Malamusi, Lidiya Malamusi & D. Kachamba).

1987c   "Musical Activities of Children Within the Eastern Angolan Culture Area." *The World of Music* 29(3):5-27.

1987d   *Nyau - Maskentänze im südlichen Malawi*. Begleitveröffentlichung zum wissenschaftlichen Film P 2058 des ÖWF, Wissenschaftlicher Film Nr. 36/7:115-23.

1987e   *Nyau - Maskenbünde im südlichen Malawi*. Veröffentlichungen der Ethnologischen Kommission Nr. 4. Österreichische Akademie der Wissenschaften, Sitzungsberichte, Band 485. Wien: Verlag der Österreichischen Akademie der Wissenschaften (author assisted by Moya Aliya Malamusi).

1987f   *Tusona -Luchazi Ideographs. A Graphic Tradition Practised by a People of West-Central Africa.* Föhrenau-Wien: E. Stiglmayr.

1988a   "Kwela, Simanje-manje und Mbaqanga - Transkulturative Prozesse in der

Musik des südlichen Afrika." *Österreichische Musikzeitschrift* 7-8:407-11.
1988b "Obituary: Daniel Kachamba 1947-1987, Malaŵian Musician-Composer."
       Jazzforschung - Jazz Research 20:174-9.
1989a *Multi-Part Singing in East and South-East Africa.* Selected Recordings of the
       East Africa Expedition Helmut Hillegeist/Gerhard Kubik, August 7, 1961 to
       January 10, 1963. Tondokumente aus dem Phonogrammarchiv der Öster-
       reichischen Akademie der Wissenschaften PHA LP 2. Wien: Verlag der
       Österreichischen Akademie der Wissenschaften.
1989b "Subjective Patterns in African Music." In: *Cross Rhythms, Papers in African
       Folklore.* Susan Domowitz, Maureen Eke & Enoch Mvula, eds. Vol. 3.
       Bloomington: African Studies Program, Trickster Press, 129-54.
1989c "The Southern African Periphery: Banjo Traditions in Zambia and Malaŵi."
       The World of Music 31(1):3-29.
1990   "Drum Patterns in the 'Batuque' of Benedito Caxias." *Latin American Music
       Review* 11(2):115-80.
1991a "Documentation in the Field. Scientific Strategies and the Psychology of Cul-
       ture Contact." In: *Music in the Dialogue of Cultures: Traditional Music and Cul-
       tural Policy.* Max Peter Baumann, ed. Intercultural Music Studies 2.
       Wilhelmshaven: Florian Noetzel, 318-35.
1991b *Extensionen afrikanischer Kulturen in Brasilien.* Edition Herodot. Aachen:
       Alano.
1991c "Muxima Ngola — Veränderungen und Strömungen in den Musikkulturen
       Angolas im 20. Jahrhundert." In *Populäre Musik in Afrika.* Veröffentlichungen
       des Museums für Völkerkunde Berlin. Neue Folge 53, Abteilung Musik-
       ethnologie VIII. Veit Erlmann, ed. Berlin: Staatliche Museen Preußischer
       Kulturbesitz, 201-71, 20-2.
1991d "Theorie, Aufführungspraxis and Kompositionstechniken der Hofmusik von
       Buganda. Ein Leitfaden zur Komposition in einer ostafrikanischen Musik-
       kultur." *Hamburger Jahrbuch für Musikwissenschaft* 11 (Für Györgi Ligeti.
       Die Referate des Ligeti Kongresses Hamburg 1988):23-162.
1992a "Analoge Strukturen im auditiven und visuellen Bereich afrikanischer
       künstlerischer Gestaltung." *Jahrbuch Bayerische Akademie der Schönen Künste*
       6. München: Oreos Verlag, 326-68.
1992b "Embaire Xylophone Music of Samusiri Babalanda (Uganda 1968)." *The
       World of Music* 34(1):57-84.
1992c "Review of: Éric de Dampierre 'Harpes Zandé', 1991." *The World of Music*
       34(3):140-1.
1993a "Die *mukanda*-Erfahrung. Zur Psychologie der Initiation der Jungen im Ost-
       Angola-Kulturraum." In *Kinder. Ethnologische Forschungen in fünf Konti-
       nenten.* Marié-José van de Loo & Margarete Reinhart, eds. München: Trick-
       ster, 309-47.
1993b *Makisi - Nyau - Mapiko. Maskentraditionen im Bantu-sprachigen Afrika.*
       München: Trickster.
Kubik, Gerhard *et al.*
1982   *Musikgeschichte in Bildern: Ostafrika.* Band 1: Musikethnologie Lieferung 10.
       Leipzig: VEB Deutscher Verlag für Musik.
1989   *Musikgeschichte in Bildern: Westafrika.* Band I: Musikethnologie. Lieferung II.
       Leipzig: VEB Deutscher Verlag für Musik.
Kubik, Gerhard; Balyebonera, Fred *et al.*
1977   *Recordings and Classification of Oral Literature in Tanzania and some Other*

Parts of Africa. Papers presented during the Seminar conducted by Dr. Gerhard Kubik at the Goethe-Institut Dar es Salaam, September 20-26, 1976, Dar es Salaam: Goethe-Institut.

Kubik, Gerhard & Donald Kachamba
1992   *Daniel Kachamba Memorial Cassette — Kaseti ya Nyimbo za Chikumbutso cha Malemu Daniel Kachamba* (Audio cassette and booklet). Zomba: Department of Fine and Performing Arts, University of Malaŵi.

Kubik, Gerhard & Moya A. Malamusi
1989   *Opeka Nyimbo. Musician-Composers from Southern Malaŵi.* Double Album, MC 15, Museum Collection. Berlin: Museum für Völkerkunde, Abteilung Musikethnologie.

Kubik, Gerhard; Lidiya Malamusi & Moya A. Malamusi
1990   "Typen der oralen Literatur im Chicheŵa/Cinyanja." In *Die Vielfalt der Kultur. Ethnologische Aspekte von Verwandschaft, Kunst und Weltauffassung.* Ernst Wilhelm Müller zum 65. Geburtstag. Karl-Heinz Kohl, Heinzarnold Muszinski & Ivo Strecker, eds. Mainzer Ethnologica Bd. 4. Berlin: Dietrich Reimer, 357-79.

Kubik, Gerhard & David Rycroft
1989   "African Arts: Music." *The New Encyclopaedia Britannica*, Vol. 13. Chicago: Encyclopaedia Britannica Inc., 144-52, 154, 173-9.

Kunst, Jaap
1936   "A Musicological Argument for Cultural Relationship Between Indonesia - Probably the Isle of Java - and Central Africa." In *Proceedings of the Musical Association,* Session LXII (1935-36). Leeds: Whitehead & Miller Ltd., 57-76.

Kyagambiddwa, Joseph
1955   *African Music from the Source of the Nile.* New York: Praeger.

Laade, Wolfgang
1971   *Neue Musik in Afrika, Asien und Ozeanien. Diskographie und historisch-stilistischer Überblick.* Heidelberg: published by the author.

Ladzekpo, S. Kobla
1971   "The Social Mechanics of Good Music: A Description of Dance Clubs Among the Anlo-Ewe-Speaking People of Ghana." *African Music* 5(1):6-13.

Ladzekpo, S. Kobla & Hewitt Pantaleoni
1970   "Takada Drumming." *African Music* 4(4):6-31.

Laurenty, Jean-Sebastian
1960   *Les Chordophones du Congo Belge et du Ruanda-Urundi.* 2 Vols. Annales du Musée Royal du Congo Belge, Tervuren. Nouvelle Série in-4 . Sciences de l'Homme. Vol. 2. Tervuren: Musée Royal du Congo Belge.

1962   *Les Sanza du Congo.* 2 Vols. Annales du Musée Royal de l'Afrique Centrale Tervuren. Nouvelle Série in-4 . Sciences Humaines 3. Tervuren: Musée Royal de l'Afrique Centrale.

Lhote, Henry
1973   *A la découverte des fresques du Tassili.* Collection Signes de Temps 3. Paris: B. Arthaud.

Linschoten, Jan Huyghen van
1596   *Itinerario, Voyage ofte Schipvaert ... , 1579-92.* Amsterdam: Claesz.

List, George
1983   *Musik and Poetry in a Colombian Village. A Tri-Cultural Heritage.* Bloomington: Indiana University Press.

Lo-Bamijoko, Joy N.
1987   "Classification of Igbo Musical Instruments, Nigeria." *African Music* 6(4):19-41.

Locke, David
1982   "Principles of Offbeat Timing and Cross-Rhythm in Southern Eʋe Dance
        Drumming." *Ethnomusicology* 26(2):217-46.
1985   "The Rhythm of Takai." *Percussive Notes* 23(4):51-4.
1990   *Drum Damba. Talking Drum Lessons.* Crown Point (Indiana): White Cliffs
        Media Company.
Locke, David & Godwin Kwasi Agbeli
1980   "A Study of the Drum Language in Adzogbo." *African Music* 6(1):32-51.
Lomax, Alan
1968   *Folk Song Style and Culture.* American Association for the Advancement of Sci-
        ence, Publication 88. Washington: American Association for the Advancement
        of Science.
1973   "Cinema, Science and Culture Renewal." *Current Anthropology* 14(4) Octo-
        ber:474-80.
Lomax, Alan *et al.*
1969   "Choreometrics: A Method for the Study of Cross-Cultural Pattern in Film."
        Research Film 6(6):505-17.
Low, John
1982a   "A History of Kenyan Guitar Music: 1945-1980." *African Music* 6(2):17-36.
1982b   *Shaba Diary.* Föhrenau-Wien: E. Stiglmayr.
Lunsonga, Cajetan
1978   "Music Education in Africa and the Africanization of Other Subjects." *Review
        of Ethnology* 5(9-10):65-76.
Lush, A. J.
1935   "Kiganda Drums." *Uganda Journal* 3(1):7-20.
Maes, J.
1921   "La Sanza du Congo Belge." *Congo* 1(4):542-72.
Makeba, Miriam
1988   *Makeba: My Story.* New York: New American Library.
Makumbi, Archibald J.
1954   *Maliro ndi myambo ya Acewa.* London: Longman.
Malamusi, Moya Aliya
1984   "The Zambian Popular Music Scene." *Jazzforschung - Jazz Research* 16:189-98.
1987   "'Sholisho' a Mobile Music Puppet ... ." Cover illustration. *African Music*
        6(4):cover.
1990   "*Nthano* Chantefables and Songs Performed by the *bangwe* Player Chitenje
        Tambala." *South African Journal of African Languages* (Contributions in Hon-
        our of David Kenneth Rycroft) 10(4): 222-38.
1991   "Samba Ng'oma Eight - the Drum-Chime of Mario Sabuneti." *African Music*
        7(1):55-71.
1992   "Thunga la ngororombe - the Panpipe Dance Group of Sakha Bulaundi." *Afri-
        can Music* 7(2):85-107.
Manima, Sese Kwaku
1976   "Precocité et étapes probables de l'acculturation tonale." *Revue Zaïroise des
        Arts* 1:23-5.
Manuel, Peter
1988   *Popular Musics of the Non-Western World: An Introductory Survey.* New York:
        Oxford University Press.
Mapoma, Mwesa I.
1980   "Zambia." In *The New Grove Dictionary of Music and Musicians.* Vol. 20.
        Stanley Sadie, ed. London: Macmillan, 630-5.

1982   *Survey of Zambian Musical Instruments. Case Study: Musical Instruments of the Lala People of Serenje District.* Lusaka: University of Zambia, Institute for African Studies.

Maraire, Abraham Dumisani
1971   *Mbira Music from Rhodesia.* LP Record and Booklet. Seattle: University of Washington Press.

Martin, Stephen
1982   "Music in Urban East Africa: Five Genres in Dar es Salaam." *Journal of African Studies* 9(3):155-63.
1991   "Brass Bands and the beni Phenomenon in Urban East Africa." *African Music* 7(1):72-81.

Matos, Mário Ruy de Rocha
1982   "(Ma)Dimba — para um estudo sistemático." *Vida & Cultura.* Suplemento do Jornal de Angola 37, Luanda, 28 de Fevereiro:4-5.

Mauch, Carl
1869-72   *Afrikanisches Tagebuch 1869-1872.* Unpublished German manuscript. Stuttgart: Linden-Museum.
1969   *The Journals of Carl Mauch. His Travels in the Transvaal and Rhodesia 1869-1872.* Transcribed from the original by Mrs. E. Bernard and translated by F. O. Bernhard. Salisbury: National Archives of Rhodesia.

Mbunga, Stephan
1959   *Misa Baba Yetu.* Peramihó: Benedictine Mission.
1963   *Church Law and Bantu Music. Ecclesiastical Documents and Law on Sacred Music as Applied to Bantu Music.* Einsiedeln: Administration de la Nouvelle Revue de Science Missionaire.

McDougall, Lorna
1975   *The Interpretation of Symbols Especially Body Symbols.* Paper presented at the ASA (Association of Social Anthropologists) Conference on "The Anthropology of the Body" in Belfast, April 1975. Typescript.
1977   "Symbols and Somatic Structures." In *The Anthropology of the Body.* A.S.A. Monograph 15. John Blacking, ed. London: Academic Press, 391-406.

Mensah, Atta Annan
1967a   "Further Notes on Ghana's Xylophone Traditions." *Research Review* 3(2):62-5.
1967b   "The Polyphony of Gyil-gu, Kudzo and Awutu Sakumo." *Journal of the International Folk Music Council* 19:75-9.
1969   "The Gyilgo - A Gonja Sansa." In *Papers in African Studies* 3. J. H. Nketia, ed. Legon: Institute of African Studies, University of Ghana, 35-41.
1970a   "Ndebele-Soli Bi-Musicality in Zambia." *Yearbook of the International Folk Music Council* 2:108-20.
1970b   "Principles Governing the Construction of the Silimba, a Xylophone Type Found Among the Lozi of Zambia." *Review of Ethnology* 3(3):17-24.
1971   "Performing Arts in Zambia, Music and Dance." *Bulletin of the International Committee on Urgent Anthropological and Ethnological Research* 13:67-82.
1971/2   "Jazz - The Round Trip." *Jazzforschung - Jazz Research* 3/4:124-37.
1982   "Gyil: The Dagara-Lobi Xylophone." *Journal of African Studies* 9(3):155-63.

Merolla, Girolamo,
1692   *Breve e svccinta Relatione del viaggio nel regno di Congo nell Africa Meridionale* ... . Napoli: Mollo.

Merriam, Alan P.
1953a   "African Music Reexamined in the Light of New Material from the Belgian

                Congo and Ruanda Urundi." *Zaire* 7(3):244-53.

1953b   "Les styles voceaux dans la musique du Ruanda-Urundi." *Jeune Afrique* 7:12-6.

1955   "Musical Instruments and Techniques of Performance Among the Bashi." *Zaire* 9(2):124-8.

1957a   *Africa South of the Sahara.* Folkways Records and Service Corp. Album notes for EFL album FE 503, New York.

1957b   "The Bashi *Mulizi* and its Music: An End-Blown Flute from the Belgian Congo." *Journal of American Folklore* 70:143-56.

1957c   "Yovu Songs from Ruanda." *Zaire* 11:933-66.

1959a   "African Music." In *Continuity and Change in African Cultures.* W. R. Bascom & M. J. Herskovits, eds. Chicago: University of Chicago Press, 49-86.

1959b   "Apports de la musique Africaine à la culture mondiale." *Jeune Afrique* 12:26-34.

1959c   "Characteristics of African Music." *Journal of the International Folk Music Council* 11:13-9.

1962a   "The African Idiom in Music." *Journal of American Folklore* 75:120-30.

1962b   "The Epudi - A Basongye Ocarina." *Ethnomusicology* 6(3):175-80.

1962c   "The Music of Africa." In *Africa and the United States: Images and Realities.* Background book for the 8th National Conference of the U. S. National Commision for UNESCO. Boston: National Comission for UNESCO, 155-64. Reprinted in *Africa Report* 7(June) 1962:15-17, 23.

1962/9   *Africa Report.* Monthly column. 7 (June) - 14 (May-June).

1963   "African Music." In *Encyclopedia International.* New York: Grolier, 148-9.

1964   *The Anthropology of Music.* Evanston: Northwestern University Press.

1965   "Music and Dance." In *The African World: A Survey of Social Research.* Robert A. Lystad, ed. New York: Praeger, 452-68.

1967   "The Use of Music as a Technique of Reconstructing Culture History in Africa." In *Reconstructing African Culture History.* Creighton Gabel & Norman R. Bennet, eds. Boston University African Research Studies No. 8. Boston: Boston University Press, 83-114.

1970   *African Music on LP: An Annotated Discography.* Evanston: Northwestern University Press.

1977a   "Musical Change in a Basongye Village (Zaïre)." *Anthropos* 72:806-46.

1977b   "Traditional Music of Black Africa." In *Africa.* P. M. Martin & P. O'Meara, eds. Bloomington: Indiana University Press, 243-58.

1980   Review of J. M. Chernoff: "African Rhythm and African Sensibility". *Ethnomusicology* 24(3):559-61.

Messomo, Albert Noah

1980   *Mendzan. Etude ethno-littéraire du xylophone des Beti.* Yaoundé: Université de Yaoundé.

Miehe, Gudrun

1983   "Akzent." In *Lexikon der Afrikanistik. Afrikanische Sprachen und ihre Erforschung.* H. Jungraithmayr & W. J. G. Möhlig, eds. Berlin: Dietrich Reimer, 26-7.

Miller, G. A. & G. Heise

1950   "The Thrill Threshold." Journal of the Acoustical Society of America 22:637-8.

Modisane, Bloke

1963   *Blame me on History.* London: Thames and Hudson.

Moorehead, Alan

1973   *The White Nile.* Harmondsworth: Penguin Books Ltd.

Msiska, Augustine W. C.
1981   "Virombo, Vimbuza and Vyanusi as Observed Among the Phoka of Rumphi, Northern Malawi." *Review of Ethnology* 7(24):185-91.
Mubitana, K.
1970   "Forms and Significance in the Art of the Lunda, Luvale, Luchazi and Chokwe of Zambia. A Boasian Approach." *Zambia Museums Journal* 1:22-7.
Mugglestone, Erica
1982   "The Gora and the 'Grand' Gom-Gom: A Reappraisal of Kolb's Account of a Khoikhoi Music Bow." *African Music* 6(2):94-115.
Mundy-Castle, A. C.
1966   "Pictorial Depth Perception in Ghanaian Children." *International Journal of Psychology* 1:290-300.
Murdock, George Peter
1959   *Africa: Its Peoples and their Culture History.* New York: McGraw Hill.
1967   *Ethnographic Atlas.* Pittsburgh: University of Pittsburgh Press.
Murray, Jocelyn (ed.)
1981   *Cultural Atlas of Africa.* Oxford: Elsevier Publishers, Phaidon Press.
Mutesa II, Edward F. (Kabaka)
1967   *Desecration of my Kingdom.* London: Constable & Company.
Mvula, Enoch Timpunza
1985   "Tumbuka Pounding Songs in the Management of Family Conflicts." *Cross Rhythms. Occasional Papers in African Folklore/Music* 2:93-113.
Mwondela, William R.
1972a   *Chiseke* Lusaka: National Educational Company of Zambia Ltd.
1972b   *Mukanda and Makishi: Traditional Education in Northwestern Zambia.* Lusaka: National Educational Company of Zambia Ltd.
n.d.   *Mukanda Syllabus - Luvale Traditional College in the Republic of Zambia.* Manuscript (ca. 1971), 9 pages. (Private archive Aliya/Kubik, Vienna.)
Mworoha, Emile
1977   *Peuples et rois de l'Afrique des lacs. Le Burundi et les royaumes voisins au XIXième siècle.* Dakar/Abidjan: Les Nouvelles Éditions Africaines.
Nadel, Siegfried Frederick
1931   *Marimba-Musik.* Akademie der Wissenschaften in Wien. Philosophisch-historische Klasse. Sitzungsberichte, 212. Band, 3. Abhandlung. Wien, Leipzig: Hölder - Pichler - Tempsky.
Nagel, Franz
1974   "Kurzberichte zur musikalischen Programmarbeit im Ausland (Nairobi)." In *Fortbildungsseminar im Programmbereich Musik vom 16.-21.9.1974.* Goethe-Institut. München: Goethe-Institut, 127-33.
Ngumu, Pie-Claude
1975/6 "Les mendzaŋ des Ewondo du Cameroun." *African Music* 5(4):6-26.
1976   *Les Mendzaŋ des chanteurs de Yaoundé. Histoire - Organologie- Fabrication - Système de Transcription.* Acta Ethnologica et Linguistica 34, Series Musicologica 2. Föhrenau-Wien: E. Stiglmayr.
1980   "Modèle standard de rangées de carreaux pour transcrire les traditions musicales africaines du Cameroun." *African Music* 6(1):52-61.
Njock, Pierre Emmanuel
1970   "Einführung in den afrikanischen Rhythmus mit Beispielen aus der Bundesrepublik Kamerun." *Zeitschrift für Kulturaustausch* 1(20):20-3.
Njungu, Agrippa
1971   "Further Notes on the Word 'inyimbo'." *Inyimbo Newsletter* 1(2):20-1.

Nketia, J. H. Kwabena
  1955   *Funeral Dirges of the Akan People.* Exeter: James Townsend & Sons.
  1956   "The Grammophone and Contemporary African Music in the Gold Coast."
          *Procedures of the 4th Annual Conference: West African Institute of Social and
          Economic Research.* Ibadan: University of Ibadan, 191-201.
  1957a   "Modern Trends in Ghana Music." *African Music* 1(4):13-7.
  1957b   "The Organization of Music in Adangme Society." *Universitas* (Accra) 3(1):9-
          11.
  1958a   "The Ideal in African Folk Music: A Note on 'Klama'." *Universitas* (Accra)
          3(2):40-2.
  1958b   "Traditional Music of the Ga People." *Universitas* (Accra) 3(3):76-80.
  1958c   "Yoruba Musicians in Accra." *Odu* (Journal of Yoruba and Related Studies)
          6:35-44.
  1959a   "African Gods and Music." *Universitas* (Accra) 4(1):3-7.
  1959b   "Changing Traditions of Folk Music in Ghana." *Journal of the International
          Folk Music Council* 11:31-5.
  1962a   *African Music in Ghana. A Survey of Traditional Forms.* London: Longmans
          Green & Co.
  1962b   "The Hocket-Technique in African Music." *Journal of the International Folk
          Music Council* 14:44-52.
  1963a   *Drumming in Akan Communities of Ghana.* Edinburgh: Thomas Nelson &
          Sons.
  1963b   *Folk Songs of Ghana.* London: Oxford University Press.
  1967   "Multi-Part Organization in the Music of the Gogo of Tanzania." *Journal of
          the International Folk Music Council* 19:79-88.
  1971a   "Surrogate Languages of Africa." In *Current Trends in Linguistics* 8. Thomas
          A. Sebeok, ed. The Hague: Mouton, 699-732.
  1971b   "The Linguistic Aspect of Style in African Languages." In *Current Trends in
          Linguistics.* Thomas A. Sebeok, ed. The Hague: Mouton, 737-47.
  1972   "The Musical Languages of Subsaharan Africa." In *African Music Meeting in
          Yaoundé* (Cameroon), 23-27 February 1970 organized by UNESCO. Paris: La
          Revue Musicale, 7-49.
  1974   *The Music of Africa.* New York: Norton & Company, Inc.
  1978   "Tradition and Innovation in African Music." *Jamaica Journal* 11(3-4):2-9.
  1982   "On the History of Music in African Cultures." *Journal of African Studies*
          9(3):101-15.
  1986   "Processes of Differenciation and Interdependency in African Music: The
          Case of Asante and her Neighbors." *The World of Music* 28(2):41-55.
van Noorden, L. P. A. S.
  1975   *Temporal Coherence in the Perception of Tone Sequences.* Eindhoven: Institute
          for Perception Research.
Nurse, George T.
  1964   "Popular Songs and National Identity in Malawi." *African Music* 3(3):101-6.
  1967   "The Name 'Akafula'." *The Society of Malaŵi Journal* 20(2):1-6.
  1968a   "Bush Roots and Nyanja Ideophones." *The Society of Malaŵi Journal* 21(1):50-
          7.
  1968b   "Ideophonic Aspects of Some Nyanja Drum Names." *African Music* 4(2):40-3.
  1970   "Cewa Concepts of Musical Instruments." *African Music* 4(4):32-6.
  1974   "Verb Species Relationships of Some Nyanja Ideophones." *African Studies*
          33(4):227-42.

Nurse, George T.; Weiner, J. S. & T. Jenkins
   1985   *The Peoples of Southern Africa and Their Affinities.* Oxford: Oxford U. Press.
Nzewi, Meki
   1971   "The Rhythm of Dance in Igbo Music." *The Conch* 3(2):104-8.
   1974   "Melo-Rhythmic Essence and Hot Rhythm in Nigerian Folk Music." *The Black Perpective in Music* 2(1):23-8.
   1977   *Master Musicians and the Music of Ese, Ukom and Mgba Ensembles in Ngwa, Igbo Society.* Ph.D. dissertation. 2 vols. Belfast: Queens University.
   1980   "Folk Music in Nigeria: A Communion." *African Music* 6(1):6-21.
   1987   "*Ese* Music: Honours for the Dead: Status for the Sponsor." *African Music* 6(4):90-107.
Obama, Jean-Baptiste
   1969   *Education musicale et modernisation des traditions folkloriques africaines.* Unpublished manuscript.
Ogot, Bethwell A.
   1967   *A History of the Southern Luo.* Vol. 1 ("Migration and Settlement 1500-1900"). Nairobi: East African Publishing House.
Ogundipe, Ayodele
   1972   "Yoruba Tongue Twisters." In *African Folklore.* Richard M. Dorson, ed. New York: Anchor Books, Doubleday, 211-20.
Ojo, Jerome O.
   1976   *Yoruba Customs from Ondo.* Acta Ethnologica et Linguistica 37. Series Africana 10. Föhrenau-Wien: E. Stiglmayr.
Ojo, Valentine
   1978   "Yoruba-Musik - gestern, heute, morgen." *Jazzforschung-Jazz Research* 9:123-43.
Okoreaffia, C. O.
   1979   "Igeri Ututu: An Igbo Folk Requiem Music Dance Ritual." In *The Performing Arts.* John Blacking & Joann W. Kealiinohomoku, eds. The Hague: Mouton.
Oliver, Paul
   1970   *Savannah Syncopators. African Retentions in the Blues.* London: November Books Ltd.
Olsen, Howard
   1980   "The Relationship Between Lyrics and Melody in Rimi Vocal Music." *African Music* 6(1):126-8.
Omibiyi-Obidike, Monsunmola
   1973/4   "A Model for the Study of African Music." *African Music* 5(3):6-11.
   1980   "Islamic Influences on Yoruba Music." *African Notes* 8(2):37-54.
   1983   "Human Migration and Diffusion of Musical Instruments in Nigeria." *Bulletin of the International Committee on Urgent Anthropological and Ethnological Research* 25:77-85.
Onibonokuta, Ademola
   1983   *A Gift of the Gods. The Story of the Invention of the "Odu" Gongs and the Rediscovery of an Ancient Lithophone.* Bayreuth: IWALEWA-Haus.
Ortiz, Fernando
   1940   *Contrapunteo cubano del tabaco y el azúcar.* La Habana.
Owour, Henry Anyumba
   1970   "The Making of a Lyre Musician." *Mila* 1(2):28-35.
   1983   "Contemporary Lyres in Eastern Africa." *African Musicology* 1(1):18-33.
Pantaleoni, Hewitt
   1970   Review of "Folk Song Style and Culture" by Alan Lomax (1968). *African Music* 4(4):130-1.

1972a   *The Rhythm of Atsiã Dance Drumming Among the Anlo (Eve) of Anyako.*
         Oneonta, New York: Pantaleoni.

1972b   "Three Principles of Timing in A<u>nlo</u> Dance Drumming." *African Music*
         5(2):50-63.

1972c   "Toward Understanding the Play of Atsime<u>v</u>u in Atsiã." *African Music* 5(2):64-
         84.

1972d   "Toward Understanding the Play of Sogo in Atsiã." *Ethnomusicology* 16(1):1-
         37.

Pearson, Emil

1970   *Ngangela - English Dictionary*, Mexico: Tipográfia Indigena, Morelos.

1977   *People of the Aurora.* San Diego (Calif.): Beta Books.

Pechuël-Loesche, Eduard

1907   *Die Loango-Expedition.* Stuttgart: Strecker & Schröder.

Phillips, Etundayo

1953   *Yoruba Music. The Blending of Speech and Song in West African Music.* Johan-
         nesburg: African Music Society.

Phillipson, David W.

1977   *The Later Prehistory of Eastern and Southern Africa.* London: Heinemann.

Phiri, Kings M.

1982   "The Historiography of Nyau." *Kalulu* (Bulletin of Oral Literature. University
         of Malawi) 3:55-8.

Pike, Kenneth L.

1954   "Emic and Etic Standpoints for the Description of Behaviour." In K. L. Pike,
         Language in Relation to a Unified Theory of the Structure of Human Behaviour.
         Preliminary Edition. Glendale: Summer Institute of Linguistics, 8-28.

Pinto, Tiago de Oliveira

1988   *Berimbau e Capoeira - BA.* Documentário Sonoro do Folclore Brasileiro 46.
         Ministério da Cultura Fundação Nacional de Arte. Rio de Janeiro: Instituto
         Nacional do Folclore. LP Record and booklet.

1991   *Capoeira, Samba, Candomblé. Afrikanische Musik im Recôncavo, Bahia.* -
         Veröffentlichungen des Museums für Völkerkunde Berlin. Neue Folge 52,
         Abteilung Musikethnologie VII. Berlin: Staatliche Museen Preußischer Kul-
         turbesitz.

Pinto, Tiago de Oliveira (ed.)

1986   *Welt Musik Brasilien. Einführung in Musiktraditionen Brasiliens.*
         Internationales Institut für Vergleichende Musikstudien und Dokumentation
         Berlin. Mainz: Schott.

Posnansky, Merrick

1969   "Bigo bya Mugenyi." *Uganda Journal* 33:125-50.

Praetorius, Michael

1620   *Syntagma musicum.* Vol. 2, De organographia. Wolfenbüttel.

Pressing, Jeff

1983   "Rhythmic Design in the Support Drums of Agbadza." *African Music* 6(3):4-
         15.

Price-Williams, D. R.

1969   *Cross-Cultural Studies.* Penguin Modern Psychology Readings. Harmonds-
         worth: Penguin.

Prinz, Armin

1978   *Azande* (Äquatorialafrika, Nordost-Zaire). Films in the Encyclopaedia
         Cinematographica, Göttingen with accompanying notes. Göttingen: Institut
         für den Wissenschaftlichen Film.

Prinz, Armin & Laku Heke
1986   "Résultats d'études ethnopharmacologiques sur les plantes toxiques et
        thérapeutiques du Haut-Zaïre." *Muntu* (Revue Scientifique et Culturelle du
        CICIBA, Libreville) 4-5:57-70.
Rahn, Jay
1987   "Asymmetrical Ostinatos in Sub-Saharan Music: Time, Pitch and Cycles
        Reconsodered." *In Theory Only* 9(7) March:23-36.
Ranger, T. O.
1975   *Dance and Society in Eastern Africa 1890-1970. The Beni Ngoma.* Berkeley:
        University of California Press.
Rauter, Eva Mahongo
1993   "Das Mädchen lernt tanzen. Die weibliche Initiation bei den Luvale." In
        Kinder. Ethnologische Forschungen in fünf Kontinenten. Marie-José van de Loo
        & Margarete Reinhart, eds. München: Trickster, 349-65.
Ray, Benjamin C.
1991   *Myth, Ritual and Kingship in Buganda.* Oxford: Oxford University Press.
Redinha, José
1948   *As gravuras rupestres do Alto Zambeze e a primeira tentativa da sua
        interpretação.* Pulicações Culturais do Museo do Dundo 2. Lisbon:
        Companhia de Diamantes de Angola.
1975   *Etnias e culturas de Angola.* Luanda: Instituto de Investigação Cientifica de
        Angola.
1984   *Instrumentos musicais de Angola. Sua construção e descrição.* Publicações do
        Centro de Estudos Africanos 3. Coimbra: Universidade de Coimbra: Instituto
        de Antropologia.
Rhodes, William
1958   Letters to the Editor. *African Music* 2(1):82-4.
Richards, Paul
1987   "Africa in the Music of Samuel Coleridge-Taylor." *Africa* 57(4):566-51.
Richardson, Irvine
1957   *Linguistic Survey of the Northern Bantu Borderland.* Vol. 2. International Afri-
        can Institute. London: Oxford University Press.
Risset, Jean-Claude
1991   "Computer, Synthesis, Perception, Paradoxes." *Hamburger Jahrbuch für
        Musikwissenschaft* 11 (Für Györgi Ligeti. Die Referate des Ligeti-Kongresses
        Hamburg 1988): 245-58.
Roberts, John Storm
1968   "Popular Music in Kenya." *African Music* 4(2):53-5.
1972   *Black Music of Two Worlds.* New York: Praeger.
Rocha Matos, Mario Ruy de
1982a   "(Ma)-Dimba - para um estudo sistemático." *Vida & Cultura* 37 (Suplemento
        do Journal de Angola, 28 de Fevereiro):4-5.
1982b   "Para um programa de pesquisas de urgencia em Angola e algumas questões
        sobre o estudo da musicologia angolana." *Bulletin of the International Com-
        mittee on Urgent Anthropological and Ethnological Research* 24:89-103.
Rock, Irvin & Stephen Palmer
1990   "The Legacy of Gestalt Psychology." *Scientific American* 263(6):48-62.
Roelko, Eckhard
1980   "Akustische Illusionen." *Die Zeit* 57(5). 8. April 1980.
Roscoe, John
1911   *The Baganda.* London: Macmillan.

Rouget, Gilbert
1961   "Un chromatisme africain." *L'Homme* 1(3):1-15.
1964   "Tons de la langue en Gun (Dahomey) et tons du tambour." *Revue de Musicologie* 50:3-29.
1965a   "Notes et documents pour servir à l'étude de la musique yoruba." *Journal de la Société des Africanistes* 35(Fasc. 1):67-107.
1965b   "Un film expérimental: Batteries Dogon. Eléments pour une étude des rythmes." *L'Homme* 5(2):126-32.
1969   "Sur les xylophones équiheptaphoniques des Malinké." *Revue de Musicologie* 55(1):47-77.
1970   "Transcrire ou décrire? Chant soudanais et chant fuégien." In *Echanges et communications. Mélanges offerts à Claude Lévi-Strauss à l'occasion de son soixantième anniversaire.* Jean Pouillon & Pierre Maranda, eds. Paris: Mouton, 1:677-706.
1971a   "Court Songs and Traditional History in the Ancient Kingdoms of Porto-Novo and Abomey." In *Essays on Music and History in Africa.* Klaus Wachsmann, ed. Evanston: Northwestern University Press, 27-64.
1971b   "Une expérience de cinéma synchrone au ralenti." *L'Homme* 11(2):113-7.
1980   *La musique et la trance.* Esquisse d'une théorie générale des relations de la musique et de la possession. Paris: Editions Gallimard.
1982a   "Cithare et glissando: Nouvelles données sur le chromatisme au Bénin." *Revue de Musicologie* 68(1-2):310-24.
1982b   "Notes sur l'accord des sanza d'Ebézagui." *Revue de Musicologie* 68(1-2):330-44.
1987   "La voix, la cloche et le pouvoir du roi ou la transformation des symboles: A la mémoire de Alohentô Gbèfa, dernier roi de Porto-Novo." In *Ethnologiques: Hommages à Marcel Griaule.* Paris: Hermann, 313-32.
Rowlands, E. C.
1969   *Yoruba. Teach Yourself Books.* London: Hodder & Stoughton Paperbacks.
Rycroft, David
1954   "Tribal Style and Free Expression." *African Music* 1(1):16-28.
1956   "Melodic Imports and Exports: A Byproduct of Recording in Southern Africa." *British Institute of Recorded Sound Bulletin* 3 (Winter):19-21.
1957   "Zulu Male Traditional Singing." *African Music* 1(4):33-6.
1958   "The New 'Town Music' of Southern Africa." *Recorded Folk Music* 1:54-7.
1959   "African Music in Johannesburg: African and Non-African Features." *Journal of the International Folk Music Council* 11:25-30.
1960   "Melodic Features in Zulu Eulogistic Recitation." *African Language Studies* 1:60-78.
1961/2 "The Guitar Improvisations of Mwenda Jean Bosco." Part 1: *African Music* 2(4):81-98. Part 2: *African Music* 3(1):86-101.
1962   "Zulu and Xhosa Praise-Poetry and Songs." *African Music* 3(1):79-85.
1962/3 *Dark Music - Ethnomusicology and its Application in Africa.* Memoirs and Proceedings of the Manchester Literary and Philosophical Society 105. Manchester.
1966   "Friction Chordophones in South-Eastern Africa." *Galpin Society Journal* 19:84-100.
1967   "Nguni Vocal Polyphony." *Journal of the International Folk Music Council* 19:88-103.
1971   "Stylistic Evidence in Nguni Song." In *Essays on Music and History in Africa.* Klaus Wachsmann, ed. Evanston: Northwestern University Press, 213-41.

1975   "A Royal Account of Music in Zulu Life, With Translation, Annotation, and Musical Transcription." *Bulletin of the School of Oriental and African Studies*, University of London 38(2):350-402.

1975/6a "Review of G. Kubik: The Kachamba Brothers' Band ..." *African Music* 5(4):151-52.

1975/6b "The Zulu Bow Songs of Princess Magogo." *African Music* 5(4):41-97.

1977a   "Evidence of Stylistic Continuity in Zulu 'Town' Music." In *Essays for a Humanist: An Offering to Klaus Wachsmann*. New York: The Town House Press, 216-60.

1977b   *Music in Southern Africa: The Music of the Zulus and their Neighbours*. Teachers' Notes Brochure. London: BBC Publications.

1978   "Comments on Bushmen and Hottentot Music Recorded by E. O. J. Westphal." *Review of Ethnology* 5(2-3):16-23.

1980   "Gora" (vol. 7:535-6) "Musical Bow." (vol. 12:811-4) "Ramkie" (vol. 15:574-5). In *The New Grove Dictionary of Music & Musicians*. Stanley Sadie, ed. London: Macmillan.

1981/2   "The Musical Bow in Southern Africa." In *Papers Presented at the Second Symposium on Ethnomusicology*. Rhodes University, Music Department. Grahamstown: International Library of African Music, 70-6.

1991   "Black South African Urban Music since the 1890's: Some Reminiscences of Alfred Assegai Kumalo." *African Music* 7(1):5-32.

Santos, Eduard dos
1961   "Contribução para o estudo das pictografias e ideogramas dos Quicos." In *Estudos, ensaios e documentos*, 84, Estudos sobre a etnologia do Ultramar Português 2. Lisbon: Junta de Investigações do Ultramar, 17-131.

Santos, Frei João dos
1609   *Ethiopia Oriental*. Evora. Second edition: Biblioteca de Clássicos Portugueses. 2 vols. Lisbon: Mello de Azevedo, 1891.

Schaeffner, André
1990   *Le sistre et le hochet: Musique, théâtre et danse dans les sociétés africaines*. Paris: Hermann.

Schmidhofer, August
1991   *Xylophonspiel in Madagaskar. Ergebnisse der Feldforschungen 1986-89*. Ph.D. dissertation, Universität Wien: Musikwissenschaftliches Institut.

Schmidt, Cynthia
1984   "Interlocking Techniques in Kpelle Music." In *Studies in African Music. Selected Reports in Ethnomusicology* 5:195-216.

Schmidt-Wrenger, Barbara
1980   "Umrisse einer afrikanischen Musikkonzeption: Terminologie und Theorie der Tschokwe-Musik." *Africa-Tervuren* 26(3):58-65.

1983   "Most of the Books Were Written by Women - Komponistinnen in Afrika." *Neuland* 4:94-106.

Schneider, Albrecht & Andreas E. Beurmann
1990   "'Okutuusa Amadinda'. Zur Frage äquidistanter Tonsysteme und Stimmungen in Afrika." In *Musikkulturgeschichte. Festschrift für Constantin Floros zum 60. Geburtstag*. Peter Petersen, ed. Wiesbaden: Breitkopf & Härtel, 493-526 (with cooperation of Gerhard Kubik, Vienna and Mpijma Wamala, Hamburg-Harburg).

1991   "Tonsysteme, Frequenzdistanz, Klangformen und die Bedeutung experimenteller Forschung für die Vergleichende Musikwissenschaft." *Hamburger*

Jahrbuch für Musikwissenschaft 11 (Für Györgi Ligeti. Die Referate des Ligeti-Kongresses Hamburg 1988): 179-223.

Schneider, Marius

1934   *Geschichte der Mehrstimmigkeit.* Band 1: Die Naturvölker. Berlin: Julius Bard.

1937   "Über die Verbreitung afrikanischer Chorformen." *Zeitschrift für Ethnologie* 69:78-88.

1951   "Ist die vokale Mehrstimmigkeit eine Schöpfung der Altrassen?" *Acta Musicologica* 23:40-50.

1960   "Lieder der Duala." *Deutsches Jahrbuch der Musikwissenschaft für 1959* 4:93-113.

1961   "Tone and Tune." *Ethnomusicology* 5(3):204-15.

Schultze, Leonhard

1928   "Zur Kenntnis des Körpers der Hottentotten und Buschmänner." *Jenaische Denkschriften* 17:147-228.

Schweinfurth, Georg

1875   *Im Herzen von Afrika. Reisen und Entdeckungen im Centralen Äquatorial-Afrika während der Jahre 1868 bis 1871.* Leipzig: A. Brockhaus.

Scott, David Clement & Alexander Hetherwick

1929   *A Dictionary of the Nyanja Language.* London: Religious Tract Society.

Senghor, Léopold Sédar

1969a   *Anthologie de la nouvelle poésie nègre et malgache de langue française.* Paris: Presses universitaires de France.

1969b   *Négritude, arabité et francité. Reflexions sur le Problème de la culture.* Beyrouth: Ed. Dar al-kitab Allubnani.

1988   *Ce que je crois. Négritude, francité et civilisation de l'universel.* Paris: Grasset.

1990   *Oeuvre poétique.* Paris: Éd. du Seuil.

Serwadda, Moses & Hewitt Pantaleoni

1968   "A Possible Notation for African Dance Drumming." *African Music* 4(2):47-52.

Seshie, Paul

1971   "The Atopani Talking Drum." *Review of Ethnology* 3(13): 103-4.

Simon, Artur

1970   "Ein Krankenheilungsritus der Digo aus musikethnologischer Sicht." In *Probleme interdisziplinärer Afrikanistik.* Edited by the Vereinigung der Afrikanisten in Deutschland. Hamburg: Buske, 107-25.

1975a   "Dahab - ein blinder Sänger Nubiens, Musik und Gesellschaft im Nordsudan." *Baessler-Archiv* N. F. 23:159-94.

1975b   "Islamische und afrikanische Elemente in der Musik des Nordsudan am Beispiel des Dikr." *Hamburger Jahrbuch für Musikwissenschaft* 1:249-78.

1979   "Probleme, Methoden und Ziele der Ethnomusikologie." *Jahrbuch für Musikalische Volks- und Völkerkunde* 9:8-52.

1989   "Trumpet and Flute Ensembles of the Berta People in the Sudan." In: *African Musicology - Current Trends.* A Festschrift presented to J. H. Kwabena Nketia, Vol. 1. Jacqueline Cogdell Djedje & William G. Carter, eds. Los Angeles: Crossroads Press, 183-217.

1990   "Sammeln, bewahren, forschen und vermitteln. Die musikalischen Traditionen in der Arbeit der Abteilung Musikethnologie des Museums für Völkerkunde." *Jahrbuch Preußischer Kulturbesitz* 27: 215-229.

1991a   "Klangkonzeptionen und Kulturanthropologie." In: *Musikwissenschaft als Kulturwissenschaft.* Festschrift zum 65. Geburtstag von Hans-Peter Reinecke.

K.-E. Behme; E. Jost; E. Kötter & H. de la Motte-Haber, eds. Regensburg: Gustav Bosse, 197-215.

1991b   "Sudan City Music." In *Populäre Musik in Afrika*. Veröffentlichungen des Museums für Völkerkunde Berlin. Neue Folge 53, Abteilung Musikethnologie VIII. Veit Erlmann, ed. Berlin: Staatliche Museen Preußischer Kulturbesitz, 165-180.

1993   "100 Jahre Ethnomusikologie. Die 'Garland Library of Readings in Ethnomusicology'." *Anthropos* 88:528-38.

Simon, Artur (ed.)

1983   *Musik in Afrika. 20 Beiträge zur Kenntnis traditioneller afrikanischer Musikkulturen*. Veröffentlichungen des Museums für Völkerkunde Berlin. Neue Folge 40, Abteilung Musikethnologie IV. Berlin: Staatliche Museen Preußischer Kulturbesitz.

Sithole, Elkin Thamsanqa

1979   "Ngoma Music Among the Zulu." In *The Performing Arts*. Sol Tax, ed. The Hague: Mouton, 277-85.

Souindoula, Simao

1982   "Genocide des Boschimans d'Angola." *Bulletin of the International Committee on Urgent Anthropological and Ethnological Research* 24:77-80.

Speke, John Hanning

1863   *Journal of the Discovery of the Source of the Nile*. Edinburgh: Blackwood. [German edition - Leipzig: Brockhaus, 1864]

Stanley, Henry Morton

1878   *Through the Dark Continent*. 2 vols. London: Low.

Stewart, Gary

1992   *Breakout. Profiles in African Rhythm*. Chicago: The University of Chicago Press.

Stockmann, Erich (ed.)

1987   *Musikkulturen in Afrika*. Berlin: Verlag Neue Musik.

Stone, Ruth

1978a   *Communication and Interaction Processes in Music Events Among the Kpelle of Liberia*. Ph.D. dissertation. Bloomington: Indiana University.

1978b   "Motion Film as an Aid in Transcription and Analysis of Music." In *Discourse in Ethnomusicology. Essays in Honor of George List*. C. Card, J. Hasse, R. Singer & R. Stone, eds. Bloomington: Ethnomusicology, Publications Group, Indiana University, 65-87.

1982   *Let the Inside be Sweet. The Interpretation of Music Event Among the Kpelle of Liberia*. Bloomington: Indiana University Press.

1985   "In Search of Time in African Music." *Music Theory Spectrum* 7:139-48.

1986   "The Shape of Time in African Music." In *Time, Science and Society in China and the West*. J. T. Fraser *et al.*, eds. Amherst: University of Massachusetts Press, 113-25.

1986   "Commentary: The Value of Local Ideas in Understanding West African Rhythm." *Ethnomusicology* 30(1):54-5.

1988a   *Dried Millet Breaking: Time, Words, and Song in the Woi Epic of the Kpelle*. Bloomington: Indiana University Press.

1988b   "Performance in Contemporary African Arts: A Prologue." *Journal of Folklore Research,* 25(1-2):3-15.

Sturtevant, William C.

1964   "Studies in Ethnoscience." *American Anthropologist* [special issue on "Transcultural Studies in Cognition"] 66(2):99-131.

Strumpf, Mitchel
1970   "Ghanian Xylophone Studies." *Review of Ethnology* 3(6): 41-5.
Sutton, John E. G.
1981   "Early Man in Africa." In *Cultural Atlas of Africa*. Joselyn Murray, ed. Oxford: Elsevier Publishers, Phaidon Press, 42-7.
Thiel, Paul van
1969   "An Attempt to a Kinyankore Classification of Musical Instruments." *Review of Ethnology* 2(13):1-5.
Thompson, Donald
1975/6   "A New World Mbira: the Carribean Marimbula." *African Music* 5(4):140-8.
Thompson, Robert Farris
1974   *African Art in Motion*. Los Angeles: University of California Press.
1984   *Flash of the Spirit*. African & Afro-American Art & Philosophy. New York: Vintage Books Edition.
Tracey, Andrew
1961   "Mbira Music of Jege A Tapera." *African Music* 2(4):44-63.
1963   "Three Tunes on the Mbira Dza Vadzimu." *African Music* 3(2):96-100.
1969   "The Tuning of Mbira Reeds. A Contribution to the Craft of Mbira Making." *African Music* 4(3):96-100.
1970a   *How to Play the Mbira Dza Vadzimu*. Roodepoort: International Library of African Music.
1970b   "The Matepe Mbira Music of Rhodesia." *African Music* 4(4):37-61.
1971   "The Nyanga Panpipe Dance." *African Music* 5(1):73-89.
1972   "The Original African Mbira?" *African Music* 5(2):85-104.
1974   "African Music." *Encyclopaedia Britannica*. Vol. 13. 15th edition. Chicago: Encyclopaedia Britannica, Inc., 246-7.
1981   "White Response to African Music." In *Papers Presented at the Symposium on Ethnomusicology*, Music Department, Rhodes University on 10th and 11th October 1980. Grahamstown: International Library of African Music, 29-35.
1989   "The System of the Mbira." *Papers presented at the Seventh Symposium on Ethnomusicology, University of Venda, 3rd - 5th September, 1988*. Grahamstown: International Library of African Music, 43-54.
1991   "Kambazithe Makolekole and his *valimba* Group: a Glimpse of the Technique of the Sena Xylophone." *African Music* 7(1):82-104.
1992   "Some Dance Steps for the nyanga Panpipe Dance." African Music 7(2): 108-18.
Tracey, Hugh
1929   "Some Observations on Native Music of Southern Rhodesia." *Nada* 27:96-103.
1948a   *Chopi Musicians. Their Music, Poetry and Instruments*. London: Oxford University Press. (2nd edition 1970, London: International African Institute.)
1948b   *Handbook for Librarians*. Roodepoort: African Music Society.
1948c   *Ngoma: An Introduction to Music for Southern Africans*. London: Longmans, Green & Co.
1950   "Recording Tour 1949." *African Music Society Newsletter* 1(3) July:33-7.
1951   "Recording Tour, May to November, 1950, East Africa." *African Music Society Newsletter* 1(4):38-51.
1952   *African Dances of the Witwatersrand Gold Mines*. Johannesburg: African Music Society.
1953   "Recording in East Africa and Northern Congo." *African Music Society Newsletter* 1(6):6-15.

1954   "The State of Folk Music in Bantu Africa." *African Music* 1(1):8-11.
1955   "Recording African Music in the Field." *African Music* 1(2):6-11.
1958a   "A Unique Set of Tuning Forks for Students of African Modality." *African Music* 2(1):77-8.
1958b   "Towards an Assessment of African Scales." *African Music* 2(1):15-20.
1961   "A Case for the Name Mbira." *African Music* 2(4):17-25.
1962   "The Arts in Africa - The Visual and the Aural." *African Music* 3(1):20-32.
1965a   "I. L. A. M. Recording Tour." *African Music* 3(4):68-70.
1965b   "Musical Appreciation Among the Shona in the Early Thirties." *African Music* 3(4):29-34.
1969a   "Measuring African Scales." *African Music* 4(3):73-4.
1969b   "The Mbira Class of Instruments in Rhodesia (1932)." *African Music* 4(3):78-95.
1973   *Catalogue of the Sound of Africa Recordings.* 210 Long play records on music and songs from Central, Eastern and Southern Africa by Hugh Tracey, Vol. I and II. Roodepoort (South Africa): The International Library of African Music.

Tracey, Hugh; Kubik, Gerhard & Andrew Tracey
1969   *Codification of African Music and Textbook Project: A Primer of Practical Suggestions for Field Research.* Roodepoort: International Library of African Music.

Trowell, Margaret & Klaus Peter Wachsmann
1953   *Tribal Crafts in Uganda.* London: Oxford University Press.

Tsukada, Kenichi
1988   *Luvale Perceptions of Mukanda in Discourse and Music.* Ph.D. dissertation, Queen's University of Belfast: Ann Arbor, University Microfilms (no. 8917245).
1990a   "*Kukuwa* and *Kachacha:* the Musical Classification and the Rhythmic Patterns of the Luvale in Zambia." In *Peoples and Rhythms.* Tetsuo Sakurai, ed. Tokyo: Tokyo Shoseki, 229-75 (in Japanese).
1990b   "Variation and Unity in African Harmony: A Study of *Mukanda* Songs of the Luvale in Zambia." In *Florilegio Musicale. Festschrift für Professor Dr. Kataoka Gido zu seinem siebzigsten Geburtstag.* Usaburo Mabuchi *et al.*, eds. Tokyo: Onagaku no Tomo, 157-97.

Tuburu, Azuka
1987   *Kinetik und soziale Funktion des Tanzes bei den Igbo (Nigeria), unter besonderer Berücksichtigung traditioneller afrikanischer Instrumentalspiel- und Bewegungsdidaktiken sowie ausgewählter Transkriptionen in Labannotation.* 2 Vols. Ph.D. dissertation. Salzburg: University of Salzburg, Musikwissenschaftliches Institut.

Tucker, Archibald Norman
1933a   "Children's Games and Songs in the Southern Sudan." *Journal of the Royal Anthropological Institute* 63:165-87.
1933b   *Tribal Music and Dancing in South Sudan at Social and Ceremonial Gatherings.* London: W. Reeves.

Turkson, A.
1982   "Effutu Asafo: Its Organization and Music." *African Music* 6(2):4-16.

Turner, Victor
1953   *Lunda Rites and Ceremonies.* The Occasional Papers of the Rhodes-Livingstone Museum, Nr. 10. Livingstone: The Rhodes-Livingstone Museum.
1967   *The Forest of Symbols. Aspects of Ndembu Ritual.* Ithaca and London: Cornell University Press.

1968   *The Drums of Affliction. A Study of Religious Processes Among the Ndembu of Zambia.* Oxford: Clarendon Press.

1977   *The Ritual Process: Structure and Anti-Structure.* Ithaca, N. Y.: Cornell University Press.

Turner, Victor & Edward Bruner (eds.)

1986   *The Anthropology of Experience.* Urbana: University of Illinois Press.

Tutuola, Amos

1952   *The Palm-Wine Drinkard and His Dead Palm-Wine Tapster in the Deads' Town.* London: Faber and Faber Ltd.

1954   *My Life in the Bush of Ghosts.* London: Faber and Faber Ltd.

Tyler, Stephen A. (ed.)

1969   *Cognitive Anthropology.* New York: Holt, Rïnehart and Winston Inc.

Vansina, Jan

1965   *Oral Tradition. A Study in Historical Methodology.* London: Routledge & Kegan Paul.

1969   "The Bells of Kings." *Journal of African History* 10(2):187-97.

Vergani, de A. Armitage

1981   *Analyse numérique des idéogrammes tshokwe de l'Angola. Expressions symboliques du nombre dans une culture traditionelle africaine.* Ph.D. dissertation. Université de Génève.

Vidal, Pierre

n.d.   *Panorama ethnique de la République Centrafricaine.* Document publié par le Service de l'Information B. P. 373, Bangui.

Voitl, Roland

1984   *Daniel Kachamba "Afro Africa".* Begleitheft zur Kassette. Tübingen: Roland Voitl Musik.

Wachsmann, Klaus P.

1939   "An Approach to African Music." *Uganda Journal* 6(3):148-63.

1950   "An Equal-Stepped Tuning in a Ganda Harp." *Nature* 165:40-1.

1953   "Musicology in Uganda." *Journal of the Royal Anthropological Institute* 83(Part I):50-7.

1954   "The Transplantation of Folk Music From One Social Environment to Another." *Journal of the International Folk Music Council* 6:41-5.

1956a   *Folk Musicians in Uganda.* Uganda Museum Occasional Papers 2.

1956b   "Harp Songs from Uganda." *Journal of the International Folk Music Council* 8:23-5.

1956c   Review of Joseph Kyagambiddwa: "African Music from the Source of the Nile." *African Music* 1(3):80-1.

1957   "A Study of Norms in the Tribal Music of Uganda." *Ethnomusicology Newsletter* 11:9-16.

1964   "Human Migration and African Harps." *Journal of the International Folk Music Council* 16:84-8.

1965a   "Some Speculations Concerning a Drum Chime in Buganda." *Man* 65(1):1-8.

1965b   "Traditional Music in Uganda." In *Creating a Wider Interest in Traditional Music.* A. Daniélou, ed. Berlin: International Institute for Comparative Music Studies and Documentation, 128-31.

1967   "Pen-Equidistance and Accurate Pitch: A Problem from the Source of the Nile." In *Festschrift für Walter Wiora zum 30. Dezember 1966.* L. Finscher & C.-H. Mahling, eds. Kassel: Bärenreiter, 583-92.

1970   "A Drum from Seventeenth Century Africa." The *Galpin Society Journal* 23:97-103.

1971   "Musical Instruments in Kiganda Tradition and their Place in the East African
        Scene." In *Essays on Music and History in Africa*. Klaus P. Wachsmann, ed.
        Evanston: Northwestern University Press, 93-134.
1973   "A 'Shiplike' String Instrument from West Africa." *Ethnos* 38(1-4):43-56.
1982   "The Changeability of Musical Experience." *Ethnomusicology* 26(2):197-215.
Wallis, Roger & Krister Malm
1983   *Big Sounds from Small Peoples: The Music Industry in Small Countries*. Lon-
        don: Constable. (1984 New York: Pendragon.)
Ward, W. E.
1927   "Music on the Gold Coast." *Gold Coast Review* 3:199-223.
Waterman, Christopher A.
1988   "Asíkó, Sákárà and Palmwine: Popular Music and Social Identity in Inter-War
        Lagos, Nigeria." *Urban Anthropology* 17(2-3):229-59.
1990a   *Jùjú: A Social History and Ethnography of an African Popular Music*. Chicago:
        University of Chicago Press.
1990b   "'Our Tradition is a Very Modern Tradition': Popular Music and the Construc-
        tion of Pan-Yoruba Identity." *Ethnomusicology* 34(3):367-79.
Waterman, Richard A.
1948   "'Hot' Rhythm in Negro Music." *Journal of the American Musicological Society*
        1(1):24-37.
1952   "African Influences on the Music of the Americas." In *Acculturation in the
        Americas*. Sol Tax, ed. Chicago: University of Chicago Press, 207-18.
Wegner, Ulrich
1984   *Afrikanische Saiteninstrumente*. Veröffentlichungen des Museums für Völker-
        kunde Berlin. Neue Folge 41, Abteilung Musikethnologie V. Berlin: Staatliche
        Museen Preußischer Kulturbesitz.
1990   *Xylophonmusik aus Buganda (Ostafrika)*. Musikbogen. Wege zum Verständnis
        fremder Musikkulturen 1. Wilhelmshaven: Florian Noetzel.
1993   "Cognitive Aspects of *amadinda* Xylophone Music from Buganda: Inherent
        Patterns Reconsidered." *Ethnomusicology* 37(2):201-41.
Welle, Jean
1952   "Rumbas congolaises et jazz americain." *African Music Society Newsletter* 1(5)
        June:42-3.
Westermann, Diedrich & Ida C. Ward
1933   *Practical Phonetics for Students of African Languages*. London: Oxford Univer-
        sity Press. Fifth edition: 1966.
Westphal, E. O.
1963   "The Linguistic Prehistory of Southern Africa: Bush, Kwadi, Hottentot and
        Bantu Linguistic Relationships." *Africa* 33(3):237-65.
1978   "Observations on Current Bushmen and Hottentot Musical Practices." *Re-
        view of Ethnology* 5(2-3):9-15.
White, C. M. N.
1961   *Elements in Luvale Beliefs and Rituals*. The Rhodes-Livingstone Papers 32.
        Manchester: Manchester University Press.
Wieschhoff, Heinz
1933   *Die afrikanischen Trommeln und ihre außerafrikanischen Beziehungen*. Stutt-
        gart: Strecker & Schröder.
Willet, Frank
1977   "A Contribution to the History of Musical Instruments Among the Yoruba."
        In *Esssays for a Humanist. An Offering to Klaus Wachsmann*. New York: The
        Town House Press, 350-89.

Wilson, Olly
   1977   *The Association of Movement and Music as a Manifestation of a Black Concep-*
           tual Approach to Music Making. Conference paper read at the 12th Congress of
           the International Musicologial Society. Berkeley. Unpublished.
Wizara ya Elimu ya Taifa Tanzania
   1977   *Elimu ya Muziki katika schule za msingi. Kiongozi cha mwalimu.* London: Ox-
           ford University Press.
Wober, Mallory
   1975   *Psychology in Africa.* London: International African Institute.
Wolf, Paul P. de
   1983   "Xhosa." In *Lexikon der Afrikanistik. Afrikanische Sprachen und ihre Erfor-*
           schung. H. Jungraithmayr & W. J. G. Möhlig, eds. Berlin: Dietrich Reimer, 270.
Yankah, Kwesi
   1985   "Beyond the Spoken Word: Aural Literature in Africa." *Cross Rhythms* 2:114-
           16.
Yotamu, Mose
   1979   "My Two Weeks Fieldwork in Ivory Coast - A Preliminary Report." *Review of*
           Ethnology 6(1-24):161-92.
Zanten, Wim van
   1980   "The Equidistant Heptatonic Scale of the Asena in Malawi." *African Music*
           6(1):107-25.
Zaslavsky, Claudia
   1979   *Africa Counts. Number and Pattern in African Culture.* Westpoint, Conn.: Law-
           rence Hill.
Zemp, Hugo
   1971   *Musique Dan. La musique dans la pensée et la vie sociale d'une société africaine.*
           Cahiers de l'Homme. Nouvelle Série 11. The Hague: Mouton.

LIST OF MUSICAL

No.	Title and/or genre	Performer(s), sex/age and instrument(s)	Language/ethnic group
1	*"Ganga alula"*	Albert Sempeke, m, 30, and group / *amadinda* (log xylophone)	Luganda/Baganda
2	*"Obukaire butusinye"*	Yonasani Mutaki, m, 25, and group / *embaire* (log xylophone), drums	Lusoga/Basoga
3	*"Njala egwire"*	- " -	Lusoga/Basoga
4	*"Sundya omulungi alya ku malagala"*	Venekenti Nakyebale, m, 25, and group / *embaire* (log xylophone), drums	Lusoga/Basoga
5	*"Empuuta"*	The Blind Musicians of Salama, m, ca. 20-30 / *akadinda* (log xylophone), rattle and drums	Luganda/Baganda and Basoga
6	*"Limbyayo"*	Bernard Guinahui and François Razia, m, ca. 30 / two *kundi* (harps)	Zande/Azande
7	*"Nginza njale kiye"*	Chief Zekpio, m, 80, *kundi* (harp) and Martin Abirase, m, 60, *manza* (log xylophone)	Zande/Azande
8	*"Aboro na li ngboro mi ni rungo"*	Raymon Zoungakpio, m, 40 / *kundi* (harp)	Zande/Azande
9	*"Boganda"*, / *kponingbo*	Anon., m, ca. 18, demonstration of *kponingbo* (log xylophone) pattern	Zande/Azande
10	*"Nzanginza mu du kporani yo"*	Maurice Gambassi, m, 16, *kundi* (harp)	Zande/Azande
11	*"Wen'ade gbua"*	Antoine Gbalagume, m, 40 / *kundi* (harp) and female chorus	Zande/Azande
12	*"Ngbadule o"*	Samuel Ouzana, m, 12 / *kundi* (harp)	Zande/Azande
13	*"Ndendelu ndendelu"*	Lupingu school boys (ca. 8-12)	Kikisi/Wakisi
14	*"Mphezi mphezi iwe!"* /*nthano* (chantefable)	Nasibeko Kachamba, f, 40, and villagers	Cinyanja/Anyanja

EXAMPLES ON CD I*

Place and date of recording	Orig. Tape No.	Dura-tion	Book page reference	No.
Kampala (Uganda) November 1967	113/I/11	2:10	66, 71, 306-7, 316	1
Bumanya, Busoga District (Uganda), January 2, 1963	R 18/II/6	1:19	66-7, 72, 273	2
- " -	R 18/II/7	1:58	68, 273	3
- " -	R 18/I/1	1:15	72, 273	4
Salama, Agricultural Training Centre for the Blind (Uganda) December 1967	114/II/3	1:48	84, 323	5
Makanza, 7 km northwest of Rafai, Central African Republic, April 1964	R 44/II/4	1:35	101, 120, 148-9	6
Dembia (between Rafai and Zemio), Central African Republic, May 1964	R 47/I/1	2:07	102-3	7
Fizane, 15 km east of Zemio, Central Afr. Rep., May 1964	R 48/II/5	1:49	105	8
- " -	R 46/I/1	0:23	106	9
- " -	R 44/II/7	1:43	114-9, 131-6	10
Djema, north of Zemio, Central African Republic, May 1964	R 46/II/3	1:27	120, 125, 150-1	11
- " -	R 45/II/5	1:28	123, 124-5, 151-4	12
Lupingu, southwestern Tanganyika, April 1960	20/II/20-21	0:54	172	13
Singano village, near Chileka, Malaŵi, March 1967	2/no.5	1:09	172	14

No.	Title and/or genre	Performer(s), sex/age and instrument(s)	Language/ ethnic group
15	*msunyunho* song	Anon., Wagogo men, ca. 20-50	Kigogo/ Wagogo
16	*"Haya Wajeremani haya!"*	Mirindi, m, 30 / *ilimba* (lamellophone)	Kigogo/ Wagogo
17	*"Nan' engongol!"*	André Mvome, m, 30, *bɛŋ* (mouth-bow) and cult participants	Faŋ
18	*"Halelanga e!"* *ekongo* (drinking songs)	Group of men, 20-50	ŋgili/ Boŋgili
19	*"Chiyongoyongo neza"* / *mwaso wa kukuwa*	Male singers (guardians, aged 20-40, and initiates, 5-8) with *mingongi* (concussion sticks) and *tutanga* suspended struck wooden slats)	Mbwela/ Vambwela
20	*"Atɛndɛ"* / *sya* (story song)	Mandali, f, 50, and villagers	Mpyɛmɔ̃
21	*"Syelinga nɛ Nkuminjɛli"* / *sya* (story song)	Ignace Bawandɔ, m, 45, and villagers	Mpyɛmɔ̃
22	*"Terekanthalo"* / *mbanda* dance	Beria Lazani, f, 30, and women with percussion bottles	Cinsenga/ Ansenga
23a	*"I//kake ku Ndyango"*	Lithundu Musumali, m, 45, with *n//kau* (gourd-resonated bow)	!Kung'
23b	(Title unknown)	- " -	!Kung'
23c	(Title unknown)	Chief Vimphulu, m, 55 / *sungu* (mouth-resonated bow)	!Kung'
24	*"Ochiyochiyo we yaya mama"*	Benson Siyemba Munitembwe, m, 50, and group / *kaŋombyo* (lamellophone), buzzing devices prominent	Silozi/ Valozi
25	*"Vashambaulu woye mwashauka"*	Patrick Kahyata, born 1960, and Peter Lijimu, born 1967 / *silimba* (xylophone; gourds damaged)	Silozi/ Valozi

Place and date of recording	Orig. Tape No.	Dura-tion	Book page reference	No.
Kintinku, Central Region, Tanganyika, May 1962	A 18/I/3	1:33	176	15
Nondwa, Central Region, Tanganyika, May 1962	A 22/II/5	1:10	180-4	16
Oyem, Gabon, July 1964	R 56/II/6	1:17	188-91, 204-5	17
Mekɔme, south of Liweso, République Congo, July 1964	R 57/II/3	1:05	192	18
Sakateke, 25 km north of Cuito-Cuanavale, southeastern Angola, August 1965	63/I/3	2:42	194-5, 196, 352-3, 365	19
Bigene, District Nola, Central Afr. Rep., June 1964	R 53/I/2	0:47	198	20
Bigene, District Nola, Central Afr. Rep., April 1966	87/I/2	0:32	198-9, 206-7	21
Origin: Siyankhuni village, Chipata, Zambia. Rec. at Chiwalo, Mulanje District, Malaŵi, May 1967	53/no.3	1:31	214	22
Camp Vimphulu, east of Cuito-Cuanavale, southeastern Angola, December 1965	76/II/14	1:09	218-9	23a
- " -	76/II/13	1:04	218-9	23b
- " -	76/II/12	0:42	218-9, 244	23c
Kasheshe village, Bukalo Boma, Caprivi Region, Namibia, August 31, 1992	92/30/9	1:24	231-2	24
Chikenge village, Kabompo District, N. W. Province Zambia, July 16, 1979	A 83/I/2	1:43	232	25

No.	Title and/or genre	Performer(s), sex/age and instrument(s)	Language/ ethnic group
26	"Kuzanga"	Beulah Dyoko, f, born 1945, mbira dza vadzimu (lamellophone)	Chishona/ Mashona
27	"Kainta a"	Nthumba, f, 50, with bavugu (stamping tube) and other women	!Kung'
28	"Olutalo olw'e Nsinsi"	Albert Sempeke, m, 30, and group / amadinda (log xylophone)	Luganda/ Baganda
29	"Olutalo olw'e Nsinsi" (four miko)	Evaristo Muyinda, m, born 1914, and group / amadinda (log xylophone). Historically valuable recordings, distortions in the originals	Luganda/ Baganda
30	"Ennyana ekutudde"	Albert Sempeke, m, 30, and group / amadinda (log xylophone)	Luganda/ Baganda
31	"Olutalo olw'e Nsinsi"	Evaristo Muyinda, m, born 1914 / ennanga (harp)	Luganda/ Baganda
32	"Akabira kange"	Abusolomu Mukasa, m, 30 / akadinda (log xylophone) and ensege (flat rattle)	Luganda/ Baganda
33	"Vanana somili" / chisimo (chantefable)	Kayoko, m, 6, and friend	Nkhangala/ Vankhangala
34	Luvimbi first type	Kufuna, m, 16, luvimbi (vibrating leaf)	Nkhangala/ Vankhangala
35	Luvimbi second type	Kayoko, m, 6, luvimbi (vibrating leaf)	Nkhangala/ Vankhangala
36	Concert for two types of maluvimbi	Kufuna, m, 16, Kayoko, m, 6, and group, maluvimbi (vibrating leaves)	Nkhangala/ Vankhangala
37	"Kambulumbumba kambulumbumba"	Kayoko, m, 6, Vibanda, m, 8, and Litwayi, m, 12 / kambulumbumba (percussion bow)	Nkhangala/ Vankhangala

Place and date of recording	Orig. Tape No.	Dura-tion	Book page reference	No.
Chitungwiza township, Harare, Zimbabwe, July 16, 1989	4/1989/1	3:28	235	26
Camp Vimphulu, east of Cuito-Cuanavale, southeastern Angola, December 1965	76/II/9	1:54	241-3	27
Kampala (Uganda), November 1967	113/I/10	0:56	261, 314	28
Nabbale, near Kampala (Uganda) 1962	A 34/I/1	1:18	262, 310, 312	29
Kampala (Uganda), November 1967	113/I/12	1:30	265, 310, 314	30
Nabbale, near Kampala (Uganda) 1962	A 34/I/2	2:20	287-9, 313	31
Salama, Agricultural Training Centre for the Blind (Uganda), December 1967	115/II/36	1:05	299-301	32
Chingangu, adm. Longa, Cuando-Cubango, Angola, October 1965	R 66/I/3	1:42	335-6	33
- " -	R 66/II/3	0:27	336-9	34
- " -	R 66/II/4	0:34	336-9	35
- " -	R 66/II/6	0:45	336-9	36
- " -	R 66/II/7	0:54	339-42	37

No.	Title and/or genre	Performer(s), sex/age and instrument(s)	Language/ ethnic group
38	"De kele ŋge kele"	Kufuna Kandonga, m, 15, with two tent pegs for percussion	Mbwela/ Tucokwe
39	"Munthembo weku-handeka"	Mose Kamwocha, m, 14	Luchazi/ Valuvale
40	"Machakili machaki-li" (drum pattern)	Terceiro, m, 5 (children's drum) and Celestino Chihinga, m, 17, percussion stick	Mbwela/ Vambwela
41	"E nany'e lelo miva-nze vange" / tuvema (women's association)	Female members, ca. 20, hand-clapping	Nkhangala/ Vankhangala
42	"Hawe, mwatambuka chongono" / makisi (masked performance)	Chileya mask and women's chorus, three vipwali (long drums)	Mbwela/ Vambwela
43	"Ndo ndo ndo nana yow'e", "Kawaly'ee!" / mukanda songs	Initiates, 5-8, inside mukanda practising the kuhunga and kundekula movement; three drums	Mbwela/ Vambwela
44	"Mwandumba Kalunga"	Kufuna Kandonga, m, 15, likembe (lamellophone) and Chimutwe Masozi, 14, percussion stick	Mbwela/ Tucokwe
45	"Manguchata kumuf-weta"	- " -	Cokwe/ Tucokwe
46	(New composition, untitled)	Kufuna Kandonga, m, 15, likembe solo	Mbwela/ Tucokwe

Place and date of recording	Orig. Tape No.	Dura-tion	Book page reference	No.
Kumboyombacho, adm. Longa, southeastern Angola, November 1965	75/I/5	0:53	341-2	38
Chikenge, Kabompo District, Zambia, September 13 and November 5, 1971	L 16/I/7 and L 24/ II/12-13	1:30	342-4	39
Kayoko, adm. Cuito-Cuanavale, southeastern Angola, August 1965	65/II/11	0:34	346	40
Sangombe, 80 km northwest of Cuito-Cuanavale, south-eastern Angola, September 1965	68/II/9	2:03	348	41
Sakateke, 25 km north of Cuito-Cuanavale, southeast-ern Angola, August 1965	63/I/1	1:21	351, 375	42
- " -	62/II/5	2:32	360-1	43
Chisende, adm. Longa, southeastern Angola, October 1965	73/I/2	2:04	385	44
- " -	73/I/1	1:54	386	45
Mupeku, adm. Longa, south-eastern Angola, November 1965	75/I/11	1:18	397-8	46

Total time: 71:26

* The CD represents a coproduction project between the International Institute for Traditional Music and DeutschlandRadio Berlin. We acknowledge with many thanks the technical assistance granted by both the Abteilung Musikethnologie of the Museum für Völkerkunde and also the Staatliche Institut für Musikforschung Preußischer Kulturbe-sitz in preparing single tracks of the CD for the mastertape.

Contents of Volume II